WORLD TRADE ORGANIZATION

Dispute Settlement Reports

2001
Volume II

Pages 411-775

CAMBRIDGE
UNIVERSITY PRESS

PUBLISHED BY THE PRESS SYNDICATE OF THE UNIVERSITY OF CAMBRIDGE
The Pitt Building, Trumpington Street, Cambridge, United Kingdom

CAMBRIDGE UNIVERSITY PRESS
The Edinburgh Building, Cambridge CB2 2RU, UK
40 West 20th Street, New York, NY 10011–4211, USA
477 Williamstown Road, Port Melbourne, VIC 3207, Australia
Ruiz de Alarcón 13, 28014 Madrid, Spain
Dock House, The Waterfront, Cape Town 8001, South Africa

http://www.cambridge.org

First published 2003

Printed in the United Kingdom at the University Press, Cambridge

French edition and Spanish edition paperbacks of this title are both available directly from WTO Publications, World Trade Organization, Centre William Rappard, 154 rue de Lausanne, CH-1211 Geneva 21, Switzerland http://www.wto.org

ISBN 0 521 82979 8 hardback

THE WTO DISPUTE SETTLEMENT REPORTS

The *Dispute Settlement Reports* of the World Trade Organization (the "WTO") include panel and Appellate Body reports, as well as arbitration awards, in disputes concerning the rights and obligations of WTO Members under the provisions of the *Marrakesh Agreement Establishing the World Trade Organization.* The *Dispute Settlement Reports* are available in English, French and Spanish. Starting with 1999, the first volume of each year contains a cumulative index of published disputes.

This volume may be cited as DSR 2001:II

TABLE OF CONTENTS

UNITED STATES – IMPORT MEASURES ON CERTAIN PRODUCTS FROM THE EUROPEAN COMMUNITIES

Report of the Panel

WT/DS165/R/Add.1

TABLE OF CONTENTS

I. PROCEDURAL BACKGROUND

1.1 This proceeding was initiated by the European Communities, as complaining party against the United States.

1.2 On 4 March 1999, the European Communities requested consultations with the United States under Article XXII:1 of the General Agreement on Tariffs and Trade 1994 ("GATT") and Article 4 of the Understanding on Rules and Procedures Governing the Settlement of Dispute ("DSU") with regard to the US decision, effective as of 3 March 1999, to withhold liquidation on imports from the European Communities of a series of products (listed in the Annex to the document WT/DS165/1), together valued at over $500 million on an annual basis, and to impose a contingent liability for 100 per cent duties on each individual importation of affected products as of this date. The European Communities claimed that according to information provided by the United States Trade Representative ("USTR"), this measure includes administrative provisions which foresee, among other things, the posting of a bond to cover the full potential liability.

1.3 On 11 May 1999, the European Communities requested the establishment of a panel pursuant to Article 6 of the DSU (WT/DS165/8).

1.4 In its panel request, the European Communities claims that:

> "I have the honour to request, on behalf of the European Communities, the establishment of a panel pursuant to Article XXIII of the General Agreement on Tariffs and Trade 1994 (GATT 1994) and Articles 4 and 6 of the Dispute Settlement Understanding (DSU) with respect to the US decision, effective as of 3 March 1999, to withhold liquidation on imports from the EC of a list of products, together valued at $520 million on an annual basis, and to impose a contingent liability for 100 per cent duties on each individual importation of affected products as of this date (annex 1). This measure includes administrative provisions that foresee, among other things, the posting of a bond to cover the full potential liability.
>
> ... When the US received WTO authorization on 19 April 1999 to suspend concessions as of that date on EC imports of products with an annual value of only $191.4 million, a more limited list of products was selected from the previous list (annex 2). At the same time, the US confirmed, despite the prospective nature of the WTOs, the liability for 100 per cent duty on the products on the list in annex 2 that had entered the US for consumption with effect from 3 March 1999.
>
> The European Communities considers that this US measure is in flagrant breach of the following WTO provisions:
>
> - Articles 3, 21, 22 and 23 of the DSU;
> - Articles I, II, VIII and XI of GATT 1994.
>
> Through these violations of fundamental WTO rules, the US measure nullifies or impairs benefits accruing, directly or indirectly, to the European Communities under GATT 1994. This measure also impedes important objectives of GATT 1994 and of the WTO."

1.5 On 16 June 1999, the Dispute Settlement Body ("DSB") established the Panel pursuant to Article 6 of the DSU. In accordance with Article 7.1 of the DSU, the terms of reference of the Panel are:

> "To examine, in the light of the relevant provisions of the covered agreements cited by the European Communities in document WT/DS165/8, the matter referred to the DSB by the European Communities in that document and to make such findings as will assist the DSB in making the recommendations or in giving the rulings provided for in those agreements."

1.6 Dominica, Ecuador, India, Jamaica, Japan, and St. Lucia, reserved their rights to participate in the Panel proceedings as third parties.

1.7 On 29 September 1999, the European Communities requested the Director-General, pursuant to Article 8.7 of the DSU, to determine the composition of the Panel. On 8 October 1999, the Director-General announced the composition of the Panel as follows:

Chairman:	Mr. Hugh McPhail
Members:	Ms. Leora Blumberg
	Mr. Peter Palečka

1.8 The Panel had substantive meetings with the parties on 16 and 17 December 1999, and 9 February 2000.

II. FACTUAL ASPECTS

A. *Factual Background to this Case*

2.1 At its meeting of 25 September 1997, the DSB adopted the Appellate Body report,[1] and the panel reports,[2] as modified by the Appellate Body report, on European Communities – *Regime for the Importation, Sale and Distribution of Bananas*.[3] The Appellate Body report recommended that the [DSB] request the European Communities to bring the measures found in this Report and in the Panel Reports ... to be inconsistent with the GATT 1994 and GATS into conformity with the obligations of the European Communities under those agreements."[4] In this case, Ecuador, Guatemala, Honduras, Mexico and the United States (the "Complainants on *EC - Bananas III*") claimed that the EC regime for the importation, sale and distribution of bananas established by the Council Regulation (EEC) 404/93, and the subsequent EC legislation, regulations and administrative measures, was inconsistent with the WTO Agreement.[5] At the DSB meeting of 16 October 1997, the European Communities confirmed that "the Communities would fully respect their international obligations with regard to this matter."[6]

2.2 On 24 October 1997, the European Communities requested consultations with the Complainants on *EC - Bananas III* in order to reach agreement on a

---

1 Appellate Body Report, *European Communities – Regime for the Importation, Sale and Distribution of Bananas* ("*EC - Bananas III*"), adopted 25 September 1997, WT/DS27/AB/R, DSR 1997:II, 591.

2 Panel Reports, *European Communities – Regime for the Importation, Sale and Distribution of Bananas* ("*EC - Bananas III*"), adopted 25 September 1997, *Complaint by Ecuador*, WT/DS27/R/ECU, DSR 1997:III, 1085; *Complaint by Guatemala and Honduras*, WT/DS27/R/GTM, WT/DS27/R/HND, DSR 1997:II, 695: *Complaint by Mexico*, WT/DS27/R/MEX, DSR 1997:II, 1803 and *Complaint by the United States*, WT/DS27/R/USA, DSR 1997:II, 943.

3 WT/DSB/M/37.

4 Appellate Body Report on *EC – Bananas III*, *supra*, footnote 1, para. 257.

5 *Ibid.*, para. 1.

6 WT/DSB/M/38.

"reasonable period of time" for the implementation of the recommendations and rulings of the DSB adopted on 25 September 1997, but these consultations did not lead to an agreement.[7] Pursuant to the request of the Complainants on *EC - Bananas III*, on 8 December 1997, the Director-General of the WTO appointed Mr. Said El-Naggar as the arbitrator.[8] On 7 January 1998, the arbitrator decided that the "'reasonable period of time' ... [was] the period from 25 September 1997 to 1 January 1999.[9]

2.3 On 20 July 1998, the Council of the European Union adopted the Regulation (EC) No. 1637/98 amending the Council Regulation (EEC) No. 404/93 on the common organization of the market in bananas. This Regulation entered into force on 31 July 1998, and later became applicable as of 1 January 1999.[10] Further, on 28 October 1998, the Commission of the European Communities adopted the Regulation (EC) No. 2362/98 laying down detailed rules for the implementation of the Council Regulation (EEC) No. 404/93 regarding imports of bananas into the European Communities. This Regulation entered into force on 1 November 1998, and later became applicable as of 1 January 1999 as well.[11]

2.4 On 18 August 1998, the Complainants on *EC - Bananas III* jointly and severally requested consultations with the European Communities in relation to the proposed banana regime.[12] Their request for consultations states as follows:

> "At [a] meeting [of 6 August 1998], the EC clarified its view that Article 21.5 requires parties to consult as a prior condition to the resort to the original panel to resolve the disagreement over the WTO-consistency of the EC measures taken to implement the DSB rulings and recommendations. ...
>
> ...
>
> We do not agree that consultations are necessary before resorting to the original panel under Article 21.5. The EC's position taken for the purposes of this dispute appears calculated to produce maximum delay and is unsupportable for the effective functioning of the dispute settlement system. ..."[13]

---

[7] Award of the Arbitrator, *European Communities – Regime for the Importation, Sale and Distribution of Bananas - Arbitration under Article 21.3(c) of the DSU ("EC - Bananas III")*, WT/DS27/15, 7 January 1998, DSR 1998:I, 3, para. 2.

[8] WT/DS27/14. This appointment was made in accordance with footnote 12 to Article 21.3(c) of the DSU.

[9] Award of the Arbitrator, *EC – Bananas III*, *supra*, footnote 7, para. 20.

[10] Communication, dated 15 December 1998, from the European Communities to the Chairman of the DSB, WT/DS27/40.

[11] *Ibid.*

[12] Communication, dated 18 August 1998, from Ecuador, Guatemala, Honduras, Mexico, and the United States to the Chairman of the DSB, WT/DS27/18.

[13] *Ibid.*

2.5 On 8 September 1998, in their joint communication to the Chairman of the DSB, the Complainants on *EC - Bananas III* claimed that since the proposed banana scheme of the European Communities was inconsistent with the WTO Agreement, and thus, "in order to ensure compliance with the DSB recommendations and ruling by the end of the reasonable period of time on 1 January, 1999, ... this matter should be referred to a panel pursuant to Article 21.5 [of the DSU]."[14] At the DSB meeting of 22 September 1998, such panel was not established.[15] At that meeting, however, the United States, on its own behalf and on behalf of the other Complainants on *EC – Bananas III* and Panama, stated as follows:

> "... The EC's insistence on consultations only delayed the process. This delay would only prolong the dispute beyond the reasonable period of time established by the arbitrator. These delaying tactics, if tolerated, would have serious consequences for the DSU and the multilateral trading system. ..."[16]

> In response, the European Communities indicated as follows:

> "The Community believed that the dispute which fell under Article 21.5 of the DSU should be resolved in accordance with the normal dispute settlement procedures except as otherwise provided in this Article. ... The normal dispute settlement procedures implied the need to hold consultations and the Community had insisted on this point. ... [T]hese were not delaying tactics but a simple application of the DSU procedures. ..."[17]

2.6 On 13 November 1998, Ecuador requested the reactivation of the 17 September 1998 consultations with the European Communities.[18] As their consultations did not result in a mutually satisfactory solution, on 18 December 1998, Ecuador requested "the WTO Dispute Settlement Body, at today's meeting, to call for the re-establishment of the Panel that originally heard the case in order to resolve the conflict with the European Communities concerning the consistency of its measures to implement the recommendations and rulings of the Dispute Settlement Body of 25 September 1997."[19] At its meeting of 12 January 1999, the DSB agreed "to refer to the original panel, pursuant to Article 21.5, the matter raised by Ecuador in document WT/DS27/41."[20]

---

[14] Communication, dated 8 September 1998, from Ecuador, Guatemala, Honduras, Mexico, and the United States, WT/DS27/21.

[15] WT/DSB/M/48.

[16] *Ibid.*

[17] *Ibid.*

[18] Communication, dated 13 November 1998, from Ecuador to the Chairman of the DSB and the European Communities, WT/DS27/30 and WT/DS27/30/Add.1.

[19] Communication, dated 18 December 1998, from Ecuador to the Chairman of the DSB, WT/DS27/41.

[20] WT/DSB/M/53.

2.7 On 14 December 1998, the European Communities requested that the DSB establish "a panel under Article 21.5 of the DSU with the mandate to find that [its new bananas import regime] must be presumed to conform to WTO rules unless [its] conformity has been duly challenged under the appropriate DSU procedures."[21] At its meeting of 12 January 1999, the DSB also agreed "to refer [the matter] to the original panel pursuant to Article 21.5 of the DSU."[22]

2.8 On 14 January 1999, pursuant to Article 22.2 of the DSU, the United States "request[ed] authorization from the Dispute Settlement Body (DSB) to suspend the application to the European Communities (EC), and Member States thereof, of tariff concessions and related obligations under the General Agreement on Tariffs and Trade 1994 (GATT), covering trade in an amount of US$520 million,"[23] claiming that the European Communities had "fail[ed] to bring its regime for the importation, sale and distribution of bananas (banana regime) into compliance, by 1 January 1999, with the GATT and the General Agreement on Trade in Services (GATS) or to otherwise comply with the recommendations and rulings of the DSB in EC - Regime for the Importation, Sale and Distribution of Bananas."[24]

2.9 On 29 January 1999, the European Communities, "[p]ursuant to Article 22.6 of the DSU, ... object[ed] to the level of suspension proposed by the United States in document WT/DS27/43," and further requested that "the matter ... be submitted to arbitration", claiming "that the Community banana import measures found to be inconsistent with WTO obligations were withdrawn by 1 January 1999 and have therefore ceased to produce their effects since the expiry of the reasonable period of time determined in accordance with Article 21, paragraph 3 [of the DSU] ...".[25]

2.10 At its meeting of 25, 28 and 29 January and 1 February 1999, the Chairman suggested, among others, as follows:

> "[A]s to bananas the original panel is now engaged in two Article 21.5 proceedings. ... [A]ssuming the EC make a request for arbitration under Article 22.6, the same individuals could be given the task of arbitrating the level of suspension. ... There remains the problem of how the panel and the arbitrators would coordinate their work, but as they will be the same individuals, the reality is that they will find a logical way forward, in consultation with the parties. In this way, the dispute settlement mechanisms of the DSU

[21] Communication, dated 14 December 1998, from the European Communities to the Chairman of the DSB, WT/DS27/40.
[22] WT/DSB/M/53.
[23] Communication, dated 14 January 1999, from the United States to the Chairman of the DSB, WT/DS27/43.
[24] *Ibid.*
[25] Communication, dated 29 January 1999, from the European Communities to the Chairman of the DSB, WT/DS27/46.

can be employed to resolve all of the remaining issues in this dispute, while recognizing the right of both parties and respecting the integrity of the DSU."[26]

The DSB then agreed "that the matter be referred to arbitration by the original panel in accordance with Article 22.6 of the DSU."[27]

2.11 On 18 February 1999, the United States,

"[p]ursuant to Article 22.7 of the [DSU], ... request[ed] authorization from the [DSB] to suspend the application to the European Communities (EC), and member States thereof, of tariff concessions and related obligations under the General Agreement on Tariffs and Trade 1994 (GATT), in an amount consistent with DSU Article 22.4, as determined by the arbitrator pursuant to DSU Article 22.7 in 'EC – Regime for the Importation, Sale and Distribution of Bananas'."[28]

The United States further explained that "[a]ccording to Article 22.6 of the DSU and the timetable for the arbitrators' work, the arbitrators' decision is to be issued by 2 March 1999."[29]

2.12 On 2 March 1999, the arbitrators, in their initial decision, requested the parties to supply them with certain additional information.[30] They indicated that "[f]ollowing our receipt and analysis of that information, we expect to be in a position to issue a final decision in this matter soon thereafter."[31]

2.13 On 3 March 1999, the United States took those actions described in Section B below. As described in Section I above, on 4 March 1999, the European Communities requested consultations with the United States on the matter under Article XXII:1 of the GATT and Article 4 of the DSU, and subsequently on 16 June 1999, pursuant to the EC request, the DSB established this Panel pursuant to Article 6 of the DSU.

2.14 On 6 April 1999, the Article 22.6 arbitrators and the Article 21.5 panels issued simultaneously to the parties, both the decision of the arbitrators, and the panel reports on the recourse to Article 21.5 by Ecuador and the European Communities.[32]

---

26 WT/DSB/M/54.

27 *Ibid.*

28 Communication, dated 18 February 1999, from the United States to the Chairman of the DSB, WT/DS27/47.

29 *Ibid.*

30 Decision by the Arbitrators, *European Communities – Regime for the Importation, Sale and Distribution of Bananas - Recourse to Arbitration by the European Communities under Article 22.6 of the DSU ("EC - Bananas III (US) (Article 22.6 – EC)")*, WT/DS27/ARB, 9 April 1999, DSR 1999:II, 725, para. 2.10.

31 WT/DS27/48.

32 See WT/DSB/M/59.

2.15 On 7 April 1999, pursuant to Article 22.7 of the DSU, the United States requested that "the DSB authorise it to suspend concessions in an amount up to US$191.4 million per year...", referring to the arbitrators' decision issued to the parties on 6 April 1999.[33]

2.16 On 9 April 1999, the following decision of the arbitrators was circulated to the Members:

> "[T]he Arbitrators determine that the level of nullification or impairment suffered by the United States in the matter European Communities – *Regime for the Importation, Sale and Distribution of Bananas* is US$191.4 million per year. Accordingly, the Arbitrators decide that the suspension by the United States of the application to the European Communities and its member States of tariff concessions and related obligations under GATT 1994 covering trade in a maximum amount of US$191.4 million per year would be consistent with Article 22.4 of the DSU."[34]

2.17 In reaching this conclusion, the arbitrators explained as follows:

> "[W]e cannot fulfil our task to assess the *equivalence* between the two levels before we have reached a view on whether the revised EC regime is, in light of our and the Appellate Body's findings in the original dispute, fully WTO-consistent. It would be the WTO-inconsistency of the revised EC regime that would be the root cause of any nullification or impairment suffered by the United States. Since the level of the proposed suspension of concessions is to be equivalent to the level of nullification or impairment, logic dictates that our examination as Arbitrators focuses on that latter level before we will be in a position to ascertain its equivalence to the level of the suspension of concessions proposed by the United States."[35]

2.18 On 12 April 1999, the panel which addressed the recourse to Article 21.5 of the DSU by the European Communities circulated a final report to the Members. In its report, the panel concluded that "we do not make findings as requested by the European Communities."[36] In this proceeding, the European Communities claimed as follows:

> "[S]ince Guatemala, Honduras, Mexico and the United States had failed to pursue any recourse to dispute settlement procedures un-

---

[33] Communication, dated 9 April 1999, from the United States to the Chairman of the DSB, WT/DS27/49.

[34] Decision by the Arbitrators, *EC - Bananas III (US) (Article 22.6 – EC)*, *supra*, footnote 30, para. 8.1.

[35] *Ibid.*, para. 4.8 (emphasis original).

[36] Panel Report, *European Communities – Regime for the Importation, Sale and Distribution of Bananas - Recourse to Article 21.5 of the DSU by the European Communities* ("*EC – Bananas III (Article 21.5 – EC)*"), WT/DS27/RW/EEC and Corr.1, 12 April 1999, DSR 1999:II, 783, para. 5.1.

der the rules and procedures of the DSU, the new EC regime for the importation, sale and distribution of bananas adopted in order to comply with the recommendations and rulings of the DSB in the three dispute settlement procedures (*'EC – Regime for Importation, Sale and Distribution of Bananas'*) had to be deemed ...in so far as [these parties to the original dispute] were concerned, to be in conformity with the WTO covered agreements so long as those original parties had not successfully challenged the new EC regime under the relevant dispute settlement procedures of the WTO."[37]

2.19 On the same day, the panel which addressed the recourse to Article 21.5 of the DSU by Ecuador circulated a final report to the Members. In its report, the panel concluded that "aspects of the EC's import regime for bananas are inconsistent with the EC's obligations under ... GATT 1994 and ... GATS."[38] This report was adopted by the DSB at its meeting of 6 May 1999.[39]

2.20 At its meeting of 19 April 1999, the DSB, "pursuant to the US request under Article 22.7 of the DSU, agree[d] to grant authorization to suspend the application to the European Communities and its member States of tariff concessions and related obligations under GATT 1994, consistent with the decision of the Arbitrators contained in document WT/DS27/ARB."[40]

B. Measure at Issue

2.21 In this case, the European Communities requested that the DSB establish a panel,

> "with respect to the US decision, effective as of 3 March 1999, to withhold liquidation on imports from the EC of a list of products, together valued at $520 million on an annual basis, and to impose a contingent liability for 100 per cent duties on each individual importation of affected products as of this date (annex 1 [to the request]). This measure includes administrative provisions that foresee, among other things, the posting of a bond to cover the full potential liability."[41]

2.22 This request corresponds to the USTR press release of 3 March 1999, which states as follows:

> "[E]ffective today, the U.S. Customs Service will begin 'withholding liquidation' on imports valued at over $500 million of selected

---

37 *Ibid.*, para. 2.22.

38 Panel Report, *European Communities – Regime for the Importation, Sale and Distribution of Bananas - Recourse to Article 21.5 of the DSU by Ecuador* ("*EC – Bananas III (Article 21.5 – Ecuador)*"), 12 April 1999, WT/DS27/RW/ECU, DSR 1999:II, 803, para. 7.1.

39 WT/DSB/M/61.

40 WT/DSB/M/59.

41 WT/DS165/8.

products from the European Union (EU), consistent with U.S. rights under the WTO agreements. Withholding liquidation imposes contingent liability for 100 per cent duties on affected products as of March 3, 1999."[42]

2.23 On 3 March 1999, Mr. Peter L. Scher, Special Trade Negotiator of the Trade Representative of the United States ("USTR"), wrote to Mr. Raymond W. Kelly, Commissioner of the US Customs Service, as follows:

"On January 14, 1999, the United States requested authorization from the World Trade Organization (WTO) to suspend the application to the European Communities (EC) of tariff concessions covering trade in an amount of US$520 million in response to the EC's failure to implement a WTO-consistent regime for the importation, sale, and distribution of bananas. The [USTR] intends to implement this suspension of tariff concessions by directing the Customs Service to impose 100 percent duties, ad valorem, on the products listed in the attachment to this letter. (See also 63 Fed. Reg. 63099 and 63 Fed. Reg. 71665 giving notice of the proposed increase in duties on selected products).

The EC requested that the U.S.-proposed level of suspension be reviewed by WTO arbitrators. The WTO dispute settlement rules require that the arbitration proceedings be completed on March 2. The arbitrators, however, failed to meet this deadline and are not expected to make their final decision until some later date. The USTR now seeks to preserve its right to impose 100 percent duties as of March 3, pending the release of the arbitrators' final decision.

Therefore, I am hereby requesting that until further notice the Customs Service withhold liquidation of entries of all articles identified in the attachment to this letter that are the products of Austria, Belgium, Finland, France, the Federal Republic of Germany, Greece, Ireland, Italy, Luxembourg, Portugal, Spain, Sweden or the United Kingdom and that are entered, or withdrawn from warehouse, for consumption, on or after March 3, 1999. I further request that the Customs Service today instruct port directors to review the sufficiency of bond posted with respect to entries described in the previous sentence, and to take steps to provide adequate or additional security in accordance with 19 C.F.R. §113.13."[43]

---

[42] USTR Press Release, dated 3 March 1999, "United States takes customs action on European imports" (EC Annex VII).

[43] Letter dated 3 March 1999 from Mr. Peter L. Scher, Special Trade Negotiator to Commissioner Raymond W. Kelly, US Customs Service (US Ex. 12).

2.24 In response to the USTR's request, Mr. Philip Metzger, Director of the Trade Compliance Division of the US Customs Service, in a memorandum regarding "European Sanctions",[44] gave the following instructions to the Customs Area and Port Directors:

> "RE: European Sanctions
>
> ...
>
> Effective for all merchandise classifiable under the Harmonized Tariff Schedule (HTS) subheadings listed below, entered, or withdrawn from warehouse, for consumption, on or after March 3, 1999, and produced in the listed countries, Area and Port Directors must require a Single Transaction Bond (STB) equal to the entered value of the merchandise. The only exception to this requirement is, at the discretion of the Port Director, the importer of record may use a continuous bond equal to 10 per cent of the total of the entered value of the covered merchandise imported by the importer for the preceding year. Ports should process increased continuous bonds immediately.
>
> No entry shall be scheduled to liquidate earlier than the 314th day, thereby ensuring the withholding of liquidation as requested by USTR. ...
>
> Affected countries*:
>
> Austria
> Belgium
> Finland
> France
> Federal Republic of Germany
> Greece
> Ireland
> Italy
> Luxembourg
> Portugal
> Spain
> Sweden
> United Kingdom
>
> *Please note that the Netherlands and Denmark are not included on this list. ...

[44] Memorandum of 4 March 1999 to Customs Area and Port Directors, CMC Directors from Trade Compliance Division, US Customs Service, Regarding European Sanctions (EC Annex VIII).

HTS Subheadings

0210.19.00

Meat of swine, salted, in brine, dried or smoked, other than hams, shoulders, and cuts thereof, with bone in, or bellies (streaky) and cuts thereof

0406.90.57

Pecorino cheese, made from sheep's milk, in original loaves, not suitable for grating

1905.30.00

Sweet biscuits; waffles and wafers

3307.30.50

Bath preparation, other than bath salts

3406.00.00

Candles, tapers and the like

3920.20.00

Other plates, sheets, film, foil and strip, noncellular and not reinforced, laminated, supported or similarly combined with other materials, of polymers of propylene

4202.22.15

Handbags, whether or not with shoulder strap, including those without handle, with outer surface of sheeting of plastic

4202.32.10

Articles of a kind normally carried in the pocket or in the handbag, with outer surface of sheeting of plastic, of reinforced or laminated plastic

4805.50.00

Uncoated felt paper and paperboard in rolls or sheets

4819.20.00

Folding cartons, boxes and cases, of noncorrugated paper or paperboard

4911.91.20

Lithographs on paper or paperboard, not over 0.51 mm in thickness, printed not over 20 years at time of importation

6110.10.10

Sweaters, pullovers, sweatshirts, waistcoats (vests) and similar articles, knitted or crocheted, wholly of cashmere

6302.21.90

Bed linen, other than knit or crocheted, printed, of cotton, other than containing any embroidery, lace, braid, edging, trimming, piping or applique work, not napped

8507.20.80

Lead-acid storage batteries, other than of a kind used for starting piston engines or as the primary source of electrical power for electrically powered vehicles of subheading 8703.90

8516.71.00

Electrothermic coffee or tea makers, of a kind used for domestic purposes"[45]

2.25 On the same day, the Customs Area and Port Directors accordingly started requiring that an importer of listed products imported from the listed EC countries lodge, in most cases, an increased continuous bond for the release of the products into the United States prior to the final liquidation in accordance with the instructions referred to in paragraph 2.24 above.

C. *US Ordinary Liquidation Procedures, Bonding Requirements and Relevant Tariff Rates*

2.26 Under US law, when a shipment reaches the United States, the importer of record (i.e. the owner, purchaser, or licensed customs broker designated by the owner, purchaser, or consignee) will file entry documents for the goods with the port director at the port of entry. Imported goods are not legally entered until after the shipment has arrived within the port of entry, delivery of the merchandise has been authorised by the Customs, and estimated duties have been paid.[46]

2.27 Liability for payment of duties is incurred at the time the goods arrive on a vessel within a Customs port when there is an intent to unload the goods at that port, or, if arrival is otherwise than by vessel, at the time of arrival within the Customs territory of the United States. The applicable rate of duty is the rate for the date the merchandise was entered for consumption or for immediate transportation of goods from one US port to another (so that Customs documentation can be submitted at the latter port).[47]

2.28 At the time of entry, importers are required to pay only estimated duties. Any other duties and fees are to be collected at the time of liquidation, i.e. when the Customs has calculated the final amount of duties on imports based upon confirmation of the correct valuation, classification and origin of the goods. Section 1504, Paragraph (a) of the Tariff Act of 1930 sets forth a time-limit on liquidation, subject to certain exceptions, as follows: "...[A]n entry of merchandise not

---

[45] *Ibid.*

[46] Excerpts from Customs Website on Entry Procedures (US Ex. 8), §2.

[47] US Responses to Questions of the Panel and the Parties, dated 13 January 1999, para. 6 (Appendix 2.4 of this Panel Report).

liquidated within one year from (1) the date of entry ...(4) ... shall be deemed liquidated at the rate of duty, value, quantity, and amount of duties asserted at the time of entry by the importer of record. ..."[48]

2.29 Before liquidation takes place, however, importers can obtain the release of their imports into the United States by submitting a bond and filing proper documentation. Section 142.4(a) of the Code of Federal Regulations ("CFR") Vol. 19, provides:

> "...[M]erchandise shall not be released from Customs custody at the time Customs receives the entry documentation or the entry summary documentation which serves as both the entry and the entry summary, as required by §142.3 unless a single entry or continuous bond on Customs Form 301 ... has been filed. ..."[49]

2.30 The amount of a continuous bond on imports is determined in accordance with the "Guidelines for Determining Amounts of Bonds" attached to the Customs Directive, which the Assistant Commissioner of the Office of Commercial Operation issued to, among others, the District/Area Directors and Port Directors on 23 July 1991.[50] The Guidelines set forth:

> "The bond limit of liability amount shall be fixed in an amount the district director may deem necessary to accomplish the purpose for which the bond is given. The non-discretionary bond amount minimum is $50,000. ...[T]he following formula shall be used.
>
> None to $1,000,000 duties and taxes – the bond limit of liability amount shall be fixed in multiples of $10,000 nearest to 10 percent of duties, taxes and fees paid by the importer or broker acting as importer of record during the calendar year preceding the date of the application.
>
> Over $1,000,000 duties and taxes – the bond limit of liability amount shall be fixed in multiples of $100,000 nearest to 10 percent of duties, taxes and fees paid by the importer or broker acting as importer of record during the calendar year preceding the date of the application."[51]

2.31 The amount of a single transaction bond is determined in accordance with the same Guidelines, which set forth:

> "Generally, a single transaction ... bond ... will be executed in an amount not less than the total entered value plus all duties, taxes, and fees which apply, unless the merchandise being imported falls

[48] 19 U.S.C. §1504 (US Ex. 11).

[49] 19 C.F.R. §142.4(a) (1999) (US Ex. 11).

[50] The Customs Directive No. 099 3510-004, *Monetary Guidelines for Setting Bond Amounts*, 23 July 1991 (the "Customs Directive") (US Ex. 4).

[51] *Ibid.*, pp. 3-4.

into one of the following categories. In these cases, the bond will be executed in an amount which is not less than three times the total entered value of the merchandise.

1. Merchandise Subject to Other Agency Requirements Where Failure to Redeliver Could Pose a Threat to the Public Health and Safety

A) Food and Drug Administration (FDA) – All

...

G) Toxic Substances Control Act (TOSCA) – All"[52]

2.32 However, Section 113.13(d) of the CFR, Vol. 19 sets forth the authority of the port director to impose additional security requirements as follows:

> "(d) Additional security. Notwithstanding the provisions of this section or any other provision of this chapter, if a port director ... believes that acceptance of a transaction secured by a continuous bond would place the revenue in jeopardy or otherwise hamper the enforcement of Customs law or regulations, he shall require additional security."[53]

2.33 Accordingly, the Guidelines provide that the standard formulas mentioned in paragraphs 2.30 and 2.31 above shall not be applied if "any district director is aware that either extraordinary circumstances or a greater risk to the government involved."[54] In such cases, the Guidelines require that:

> "the district director with such knowledge shall contact the district where the bond is filed and convey the supporting facts so that appropriate action, if required, can be taken. For example, where the amount of a continuous bond does not cover the duty on a particular shipment and the district director suspects that a greater risk to the government is involved, the district director shall:
>
> 1. secure, at the time of release, deposit of the estimated duty due on the shipment, or,
>
> 2. request a single entry bond for that shipment, or
>
> 3. request that a new continuous bond in a higher amount be filed."[55]

2.34 Based upon the US data for February 1999, continuous bonds were used for approximately 97 per cent of all entries made in that month, versus 3 per cent use of single transaction bonds. For entries from EC countries, approximately 94

---

52 *Ibid.*, pp. 4-5.
53 19 C.F.R. §113.13(d) (1999) (US Ex. 6).
54 Customs Directive, op. cit., p. 3.
55 *Ibid.*

per cent of entries in February 1999 were made using continuous bonds, versus 6 per cent use of single transaction bonds.[56]

2.35 As of 3 March 1999, the binding tariff rates and applicable tariff rates of the United States with respect to the listed products were as follows:

Products	**HTS Number**	**Binding /Applied Rate**
Pork, dried smoked	0210.19.00	$0.015/kg
Pecorino cheese	0406.90.57	Free
Sweet biscuit	1905.30.00	Free
Bath preparations	3307.30.50	4.9%
Candles, tapers	3406.00.00	Free
Plates, sheets, film	3920.20.00	4.2%
Handbags, plastic	4202.22.15	18%
Pocketbooks, plastic	4202.32.10	$0.121/kg + 4.6%
Felt paper and paperboard	4805.50.00	Free
Folding cartons	4819.20.00	1.4%
Lithographs	4911.91.20	$0.066/kg
Sweaters, cashmere	6110.10.10	5.8%
Bed linen, cotton	6302.21.90	7.2%
Lead-acid storage batteries	8507.20.80	3.5%
Coffee or tea makers	8516.71.00	3.7%

*US Ex. 7.

D. Developments in the United States after 3 March 1999

2.36 On 19 April 1999, the USTR determined that "effective April 19, 1999, a 100 per cent *ad valorem* rate of duty shall be applied to [certain] articles that are of the products of certain EC member States",[57] following which the port directors were instructed to assess 100 per cent duties on those products, and accordingly 100 per cent duty deposits were required at the time of entry from 19 April 1999.[58] The selected products were (i) bath preparations, other than bath salts; (ii) handbags, plastic; (iii) pocketbooks, plastic; (iv) felt paper and paperboard; (v) folding cartons; (vi) lithographs, (vii) bed linen, cotton; (viii) lead-acid storage batteries; and (ix) coffee or tea makers (except for those from Italy).[59]

2.37 The following charts indicate the fluctuations (on a monthly basis and on the basis of the average of a preceding 12-month period) in the total value of imports from the European Communities during the period from January 1997 to September 1999, with respect to (i) those products contained in the 3 March list,

---

[56] US Responses to Additional Questions of the Panel, dated 10 February 2000 (Appendix 2.10 to this Panel Report), para. 13.
[57] 64 Fed. Reg. 19209 (EC Annex X).
[58] US Responses to Additional Questions of the Panel, dated 8 February 2000, para. 20 (Appendix 2.6 to this Panel Report).
[59] US Ex. 7.

and subject to the 19 April action (Chart A)[60], and (ii) those products contained in the 3 March list but not subject to the 19 April action (Chart B)[61]:

60 Chart A is derived from the data contained in US Ex. 5.

61 Chart B is derived from the data contained in US Ex. 10.

CHART A

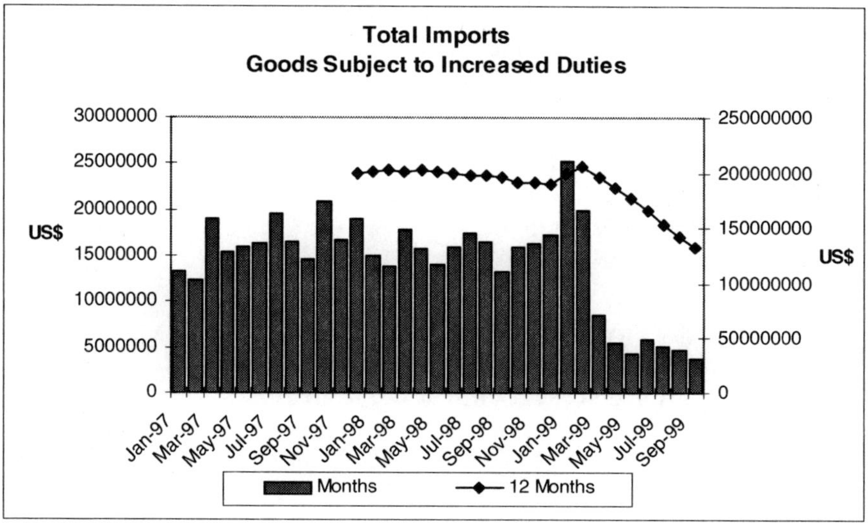

CHART B

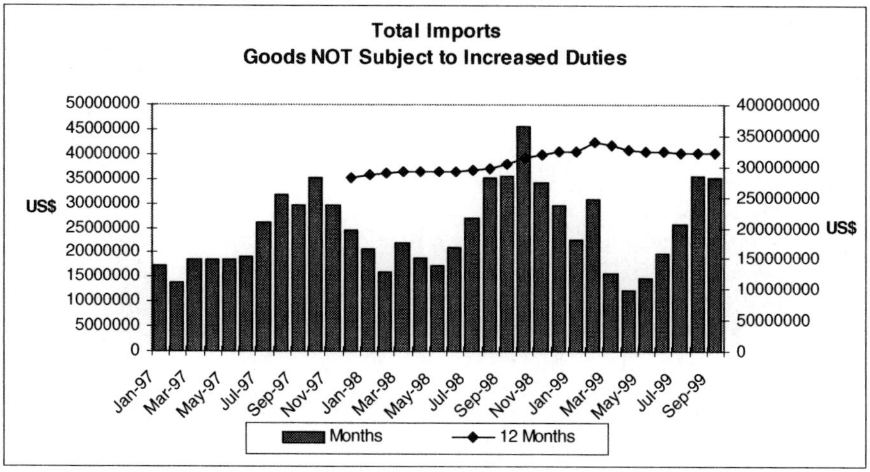

III. ARGUMENTS OF THE PARTIES

3.1 The arguments of the parties are set out in their submissions to the Panel (see Appendices 1.1 through 1.10 for the European Communities and Appendices 2.1 to 2.10 for the United States, to this Panel Report).

IV. ARGUMENTS OF THE THIRD PARTIES

4.1 The arguments of the third parties are set out in their submissions to the Panel (see Appendix 3 for Dominica and St. Lucia, Appendix 4 for Ecuador (original Spanish), Appendix 5 for India, Appendix 6 for Jamaica, and Appendix 7 for Japan, to this Panel Report.

V. INTERIM REVIEW

5.1 On 27 March both the United States and the European Communities requested the Panel to review the interim report which had been issued to the parties on 13 March 2000. On 29 March, the European Communities reacted in writing to the US request. On 30 March the United States requested permission from the Panel to respond to the latest EC comments within 5 days. On 31 March the Panel granted this request and invited the United States to send its response to the EC comments by 4 April. On 4 April the United States sent us its last set of comments.

5.2 In its request for review, the United States submitted four main comments and suggested other changes to our description of the facts of this case. The European Communities, in addition to commenting on the US request for review, also requested the Panel to review mainly two aspects of the Panel's findings.

5.3 First, the United States argued that in the interim report the Panel reached conclusions on Articles 3.7 and 23.2(a) of the DSU for which the European Communities has not submitted any claim or any arguments.

5.4 With reference to Article 23.2(a), the European Communities responded that the United States was attempting to redefine the scope of this dispute and reargue Article 23.2(a). It insisted that in its written and oral submissions it referred to all the discussions and conclusions of the Panel Report on *US - Section 301*. In particular, the European Communities quoted paragraph 20 of its first written submission:

> "... This course of events confirms that the USTR implemented the further action (*unilaterally*) *decided upon only on the basis of its domestic legislation* and thus *irrespective* of whether that action

conformed to the requirements of Article 23; paragraphs 1 and 2, of the DSU."[62] (underlined on the EC original, italics added)

The European Communities reiterated paragraph 14 of its oral presentation at the first substantive meeting to the effect that:

> "The guiding principle of Article 23 is contained in paragraph 1 which also governs the more detailed provisions of paragraph 2 since this paragraph starts with the words "In such cases, Members shall" by which paragraph 1 is incorporated into paragraph 2. As the panel on Sections 301-310 has stated, Article 23.1 of the DSU prescribes that 'Members have to have recourse to the DSU dispute settlement system to the exclusion of any other system, *in particular a system of unilateral enforcement of WTO rights and obligations*'."[63] (underlined on the EC original)

Finally, the European Communities referred to the various notices published in the Federal Register on this case (EC Annexes I, II and III), which deal expressly with both the unilateral determination of incompatibility and the unilateral implementation of trade sanctions.

5.5 For the United States, the above references are not sufficient for the present Panel to reach the conclusion that the 3 March Measure was "contrary to Articles 23.2(a) and 21.5, first sentence, together with Article 23.1 of the DSU". Inasmuch as it had no notice that Article 23.2(a) would be the subject of Panel findings, the United States claimed that it did not make any arguments on this subject.

5.6 Second, on the substance of the Panel's discussion regarding the scope of Article 23.2(a) of the DSU, the United States argued that statements made by USTR representatives had no legal significance and cannot themselves constitute "determinations". For the United States, the ability to take such a position for the purposes of asserting its rights under Article 22 of the DSU, is an inherent part of the exercise by a Member of its rights under the DSU. The European Communities responded that public statements constitute evidence of the nature of the 3 March Measure but are not measures themselves.

5.7 Third, the United States reiterated that the increased bonding requirements of the 3 March Measure did not create any liability additional to the US tariff bindings. The European Communities agreed with the conclusions reached by the Panel on this matter.

5.8 The Panel notes that in its request for establishment of a panel the European Communities claimed violations of Articles ***3***, 21, 22 and ***23*** of the DSU.[64] Section 3.3 of the EC first submission is entitled "The violation of Article 23 and

[62] EC First Submission, para. 20 (Appendix 1.1 to this Panel Report).

[63] EC Oral Presentation at the First Substantive Meeting, para. 14 (Appendix 1.2 to this Panel Report).

[64] WT/DS165/8.

Article 3 of the DSU".[65] For us the ordinary meaning of the last sentence of Article 3.7 of the DSU is clear when it provides that the suspension of concessions or other obligations is to be used as a last resort "subject to authorization by the DSB of such measures". In paragraph 5 of its first submission, the European Communities refers to the three notices in the US Federal Register and states that "This proposed action was based on the unilateral determination by the United States that "the measures the EC has undertaken to apply as of January 1, 1999 fail to implement the WTO recommendations concerning the EC banana regime".[66] In its first submission, the European Communities refers to the US measures being in contravention of the requirements of Article 23, paragraphs 1 *and* 2.[67] In paragraph 86 of its rebuttals, the European Communities argues that "Article 23.1 and 23.2(a) of the DSU specify that such a finding (which in the terminology of Article 23 is called a 'determination') can only be made under the rules and procedures of the DSU".[68] The Panel also notes the arguments made by the European Communities, as quoted above in paragraph 5.4.

5.9 In paragraph 6.17 of our findings, we state that Article 23.1 contains a general obligation that any Member that "seeks the redress" of a WTO violation shall do so within the institutional framework of the WTO. We also reiterate the conclusions of the *US - Section 301* Panel Report that paragraph 2 of Article 23 only provides "examples" of conduct that may contravene the rules of the DSU and which, if they take place when a Member is seeking to redress a WTO violation, constitute a violation of Article 23.1.[69] In other words, as we discuss in our findings, when a measure is taken in the context described in the first paragraph of Article 23 – i.e., when a Member is seeking the redress of a WTO violation – such measure, if taken outside the institutional framework of the WTO or in a manner inconsistent with the DSU, violates Article 23.1 of the DSU.

5.10 In the Panel's view, the main claim of the European Communities is that on 3 March 1999 the United States acted unilaterally, contrary to the fundamental obligation of Article 23 of the DSU. We recall that Article 23.1 provides that when a Member seeks the redress of a WTO violation it shall have recourse to and abide by the DSU. The more specific allegations of DSU inconsistencies only serve to provide examples of how the United States did not "abide by" the rules of the DSU. Since, in our view, the 3 March Measure is inconsistent with Articles 3.7, last sentence, 22.6, 23.2(c), 21.5 and 23.2(a), the United States by introducing the 3 March Measure did not abide by the DSU. Given that the 3 March Measure took place while the United States was seeking to redress a WTO violation, the United States violated Article 23.1 of the DSU.

---

65 EC First Submission (Appendix 1.1 to this Panel Report).

66 *Ibid.*, para. 5.

67 *Ibid.*, para. 20.

68 EC Rebuttal Submission, para. 86 (Appendix 1.5 to this Panel Report).

69 Panel Report, *United States – Sections 301-310 of the Trade Act of 1974* ("*US – Section 301*"),WT/DS152/R, adopted 27 January 2000, DSR 2000:II, 815, para. 7.39.

5.11 In addition, as we stated throughout our findings, we consider that the very wording of Article 23.1 covers situations where a Member seeks to redress any WTO violation, whether determined by a WTO adjudicating body or unilaterally. It would be ludicrous if the first paragraph of Article 23, which contains the general prohibition against unilateral actions, condemned only situations where a Member takes unilateral sanctions following a WTO - determined violation, without prohibiting situations where a Member determines unilaterally that a WTO violation has taken place before taking unilateral trade sanctions. For us, therefore, the prohibition against unilateral determination is contained in the first paragraph of Article 23 and the European Communities has clearly made claims under Article 23 paragraphs 1 and 2.

5.12 The United States seems to be arguing that had it known that there was a claim challenging its 3 March unilateral action, it would have been able to defend itself better. We consider, on the contrary that the United States was given ample opportunities to defend itself. In its first submission, the European Communities presented the dispute as one where USTR had "imposed trade sanction by effectively stopping trade. This course of events confirms that the USTR implemented the further action (unilaterally) decided upon only on the basis of its domestic legislation and thus irrespective of whether that action conformed to the requirements of Article 23, paragraphs 1 and 2".[70] In its oral statements to the Panel at the first substantive meeting and in its rebuttals the European Communities refers to various official statements from USTR all of which provide clear evidence of the nature of the EC claims.[71]

5.13 Notwithstanding the serious allegations of violation of Article 23 of the DSU, throughout this panel process the United States concentrates its arguments and discussions on the technicalities of its Customs Service's bonding requirements and the changes it put in place as of 3 March 1999 on listed imports from the European Communities. However, the issues before this Panel are not limited to bonding requirements. The evidence before us demonstrates that the United States was seeking to impose trade sanctions against the European Communities. In this respect, we recall that the ordinary meaning of the terms "***seek*** the redress" (the term used in Article 23.1) is "look for, try to obtain or bring about"[72], implying a desire, an effort (successful or not) to "redress". For us, it is clear from the evidence that the United States was trying to impose trade sanctions - the ultimate remedy under WTO law - against listed imports from the European Communities. The various statements, declarations and other internal memos of USTR and the US Customs Services confirm the context of the 3 March Measure, as a measure whereby the United States was seeking the redress of what it had unilaterally determined to be a WTO violation.

[70] EC First submission, para. 20 (Appendix 1.1 to this Panel Report).

[71] E.g. EC Oral Presentation at the First Substantive Meeting, para. 10 (Appendix 1.2 to this Panel Report), and EC Rebuttal Submission, para. 2 (Appendix 1.5 to this Panel Report).

[72] The New Little Oxford Dictionary.

5.14 In addition, even if we were to accept the US argument that the ability to take such a public position (that the EC implementing measure violated the DSU) for the purposes of asserting its rights under Article 22 of the DSU, is an inherent part of the exercise by a Member of its rights under the DSU, we are of the view that the unilateral determination made with the 3 March Measure was not of the nature of what was necessary for the United States to assert and exercise its rights under Article 22. Article 23.2(a) *a contrario* authorises Members to make determinations through recourse to the DSU and consistent with findings of panels, the Appellate Body or arbitration. When, in January 1999, the United States required a DSB authorization pursuant to Article 22, it had to have reached an internal decision that the EC implementing measure was WTO inconsistent. (Since the United States needed to come up with a proposal for sanctions, it means that the United States needed to have decided previously that the implementing measure was, in its view, WTO inconsistent.) This US decision was a form of "determination", but one that is legal since made "through recourse to dispute settlement in accordance with" the DSU, namely, as required under Article 22. However on 3 March, when the United States decided to act outside of the DSU process, it made a unilateral determination that the EC implementing measure was WTO inconsistent. In doing so, the United States was not (anymore) making a determination through the recourse of the DSU; in doing so the United States did not abide by the DSU. The 3 March Measure in seeking the redress of a unilaterally determined WTO violation was inconsistent with Articles 23.2(a) and 21.5, and thus necessarily violated Article 23.1.

5.15 We reiterate that on 3 March the United States had no right - no DSB authorization - to collect import duties above its bindings. In putting in place increased bonding requirements to secure, as of 3 March, the payment of tariff duties up to 100 percent on listed imports from the European Communities, the United States unilaterally began enforcing a right that it did not have, as bonding requirements are of the nature of a security and an enforcement mechanism.

5.16 Fourth, the United States also challenges our understanding of the US interpretation of the mandatory nature of the 60 day time-period within which an arbitration pursuant to Article 22.6 is to take place. For us this US interpretation was clear from the public records of the minutes of the DSB and the Article 22.6 DSU Decision of the Arbitrators of 9 April 1999[73] in *EC – Bananas III*. The main point of our findings is that on 3 March, when it put in place the increased bonding requirements, the United States had not requested the retroactive application of the suspension of concessions and should have known that. On 3 March, therefore, it could not claim that it was entitled to secure an eventual retroactive right to collect 100 per cent import tariffs on listed imports from the European Communities.

[73] Decision by the Arbitrators, *EC - Bananas III (US) (Article 22.6 – EC)*, *supra*, footnote 30.

5.17 The United States also argues that there is no evidence that there were any interest charges, costs or fees. We refer the United States to paragraph 6.42 below where the Panel proceeds to an estimation of the costs of any such 3 March increased bonding requirements based on the evidence submitted by the United States. With regard to the United States' discussion relating to the ordinary US Customs Service practices and what is allowed under Article 13 of the Agreement on Customs Valuation, we reiterate, again, that it is not our mandate to assess the bonding requirements practices of the US Customs Services in general.

5.18 With a view to ensuring the clarity of this Panel Report, and taking into account our discussion on the nature of the first sentence of Article 21.5 prohibiting unilateral determination of the WTO inconsistency of implementing measures, we have revised our findings in line with the above discussion. We have also taken into account other comments made by the United States, including calculation mistakes and improved our findings accordingly.

5.19 The European Communities is asking us to review our description of its claim with reference to the WTO inconsistency of some of the aspects of the Article 22.6 Arbitration Decision of 9 April (WT/DS27/ARB). The European Communities has also asked us to make others changes to our description of some of its arguments. We have carefully reviewed the submissions and oral statements of the European Communities and revised our draft accordingly. We would like, however, to emphasise some points.

5.20 In its rebuttals, the European Communities argues that the US action of 19 April was nothing but a confirmation of the 3 March measure[74]. The European Communities continues and argues that the "United States in the *Bananas* dispute [had] recourse to a request for authorization of the suspension of concessions or other obligations based on a unilateral determination that the EC failed to honour its WTO obligations".[75] For the European Communities this was so because the United States had not in hand an Article 21.5 panel report on the assessment of the WTO compatibility of the EC implementing measure when it requested the DSB authorization to retaliate. The European Communities then argues that because on 3 March the United States was in violation of Article 21.5, and because the 19 April action is only a confirmation of the 3 March Measure, on 19 April the United States was still in violation of Article 21.5. In other words, the 3 March violation was of a continuing nature. The European Communities claims that a refusal from this Panel to answer its request as to

[74] This was a reiteration of the EC argument developed in its rebuttals. See para. 20 of the EC Rebuttal Submission (Appendix 1.5 to this Panel Report).

[75] EC Oral Presentation at the Second Substantive Meeting, §II (Appendix 1.8 to this Panel Report).

the nature of the 3 March Measure's violation would constitute a denial of justice.[76]

5.21 We recall that the reason why the European Communities considers that the 3 March Measure violates Article 21.5 of the DSU is because the European Communities is of the view that a determination of the WTO compatibility of the EC implementing measure can only be done by an Article 21.5 panel and cannot be performed by the original panel through an arbitration procedure pursuant to Article 22.6 of the DSU. In this respect, the European Communities considers that the determination of the WTO compatibility of the EC implementation measure performed by the Article 22.6 Arbitration Decision of 9 April 1999 is thus invalid. This is why the European Communities takes the position that this Panel did not even need to mention the Article 22.6 Arbitration Decision given that for the European Communities that 9 April Arbitration Decision was concerned exclusively with the level of nullification and impairment of the revised EC Bananas regime.

5.22 We disagree with the European Communities. We rather find that on 3 March there was a valid ongoing WTO adjudicating process on the determination of the WTO compatibility of the EC implementing measure. But on 3 March, contrary to what was the case on 19 April, this adjudicating body (the Arbitration panel acting pursuant to Article 22.6) had not completed its work.

5.23 We have therefore changed the wording of some paragraphs of this panel report to ensure a better understanding of our discussion. We have also taken into

---

[76] The statement of the European Communities to the Panel was: "This aspect of the present case has a bearing not only on the legal basis for the violations about which the EC complains, but also on the question whether the violation is of a continuing nature. As the Panel will easily understand, this aspect of the case is therefore of fundamental importance for the EC. If the Panel finds in favour of the EC on this decisive point, the suspension of concessions is and remains inconsistent with the US obligations both for the initial list of 3 March 1999, which constitutes Annex 1 to the EC's request for the establishment of the Panel, and for the reduced list of 19 April 1999 which constitutes Annex 2 to the EC's request for the establishment of the Panel. The EC believes that it is entitled to receive an answer from the Panel with regard to this important claim on which the parties clearly have a disagreement with very important legal and practical consequences in the present case. A denial of justice on this point would necessarily lead to continuing legal uncertainty and more litigation. The EC has already pointed out in its written submissions that there was no justification to resort to the suspension of concessions or other obligations in the present case, neither on 3 March 1999 nor on 19 April 1999. The WTO-inconsistency of the 3 March measure could not "healed", by the authorization of the DSB of 19 April 1999 simply because it was legally flawed from the outset. The EC repeats that in this context, the DSB authorization of 19 April 1999 was a necessary, but not a sufficient prerequisite for the suspension of concessions or other obligations." EC Final statement 2nd meeting. This statement was a reiteration of the EC's arguments contained in its rebuttals. See for instance paras. 78, 81 and 82 of the EC Rebuttal Submission (Appendix 1.5 to this Panel Report): "However, in the case of the US, such a decision by the DSB [speaking of Article 21.5 of the DSU] was missing on 3 March, was also missing on 19 April and is still missing today... In conclusion, the EC reiterates that the contested US measure of 3 March 1999, confirmed on 19 April 1999, is inconsistent with Article 21.5 of the DSU. This inconsistency ... was equally not healed by the authorization... granted by the DSB on 19 April 1999".

account other comments made by the European Communities and revised our findings accordingly.

VI. FINDINGS

A. *Introduction*

6.1 This dispute concerns an alleged unilateral retaliation measure[77] taken on 3 March 1999 by the United States against listed imports from the European Communities, contrary to the WTO Agreement.

6.2 On 3 March the USTR press release provided as follows:

> "United States Takes Customs Action on European Imports
>
> [E]ffective today, the U.S. Customs Service will begin 'withholding liquidation' on imports valued at over $500 million of selected products from the European Union (EU), consistent with U.S. rights under the WTO agreements. Withholding liquidation imposes contingent liability for 100 per cent duties on affected products as of March 3, 1999."[78]

6.3 On 4 March 1999, the European Communities requested consultations with the United States with regard to a US decision effective as of 3 March 1999 requiring additional bonding requirements in respect of listed imports from the European Communities upon importation.[79]

6.4 The European Communities requested that the DSB establish a panel:

> "with respect to the US decision, effective as of 3 March 1999, to withhold liquidation on imports from the EC of a list of products, together valued at $520 million on an annual basis, and to impose a contingent liability for 100 per cent duties on each individual importation of affected products as of this date (annex 1 [to the request]). This measure includes administrative provisions that foresee, among other things, the posting of a bond to cover the full potential liability."[80]

The measure at issue is hereinafter referred to as the "3 March Measure" and is described in paragraphs 1.4 and 1.5 of this Panel Report. We note that the 3 March Measure was put in place as of 3 March pending the release of the Arbi-

---

77 In its First Submission, para.20 (Appendix 1.1 to this Panel Report), the European Communities makes allegation of "trade sanctions" imposed by the United States. We discuss briefly these various concepts hereinafter.

78 USTR Press Release, dated 3 March 1999, "United States Takes Customs Action on European Imports" (EC Annex VII).

79 See WT/DS165/1 and para. 1.2 of this Panel Report.

80 WT/DS165/8.

trators' final decision.[81] We are also aware that on 19 April the United States took a distinct legal action against a reduced list of imports from the European Communities pursuant to the 19 April DSB authorization[82].

6.5 On 16 June 1999 the Dispute Settlement Body (DSB) established the present Panel with the mandate to examine the request of the European Communities. The European Communities claims that the 3 March Measure is inconsistent with Articles 23.1 and 23.2 (in particular 23.2(c)), 3.7, 21.5, and 22.6 of the DSU and with Articles I, II, VIII and XI of GATT.

6.6 The 3 March Measure resulted[83], in most cases, in increased levels of bonding requirements on listed imports (which the United States calls the "retaliation list" [84]) from the European Communities (hereinafter referred to as "the EC listed imports"). The bonding requirements generally applicable to the EC listed imports and the 3 March increased bonding requirements are described in paragraphs 2.24 to 2.34 of this Panel Report[85].

B. EC Claims and US Defenses under the DSU and GATT 1994

1. The EC Claims

6.7 We understand the EC claims as being three-fold. First, the European Communities argues that on 3 March 1999 the United States "imposed trade sanctions by effectively stopping trade"[86]. In doing so, the United States acted unilaterally, contrary to Articles 23.1 and 23.2, and 3.7 of the DSU and Articles I, II, VIII and XI of GATT 1994. Secondly, the 3 March Measure contravenes the provisions of Article 22.6 in that it constitutes a suspension of concessions or other obligations which was imposed by the United States while the arbitration process pursuant to Article 22.6-22.7 of the DSU was still ongoing. Thirdly, the European Communities submits that the United States also violated Article 21.5 of the DSU because it had not exhausted this procedure when it requested DSB permission to suspend concessions or other obligations in respect of the EC listed imports. For the European Communities such a violation is of a continuing nature. For the European Communities, the 19 April action is only a confirmation of the US Measure of 3 March and it argues that a "[DSB decision adopting an Article 21.5 panel report] was missing on 3 March, was also missing on 19 April

---

[81] See the USTR Press Release, dated 3 March 1999, "United States Takes Customs Action on European Imports" (EC Annex VII).

[82] WT/DSB/M/59.

[83] US First Submission, paras. 33-34 (Appendix 2.1 to this Panel Report), and US Responses to Additional Questions of the Panel, dated 8 February 2000, paras. 3 to 5 (Appendix 2.6 to this Panel Report).

[84] Expression used by Deputy USTR, EC Annex X. See the list of such identified imports from the European Communities at para. 2.24 of this Panel Report.

[85] We further discuss our understanding of the 3 March increased bonding requirements in paras. 6.46 to 6.51 of this Panel Report.

[86] EC First submission, para. 20 (Appendix 1.1 to this Panel Report).

and is still missing today"[87]. In the European Communities' view, the WTO inconsistency of the 3 March Measure could not have been healed by the DSB authorization of 19 April because it was flawed from the outset: the DSB authorization of 19 April 1999 was a necessary, but not a sufficient prerequisite for the US suspension of concessions or other obligations.

2. *The US Defenses*

6.8 The United States' response is that the 3 March Measure did not constitute a suspension of concessions or other obligations: requiring bonds upon importation is a normal practice of the US Customs Service (and of many other Members including the European Communities), and is explicitly authorised by Article 13 of the Customs Valuation Agreement. For the United States, the 3 March Measure did not violate Articles I, II and VIII or XI of GATT. The United States argues that it did not violate Article 23 of the DSU: it only took action in order "to preserve its rights" to collect duties as of 3 March and duties were neither assessed nor collected on 3 March. The United States adds that it did not violate Article 21.5 because there is a conflict between the time prescriptions of Article 21.5 and those of Article 22 which should be resolved in favour of the US interpretation, since it is clear that the DSB must be requested to authorise suspension within 30 days of the expiry of the reasonable period of time. Otherwise, according to the United States, the reverse consensus rule would no longer apply. For the United States, the US action of 19 April and the 19 April DSB authorization are not matters before this Panel. Finally, the United States submits that the European Communities unduly delayed both the US request for an Article 21.5 WTO compatibility assessment before the expiry of the reasonable period of time and the Article 22.6 arbitration process. For the United States, if the DSU procedural stages had been respected, the arbitration report authorising WTO compatible suspension of concessions or other obligations would have been issued to the parties before 3 March 1999.

C. *US Request for a Preliminary Ruling*

6.9 On 21 January 2000, in the cover letter of its Rebuttal Submission, the United States requested "the Panel to clarify, prior to the outset of the second substantive meeting, the measures that it considers to be within the Panel's terms of reference...".

6.10 The European Communities responded, in its letter dated 24 January 2000, that the "Panel should not accede to this request at this late stage of the proceedings before it (...) unless the United States was able to show 'good cause' for granting an exception".[88]

---

[87] EC Second submission, paras. 77-78 (Appendix 1.5 to this Panel Report).

[88] EC Letter dated 24 January 2000 (Appendix 1.6 to this Panel Report).

6.11 On 9 February 2000 (at the beginning of the second substantive meeting of the Panel), the Panel heard the views of the parties on this matter. On the same day, the Panel ruled that:

> "9. Implicit in the US request for this ruling would appear to be a concern that this Panel may be going beyond its terms of reference, namely in examining measures other than that of 3 March 1999.
>
> 10. The claims from the European Communities as well as the defense submitted by the United States oblige us to understand what was effectively done on 3 March, if anything, in comparison with what is usually done on those listed imports or what was done on the same listed imports on 19 April 1999. The EC claims also oblige us to be fully informed of the sequence of events that surrounded the 3 March decision, including that of 19 April.
>
> 11. Some of the Panel's questions to the parties, and in particular to the United States, relate to the normal US bonding requirements, the bonding requirements imposed as of 3 March on listed imports, and any subsequent US actions that may clarify the nature and effect of the 3 March Measure. The Panel considers that the US replies to these questions are important to the Panel's understanding of the matter at issue.
>
> 12. We note that in its report on *Argentine – Measures Affecting Imports of Footwear, Textiles, Apparel and Other Items* (WT/DS56/R, para. 6.63) the panel did examine events that took place after the date of the measure at issue for the purpose of understanding the way the Argentinian tariff system worked.
>
> 13. Accordingly, we shall continue to limit ourselves to our terms of reference and to the measure therein identified, keeping in mind that events surrounding the 3 March Measure may have to be addressed in order for the Panel to provide an answer to the claims at issue.
>
> 14. Finally, we are aware of our duties, pursuant to Article 11 of the DSU, to perform an objective assessment of the facts and the law applicable to the matter at issue."

D. *EC Claims that the 3 March Measure Violated Articles 23 and Others of the DSU*

1. *Claims under Article 23*

(a) Article 23 of the DSU as a Whole

6.12 We understand that the core of the EC claims is that the 3 March Measure is a 'trade sanction' that contravenes Article 23, first and second paragraphs.

6.13 The Panel believes that the adopted Panel Report on United States – *Sections 301-310 of the Trade Act of 1974* ("*US – Section 301*")[89] has confirmed the crucial importance that WTO Members place on the dispute settlement system of the WTO, as the exclusive means to redress any violations of any provisions of the WTO Agreement.[90] This fundamental principle is embedded in Article 23 of the DSU:

> "*Strengthening of the Multilateral System*
>
> 1. When Members seek the redress of a violation of obligations or other nullification or impairment of benefits under the covered agreements or an impediment to the attainment of any objective of the covered agreements, they shall have recourse to, and abide by, the rules and procedures of this Understanding.
>
> 2. In such cases, Members shall:
>
> (a) not make a determination to the effect that a violation has occurred, that benefits have been nullified or impaired or that the attainment of any objective of the covered agreements has been impeded, except through recourse to dispute settlement in accordance with the rules and procedures of this Understanding, and shall make any such determination consistent with the findings contained in the panel or Appellate Body report adopted by the DSB or an arbitration award rendered under this Understanding;
>
> (b) follow the procedures set forth in Article 21 to determine the reasonable period of time for the Member concerned to implement the recommendations and rulings; and
>
> (c) follow the procedures set forth in Article 22 to determine the level of suspension of concessions or other obligations and obtain DSB authorization in accordance with those procedures before suspending concessions or other obligations under the covered agreements in response to the failure of the Member concerned to implement the recommendations and rulings within that reasonable period of time."

6.14 An important reason why Article 23 of the DSU must be interpreted with a view to prohibiting any form of unilateral action is because such unilateral actions threaten the stability and predictability of the multilateral trade system, a necessary component for "market conditions conducive to individual economic

---

89 Panel Report, *US – Section 301*, *supra*, footnote 69.

90 See the numerous statements of Members at the DSB meeting of 27 January 2000, WT/DSB/M/74 approving the content of that Panel Report.

activity in national and global markets"[91] which, in themselves, constitute a fundamental goal of the WTO. Unilateral actions are, therefore, contrary to the essence of the multilateral trade system of the WTO. As stated in the Panel Report on *US – Section 301*:

> "7.75 Providing security and predictability to the multilateral trading system is another central object and purpose of the system which could be instrumental to achieving the broad objectives of the Preamble. Of all WTO disciplines, the DSU is one of the most important instruments to protect the security and predictability of the multilateral trading system and through it that of the market-place and its different operators. DSU provisions must, thus, be interpreted in the light of this object and purpose and in a manner which would most effectively enhance it."[92]

6.15 In the *US - Section 301* dispute, the Panel was convinced that the legislation at issue had to be examined both from the perspective of the damage it causes to Member governments and from the perspective of the damages caused to the market-place itself. The following statement regarding the mere existence of a law that would allow for some unilateral actions to be taken, is even more relevant in specific instances of unilateral measures, such as those at issue in the present case:

> "...[unilateral actions] may prompt economic operators to change their commercial behaviour in a way that distorts trade. Economic operators may be afraid, say, to continue ongoing trade with, or investment in, the industries or products threatened by unilateral measures. Existing trade may also be distorted because economic operators may feel a need to take out extra insurance to allow for the illegal possibility that the legislation contemplates, thus reducing the relative competitive opportunity of their products on the market. Other operators may be deterred from trading with such a Member altogether, distorting potential trade...."[93]

6.16 The ordinary meaning of the terms used in Article 23.1 is plain and clear:

> 23.1 When Members ***seek the redress of a violation*** of obligations or other nullification or impairment of benefits under the covered agreements or an impediment to the attainment of any objective of the covered agreements, ***they shall have recourse to, and abide by***, the rules and procedures of this Understanding. (emphasis added)

---

[91] Panel Report on *US – Section 301*, *supra*, footnote 69, para. 7.71. "The purpose of many of the GATT/WTO disciplines, indeed one of the primary objects of the GATT/WTO as a whole, is to produce certain market conditions which would allow this ... activity to flourish." *Ibid.*, para.7.73.

[92] *Ibid.*, para. 7.75.

[93] *Ibid.*, para. 7.90.

6.17 The structure of Article 23 is that the first paragraph states the general prohibition or general obligation, i.e. when Members seek the redress of a WTO violation[94], they shall do so only through the DSU. This is a general obligation. Any attempt to seek "redress" can take place only in the institutional framework of the WTO and pursuant to the rules and procedures of the DSU.

6.18 The prohibition against unilateral redress in the WTO sectors is more directly provided for in the second paragraph of Article 23. From the ordinary meaning of the terms used in the chapeau of Article 23.2 ("in such cases, Members shall"), it is also clear that the second paragraph of Article 23 is "explicitly linked to, and has to be read together with and subject to, Article 23.1"[95]. That is to say, the specific prohibitions of paragraph 2 of Article 23 have to be understood in the context of the first paragraph, i.e. when such action is performed by a WTO Member with a view to redressing a WTO violation.

6.19 We also agree with the *US – Section 301* Panel Report that Article 23.2 contains "egregious examples of conduct that contradict the rules of the DSU"[96] and which constitute more specific forms of unilateral actions, otherwise generally prohibited by Article 23.1 of the DSU.

> "[t]hese rules and procedures [Article 23.1] clearly cover much more than the ones specifically mentioned in Article 23.2. There is a great deal more State conduct which can violate the general obligation in Article 23.1 to have recourse to, and abide by, the rules and procedures of the DSU than the instances especially singled out in Article 23.2. "(Footnotes omitted)[97]

The same Panel identified a few examples of such instances where the DSU could be violated[98] contrary to the provisions of Article 23. Each time a Member seeking the redress of a WTO violation is not abiding by a rule of the DSU, it thus violates Article 23.1 of the DSU.

6.20 In order to verify whether individual provisions of Article 23.2 have been infringed (keeping in mind that the obligation to also observe other DSU provisions can be brought under the umbrella of Article 23.1), we must first determine whether the measure at issue comes under the coverage of Article 23.1. In other words, we need to determine whether Article 23 is applicable to the dispute before addressing the specific violations envisaged in the second paragraph of Article 23 of the DSU or elsewhere in the DSU.

---

[94] Article 23.1 of the DSU refers more accurately to "seek the redress of a violation of obligations or other nullification or impairment of benefits under the covered agreements or an impediment to the attainment of any objective of the covered agreements", i.e. the three causes of actions under WTO. In this Panel Report, the expression "WTO violation(s)" refers to all three causes of actions mentioned in Article 23.1 of the DSU.

[95] Panel Report on *US – Section 301, supra*, footnote 69, para 7.44.

[96] *Ibid.*, para. 7.45.

[97] *Ibid.*

[98] See ibid., footnotes 655 and 656 to para. 7.45.

(b) The Application of Article 23 to the Present Dispute

6.21 Article 23.1 of the DSU provides that the criterion for determining whether Article 23 is applicable is whether the Member that imposed the measure was "seeking the redress of" a WTO violation. The measure in the present dispute is increased bonding requirements as of 3 March on EC listed imports.

6.22 The term "seeking" or "to seek" is defined in the *Webster New Encyclopedic Dictionary* as: "to resort to, ... to make an attempt, try". This term would therefore cover situations where an effort is made to redress WTO violations (whether perceived or WTO determined violations). The term "to redress" is defined in the *New Shorter Oxford English Dictionary* as "repair (an action); atone for (a misdeed); remedy or remove; to set right or rectify (injury, a wrong, a grievance etc.); obtaining reparation or compensation". The term "redress" is defined in the *New Shorter Oxford English Dictionary* as: "reparation of or compensation for a wrong or consequent loss; remedy for or relief from some trouble; correction or reformation of something wrong". The term 'redress' implies, therefore, a reaction by a Member against another Member, because of a perceived (or WTO determined) WTO violation, with a view to remedying the situation.

6.23 Article 23.1 of the DSU prescribes that when a WTO Member wants to take any remedial action in response to what it views as a WTO violation, it is obligated to have recourse to and abide by the DSU rules and procedures. In case of a grievance on a WTO matter, the WTO dispute settlement mechanism is the only means available to WTO Members to obtain relief, and only the remedial actions envisaged in the WTO system can be used by WTO Members.[99] The remedial actions relate to restoring the balance of rights and obligations which form the basis of the WTO Agreement, and include the removal of the inconsistent measure, the possibility of (temporary) compensation and, in last resort, the (temporary) suspension of concessions or other obligations authorised by the DSB (Articles 3.7 and 22.1 of the DSU). The latter remedy is essentially retaliatory in nature.[100]

---

[99] This mechanism allows, of course, for consultations to be held outside the WTO.

[100] We note that the United States often uses the term "to retaliate" or "retaliation". The terms 'retaliation' or 'to retaliate' is defined in the *Webster New Encyclopedic Dictionary* as "to return like for like, to get even". In the *Black Law Dictionary* (6th Ed.) retaliation refers to *lex talionis* which it self is defined as: "The Law of retaliation; which requires the infliction upon a wrongdoer of the same injury which he has caused to another". Under general international law, retaliation (also referred to as reprisals or counter-measures) has undergone major changes in the course of the XX century, specially, as a result of the prohibition of the use of force (*jus ad bellum*). Under international law, these types of countermeasures are now subject to requirements, such as those identified by the International Law Commission in its work on state responsibility (proportionality etc... see Article 43 of the Draft). However, in WTO, countermeasures, retaliations and reprisals are strictly regulated and can take place only within the framework of the WTO/DSU. Elagab Omer Youssif, "*The Legality of Non-Forcible Counter-Measures in International Law* (1988), Oxford University Press; Boisson de Charzournes Laurence, *Les contre-mesures dans les relations économiques internationales*, (1992)

(i) Was the *3 March* Measure a Measure 'Seeking the Redress of' a WTO Violation?

6.24 We consider that there is ample evidence before us which demonstrates that when it took the 3 March Measure, the United States was seeking redress for a perceived WTO violation by the European Communities, within the meaning of Article 23.1 of the DSU.

6.25 The USTR Press Release announcing the 3 March Measure confirms its retaliatory nature, as a measure seeking to redress. The official USTR Press Release of 3 March 1999 reads as follows:

"United States ***Takes Customs Action*** on European Imports

[E]ffective today, the U.S. Customs Service will ***begin*** 'withholding liquidation' on imports valued at over $500 million of ***selected products from the European Union*** (EU), consistent with ***U.S. rights*** under the WTO agreements. Withholding liquidation imposes ***contingent liability for 100 per cent duties*** on affected products as of March 3, 1999...

January 1, 1999, was the deadline for the EU to implement a WTO-consistent banana regime. The EU failed to honor this deadline, thereby entitling the United States to suspend tariff concessions as early as February 1st on selected European products with the WTO's blessing."[101] (emphasis added)

6.26 On its face, this description of the 3 March Measure shows that, because of the US perceived WTO inconsistency of the 1998 Bananas regime put in place by the European Communities as a measure taken to implement the Panel and Appellate Body recommendations[102] (the "EC implementing measure"), the United States imposed an increased contingent liability on EC listed imports only. This 3 March Measure was, therefore, discriminatory and aimed at the European Communities exclusively. The unilateral imposition of a liability for 100 per cent duty as of 3 March (well above the bound rates of tariffs) constitutes the imposition of a debt on such imports, and adds further obligations on such imports, even if the full effect of such liability is suspended until a future liquidation date. This debt, this liability, this additional obligation imposed on listed EC

A Pedone; Henkin L, Pugh R.C., Schacter O. and Smit H., *International Law* (1993), West Publishing, p.570-571 and Chapter 11.

[101] USTR Press Release, dated 3 March 1999, "United States takes customs action on European imports" (EC Annex VII).

[102] Panel Reports, *EC – Bananas III*, *supra*, footnote 2 and Appellate Body Reports on *EC – Bananas III*, *supra*, footnote 1; for a description of the 1998 EC Bananas Regime, see the EC First submission, para. 3 and the US First submission, paras. 15-17 (Appendices 1.1. and 2.1 to this Panel Report).

imports[103], is evidence that the United States wanted to remedy, was 'seeking to redress', what it perceived to be a WTO violation.

6.27 The request from USTR to the US Customs Service is also revealing. On 3 March 1999, Mr. Peter L. Scher, Special Trade Negotiator of the USTR, wrote to Mr. Raymond W. Kelly, Commissioner of the US Customs Service, as follows:

".... The [USTR] intends to implement this suspension of tariff concessions by directing the Customs Service to impose 100 percent duties, *ad valorem*, on the products listed in the attachment to this letter. (See also 63 Fed. Reg. 63099 and 63 Fed. Reg. 71665 giving notice of the proposed increase in duties on selected products).

.... The USTR now ***seeks to preserve its right*** to impose 100 percent duties as of March 3, pending the release of the arbitrators' final decision.

Therefore, ... I further request that the Customs Service today instruct port directors to review the sufficiency of bond posted with respect to entries described in the previous sentence, and to take steps to provide adequate or additional security in accordance with 19 C.F.R. §113.13." [104] (emphasis added)

6.28 It becomes evident that the 3 March increased bonding requirements on EC listed imports was part of the retaliation scheme that the United States had triggered with the Section 301-310 notifications in the Federal Register.[105] Although the United States argues that the 3 March Measure was taken pursuant to Article 13(d) of the Code of Federal Regulation[106], and not pursuant to the Sections 301-310, it is now clear to us that the United States took the 3 March Measure in the context of the US Section 301 process.[107] This is also evidence that the

---

[103] In paras. 6.46 to 6.51 of this Panel Report, we further discuss our understanding of the actual increased of bonding requirements resulting from the 3 March Measure.

[104] Letter dated 3 March 1999 from Mr. Peter L. Scher, Special Trade Negotiator to Commissioner Raymond W. Kelly, US Customs Service (US Ex. 12).

[105] Notification of the USTR, Doc. No. 301-100a, 22 October 1998, 63 Fed. Reg. 56687; Notification of the USTR, Doc. No. 301-100a, 10 November 1998, 63 Fed. Reg. 63099; and Notification of the USTR, Doc. No. 301-100a, 29 December 1998, 63 Fed. Reg. 71665 (EC Annexes I, II and III). We recall the definition of retaliation in paras.6.22 and 6.23 of this Panel Report.

[106] US First Submission, para.33 (Appendix 2.1 of this Panel Report) and US Responses to Questions of the Panel and the Parties, dated 13 January 2000, para. 53 (Appendix 2.4 of this Panel report).

[107] We recall that the Notifications of the USTR in the Federal Register provided that on 3 March some action had to be taken. For example, "The dates on which the USTR intends to implement action – February 1 or not later than March 3 ..." Notification of the USTR, Doc. No. 300-100a, 10 November 1998, 63 Fed. Reg. 63099 (1998). *On its face* Section 306(b) of the Trade Act requires the USTR to determine what further action it shall take under Section 301(a) if the USTR considers that a foreign country has failed to implement a recommendation made pursuant to dispute settlement proceedings under the WTO. The USTR shall make this determination no later than thirty days after the expiry of the reasonable period of time provided for such implementation under Article 21.3 of the DSU, which is January 31, 1999 in this case. Section 305(a)(I) requires USTR normally to implement such action by no later than thirty days after the date on which that determination is

United States was seeking to "redress a WTO violation". With its 3 March increased bonding requirements, the United States put in place an enforcement remedy, effective as of 3 March.

6.29 In response to the USTR's request, Mr. Philip Metzger, Director of the Trade Compliance Division of the US Customs Service, in a memorandum of 4 March 1999,[108] gave the following instructions to the Customs Area and Port Directors. We note that the subject of this memo is concerned exclusively with the 3 March Measure and is entitled "European Sanctions".[109] This shows that the United States was 'seeking' to redress a WTO violation:

"RE: European Sanctions…

Effective for all merchandise classifiable under the Harmonized Tariff Schedule (HTS) subheadings listed below, entered, or withdrawn from warehouse, for consumption, on or after March 3, 1999, and produced in the listed countries, Area and Port Directors must require a Single Transaction Bond (STB) equal to the entered value of the merchandise. The only exception to this requirement is, at the discretion of the Port Director, the importer of record may use a continuous bond equal to 10 per cent of the total of the entered value of the covered merchandise imported by the importer for the preceding year. Ports should process increased continuous bonds immediately.

> No entry shall be scheduled to liquidate earlier than the 314th day, thereby ensuring the withholding of liquidation as requested by USTR. … "[110] (emphasis added)

6.30 On 16 March 1999, Mr. Philip Metzger, Director of the Trade Compliance Division issued a memorandum regarding "Clarification of Bond Requirements for ***European Sanctions***" (emphasis added) to the port directors.[111] This memorandum indicates that the US authorities considered that the increased

---

made, or March 2 in this case. See also Bill H.R. 4761, 9 October 1998, "To require the United States Representative to take certain actions ***in response to the failure of the European Union to comply with the rulings of the World Trade Organization***" where Section 3 *para.* (F) where the Trade Representative is mandated to suspend liquidation on EC listed imports "in no event later than 2 March 1999. Although a Bill is not binding, it demonstrates that the United States was "seeking to redress a WTO violation". (EC Annex V)

108 Memorandum of 4 March 1999 to Customs Area and Port Directors, CMC Directors from Trade Compliance Division, US Customs Service, Regarding European Sanctions (EC Annex VIII).

109 In the *New Shorter Oxford English Dictionary*, the term "sanction" is defined as "a penalty enacted in order to enforce obedience of a law; later more widely, a punishment or reward for disobedience or obedience of a law." In *Webster's New Encyclopedic Dictionary*, it is defined as "an economic or military measure adopted usually by several nations against another nation violating international law."

110 Memorandum of 4 March 1999 to Customs Area and Port Directors, CMC Directors from Trade Compliance Division, US Customs Service, Regarding European Sanctions (EC Annex VIII).

111 Memorandum to Customs Area and Port Directors, CMC Directors from Trade Compliance Division, US Customs Service, Regarding Clarification of Bond Requirements for European Sanctions, dated 16 March 1999 (US Ex. 15).

bonding requirements had been imposed as a 'sanction' against the European Communities. It reads as follows:

"This memorandum is being issued as result of the large number of questions that we have received regarding bond sufficiency requirements for merchandise ***subject to European sanctions***. In an effort to establish uniformity for importers and ports, the following bond sufficiency requirements should be adhered to by all ports:

> If the importer of record provides a statement at the time of entry (release) certifying that it has reviewed its continuous bond and has added to it an amount equal to 10 percent of the total of the entered value imported by the importer for the preceding year of the ***merchandise presently subject to the sanctions***, the Port Director will accept the continuous bond."[112] (emphasis added)

6.31 The Press Conference given by Deputy USTR P. Scher on 3 March is another piece of evidence that confirms that the 3 March Measure was seeking redress. Below are some relevant excerpts:

> "Q. Does the withholding of liquidation fulfill the terms of the Bowles letter which says "If the EU seeks arbitration ... the retaliatory action will go into effect on the date that arbitration is concluded, but in no event later than March 3, 1999?
>
> A. ... ***We retaliated by effectively stopping trade*** as of 3 March in ***responding to*** the harm caused by the ***EC's WTO inconsistent*** banana regime. That purpose is achieved by withholding liquidation on the products on the ***retaliation list*** ...
>
> Q. What is the difference between imposing duties and withholding liquidation?
>
> A. ***There is little difference***. Withholding will, ***we expect, effectively stop imports just as immediately imposing duties would***. Importers are going to be ***no more prepared to accept the contingent 100 per cent duty liability, as they would to pay 100 per cent duties. They will wait for certainty.***
>
> Q. Why aren't you keeping the White House commitments?
>
> A. ... ***We are effectively stopping trade as of* 3 March**....
>
> Q. How do you expect the EC to react?
>
> A. ... But our action makes it crystal clear that ***there are consequences for failure to comply with WTO rulings***. ...
>
> Q. How is this consistent with the White House letter and the WTO?

---

[112] *Ibid.*

A. The White House letter commits the Administration ***to retaliate effective March 3; we have done that***."[113] (emphasis added)

6.32 The content of this Press Conference speaks for itself. With the increased bonding requirements, the United States ***was expecting to and wanted to stop trade***. The United States wanted to effectively retaliate against the European Communities for its alleged WTO incompatible implementing measure.

6.33 It seems that the United States specifically chose the increased bonding requirements as a retaliation measure, because it considered that it would have an effect similar to that of increased import tariffs and would therefore stop trade. The choice of that particular measure, i.e. the fact that an additional bonding requirements increase costs to exporters/importers but do not bring any fiscal or other advantages to the United States, is another element that confirms the retaliatory nature of the 3 March Measure, i.e. redress, in that its only object is to impose administrative and financial burdens on EC listed imports, so as to effectively stop trade.

6.34 We conclude that with the 3 March Measure, the United States was seeking to redress a perceived WTO violation by the European Communities. The additional burdens imposed by the additional bonding requirements, and the declared purpose and intent of the United States when it effectively began, through the additional bonding requirements, to enforce the imposition of 100 per cent duties on EC listed imports, demonstrate that the 3 March Measure was an action seeking to redress a perceived WTO violation, within the meaning of Article 23.1 of the DSU. Having found that Article 23 applies to the 3 March Measure, we shall now proceed to examine the claims of the European Communities.

2. *Article 23.1 Together with Articles 23.2(c), 3.7 and 22.6 of the DSU*

6.35 Articles 23.2(c), 22.6 and 3.7 of the DSU prohibit any unilateral suspension of GATT/WTO concessions or obligations, without a DSB authorization. We recall that violations of Article 23.2 will take place when the measure at issue is taken in the context described in the first paragraph of Article 23[114], i.e. as a measure seeking to redress a WTO violation. We recall also that there are more violations of the DSU that can be captured by the general prohibition of Article 23.1 than those listed in paragraph 2 of Article 23.

6.36 Since we have already concluded that the 3 March Measure constituted a measure taken to redress a WTO violation (covered by Article 23.1), we proceed to examine whether the same 3 March Measure violated the provisions of the sub-paragraph 2(c) of Article 23 of the DSU, as well as Articles 3.7 and 22.6 of the DSU.

---

[113] See EC Annex X.

[114] See paras. 6.18 to 6.20 of this Panel Report.

6.37 Article 23.2(c) prohibits any suspensions of concessions or other obligations (taken as measures seeking to redress a WTO violation), prior to a relevant DSB authorization. Article 3.7 provides that suspension of concessions or other obligations should be used as a last resort, and subject to a DSB authorization. In Article 22.6, the suspension of concessions or other obligations is prohibited during the arbitration process which can only take place before the DSB authorization. Articles 3.7, 23.2(c) and 22.6 read as follows:

3.7 "...The last resort which this Understanding provides to the Member invoking the dispute settlement procedures is the possibility of ***suspending the application of concessions or other obligations*** under the covered agreements on a discriminatory basis vis-à-vis the other Member, subject to authorization by the DSB of such measures." (emphasis added)

23.2(c) "... Member shall: ... follow the procedures set forth in Article 22 to determine the level of suspension of concessions or other obligations and ***obtain DSB authorization in accordance with those procedures before suspending concessions or other obligations*** under the covered agreements in response to the failure of the Member concerned to implement the recommendations and rulings within that reasonable period of time." (emphasis added)

22.6 " ... Concessions or other obligations shall not be suspended during the course of the arbitration."

6.38 In the context of these provisions, any WTO suspension of concessions or other obligations without prior DSB authorization is explicitly prohibited. On 3 March there was no relevant DSB authorization of any sort. The remaining issue is, therefore, whether the United States, through its 3 March Measure, suspended any concessions or other obligations *vis-à-vis* imports from the European Communities. If so, there would be a violation of the DSU provisions quoted above. Did the 3 March increased bonding requirements on EC listed imports constitute a suspension of GATT/WTO concessions (a violation of Article II) or other obligations (violation of Articles I, VIII and XI)? A response to this question will also provide the answer to the European Communities' claims that the 3 March Measure constituted a violation of Articles I, II, VIII and XI of GATT.

(a) Did the 3 March Measure Constitute a Suspension of GATT/WTO Concessions or other Obligations? (EC claims that the 3 March Measure Violated Articles I, II, VIII and XI of GATT)

6.39 In this dispute the measure alleged to constitute a suspension of WTO concessions or other obligations is a decision to increase bonding requirements to secure the collection of up to 100 per cent duties on listed imports from the European Communities.

6.40 In this context, we need to understand what the object of bonding requirements is and for what purpose they are used by importing authorities. In addition, the United States focuses its defense on the normal and specific bonding requirements of the US Customs Service in arguing that the 3 March increase in bonding requirements on EC listed imports did not constitute a WTO suspension of concessions or other obligations under the WTO Agreement. We are well aware that it is not in our terms of reference to assess the bonding requirement practices of the US Customs Service in general. We have looked at the US bonding requirement mechanism and the trade effects of the action taken by the United States on 3 March, only to understand the nature of the 3 March Measure. Our assessment of the WTO compatibility of the 3 March increased bonding requirements is based exclusively on the evidence submitted by the United States.

6.41 Bonds are a means of securing and guaranteeing the exercise of certain rights/obligations. Bonds are, therefore, required by the importing Member to guarantee the performance of that importing Member's specific rights (which constitute obligations for other Members). For instance, many Members require bonds upon importation to guarantee the payment of the applicable duties or compliance with some internal regulation.

6.42 Two different aspects of the additional bonding requirements of the 3 March Measure should be assessed. One aspect of the 3 March Measure that has to be examined is the increased bonding requirements as such, in relation to the tariffs they are supposed to guarantee. The other aspect of the 3 March Measure which we will examine is whether it led to increased costs to obtain such additional bonds. The United States suggests that such costs typically would (1) for single bonds purchased for an entry of listed imports valued at $50,000, be approximately $175.00, assuming a rate of $3.50 per thousand dollars of bond value and (2) for continuous bonds calculated based on prior year listed imports of $50,000, $50 to $100 assuming a rate of $10 to $20 per thousand dollars of bond value.[115] These costs are not payable to the United States, but to the institution that provides the bond. We shall, therefore, examine both aspects of the 3 March Measure.

(i) The Increased Bonding Requirement Itself

6.43 A bonding requirement is essentially an enforcement mechanism accessory to the right that it aims at protecting. As discussed below, GATT jurisprudence also concludes that bonding requirements are enforcement mechanisms and that their GATT compatibility should be assessed together with the principal rights/obligations they aim to guarantee. In other words, a bonding requirement

[115] US Responses to Additional Questions of the Panel, dated 10 February 2000, para.5 (Appendix 2.10 to this Panel Report). However, on the basis of the example described in paras. 6.46 to 6.51 of this Panel Report, hereinafter, there would appear to be the potential for a more significant increase in costs, from at least $500 prior to 3 March to $10,000 after 3 March for continuous bonds.

does not have any separate legal *raison d'être* apart from the main right/obligation it guarantees; a bond is therefore part of and included in the right it aims to guarantee. In the present dispute, the United States alleges that the 3 March additional bonding requirements were put in place to secure the payment of 100 per cent duties and, as noted by Deputy USTR P. Scher on 3 March[116], there is little difference between imposing 100 per cent duties and imposing a contingent liability of 100 per cent of the value of the imports. We should, therefore, assess the WTO compatibility of the specific 3 March bonding requirements in light of the tariff rights (obligations) they seek to securing.

6.44 The GATT jurisprudence confirms our understanding of the legal nature of bonding requirements. In the adopted Panel Report on *EEC – Measures on Animal Feed Proteins*,[117] the Panel concluded that "the security deposit, including any associated cost, was only an enforcement mechanism for the purchase requirement and, as such, should be examined with the purchase obligation" (under Article III of GATT).[118] The adopted Panel Report on *EEC – Programme of Minimum Import Price, Licences and Surety Deposits for Certain Processed Fruits and Vegetables*[119] also concluded that the security system was necessary for the enforcement of the minimum import price and should be assessed together with it. In that case, the Panel concluded that "the minimum import price and associated additional security system did not qualify for the exemptions provided by Article XI:2(c)(i) and (ii) from the provisions of Article XI:1... this system was inconsistent with ...Article XI".[120]

6.45 In the adopted Panel Report on United States - *Section 337 of the Tariff Act of 1930*[121], the Panel examined the US Section 337, the purpose of which was to enforce the US patent law against imports. The Panel stated that "enforcement procedures cannot be separated from the substantive provisions they serve to enforce", and examined whether such enforcement procedures benefitted from an Article XX(d) exception (as Section 337 together with the patent law it enforced, violated Article III:4). The Panel concluded in the negative. The final conclusion of the Panel Report was that the US Section 337 as such (i.e. the enforcement mechanism), was inconsistent with Article III:4 of GATT.

6.46 We note that on 3 March the bound tariff rates on EC listed imports were those listed in paragraph 2.35 of this Panel Report, all of which are well below 100 per cent *ad valorem*. As of 3 March 1999, the US increased bonding re-

---

116 See para. 6.31 of this Panel Report.

117 Panel Report on *EEC – Measures on Animal Feed Proteins* ("*Animal Feed Proteins*"), adopted on 14 March 1978, BISD25S/49.

118 *Ibid.*, para. 4.4.

119 Panel Report on *EEC – Programme of Minimum Import Price, Licences and Surety Deposits for Certain Processed Fruits and Vegetables* ("*Minimum Import Price*"), adopted on 18 October 1978, BISD 25S/68.

120 *Ibid.*, para. 4.14.

121 Panel Report on United States - *Section 337 of the Tariff Act of 1930*, adopted on 7 November 1989, BISD 36S/345.

quirements to guarantee payment of 100 per cent duties on $520 million of EC listed imports. It is helpful to examine, through an example, the actual effect of this 3 March Measure, taking annual imports of $10,000,000 (all being EC listed imports), subject to, say, 5 per cent bound duties ($500,000), for both continuous and single bonding requirements and for imports that are covered by the US Food and Drugs Act. From the submissions of the United States and its responses to our questions, our understanding of the 3 March increased bonding requirements is the following.

6.47 The normal practice of the US Customs, with regard to the bonding requirements, is as follows:

(i) For most products except those covered by a Food and Drug provision:

- A continuous bond has to cover 10 per cent of the duties, taxes and fees for all the products during the preceding year and is to be no less than $50,000.
- A single transaction bond has to cover the entered value plus any duties, taxes and fees for the entry of the merchandise;

(ii) For products covered by an additional Food and Drug requirement:

- A continuous bond has to cover 10 per cent of the duties, taxes and fees for all the products during the preceding year and is to be no less than $50,000.
- A single transaction bond has to cover three times the amount of the entered value of the merchandise.

It is our understanding that, as of 3 March 1999, the bonding requirements for the EC listed imports were:

(iii) For most products, except those covered by a Food and Drug provision:

- A continuous bond has to cover 10 per cent of the entered value of covered goods in the preceeding year.
- A single transaction bond has to cover the amount of the entered value of the merchandise.

(iv) For products covered by an additional US Food and Drug Act requirement:

- A continuous bond has then to cover 10 per cent of the entered value of covered goods in the preceeding year.
- A single transaction bond has to cover three times the amount of the entered value of the merchandise.

6.48 Taking imports not subject to the US Food and Drug requirements, before 3 March, for a continuous bond, our example of $10,000,000 value of imports would have been subject to 10 per cent of the duties of $500,000 (ignoring taxes and fees for the purposes of this example), so the amount of the bond would have been $50,000. As of 3 March, the bonding requirement was 10 per cent of the entered value of covered goods in the previous year. In our example the bonding requirement would, therefore, increase from $50,000 to $1,000,000. This would appear to be consistent with the Customs Services Memorandum referred to in paragraph 2.24 above.

6.49 Before 3 March, for a single transaction bond, and assuming 50 individual shipments valued at $200,000 each, the bonding requirement was the entered value, $200,000 plus any duties (5 per cent - $10,000), so a total of $210,000. As of 3 March, the bonding requirement was the amount of the entered value, so that the amount of the bond would have been $200,000 for each shipment, i.e. a decrease. In those cases where importers were permitted to take out a single transaction bond for a shipment rather than increase the continuous bond, there would be an increase, i.e. to the extent of the full amount of the single transaction bond (in our example, $200,000), which is less of an increase than the alternative of a continuous bond of $1,000,000).

6.50 Bonding requirements on imports subject to the US Food and Drug requirements were unchanged for single transaction bonds at three (3) times the entered value. For continuous bonds, the situation would be as described in paragraph 6.48 above.

6.51 We recall that approximately 93 per cent of the EC imports (and assuming therefore approximately 93 per cent of the EC listed imports) were subject to continuous entry bonds.[122] From the evidence before us, we believe that in most cases of EC listed imports the 3 March Measure led to increased bonding requirements. There may, however, be situations where the 3 March additional bonding requirements were negligible or did not increase. We consider, however, that the object of our examination is the mechanism put in place through the 3 March Measure as a whole.

6.52 In this context, we recall the conclusions of the Appellate Body in *Argentina – Measures Affecting Imports of Footwear, Textiles, Apparel and other Items* ("*Argentina – Textiles*")[123] that if the possibility remains that Article II be violated, the tariff mechanism in place should be considered to be in violation of Article II:

> "53. In the light of this analysis, we may generalize that under the Argentine system, whether the amount of the DIEM is determined by applying 35 per cent, or a rate less than 35 per cent, to the representative international price, ***there will remain the possibility*** of a price that is sufficiently low to produce an *ad valorem*

[122] US Responses to Additional Questions of the Panel, dated 8 February 2000, para. 13 (Appendix 2.6 to this Panel Report).

[123] Appellate Body Report, *Argentina – Measures Affecting Imports of Footwear, Textiles, Apparel and other Items* ("*Argentina – Textiles*"), WT/DS56/AB/R and Corr. 1, adopted 22 April 1998, DSR 1998:III, 1003.

equivalent of the DIEM that is greater than 35 per cent. In other words, the structure and design of the Argentine system is such that for any DIEM, no matter what *ad valorem* rate is used as the multiplier of the representative international price, the possibility remains that there is a "break-even" price below which the *ad valorem* equivalent of the customs duty collected is in excess of the bound *ad valorem* rate of 35 per cent.

...

62. We recall our finding that the DIEM regime, by its structure and design, results in the application of specific duties with ad valorem equivalent exceeding 35 per cent ... We agree with Argentina, therefore, that the application of the DIEM does not result in a breach of Article II for *each and every* import transaction in a given tariff category. At the same time, however, we agree with the Panel that there are sufficient reasons to conclude that the ***structure and design*** of the DIEM will result, ***with respect to a certain range of import price***s within a relevant tariff category, in an infringement of Argentina's obligations under Article II:1 for all tariff categories in Chapters 51 to 63 of the N.C.M.."[124] (emphasis added)

6.53 The European Communities claims that the 3 March Measure violated Article I of GATT, as it was applicable only to EC products and not to other like products from other WTO Members.

6.54 We find that the 3 March additional bonding requirements violated the most-favoured-nation clause of Article I[125] of GATT, as it was applicable only to imports from the European Communities, although identical products from other WTO Members were not the subject of such an additional bonding requirements. The regulatory distinction (whether an additional bonding requirement is needed) was not based on any characteristic of the product but depended exclusively on the origin of the product and targeted exclusively some imports from the European Communities.[126]

---

124 *Ibid.*, paras. 53 and 62.

125 Article I:1 of GATT reads as follows: "With respect to customs duties and charges of any kind imposed on or in connection with importation or exportation or imposed on the international transfer of payments for imports or exports, and with respect to the method of levying such duties and charges, and with respect to all rules and formalities in connection with importation and exportation, and with respect to all matters referred to in *paras.* 2 and 4 of Article III, any advantage, favour, privilege or immunity granted by any contracting party to any product originating in or destined for any other country shall be accorded immediately and unconditionally to the like product originating in or destined for the territories of all other contracting parties."

126 Panel Report, *Indonesia – Certain Measures Affecting the Automobile Industry* ("*Indonesia – Autos*"), WT/DS54/R and Corr. 1,2,3,4, WT/DS55/R and Corr. 1,2,3,4,, WT/DS59/R and Corr. 1,2,3,4, WT/DS64/R and Corr. 1,2,3,4, adopted 23 July 1998, DSR 1998:VI, 2201, para.14.147: "For the reasons discussed above, we consider that the June 1996 car programme which introduced

6.55 The European Communities also claims that the 3 March Measure violated Article II of GATT which reads as follows:

> "1. (*a*) Each contracting party shall accord to the commerce of the other contracting parties treatment no less favourable than that provided for in the appropriate Part of the appropriate Schedule annexed to this Agreement.
>
> (*b*) The products described in Part I of the Schedule relating to any contracting party, which are the products of territories of other contracting parties, shall, on their importation into the territory to which the Schedule relates, and subject to the terms, conditions or qualifications set forth in that Schedule, be exempt from ordinary customs duties in excess of those set forth and provided therein. Such products shall also be exempt from all other duties or charges of any kind imposed on or in connection with the importation in excess of those imposed on the date of this Agreement or those directly and mandatorily required to be imposed thereafter by legislation in force in the importing territory on that date."

6.56 We have already discussed the nature of bonding requirements and concluded that their WTO compatibility should be assessed together with the rights or obligations they aim at securing. In particular, when used to guarantee the payment of customs duties, the bonding requirement becomes part of, and is included in, the right to collect customs duties (and the enforcement of this right/obligation). Bonds are required to cover the payment of tariffs, and are nothing but the mechanisms relating to the collection of the customs duties, with no legally autonomous existence. In the present dispute, the additional bonding requirements are said to have been put in place to secure the payment of increased tariffs; their WTO compatibility is, therefore, to be determined with reference to the disciplines of Article II.

6.57 We recall that the fundamental purpose of Article II is to preserve the value of tariff concessions negotiated by a Member with its trading partners, and bound in that Member's Schedule. We agree with the Appellate Body statement in *Argentina – Textiles*:

> "47. In accordance with the general rules of treaty interpretation set out in Article 31 of the *Vienna Convention*, Article II:1(b), first sentence, must be read in its context and in light of the object and purpose of the GATT 1994. Article II:1(a) is part of the context of Article II:1(b); it requires that a Member must accord to the com-

discrimination between imports in the allocation of tax and customs duty benefits based on various conditions and other criteria not related to the imports themselves and the February 1996 car programme which also introduced discrimination between imports in the allocation of customs duty benefits based on various conditions and other criteria not related to the imports themselves, are inconsistent with the provisions of Article I of GATT."

> merce of the other Members "treatment no less favourable than that provided for" in its Schedule. ... A basic object and purpose of the GATT 1994, as reflected in Article II, ***is to preserve the value of tariff concessions negotiated by a Member with its trading partners, and bound in that Member's Schedule***."[127] (emphasis added)

6.58 We consider, therefore, that the purpose of Article II is to prohibit any liability for customs duties above the maximum level recorded in a Member's Schedule. The 3 March additional bonding requirements were established at a level which would guarantee the collection of 100 per cent duties. We have found that the bonding requirements should be assessed together with the rights/obligations they purport to protect, being in this case, the right to collect tariffs at bound levels. The 3 March Measure imposed additional bonding requirements to guarantee collection of 100 per cent tariff duty. The 3 March additional bonding requirements increased the contingent tariff liability for EC listed products above their bound levels, all of which are much lower than 100 per cent *ad valorem* (the highest is 18 per cent). In fact, on 3 March, with the additional bonding requirements on EC listed imports, the United States began 'enforcing' the imposition of 100 per cent tariff duties on the EC listed imports, contrary to the levels bound in its Schedule.

6.59 We find that the increased bonding requirements of the 3 March Measure, as they provided a treatment less favourable than in the United States' Schedules, violated Article II:1(a) of GATT. The 3 March Measure also violated Article II:1(b), first sentence, as it was guaranteeing and, therefore, enforcing tariffs above their bound levels.

One Panelists' View

6.60 One Panelist is of the view that bonding requirements can legitimately be in place to enforce WTO compatible rights and obligations. Such bonding requirements could benefit from the application of Article XX(d), as "measures necessary to secure compliance with laws or regulations which are not inconsistent with the provisions of this Agreement", assuming they support WTO compatible rights/obligations and they are not inconsistent with the provisions of the chapeau of Article XX). If bonding requirements are used to secure the respect of WTO compatible rights/obligations, they would not appear to be inconsistent with the WTO Agreement. However, if not, they could be viewed as effectively imposing a form of 'restriction' contrary to Article XI of GATT.[128]

---

[127] Appellate Body Report, *Argentina – Textiles*, *supra*, footnote 123, para. 47.

[128] Article XI:1 of GATT reads as follows: "No prohibitions or restrictions other than duties, taxes or other charges, whether made effective through quotas, import or export licences or other measures, shall be instituted or maintained by any Member on the importation of any product of the territory of any other Member or on the exportation or sale for export of any product destined for the territory of any other Member."

6.61 In the present dispute, the increased bonding requirements did not enforce any legitimate WTO tariff rights and therefore could not be considered as "necessary to secure compliance with laws or regulations which are not inconsistent" with GATT. On 3 March, the tariffs were bound at levels below 100 per cent (the highest level is 18 per cent). Any bonding requirements to cover the payment of tariffs above their bound levels cannot be viewed as a mechanism in place to secure compliance with WTO compatible tariffs and constituted, therefore, import restrictions for which there was no justification. The actual trade effects of the 3 March Measure, which are reflected on the charts contained in paragraph 2.37 of this Panel Report, confirm its restrictive nature and effect. One Panelist found, therefore, that the 3 March Measure constituted a "restriction", contrary to Article XI of GATT, rather than a duty or charge under Article II.

(ii) Interest Charges, Costs and Fees in Connection with the Lodging of the Additional Bonding Requirement

6.62 The other aspect of the 3 March Measure that we must examine is whether the increased interest charges, costs and fees constituted "other duties and charges" collected by the United States on EC listed imports contrary to Article II:1(b) last sentence, as claimed by the European Communities.[129] The United States submits that the costs of obtaining an additional bonding requirement are not charges, within the meaning of Article II:1(b) last sentence, because they are not paid to the United States but to an independent entity.

6.63 Article II:1(b) of GATT prohibits the imposition of other duties and charges in excess of the customs duties.[130] Article II:1(b), second sentence reads as follows:

> "Such products shall also be exempt from all other duties or charges of any kind imposed on or in connection with the importation in excess of those imposed on the date of this Agreement or those directly and mandatorily required to be imposed thereafter by legislation in force in the importing territory on that date."

6.64 We note that nothing in Article II:1(b), second sentence provides that only charges paid to the importing country are to be covered by the terms "charges of any kind imposed on or in connection with the importation". The GATT/WTO jurisprudence has consistently ruled that any governmental "measure" can be challenged before the GATT/WTO. The 3 March Measure was a governmental measure. It would be too easy for Members to avoid the disciplines of Article II:1(b) if any charges required to be paid upon importation were exempted from

[129] For an evaluation of such costs we refer to our approximations in para. 6.42 above.

[130] The GATT 1994 Understanding imposes the obligation to record such "other duties and charges" in a Member's Schedule. Such additional charges resulting from the 3 March Measure could not have been recorded in the United States Schedules of GATT 1994.

the application of Article II:1(b) when the payment is to be made to another designated entity.

6.65 We note that a similar issue was discussed in the adopted Panel Report on *EEC – Programme of Minimum Import Price, Licences and Surety Deposits for Certain Processed Fruits and Vegetables*:

> "4.15 The Panel next examined the status of ***the interest charges and costs in connection with the lodging of the additional security*** associated with the minimum import price for tomato concentrates in relation to the obligations of the Community under Article II:1(b). The Panel noted the argument by the representative of the United States that the interest charges and costs associated with the lodging of the additional security were charges on or in connection with importation in excess of those allowed by Article II:1(b). The Panel further noted ***that the minimum import price and additional security system*** for tomato concentrates had ***not*** been found to be ***consistent with Article XI***, nor had any justification been claimed by the Community under any other provision of the General Agreement. The Panel considered that these interest charges and costs were "other duties or charges of any kind imposed on or in connection with importation" in excess of the bound rate within the meaning of Article II:1(b). Therefore, the Panel concluded that the ***interest charges and costs in connection with the lodging of the additional security associated with the minimum import price for tomato concentrates were inconsistent with the obligations of the Community under Article II:1(b).***"[131] (emphasis added)

6.66 The United States has confirmed that the additional bonding requirements did result in increased costs.[132]

6.67 We find, therefore, that any additional interest, charges and costs incurred in connection with the lodging of the additional bonding requirements of the 3 March Measure violated Article II:1(b) of GATT.

6.68 The European Communities also claims that the 3 March Measure violated Article VIII of GATT. We do not see how the costs relating to the bonding requirements upon importation could constitute the "approximate cost of services rendered", in the sense of Article VIII.

6.69 The meaning of Article VIII was examined in the adopted Panel Report on United States - *Customs Users Fee*[133] and in the adopted Appellate Body and Panel Reports on *Argentina – Textiles.* It was found that Article VIII's requirement that the charge be "limited in amount to the approximate cost of services rendered" is

---

[131] Panel Report on *Minimum Import Price*, op. cit., para. 4.15.

[132] See para. 6.42 of this Panel Report.

[133] Panel Report on United States - *Customs Users Fee* ("*US – Customs Users Fee*"), adopted on 2 February 1988, 35S/245.

"actually a dual requirement, because the charge in question must first involve a 'service' rendered, and then the level of the charge must not exceed the approximate cost of that 'service'."[134] The term "services rendered" means "services rendered to the individual importer in question."[135]

6.70 Although very briefly in its rebuttals[136], the United States argued that bonding requirements could be viewed as a form of fee for services rendered (the services being the "early release of merchandise") and therefore should benefit from the carve-out of Article II:2(c) of GATT, the United States has not submitted any data on the second requirement. There is no evidence that what was required from importers represented any such approximate costs of any service. It is also difficult to understand why the costs of such service would have suddenly increased on 3 March (did the United States provide more services to importers on 3 March?), and then only for listed imports from the European Communities.

6.71 We recall that the European Communities had the burden to convince us that Article VIII was applicable to the present dispute, which we consider it has failed to do. We consider that Article VIII is not relevant to the present dispute and, accordingly, we reject this EC claim.

6.72 We thus find that *prima facie* the increased bonding requirements of the 3 March Measure violated Article II:1(a) and II:1(b), first sentence of GATT. One Panelist was of the view that the increased bonding requirements of the 3 March Measure rather violated Article XI of GATT, in imposing an unjustified restriction on imports. We find that the additional interest charges, costs and fees incurred in connection with the lodging of the additional bonding requirements violated Article II:1(b), second sentence of GATT. We also find that the 3 March Measure violated Article I of GATT.

6.73 We conclude, therefore, that *prima facie* the 3 March Measure constituted a "suspension of concessions or other obligations" for the purpose of Articles 3.7, 22.6 and 23.2(c) of the DSU.

(b) US Defences

6.74 The United States contests the EC claims and argues that the 3 March Measure did not constitute a suspension of GATT/WTO concessions or other obligations. The US defense seems to be two-fold. The United States argues that the 3 March Measure, the (increased) bonding requirements, is explicitly authorised by Article 13 of the Agreement on Implementation of Article VII of GATT ("Customs Valuation Agreement"). The United States seems also to argue that it had the right to take the 3 March Measure because those imports represented an increased "risk", taking into account the (potential) eventual DSB authorization

---

[134] *Ibid.*, para. 69.
[135] *Ibid.*, para. 80.
[136] US Rebuttal Submission, paras. 29 and 30 (Appendix 2.5 to this Panel Report).

to suspend concessions and other obligations on the EC listed imports. First, we address the US defense based on Article 13 of the Customs Valuation Agreement. Secondly, we examine whether the rules of the DSU would provide the United States with a right, on 3 March 1999, to increase its tariffs on EC listed imports above its bindings, so that such right needed to be guaranteed.

(i) The US Defence Based on Article 13 of the CV Agreement

6.75 As further discussed below, the United States argues that the non-compliance by the European Communities created a risk, which allowed the United States to have concerns over its ability to collect the full amount of duties which might be due. In this respect, the United States went to great lengths to explain to the Panel that its entry system is consistent with Article 13 of the Customs Valuation Agreement. It is sufficient to note that the Customs Valuation Agreement deals with issues relating to the customs value of imported products (i.e. whether, for example, the customs value of an import is $150 or $175), not with how to determine the level of applicable tariffs (whether tariffs are 10 per cent or 25 per cent).

6.76 Article 13 of the Customs Valuation Agreement reads as follows:

> "If, ***in the course of determining the customs value of imported goods***, it becomes necessary to delay the final determination of such ***customs value***, the importer of the goods shall nevertheless be able to withdraw them from customs if, where so required, the importer provides sufficient guarantee in the form of a surety, a deposit or some other appropriate instrument, covering the ultimate payment of customs duties for which the goods may be liable. The legislation of each Member shall make provisions for such circumstances." (emphasis added)

6.77 In the present dispute the United States is not claiming that, as of 3 March, it required additional guarantees because the customs value of the EC listed imports had increased or changed on 3 March 1999. In the present dispute, there is no disagreement between the parties on the customs value of the EC listed imports. Article 13 of the Customs Valuation Agreement allows for a guarantee system when there is uncertainty regarding the customs value of the imported products, but is not concerned with the level of tariff obligations as such. Article 13 of the Customs Valuation Agreement does not authorise changes in the applicable tariff levels between the moment imports arrive at a US port of entry and a later date once imports have entered the US market. As we discuss further below, the applicable tariff (the applicable WTO obligation, the applicable law for that purpose[137]), must be the one in force on the day of importation, the day the tariff is applied. In other words, Article 13 of the Customs Valuation Agreement is of no relevance to the present dispute. We reject, therefore, this US defense.

(ii) The US Defence Based on the Increased "risk" that those EC Listed Imports Represented

6.78 In its first set of answers, the United States confirmed that the date of application of its tariffs is the date on which "goods arrive on a vessel within a Customs port" not a later date if a later event takes place.[138]

6.79 According to the United States, as of 3 March, the applicable tariff duty on EC listed imports could vary depending upon a future event, i.e. a DSB authorization to suspend concessions or other obligations on the same EC listed imports. This variation in the tariff level constituted a 'risk' which, we understand under US law, provided a justification for the Customs Service to change bonding requirements on those EC listed imports.

6.80 We understand that, generally, the customs clearance is based on two different types of factors: (1) factors relating to the assessment of the correct classification, customs valuation and origin of the goods: this depends on the specificities of each individual import operation which must be declared by the importer; and (2) factors determined by the relevant customs legislation applicable on the date on which the customs liability is incurred, i.e. in the case of the United States, the date of entry into the US customs territory. That legislation sets among other things the applicable duty rate.

6.81 Bonding requirements often serve the purpose of guaranteeing the correctness of the operators' declarations concerning the first set of factors (customs value, classification, origin of the imports). However, the 3 March Measure did not impose increased bonding requirements in order to guarantee payment of increased duties that would result from any uncertainty regarding the customs value, classification or origin of the imports. The change, the risk that is alleged to be the legal basis of the 3 March Measure, is a risk under US law, arising, according to the United States, from a possible future change of the WTO legal situation of the United States and the European Communities. The national law

[137] Appellate Body Report, *European Communities – Customs Classification of Certain Computer Equipment* ("*EC – LAN*"), WT/DS62/AB/R, WT/DS67/AB/R and WT/DS68/AB/R, adopted 22 June 1998, DSR 1998:V,1851, para. 84: "[T]he concessions provided in that Schedule are part of ***the terms of the treaty***. As such, the only rules which may be applied in interpreting the meaning of a concession are the general rules of treaty interpretation set out in the Vienna Convention." (emphasis added)

[138] US Responses to Questions of the Panel and the Parties, dated 15 January 2000, paras. 6 and 7 (Appendix 2.4 to this Panel Report). We note that the Kyoto Convention obliges to "specify the point in time to be taken into consideration for the purpose of determining the rates of import duties and taxes chargeable on goods declared for home use." (Standard 47 of Annex B.1)

of the United States cannot justify any WTO inconsistency[139]. No provisions of any WTO agreement refer to such risks or allow Members to create or maintain uncertainty with regard to the upper limit of the applicable duty rate. When a WTO agreement allows importers to apply measures to protect themselves against a situation 'threatening to occur' (a concept distinct from that of risk), it does provide so explicitly.[140]

6.82 We note also that the principal object and purpose of DSB authorised suspension of concessions or other obligations is not to obtain monetary compensation for an amount equivalent to the lost trade (caused by the WTO incompatible measure), but rather to restrict trade to an extent equivalent to the trade affected by the incompatible measure. Even in situations of WTO authorised suspensions of concessions, those enterprises that suffer from the consequences of the incompatible measures do not get any form of compensation out of the suspension of concessions. The purpose of such DSB authorised retaliatory measure is not to collect duties to be redistributed to exporters who lost trade opportunities because of the WTO incompatible measure of another Member. The major purpose of the WTO compatible suspension of concessions is to involve other interest groups from the Member at fault in order to induce compliance of that Member. The ultimate object of WTO authorised suspensions of concessions or other obligations is to remove WTO benefits and, therefore, probably to stop some trade. It is difficult to understand how a Member can obtain a retroactive permission to stop trade: either trade has been stopped or it has not. It would be absurd to imagine a situation where a Member would effectively stop trade while waiting for a DSB permission that may never come. What would have initially been a measure to stop trade while waiting for a 'retroactive' DSB permission, would then become a unilateral action, contrary to Article 23. Article 23 of the DSU is categorical: unilateral actions are prohibited at all times. If trade has been stopped before a DSB authorization, there is a violation of Article 23; if trade has not been stopped, the DSB cannot stop trade retroactively, it is physically impossible.

6.83 Finally, how can the United States, on 3 March, claim that there was a risk that the EC listed imports become retroactively subjected to WTO compatible higher duties (100 per cent) as of 3 March when its requests for the DSB authorization to suspend concessions or other obligations (14 January 1999 and 18 February 1999) did not even ask for the retroactive application of suspension of concessions or other obligations? Even if it were possible to obtain such a retroactive authorization, on 3 March the United States had not requested it.[141]

---

[139] Article 27 of the Vienna Convention on the Law of Treaties (the "Vienna Convention").

[140] See for instance Article 3.7 and footnote 9 of the Agreement on the Implementation of Article VI of GATT 1994, Article 15 and footnote 45 of the Agreement on Subsidies and Countervailing Duties and Article 4.1 of the *Agreement on Safeguards*.

[141] The Panel recalls the considerations set out in para. 6.106 of this Panel Report and its footnotes.

6.84 We thus reject the US defense to the effect that on 3 March it had a right to secure, through an additional bonding requirement, the payment of 100 per cent duties because there was a risk that pursuant to the DSU, the United States would be retroactively authorised to suspend concessions or other obligations against EC listed imports.

(c) Conclusion

6.85 We find that the 3 March Measure violated Articles I, II:1(a) and II:1(b) of the GATT and, therefore, constituted a suspension of concessions or other obligations within the meaning of Articles 23.2(c), 22.6 and 3.7 of the DSU.

6.86 To the extent that the 3 March Measure constituted a GATT/WTO suspension of concessions or other obligations, it could take place only pursuant to a DSB authorization. On 3 March 1999, the United States did not have any DSB authorization to suspend any tariff concession or any other obligation in response to the alleged WTO violation by the European Communities. In fact, on 3 March no WTO adjudicating body had yet determined (i) whether the EC implementing measure nullified any WTO benefits, (ii) the level of such nullification, if any, or (iii) the level of suspension that should be authorised, if any. On 3 March, bonding requirements on EC listed imports were increased but there were no related additional tariff rights to justify such an additional enforcement mechanism. On 3 March, the United States had no right to impose 100 per cent duties on the EC listed imports therefore no right to begin enforcing the imposition of 100 per cent duty on EC listed imports. On 3 March, the United States unilaterally suspended concessions or other obligations on EC listed imports, without DSB authorization.

6.87 We find, therefore, that the 3 March Measure constituted a suspension of concessions or other obligations within the meaning of Articles 23.2(c), 3.7 last sentence and 22.6 last sentence, since (i) the increased bonding requirements of the 3 March Measure violated Articles II:1(a) and II:1(b), first sentence (one Panelist is of the view that the 3 March Measure violated rather Article XI of GATT), (ii) the additional interest charges, costs and fees resulting from the 3 March Measure violated the second sentence of Article II:1(b) of GATT and (iii) the 3 March Measure violated Article I of GATT. Having reached the prior conclusion that the 3 March Measure was a measure seeking to redress a WTO violation within the meaning of Article 23.1, we find that when it put in place the 3 March Measure, prior to any DSB authorization and while the *EC - Bananas III* (22.6-7) Arbitration process was still ongoing, the United States did not abide by the rules of the DSU - violating Articles 23.2(c), 3.7 and 22.6 of the DSU – and was therefore in violation of Article 23.1.

3. *Article 23.1 together with Articles 21.5 and 23.2(a) of the DSU*

6.88 The European Communities claims that the 3 March Measure violated Article 21.5 of the DSU, because on 3 March the United States had not exhausted the procedure of Article 21.5, which, the European Communities argues, should have been completed before the United States requested the DSB permission to suspend concessions or other obligations. For the European Communities, such violation is of a continuing nature: the US suspension of concessions or other obligations of 3 March is and remains inconsistent with the WTO Agreement. In the European Communities' view, the 19 April action is only a confirmation of the US 3 March action and it argues that a "[DSB decision adopting an Article 21.5 panel report] was missing on 3 March, was also missing on 19 April and is still missing today"[142]. For the European Communities, the WTO inconsistency of the 3 March Measure (and the 19 April US action) could not have been healed by the DSB authorization of 19 April because it was flawed from the outset: the DSB authorization of 19 April 1999 was a necessary, but not a sufficient prerequisite for the US suspension of concessions or other obligations.

6.89 We recall that the US action of 19 April is not included in our terms of reference. We consider that the 19 April action is a legally distinct measure and we disagree with the EC argument that the 19 April action is only a confirmation of the 3 March Measure. We may examine the 19 April DSB authorization to the United States to suspend concessions and other obligations only to assess the US defence that the authorization may have cured any prior WTO inconsistency of the 3 March Measure.

6.90 We recall that we have reached the prior conclusion that the 3 March Measure constituted a measure seeking to redress a WTO violation within the meaning of Article 23.1 of the DSU. If we find that Article 21.5 of the DSU contains an obligation, its violation could be viewed as one of those DSU obligations which, although not explicitly listed in Article 23.2, are covered by Article 23.1 (which mandates the respect of rules and procedures of the DSU). We examine therefore the meaning of Article 21.5 of the DSU.

6.91 The first sentence of Article 21.5 reads as follows:

> "Where there is disagreement as to the existence or consistency with a covered agreement of measures taken to comply with the recommendations and rulings such dispute ***shall*** be decided through recourse to ***these*** dispute settlement procedures, ***including*** wherever possible resort to the original panel." (emphasis added)

6.92 This sentence confirms that when an assessment of the WTO compatibility of a measure taken to comply with panel and Appellate Body recommendations (an "implementing measure") is necessary (because parties disagree), such

[142] US Second submission, paras. 77-78 (Appendix 2.5 to this Panel Report).

determination can only be made through the WTO dispute settlement procedures. Pursuant to Article 23.2(a), Members are obliged to have recourse exclusively to a WTO/DSU dispute settlement mechanism to obtain a 'determination' that a measure is WTO inconsistent. We consider that the obligation to use the WTO multilateral dispute settlement mechanism (i.e. as opposed to unilateral or even regional mechanisms) to obtain any determination of WTO compatibility, is a fundamental obligation that finds application throughout the DSU. For us, the prohibition against unilateral determinations of WTO violation contained in the first sentence of Article 21.5 of the DSU is comparable to that of Article 23.2(a) of the DSU.[143] We consider that the ordinary meaning of the terms of the first sentence of Article 21.5 is that in case of disagreement between the parties, the determination of the WTO compatibility of implementing measures shall be made through recourse to the WTO dispute settlement procedures. Therefore, we do not consider that the first sentence of Article 21.5 is only of a procedural nature but rather contains a substantive obligation similar to that of Article 23.2(a) of the DSU.

6.93 Article 22.8 of the DSU, which forms part of the context of Article 21.5, provides that "the suspension of concessions or other obligations shall be temporary and shall only be applied until such time as the ***measure found to be inconsistent*** ... has been removed". The term "measure found to be inconsistent" (which in the framework of Article 21.5 relates to the implementing measure) assumes an adjudicating process and must be read together with Article 23.2(a)[144] that also mandates WTO adjudication to determine whether a WTO violation has occurred. Article 23.2(a) also forms part of the context of Article 21.5. For us, the first sentence of Article 21.5 is simply a more specific provision reiterating, in the specific context of implementing measures, the general prohibition against unilateral determination of WTO violations contained in Articles 23.1 and 23.2(a) of the DSU.

6.94 In our view, this interpretation preserves the security and predictability of the WTO dispute settlement mechanism and the multilateral trade system it supports. The determination of whether an implementing measure is WTO inconsistent is a matter for the entire membership, and therefore should be assessed through the WTO institutional framework. Many elements in Article 21 of the DSU, entitled "Surveillance of Implementation of Recommendations and Rulings", confirm that implementation of Panel and the Appellate Body recommendations is a systemic concern and that any WTO Member is directly concerned and interested in the implementation process of any other Member. To ensure effective surveillance, implementation remains on the DSB Agenda as long as the

[143] Article 21.5, first sentence is one of those DSU provisions whose violations, although not listed in Article 23.2 that contain egregious examples, may lead to a violation of Article 23.1.

[144] Article 23 is included in the context of Article 22.8 which must be taken into account when interpreting the ordinary meaning of the terms used in Article 22.8 of the DSU, Article 31.1 and 31.2 of the Vienna Convention.

matter is not resolved. The implementing Member is also obliged to report periodically to the DSB and produce reports on the status of its implementation[145].

6.95 Based on the evidence below, we are of the view that on 3 March the United States made a unilateral determination that the EC implementing measure violated the WTO; the United States did not make this determination through the recourse to the rules of the DSU or following the conclusions of a Panel, the Appellate Body or Arbitration report (Article 23.2(a)), or through recourse to any of the dispute settlement procedures of the WTO.

6.96 We recall that Article 23.2(a) reads as follows:

> "2. In such cases, Members shall:
>
> (a) not make a determination to the effect that a violation has occurred, that benefits have been nullified or impaired or that the attainment of any objective of the covered agreements has been impeded, except through recourse to dispute settlement in accordance with the rules and procedures of this Understanding, and shall make any such determination consistent with the findings contained in the panel or Appellate Body report adopted by the DSB or an arbitration award rendered under this Understanding;"

6.97 Article 23.2(a) of the DSU confirms the general obligation of Article 23.1 and prohibits more explicitly any unilateral determination that a WTO violation has occurred in providing that all determinations of whether a WTO violation has occurred can only be made pursuant to the DSU process.[146]

---

145 See Article 21.6 of the DSU: "The ***DSB shall keep under surveillance the implementation*** of adopted recommendations or rulings. The issue of implementation of the recommendations or rulings may be raised at the DSB by ***any Member*** at any time following their adoption. Unless the DSB decides otherwise, the issue of implementation of the recommendations or rulings shall be placed on the agenda of the DSB meeting after six months following the date of establishment of the reasonable period of time pursuant to *para.* 3 and ***shall remain on the DSB's agenda until the issue is resolved***. At least 10 days prior to each such DSB meeting, the Member concerned shall provide the DSB with a ***status report*** in writing of its progress in the implementation of the recommendations or rulings." (emphasis added)

146 The Panel Report on *US – Section 301* suggested that four elements must be satisfied for a specific act in a particular dispute to breach Article 23.2(a) of the DSU: "(a) the act is taken 'in such cases' (*chapeau* of Article 23.2), i.e. in a situation where a Member 'seek[s] the redress of a violation of obligations or other nullification or impairment of benefits under the covered agreements or an impediment to the attainment of any objective of the covered agreements', as referred to in Article 23.1; (b) the act constitutes a 'determination'; (c) the 'determination' is one 'to the effect that a violation has occurred, that benefits have been nullified or impaired or that the attainment of any objective of the covered agreements has been impeded'; (d) the 'determination' is either *not* made 'through recourse to dispute settlement in accordance with the rules and procedures of [the DSU]' or *not* made 'consistent with the findings contained in the panel or Appellate Body report adopted by the DSB or an arbitration award rendered under [the DSU]'." The two elements of this requirement are cumulative in nature. Determinations are only allowed when made through recourse to the DSU *and* consistent with findings adopted by

6.98 The term "determination" is defined in the *New Shorter Oxford English Dictionary* as "The action of coming to a decision; the result of this; a fixed intention. The action of definitely ... establishing the nature of something [under 23.2(a) it would be the nature of a WTO violation]; exact ascertainment." In the context of the WTO, we consider that a 'determination' that a WTO violation has occurred is a decision that a WTO Member has violated the WTO Agreement and which bears consequences in WTO trade relations.

6.99 We note that Article 23.2(a) *a contrario* means that determinations made by Members through recourse to the DSU and following findings by panels, the Appellate Body and arbitration are WTO compatible. For instance, when, in January 1999, the United States requested an Article 22 procedure, it had made an internal 'determination' that the EC implementation measure was WTO incompatible and requested a WTO adjudication on this matter. This US determination was made in the context of a DSU procedure and was obviously not in violation of Article 23. However, on 3 March, as further discussed below, the United States decided to act outside of the DSU process.

6.100 For us there is ample evidence that the 3 March Measure constituted a unilateral determination by the United States that a WTO violation had occurred for which the United States determined that a remedial action was needed. When on 3 March the United States decided to take a remedial action against EC listed imports, there was no WTO determination (no findings by a panel, Appellate Body or arbitration body) concluding that the EC implementing measure was incompatible with the WTO Agreement. The unilateral action (as we concluded above in paragraph 6.86) taken by the United States implies necessarily a prior US unilateral determination that the EC implementing measure was inconsistent with the WTO. When the United States refers to its "rights" and the need to preserve its rights to collect higher duties, this US determination of its rights was, therefore, unilateral. The USTR official announcement stated:

"United States ***Takes Customs Action*** on European Imports

[E]ffective today, the U.S. Customs Service will ***begin*** 'withholding liquidation' on imports valued at over $500 million of ***selected products from the European Union*** (EU), consistent with ***U.S. rights*** under the WTO agreements. Withholding liquidation imposes ***contingent liability for 100 per cent duties*** on affected products as of March 3, 1999...

> January 1, 1999, was the deadline for the EU to implement a WTO-consistent banana regime. ***The EU failed to honor this deadline,*** thereby entitling the United States to suspend tariff con-

---

the DSB or an arbitration award under the DSU." Panel Report, *US – Section 301*, *supra*, footnote 69, footnote 657.

cessions as early as February 1st on selected European products with the WTO's blessing."[147] (emphasis added)

6.101 The United States' unilateral determination that the EC implementing measure was WTO inconsistent (and therefore should be redressed) is also evident from the Press Conference given by Deputy USTR P. Scher on 3 March:

> "Q. Does the withholding of liquidation fulfill the terms of the Bowles letter which says 'If the EU seeks arbitration … the retaliatory action will go into effect on the date that arbitration is concluded, but in no event later than March 3, 1999'?
>
> A. … ***We retaliated by effectively stopping trade*** as of 3 March in ***responding*** to the harm caused by the ***EC's WTO inconsistent*** banana regime. ***That purpose is achieved by*** withholding liquidation on the products on the ***retaliation list*** …
>
> …
>
> Q. How do you expect the EC to react?
>
> A. … But our action makes it crystal clear that ***there are consequences for failure to comply with WTO rulings.*** …"[148] (emphasis added)

6.102 The fact that on 3 March the United States was saying that it was responding to a WTO violation when, on 3 March the WTO had not yet determined that there was a violation, confirms that the United States made a unilateral determination that the European Communities had committed a WTO violation.

6.103 The request from USTR to the US Customs Service is also revealing:

"…. The [USTR] intends to implement this suspension of tariff concessions by directing the Customs Service to impose 100 percent duties, *ad valorem*, on the products listed in the attachment to this letter. (See also 63 Fed. Reg. 63099 and 63 Fed. Reg. 71665 giving notice of the proposed increase in duties on selected products).

…. The USTR now ***seeks to preserve its right*** to impose 100 per cent duties as of March 3, pending the release of the arbitrators' final decision." [149] (emphasis added)

6.104 The United States asserts that it seeks to preserve its right to impose 100 per cent duties (the same reference to the US right exists in the Official USTR Press release). However, on 3 March 1999 the United States did not have any such right against any imports from the European Communities, as the determination of whether the EC implementing measure was WTO compatible was still

---

[147] USTR Press Release, dated 3 March 1999, "United States Takes Customs Action on European Imports" (EC Annex VII).

[148] See EC Annex X.

[149] Letter dated 3 March 1999 from Mr. Peter L. Scher, Special Trade Negotiator to Commissioner Raymond W. Kelly, US Customs Service (US Ex. 12).

under consideration by the relevant WTO adjudicating body. On 3 March the United States may have had very strong expectations that its request for suspension of concessions or other obligations would be authorised, but to preserve a right, one must have this right first. When the United States declared that it needed to preserve its rights, such a right (to 100 per cent duties) can only have been determined unilaterally by the United States, contrary to Article 23.2(a) and 21.5 of the DSU. This is evidence that on 3 March the United States took a unilateral action with a view to redressing the EC implementing measure which the United States had unilaterally determined to be in violation of the WTO Agreement.

6.105 In fact, it is only because the United States had unilaterally determined that the European Communities had violated the WTO Agreement that the United States considered that it had the right to put in place additional bonding requirements, the nature of which is to secure compliance with a WTO compatible rights/obligations. The very choice of the measure, additional bonding requirements on EC listed imports, because its purposes are to secure rights, suffices to demonstrate that on 3 March the United States made a unilateral determination that the EC implementing measure violated the WTO Agreement and that it had a right to "take action".[150]

6.106 There is also another very important element that demonstrates that the United States took the 3 March Measure after having *unilaterally* determined that it had the right to take remedial action as of 3 March. The wording of the 3 March Measure leaves the impression that the United States expected some form of retroactive right to collect increased duties. The remedy chosen on 3 March was part of the remedy that the United States alleged would be authorised by the DSB later on. There are, however, no explicit DSU provisions provid-

[150] See the title of the 3 March USTR Press Release: "United States Takes Customs Action on European Imports" (EC Annex VII). We note in this context that the Notification in the Federal Register of 10 November 1998 provided that "The dates on which the USTR intends to implement action – February 1 or not later than March 3 ..." Notification of USTR, Doc. No. 301-100a, 10 November 1998, 63 Fed. Reg. 63099 (1998) (EC Annex II). On its face, Section 306(b) of the Trade Act requires the USTR to determine what further action it shall take under Section 301(a) if the USTR considers that a foreign country has failed to implement a recommendation made pursuant to dispute settlement proceedings under the WTO. The USTR shall make this determination no later than thirty days after the expiry of the reasonable period of time provided for such implementation under Article 21.3 of the DSU, which is January 31, 1999 in this case. Section 305(a)(I) requires USTR to implement such action by no later than thirty days after the date on which that determination is made, or March 2 in this case. We recall that the Panel on *US – Section 301* had reached the conclusion that (irrespective of whether the US or EC approach to Article 21.5 and 22 is followed), Section 306 through which the USTR can make a determination that a Member's implementation has failed within 30 days after the expiry of the reasonable period of time, is *prima facie* inconsistent with Article 23.2(a) of the DSU. We recall also that the Panel concluded that when USTR determines that an action is needed because there is "a 'consideration' that implementation failed, automatically and as a *conditio sine qua non* leading to a decision on action under Section 301, that determination meet the threshold of firmness and immutability required for a 'determination' under Article 23.2(a)". Panel Report, *US – Section 301, supra*, footnote 69, paras. 7.142-147.

ing for retroactive application of retaliatory measures; to the contrary, Article 22.6 explicitly prohibits such GATT/WTO sanctions during the arbitration process. Nor are there any DSU provisions allowing for measures to be taken to 'preserve' a right to suspend concessions or other obligations. The US requests for DSB authorization to suspend concessions or other obligations[151] did not contain a claim for retroactive application of the authorization. If, arguably, the United States was entitled, when it made its requests (first, on 14 January 1999 for consideration by the DSB on 25 January 1999, and second, on 18 February 2000), to expect that the arbitration panel would respect general time limits of Article 22.6, it could not assume, on 3 March, that it would benefit eventually from a DSB retroactive right.[152] The United States did not request retroactivity, and retroactive remedies are alien to the long established GATT/WTO practice where remedies have traditionally been prospective. On 3 March the United States had no WTO compatible 'right' (even potential) to any suspension of concessions or other obligations that could be retroactively confirmed. Therefore, the US assertion that it had such a right could only have been unilaterally determined.

6.107 We conclude, therefore, that the 3 March measure constituted a unilateral determination contrary to Article 23.2(a) and 21.5 of the DSU. As discussed above we consider that Articles 23.2(a) and 21.5 make it clear that the determination of the WTO compatibility of implementing measures can only be made through recourse to the DSU. On 3 March such WTO determination did not exist. The European Communities claim that the United States should be blamed. But who should trigger this WTO determination of the WTO compatibility of an implementing measure?

6.108 The European Communities and the United States disagree as to which party bears the burden of demonstrating compliance or non-compliance of such an implementing measure. We consider that to the extent that there is a measure taken to comply with the Panel and Appellate Body recommendations (an implementing measure), and that the content of such an implementing measure is distinct from the measure that was the object of the Panel and Appellate Body

---

[151] WT/DS27/43 and WT/DS27/47.

[152] On 3 March, the United States had not requested any retroactive DSB permission and the arbitrator had not lost jurisdiction over the matter. We recall the conclusion of the Arbitrators in the Article 22.6 Decision on *EC – Bananas III, supra,* footnote 30: " On the face of it, the 60-day period specified in Article 22.6 does not limit or define the jurisdiction of the Arbitrators *ratione temporis*. It imposes a *procedural* obligation on the Arbitrators in respect of the conduct of their work, not a *substantive* obligation in respect of the validity thereof. In our view, if the time-periods of Article 17.5 and Article 22.6 of the DSU were to cause the lapse of the authority of the Appellate Body or the Arbitrators, the DSU would have explicitly provided so. Such lapse of jurisdiction is explicitly foreseen, e.g. in Article 12.12 of the DSU which provides that "if the work of the panel has been suspended for more than 12 months, the authority for establishment of the panel shall lapse". We recall a similar conclusion reached by the Panel Report, *US – Section 301, supra,* footnote 69, para. 7.31. The United States must have known that such 3 March Measure was unilateral and not based on any reasonable expectation of retroactive application.

recommendations, Article 21.5 mandates the WTO determination of whether such an implementing measure is WTO compatible. We note that the existence of a measure, i.e. the issue whether a new measure has effectively been adopted to comply with Panel and the Appellate Body recommendations, is a matter that must also be determined by the DSB and not unilaterally.

6.109 It would be, therefore, for the Member challenging the WTO consistency of the implementing measure (or challenging the very existence of an authentic implementing measure) to request that the matter be brought under a WTO/DSU dispute settlement procedure (that Member is obligated to do so pursuant to Articles 21.5 and 23.2(a) of the DSU), in particular before the original panel if available. Traditionally in GATT/WTO, it is for the country that seeks the application of a specific provision or right, to ask for it. We note, in this context, that it is relatively simple (and there is no need for any special legal interest and the 'standing' requirement is only one of 'potential' market interest.[153]) to initiate a dispute settlement procedure pursuant to the DSU. The Member intending to request DSB permission to suspend concessions or other obligations must, therefore, in the event of a disagreement between the parties, challenge the implementing measure and trigger the WTO dispute settlement mechanism to obtain a WTO determination that the implementing measure is WTO inconsistent. As under general WTO rules[154], that Member will bear the burden of proving that the new implementing measure violates provisions of the WTO Agreement.

6.110 Our position is confirmed by the following statement of the Appellate Body in *Chile – Taxes on Alcoholic Beverages*,

> "74. ... Members of the WTO should not be assumed, in any way, to have ***continued*** previous protection or discrimination

[153] See for instance the following clear statement of the Appellate Body in *EC – Bananas III*: "132. ... We do not accept that the need for a 'legal interest' is implied in the DSU or in any other provision of the *WTO Agreement*... 135. Accordingly, we believe that a Member has broad discretion in deciding whether to bring a case against another Member under the DSU. The language of Article XXIII:1 of the GATT 1994 and of Article 3.7 of the DSU suggests, furthermore, that a Member is expected to be largely self-regulating in deciding whether any such action would be 'fruitful'. (...) 136. We are satisfied that the United States was justified in bringing its claims under the GATT 1994 in this case. The United States is a producer of bananas, and a potential export interest by the United States cannot be excluded". Appellate Body Report, *EC – Bananas III*, *supra*, footnote 1, paras. 132, 135 and 136.

[154] See the well-established principle to that effect in the Appellate Body Report, *United States – Measure Affecting Imports of Woven Wool Shirts and Blouses from India* ("*US –Shirts and Blouses*"), WT/DS33/AB/R and Corr. 1, adopted 23 May 1997, DSR 1997:I, 323, at 335: "In addressing this issue, we find it difficult, indeed, to see how any system of judicial settlement could work if it incorporated the proposition that the mere assertion of a claim might amount to proof. It is, thus, hardly surprising that various international tribunals, including the International Court of Justice, have generally and consistently accepted and applied the rule that the party who asserts a fact, whether the claimant or the respondent, is responsible for providing proof thereof. Also, it is a generally-accepted canon of evidence in civil law, common law and, in fact, most jurisdictions, that the burden of proof rests upon the party, whether complaining or defending, who asserts the affirmative of a particular claim or defence".

> through the adoption of a new measure. This would come close to a presumption of bad faith."[155] (emphasis in original)

and by the following conclusion of the *Hormones* Arbitration Report:

> "9. WTO Members, as sovereign entities, can be ***presumed*** to act in conformity with their WTO obligations. A party claiming that a Member has acted ***inconsistently*** with WTO rules bears the burden of proving that inconsistency."[156] (emphasis in original)

6.111 Our interpretation of the burden of proof will not favour the adoption of 'scam' implementing measures. To the contrary, we are well aware that immediate implementation of DSB recommendations is the relevant standard, explicitly repeated in Articles 3.7, 21.1 and 21.3 of the DSU. In this context, we refer to the consistent jurisprudence of arbitrators pursuant to Article 21.3(c) of the DSU that "... the first objective is usually the *immediate removal* of the measure judged to be inconsistent ... Only if it is impracticable to do so, is the Member concerned entitled to a reasonable period of time"[157]. It seems therefore clear that implementation shall proceed expeditiously.

6.112 If the implementing Member abuses its right to implement the recommendations of Panels and Appellate Body within the reasonable period of time, such implementing Member will not benefit from the adoption of any scam measure, as it seems clear that it bears the burden of proving that the initial DSB authorised level of suspension of concessions and other obligations should be reduced (pursuant to the adoption of a new WTO compatible measure). This is consistent with the rule that the burden of proof always rests on the Member challenging the WTO compatibility of a measure. Once a Member imposes DSB authorised suspensions of concessions or obligations, that Member's measure is WTO compatible (it was explicitly authorised by the DSB). If the Member affected by that other Member's measure (imposing suspension of concessions or obligations) wants to challenge the WTO compatibility of such measure (e.g. its level is no longer equivalent to the level of nullification), it is for that affected Member to bear the related burden of proof.

---

[155] Appellate Body Report, *Chile – Taxes on Alcoholic Beverages* ("*Chile – Alcoholic Beverages*"), WT/DS87/AB/R, WT/DS110/AB/R, adopted 12 January 2000, DSR 2000:I, 281, para. 74.

[156] Decision by the Arbitrators, *European Communities – Measures Concerning Meat and Meat Products (Hormones) – Original Complaint by the United States - Recourse to Arbitration by the European Communities under Article 22.6 of the DSU*, ("*EC – Hormones (US) (Article 22.6 – EC)*"), WT/DS26/ARB, 12 July 1999, DSR 1999:III, 1105. para. 9.

[157] Award of the Arbitrator, *Australia - Measures Affecting Importation of Salmon, Arbitration under Article 21.3(c) of the DSU* ("*Australia – Salmon*"), WT/DS18/9, 23 February 1999, DSR 1999:I, 267, paras. 28-30. See also Award of the Arbitrator, *EC Measures Concerning meat and Meat Products (Hormones) - Arbitration under Article 21.3(c) of the DSU* ("*EC – Hormones*"), WT/DS26/15, WT/DS48/13, 29 May 1998, DSR 1998:V, 1833, para. 26 and Award of the Arbitrator, *Indonesia – Certain Measures Affecting the Automobile Industry - Arbitration under Article 21.3(c) of the DSU ("Indonesia – Autos")*, WT/DS54/15, WT/DS55/14, WT/DS59/13, WT/DS64/12, 7 December 1998, DSR 1998:IX, 4029.

6.113 We consider that our interpretation is consistent with the terms of Article 22.8 of the DSU, which is very specific on this matter, and which provides:

> "22.8 The suspension of concessions or other obligations shall be temporary and shall only be applied ***until such time*** as the measure found to be inconsistent with a covered agreement has been removed, or the Member that must implement recommendations or rulings provides a solution to the nullification or impairment of benefits, or a mutually satisfactory solution is reached." (emphasis added)

6.114 It is only logical that the Member, author of the said measure found inconsistent, is in the best position to know whether the situation has changed, i.e. whether the measure (or part of it) was removed and, consequently, whether the measure imposing the suspension should be challenged. That same Member should bear the burden of proving that the suspension measure is not WTO compatible anymore because its level is not equivalent to the level of nullification of WTO benefits. Our interpretation is consistent with the fundamental WTO/DSU rule that Panel and Appellate Body recommendations must be implemented "immediately" (21.3(c) of the DSU) and that, at the latest at the expiry of the reasonable period, the WTO/DSU implementation mechanism can be triggered by an interested Member.

6.115 Having found that the first sentence of Article 21.5 mandates the WTO compatibility assessment of an implementing measure through the exclusive recourse to the WTO dispute settlement mechanism, and that it is for the Member challenging the WTO compatibility of any measure to trigger such process, we must address the issue of which WTO dispute settlement procedures can be used.

6.116 The European Communities claims that the United States violated Article 21.5 because on 3 March it did not have at hand an Article 21.5 panel report. The European Communities goes further and argues that the United States should have had at hand an Article 21.5 panel report when it requested an Article 22 procedure to the DSB, (or at least when on 19 April the DSB authorised suspension of concessions and other obligations by the United States). In the European Communities' view the 3 March violation is of a continuing nature and since the 19 April action is a confirmation of the 3 March measure which it self is inconsistent with the DSU, the 19 April action is a nullity under the DSU.

6.117 First, we examine whether an Article 21.5 determination can be made by an arbitration body through the Article 22.6 procedure. In application of the principle clearly expressed in the first sentence of Article 21.5, the end of the first sentence (and the second sentence) of Article 21.5 refers to the specific 'possibility' of referring the matter to the original Panel, as one of the WTO dispute settlement procedures available to determine such WTO compatibility of implementing measures:

> "Where there is disagreement as to the existence or consistency with a covered agreement of measures taken to comply with the recommendations and ruling such dispute ***shall*** be decided through

> recourse to ***these*** dispute settlement procedures, ***including*** wherever possible resort to the original panel.
>
> The panel shall circulate its report within 90 days after the date of referral of the matter to it. When the panel considers that it cannot provide its report within this time frame, it shall inform the DSB in writing of the reasons for the delay together with an estimate of the period within which it will submit its report." (emphasis added)

6.118 For us, this sentence confirms that if an assessment of the WTO compatibility of an implementing measure is necessary (because parties disagree) such a determination can only be obtained through the WTO dispute settlement procedures. But what do "these dispute settlement procedures" refer to? There is no other indication on that matter in Article 21.5. We must continue our examination of the ordinary meaning of the terms used in Article 21.5 of the DSU.

6.119 If we examine the context of Article 21.5 (including the provisions of the DSU surrounding Article 21.5) and the object and purpose of the DSU, we note that there are several different types of WTO dispute settlement procedures under the DSU that could be used to assess the WTO compatibility of the new implementing measure. We recall that the first sentence of Article 21.5 refers to "***including*** recourse to the original panel". Although the panel (and Appellate Body) process is the most commonly used WTO dispute settlement procedure, Article 25 of the DSU, for example, explicitly provides for arbitration as a means of adjudicating WTO related disputes. Article 25.4 provides for the applicability of Articles 21 and 22 of the DSU to the results of such arbitration. There is no reason why the WTO assessment of the compatibility of an implementing measure could not be determined by an Article 25 arbitration, as one of the WTO dispute settlement procedures.

6.120 We note that the drafting history of Article 21.5 seems to confirm our interpretation based on the ordinary meaning of the terms used in their context. In the Dunkel Draft, what was then Article 19.5 used the words "***involving*** resort to the original panel wherever possible"[158]. Earlier, the Swiss delegate had put forward a proposal to introduce arbitration under the DSU[159]. It seems that negotiators may have wanted to reflect this expansion of "WTO dispute settlement procedures" when they favoured the use of the term "***including*** recourse to the original panel" instead of "***involving*** recourse to the original panel" for the first sentence of Article 21.5 of the DSU.

6.121 We are aware that the arbitration process of Article 25 is distinct from that of Articles 21.3(c) or 22.6 of the DSU. Our point is that 'panel' procedure is not the only dispute settlement procedure under the DSU. We consider that the arbi-

---

[158] MTN.TNC/W/FA. Emphasis added by the Panel.

[159] See *Arbitration within GATT, Communication from Switzerland,* GATT Doc. No. MTN.GNG/NG13/W/33. See also Terrence Stewart, *The GATT Uruguay Round: A Negotiating History, Vol. II,* (1993), Kluwer Law and Taxation, p. 2772.

tration process pursuant to Article 22 may constitute a proper WTO dispute settlement procedure to perform the WTO assessment mandated by the first sentence of Article 21.5 of the DSU. We think that the WTO compatibility determination of an implementing measure can be performed through an Article 22.6-22.7 arbitration when assessing the "equivalent level of suspension of concessions"[160]. We believe that the ordinary meaning of the terms "determine whether the level of such suspension is ***equivalent*** to the level of nullification or impairment" confirms that the equivalence between the two levels cannot be fulfilled before the WTO compatibility of the implementing measure has been assessed.[161] In our view, this provision also confirms that the determination of whether the implementing measure nullifies any WTO benefit, must take place before the level of suspension of concessions or obligations can be assessed (and eventually authorised by the DSB).[162] More importantly, however, this provision gives the arbitration panel the mandate and the authority to assess the WTO compatibility of the implementing measure. Since the Article 22.6 arbitration was given the authority to determine "a level of suspension equivalent to the level of nullification", it has the authority to assess both variables of the equation.

6.122 We are well aware that it is not our mandate to assess the DSU compatibility of what was done in the *EC - Bananas III* implementation panel and arbitration reports[163]. We consider, nonetheless, that if, at the time when the Article 22.6 arbitration is requested, no WTO determination of the compatibility of the implementing measure has yet taken place, those acting in arbitration are obliged to assess first whether the implementing measure nullifies or impairs the WTO rights of the Member requesting DSB permission to retaliate. This is a matter of simple legal logic: it is legally impossible to assess the level of suspension based on the level of nullification before assessing whether the implementing measure nullifies or impairs WTO rights. Only after having assessed the WTO compatibil-

---

[160] Article 22.7 of the DSU reads as follows: "The arbitrator acting pursuant to *para.* 6 shall not examine the nature of the concessions or other obligations to be suspended but shall ***determine whether the level of such suspension is equivalent to the level of nullification or impairment***. The arbitrator may also determine if the proposed suspension of concessions or other obligations is allowed under the covered agreement. However, if the matter referred to arbitration includes a claim that the principles and procedures set forth in *para.* 3 have not been followed, the arbitrator shall examine that claim. In the event the arbitrator determines that those principles and procedures have not been followed, the complaining party shall apply them consistent with *para.* 3. The parties shall accept the arbitrator's decision as final and the parties concerned shall not seek a second arbitration. The DSB shall be informed promptly of the decision of the arbitrator and shall upon request, grant authorization to suspend concessions or other obligations where the request is consistent with the decision of the arbitrator, unless the DSB decides by consensus to reject the request." (footnote omitted and emphasis added)

[161] In this context, we agree with the discussions and conclusions of the Arbitrators in *EC – Bananas III (US) (Article 22.6 – EC), supra*, footnote 30, paras 4.1 to 4.8.

[162] Decision by the Arbitrators, *EC – Bananas III (US) (Article 22.6 – EC), supra*, footnote 30, and Panel Report, *EC – Bananas III (Article 21.5 – EC), supra*, footnote 36, and Panel Report, *EC – Bananas III (Article 21.5 – Ecuador), supra*, footnote 38.

[163] *Ibid.*

ity of the implementing measure can a WTO adjudicating body assess the impact of any such WTO incompatibility, which will indicate the "equivalent level of suspension of concessions and other obligations". Since the Article 22.6 arbitration process was given the authority to determine "a level of suspension equivalent to the level of nullification", it has the authority to assess both variables of the equation, including whether the implementing measure nullifies any benefit and the level of such nullified benefits.

6.123 We note also that both Article 22.6 and the first sentence of Article 21.5 refer to the possibility of recourse to the original panel; there is only one original panel for each dispute. It is, therefore, not unreasonable to consider that the same original panel, through its arbitration procedure would, first, assess the WTO compatibility of the new measure, secondly, assess the impact, if any, of such WTO incompatible measure and thirdly determine the equivalent level of suspension of concessions or other obligations. We understand that such is the present practice of the DSB as it has developed under the DSU: the members of the original panel are mandated to act pursuant to Articles 21.5 and/or 22.6-22.7 of the DSU.[164] It is therefore reasonable to interpret the DSU so as to allow a single WTO adjudication body to perform both the WTO compatibility determination of the implementing measure (Articles 21.5 and 23.2(a)) and the assessment of the appropriate level of suspension (pursuant to Article 22.6-22.7).[165]

---

[164] In the following cases, the DSB decided that the matter would be referred to the original panel under Article 21.5 of the DSU: (i) *EC – Bananas III*, Recourse to Article 21.5 by Ecuador (Communication dated 18 December 1998, WT/DS27/41), WT/DSB/M/53; (ii) *EC – Bananas III*, Recourse to Article 21.5 by the European Communities, WT/DSB/M/53; (iii) *Australia – Salmons*, Recourse to Article 21.5 by Canada (Communication dated 3 August 1999, WT/DS18/14), WT/DSB/M/66; (iv) *Canada – Measures Affecting the Export of Civilian Aircraft*, Recourse to Article 21.5 by Brazil (Communication dated 26 November 1999, WT/DS46/13), WT/DSB/M/72; (v) *Brazil – Export Financing Programme for Aircraft*, Recourse to Article 21.5 by Canada (Communication dated 23 November 1999, WT/DS70/9), WT/DSB/M/72; and (vi) *Australia – Subsidies Provided to Producers and Exporters of Automotive Leather*, Recourse to Article 21.5 by the United States (Communication dated 4 October 1999, WT/DS126/8), WT/DSB/M/69. In those cases except for (ii) above, the Member invoking the procedure requested specifically that the matter be referred to the original panel. Also, in the following arbitration procedures under Article 22.6, the original panel members were appointed as arbitrators: (i) *EC – Bananas III*, Recourse to Arbitration by the European Communities under Article 22.6 of the DSU, WT/DSB/M/54; (ii) *Australia – Salmons*, Recourse to Arbitration by Australia under Article 22.6 of the DSU, WT/DS18/16; and (iii) Decision by the Arbitrators, *EC – Hormones (US) (Article 22.6 – EC), supra*, footnote 156, para. 2. In the case (i) above, the European Communities specifically requested that the original panel carry out the arbitration. Communication, dated 3 February 1999, from the European Communities to the Chairman of the DSB, WT/DS27/46.

[165] Adjudication of both whether the implementing measure nullifies WTO rights and whether the level of suggested sanctions is equivalent to the level of nullification is very burdensome exercise and may sometimes lead to delay in the issuance of the arbitration report on this matter. We note in this context, as did the Panel in *US – Section 301*, *supra*, footnote 69, para. 7.180 and footnote 720, as well as the arbitration panel in *Bananas III*, *supra*, footnote 30, footnote 7 that on its face the 60-day period specified in Article 22.6 does not limit or define the jurisdiction of arbitrators *ratione temporis*. We discuss this point further when we address the US defense that if the Euro-

6.124 We do not agree with the European Communities' argument that because arbitration reports are not "adopted" by the DSB, arbitration is not covered by the terms "these dispute settlement procedures" in the first sentence of Article 21.5. Adoption is not the only institutional means of action of the DSB. It is the DSB that refers any matter to arbitration pursuant to Article 22.6. It is the DSB that takes note of the arbitration report under Article 22.6, and the results of such arbitration decision will lead to a level of suspension that institutionally will be authorised by the WTO/DSB. We consider that the arbitration process under Article 22.6 is a form of WTO/DSU approved adjudication mechanism. Nor do we agree with the European Communities' argument that those acting through arbitration pursuant to Article 22.6 do not have the mandate to examine the WTO compatibility of an implementing measure. A determination of the "equivalent level of suspensions" necessitates a prior WTO determination of the level of nullification, if any, and those acting pursuant to Article 22.6 of the DSU have the authority to make such a determination. With the DSU, as it stands now, we consider that a determination whether the implementing measure nullifies or impairs WTO benefits can only be performed by a WTO adjudicating body.[166]

6.125 We are also well aware that WTO Members disagree on the relationship between one of the possible dispute settlement procedures that may be used, i.e. the recourse to the original panel which should issue its report within 90 days, and the timing of the right to request DSB authorization to suspend obligations and concessions. We note the efforts made by Members to solve this issue in the context of the DSU review[167]. We consider that it may be possible to assess the WTO compatibility of an implementing measure before the end of the reasonable period of time. For the WTO compatibility of a measure to be assessed, such measure must have a certain degree of firmness. We consider that as soon as a measure offers a sufficient level of certainty so that adjudication of that measure's feature is legally possible, its WTO compatibility can be assessed.[168]

6.126 We reject, therefore, the EC claim that because the United States had not exhausted the Article 21.5 procedure when it requested DSB permission to suspend concessions or other obligations in respect of EC listed imports, it violated

pean Communities has not unduly delayed the procedures, the United Sates would have been entitled at the expiry of the 60 days (on 3 March) to obtain a DSB authorization to retaliate.

[166] Of course Members may agree to limit or further regulate which procedure should be used to obtain such determination.

[167] US Ex. 3.

[168] As to the US argument that it had to file its Article 22.2-22.6 request within 30 days following the expiry of the reasonable period so as not to lose the benefit of reversed consensus decision making, we note also that Article 2.4 of the DSU is categorical: DSB decision-making shall be done by consensus. We note, however, that even if the United States were correct and that a request under Article 22.2 has to be filed within 30 days, we do not understand how this would justify a unilateral suspension of concessions or other obligations without DSB authorization. We agree with the United States that there is room for more coherence between the various procedural stages envisaged in the DSU. In any case it is not our mandate to provide answers to all issues still open for negotiation in the context of the DSU review exercise.

Article 21.5 of the DSU. On the contrary we consider that the WTO compatibility determination mandated by the first sentence of Article 21.5 can be performed by the original panel or other individuals through the Article 22.6-7 arbitration process. We find that an Article 22.6 Arbitration panel is a valid WTO adjudicating body to perform the task mandated by Articles 23.2(a) and 21.5 of the DSU. Consequently, we also reject the European Communities' claim that such a violation of Article 21.5 is of a continuing nature, as we believe that the then ongoing arbitration 'process' and the 9 April Decision was fully WTO/DSU compatible. The reason why the United States violated the first sentence of Article 21.5 (and Article 23.2(a)) is because when it put in place the 3 March Measure there was no WTO adjudicating body that had determined that the EC implementing measure violated the WTO Agreement. We recall again that the US action of 19 April is not part of our terms of reference.

6.127 Notwithstanding the lacunae of the DSU drafting and the solutions suggested in the DSU Review process, we consider that there is no exception to the fundamental prohibition against unilateral determination of WTO inconsistency of any measure, including a measure adopted to comply with Panel and Appellate Body recommendations. All such determinations must be made using the DSU as only WTO adjudicating bodies can determine that a measure (or an implementing measure) violates the WTO Agreement, and in such cases, remedial actions taken by a Member in response to such violation can only take place within the institutional framework of the WTO and pursuant to the various requirements of the DSU.

6.128 We consider that nothing in the DSB authorization of 19 April[169] or in the 19 April US action against the EC listed imports has cured the WTO inconsistencies of the 3 March Measure. We recall, however, that it is not in our mandate to assess the WTO compatibility of the legally distinct US action of 19 April imposing DSB authorised suspension of concessions or other obligations against the EC listed imports. Again, for us the 19 April action is not a confirmation of the 3 March action, but a distinct legal measure.

6.129 We conclude, therefore, that Article 21.5, first sentence is another DSU obligation (similar to Article 23.2(a)) which, although not explicitly listed in Article 23.2, is covered by Article 23.1, when the measure at issue was seeking to redress a WTO obligation.

6.130 Having reached the prior conclusion that the 3 March Measure constituted a measure seeking to redress a WTO violation within the meaning of Article 23.1, we find that when the United States put in place the 3 March Measure, no WTO adjudicating body had determined that the EC implementing measure was WTO incompatible. The United States, therefore, when it put in place the 3 March Measure violated Article 21.5 of the DSU and in so doing, it refused to abide by the rules of the DSU, in violation of Article 23.1 of the DSU.

---

[169] WT/DSB/M/59.

E. *EC Claims that the 3 March Measure Violated Articles I, II, VIII and XI of GATT*

6.131 We have already found above that the 3 March Measure constituted a suspension of concessions or other obligations in that (i) the increased bonding requirements of the 3 March Measure violated Articles I, II:1(a) and II:1(b), first sentence of GATT (One Panelist was of the view that such increased bonding requirements led, rather, to violations of Article XI of GATT) and (ii) the additional interest charges, costs and fees resulting from the increased bonding requirements violated the second sentence of Article II:1(b) of GATT. We also found that the 3 March Measure violated Article I of GATT. Finally we rejected the EC claim that the 3 March Measure violated Article VIII of GATT.

F. *US Defense Based on the European Communities' Delaying Tactics*

6.132 The United States argues that the European Communities frustrated and delayed all the US efforts to comply with the DSU. The United States seems to be claiming that the European Communities violated rules of the DSU and of the DSB meetings, and this would, somehow, excuse the US (unilateral) action.

6.133 Even if it were true that the European Communities delayed DSB meetings and the arbitration process (and arguably violated the DSU and rules of the DSB meetings), it is clear that a Member cannot find in another Member's violation a justification to set aside the prescriptions of the DSU. The US argument (which implies that it considers itself justified to do what it did because what the European Communities would have done was WTO illegal) is exactly what is prohibited by Article 23 of the DSU: unilateral determination that a WTO violation has occurred and the unilateral imposition of suspensions of concessions or other obligations. In short the regime of counter-measures, reprisals or retaliatory measures has been strictly regulated under the WTO Agreement. It is now only in the institutional framework of the WTO/DSB that the United States could obtain a WTO compatible determination that the European Communities violated the WTO Agreement, and it is only in the institutional framework of the WTO/DSB that the United States could obtain the authorization to exercise remedial action.[170]

6.134 The United States also argues that the European Communities unduly delayed the Article 22.6 arbitration panel with the consequence that it was not able to issue its final decision on 3 March. The United States seems to be suggesting that the European Communities should accept the consequence of this delay, and

[170] Therefore, in the WTO context, the provision of Article 60 of the Vienna Convention on the Laws of Treaties (1969) on this matter does not apply since the adoption of the more specific provisions of Article 23 of the DSU.

bear the consequences of the US unilateral actions which would not have taken place if the arbitration panel had proceeded expeditiously.

6.135 We will offer only two brief comments on this defense. First, ***no*** WTO violation can justify a unilateral retaliatory measure by another Member; this is the object of the prohibitions contained in Article 23.1 of the DSU. If Members disagree as to whether a WTO violation has occurred, the only remedy available is to initiate a DSU/WTO dispute process and obtain a WTO determination that such a WTO violation has occurred. Secondly, as noted by the Panel in *US – Section 301*, most of the time-limits in the DSU are either minimum time-limits without ceilings or maximum time-limits that are, nonetheless, indicative only. In *EC - Bananas III*, the arbitration panel explicitly stated that the 60-day period specified in Article 22.6 "does not limit or define the jurisdiction of the Arbitrators' *ratione temporis*. It imposes a procedural obligation on the Arbitrators in respect of the conduct of their work, not a substantive obligation in respect of the validity thereof."[171] Delays in dispute settlement procedures can always happen. The fundamental obligation of Article 23 of the DSU would be a farce if every time there is a delay in a panel or arbitration process, the unsatisfied Member could simply unilaterally determine that a violation has occurred and unilaterally impose any remedy. We reject, therefore, this US defense.

VII. CONCLUSIONS AND RECOMMENDATIONS

7.1 Although the 3 March Measure is no longer in existence, we conclude that:

(a) The 3 March Measure was seeking to redress a WTO violation and was thus covered by Article 23.1 of the DSU; when it put in place the 3 March Measure the United States did not abide by the rules of the DSU, in violation of Article 23.1.

(b) By putting into place the 3 March Measure, the United States made a unilateral determination that the EC implementing measure violated the WTO, contrary to Articles 23.2(a) and 21.5, first sentence. In doing so the United States did not abide by the DSU and thus violated Article 23.1 together with Article 23.2(a) and 21.5 of the DSU;

(c) The increased bonding requirements of the 3 March Measure as such led to violations of Articles II:1(a) and II:1(b), first sentence; the increased interest charges, costs and fees resulting from the 3 March Measure violated Article II:1(b) last sentence. The 3 March Measure also violated Article I of GATT;

[171] Decision by the Arbitrators, *EC – Bananas III (US) (Article* 22.6 - *EC) supra*, footnote 30, footnote 7.

(d) In view of our conclusions in paragraph (c) above, the 3 March Measure constituted a suspension of concessions or other obligations within the meaning of Articles 3.7, 22.6 and 23.2(c) imposed without any DSB authorization and during the ongoing Article 22.6 arbitration process. In doing so the United States did not abide by the DSU and thus violated Article 23.1 together with Articles 3.7, 22.6 and 23.2(c) of the DSU.

With reference to paragraph (c) above, one Panelist is of the view that such increased bonding requirements of the 3 March Measure rather violated Article XI of GATT.

7.2 Under Article 3.8 of the DSU, in cases where there is infringement of the obligations assumed under a covered agreement, the action is considered *prima facie* to constitute a case of nullification or impairment of benefits under that agreement. Accordingly, we conclude that, to the extent that the United States has acted inconsistently with the provisions of covered agreements, as described in the preceding paragraphs, it has nullified or impaired the benefits accruing to the complainant under those agreements.

7.3 The Panel recommends that the Dispute Settlement Body request the United States to bring its measure into conformity with its obligations under the WTO Agreement.

UNITED STATES – IMPORT MEASURES ON CERTAIN PRODUCTS FROM THE EUROPEAN COMMUNITIES

Report of the Panel

Addendum

WT/DS165/R/Add.1

The present Addendum contains the Appendices of the Report of the Panel which is contained in document WT/DS165/R.

Appendix 1.1	The First Submission of the European Communities (10 November 1999)
Appendix 1.2	The EC oral presentation at the First Substantive Meeting (16 December 1999)
Appendix 1.3	The EC final statement at the First Substantive Meeting (17 December 1999)
Appendix 1.4	The EC Responses to Questions of Panel and Parties (13 January 2000)
Appendix 1.5	Rebuttal Submission of the European Communities (21 January 2000)
Appendix 1.6	The EC letter dated 25 January 2000 concerning the scope of the Panel's terms of reference (25 January 2000)
Appendix 1.7	The EC Responses to Additional Questions of Panel (8 February 2000)
Appendix 1.8	The EC oral presentation at the Second Substantive Meeting (9 February 2000)
Appendix 1.9	The EC final statement at the Second Substantive Meeting (9 February 2000)
Appendix 1.10	The EC Responses to Additional Questions of Panel (10 February 2000)
Appendix 2.1	The First Submission of the United States (6 December 1999)
Appendix 2.2	The US oral presentation at the First Substantive Meeting (16 December 1999)
Appendix 2.3	The US closing remarks at the First Substantive Meeting (17 December 1999)
Appendix 2.4	The US Responses to Questions of Panel and Parties (13 January 2000)

Appendix 2.5	Rebuttal Submission of the United States (including its cover letter) (21 January 2000)
Appendix 2.6	The US Responses to Additional Questions of Panel (8 February 2000)
Appendix 2.7	The US oral presentation on matters relating to the scope of this dispute at the Second Substantive Meeting (9 February 2000)
Appendix 2.8	The US oral presentation at the Second Substantive Meeting (9 February 2000)
Appendix 2.9	The US closing statement at the Second Substantive Meeting (9 February 2000)
Appendix 2.10	The US Responses to Additional Questions of Panel (10 February 2000)
Appendix 3	Oral presentation of Dominica and St. Lucia at Third Party session (17 December 1999)
Appendix 4	Oral presentation of Ecuador at Third Party session (17 December 1999)
Appendix 5	Third Party Submission of India (10 December 1999)
Appendix 6	Third Party Submission of Jamaica (8 December 1999)
Appendix 7	Oral presentation of Japan at Third Party session (17 December 1999)

Appendix 1.1
First Submission of the European Communities
(10 November 1999)

I. THE SCOPE OF THIS PROCEDURE AND THE OBJECTIVE PURSUED BY THE EC

1. The European Communities have requested the DSB to establish the present Panel against the United States with a view to arrive at a ruling recommending the US to withdraw the illegal trade measure taken on 3 March 1999 and confirmed on 19 April 1999 (hereinafter: the "Measure"), limiting the importation of selected products originating in the European Communities. The EC considers that the facts of the case are straightforward and do not need, therefore, lengthy debates. The EC accordingly requests the Panel to proceed expeditiously within the shortest possible time-frame with the examination of the matter under its terms of reference. In this respect, the EC would like to draw the Panel's attention to the fact that the illegal US measures continue to deploy their detrimental effects on the EC economic operators.

II. THE FACTS AT ISSUE

2. On 7 January 1998, the Arbitrator Dr. El-Naggar ruled that

> "...pursuant to Article 21.3 (c) [of the DSU], the 'reasonable period of time' for the European Communities to implement the recommendations and rulings of the DSB adopted on 25 September 1997 in European Communities - Regime for Importation, Sale and Distribution of Bananas, shall be the period from 25 September 1997 to 1 January 1999"[1].

3. The Council of the European Union adopted Regulation (EC) No. 1637/98 of July 20, 1998 amending Regulation (EEC) 404/93 on the common organisation of the market in bananas (OJ L 210 of July 27, 1998). Regulation 1637/98 entered into force on July 31, 1998 and was applicable as from January 1, 1999. Making use of the delegated powers attributed to it by the Council, the European Commission adopted Commission Regulation (EC) No. 2362/98 of October 28, 1998 laying down detailed rules for the implementation of Council Regulation (EEC) No. 404/93 regarding the imports of bananas into the Commu-

---

[1] Award of the Arbitrator, *European Communities – Regime for the Importation, Sale and Distribution of Bananas - Arbitration under Article 21.3(c) of the DSU ("EC - Bananas III")*, WT/DS27/15, 7 January 1998, DSR 1998:I, 3, para. 20.

nity (OJ L 293 of October 31, 1998). It entered into force on 1 November 1998 and was applicable in its entirety as from 1 January 1999.

4. The modifications introduced by these Regulations created a completely new set of rules addressing specifically those elements of the previous banana regime which were found to be incompatible with WTO rules both with respect to GATT and to GATS.

5. Well before the conclusion of the reasonable period of time granted by the Arbitrator to the EC, and at a time when the EC had not yet adopted the entirety of the envisaged measures in order to comply with the recommendations and rulings of the DSB adopted on 27 September 1997, the United States published three notices in the US Federal Register respectively on 22 October, 10 November and 29 December 1998[2] (EC Annex I, II and III) of proposed determination of action by imposing prohibitive (100 per cent *ad valorem*) duties on selected products from the European Communities. This proposed action was based on the unilateral determination by the United States that «the measures the EC has undertaken to apply as of January 1, 1999 fail to implement the WTO recommendations concerning the EC banana regime». The actions proposed are intended to be in place «beginning as early as February 1, 1999».

6. The publication of the above-mentioned notices was the enactment of a political commitment taken by the US president vis-à-vis the US congress (EC Annex IV), which explicitly refers to a bill which was discussed at that time in the US congress. The commitment made in the letter was thus clearly aimed at preventing the US legislator to adopt legislation imposing immediate economic sanctions against the EC (EC Annex V and VI).

7. On 14 January 1999, without having requested a dispute settlement procedure as it was required to do under Article 21.5 of the DSU, the US nevertheless requested authorisation from the DSB under Article 22 of the DSU to suspend the application to the EC of tariff concessions and related obligations under the GATT.

8. After thorough debates in the DSB and in the General Council that underlined the extraordinary nature of the US request and the danger that such action was creating for the WTO dispute settlement system[3], in order to limit as much as possible the damage for its economic operators, on 29 January 1999 the EC objected to the level of suspension proposed by the United States and the matter was referred to arbitration pursuant to article 22.6 of the DSU.

9. On 2 March 1999, the Arbitrator issued an "initial" decision[4]. The cover letter sent to the parties to the procedure stated the following

[2] Vol. 63, page 56687, page 63099 and page 71665.

[3] See WTO doc. WT/DSB/M/54, in particular page 30 *et sequitur*.

[4] WT/DS27/48.

"I write to inform you that the Arbitrators have today issued an initial decision to the parties in which we rule on matters related to the scope of our work and to certain aspects of the methodology and calculations of the United States for determining the level of suspension of concessions. In addition, we have requested the parties to supply us with additional information. This information should enable us to take a final view on the level of nullification or impairment based on the WTO inconsistency, if any, of the revised EC banana regime, and, if relevant, to determine the level of suspension of concessions or other obligations equivalent to the level of such nullification or impairment. Following our receipt and analysis of that information, we expect to be in a position to issue a final decision in this matter soon thereafter."

10. Notwithstanding this very clear statement by the Arbitrator, on the basis of its *unilateral* determination that the European Communities had failed to implement the DSB's recommendations on this regime, the USTR announced on the following day (3 March 1999) that the U.S. Customs Service would begin as of that date withholding liquidation and reviewing the sufficiency of bonds on imports of selected European products covering trade in an amount of $520 million (EC Annex VII).

Normally, a customs debt is incurred upon importation of goods liable to import duties and is established on the basis of the duty applicable to the product that is currently imported. The level of the duty is the one determined in the US tariff nomenclature and its level should not exceed the level set out in the US WTO Schedule of commitments.

In practice, the US measure suspended the liquidation of a customs debt on importation according to the normal rules, rendering thus impossible the payment of duties as they appeared in the US customs nomenclature. In addition to this action, the US measure imposed the deposit of a bond (or security), which could not be released until such time as the customs debt in respect of which it was given was extinguished or could no longer arise. The level of the security was calculated not on a level derived from but not exceeding the US bound duties (i.e. the ordinary customs debt), but to a level far higher, in fact at 100% *ad valorem* (i.e. the arbitrary level of retaliation unilaterally set by the US) (EC Annex VIII).

In addition, the decision to withhold customs liquidation on 3 March 1999 imposed upon importers of selected European products a contingent duty liability of 100 percent *ad valorem*, discriminated against European products and importers since importers of like products of other origins were only exposed to a duty liability corresponding to the bound customs tariff.

11. On 9 April 1999, the Arbitrator issued a decision determining the level of nullification or impairment of the US at US $191.4 million[5]. On the same day (9 April 1999), the United States requested the DSB authorisation to suspend concessions or other obligations to the EC for that amount. The authorisation was granted on 19 April 1999[6].

12. Effective as from 19 April 1999, the USTR confirmed (EC Annex IX and X) that a 100% *ad valorem* rate of duty is applied retroactively to the EC products listed in the notice that had entered, or withdrawn from warehouse, for consumption *on or after 3 March 1999.*

III. THE VIOLATION OF US WTO OBLIGATIONS

A. *The Violation of Article 22 of the DSU*

13. According to Article 22.6, last sentence, of the DSU

> "Concessions or other obligations shall not be suspended during the course of the arbitration".

14. By implementing its 3 March measure, the US has breached this rule. In fact, while the arbitration procedure was still on-going, the US imposed a requirement exclusively on products imported from the EC of a contingent duty liability of 100 percent, while importers of like products of other origins were subject to a duty liability corresponding to the bound customs tariff. The bonds on imports from the EC corresponded (or were committed as to correspond) to that higher contingent duty liability covering trade in an amount of $520 million.

15. The real purpose and effect of the measure was to deter imports altogether, as importers would logically be very reluctant to accept a risk of having to pay 100% *ad valorem* duties retroactively. As the Deputy USTR P. Scher indicated at a press conference held on 3 March 1999 (EC Annex XI),

> "we retaliated by effectively stopping trade as of March 3 in response to the harm caused by the EC's WTO-inconsistent banana regime".

Moreover, as is demonstrated by the Arbitrator's final decision, the amount of US$ 520 millions of the value of EC imports subject to suspension of concessions or other obligations, unilaterally determined by the US authorities, has no basis under WTO law.

---

[5] Decision by the Arbitrators, *European Communities – Regime for the Importation, Sale and Distribution of Bananas - Recourse to Arbitration by the European Communities under Article 22.6 of the DSU ("EC - Bananas III (US) (Article 22.6 – EC)")*, WT/DS27/ARB, 9 April 1999, DSR 1999:II, 725,

[6] WT/DSB/M/59, at page 11.

B. *The Violation of Articles I, II, XI and VIII of the GATT 1994*

16. In addition, it is evident from the facts mentioned above that the Measure at issue is inconsistent with:

(a) Article I of the GATT 1994 since it discriminates *between* products originating in the EC *and* the products originating in all other countries. On 3 March 1999 only selected products originating in the EC were burdened by the US measure while other Members' like products were not;

(b) Article II of the GATT 1994 insofar as it denies as from 3 March 1999 the unconditional right to import the selected EC products at a tariff not in excess of that set forth and provided in the US Schedule. The US measure meant that every EC operator importing one of the products unilaterally targeted by the US measure was liable to pay a tariff incomparably higher than the duty bound in the US Schedule;

(c) Article XI of the GATT 1994, insofar as the consequence of the "retaliatory" measure was, in the Deputy USTR's own language, to "effectively stopping trade as of March 3";

(d) Articles II.2(a) and VIII.1 of the GATT 1994, insofar as the requirement to submit or commit bonds beyond the bound rate duty upon importation of selected EC products results in increased costs for importers that constitute "other charges" imposed in connection with importation that are prohibited. It is undeniable that the deposit of a security (or posting of a bond) necessarily imposes a financial burden since each and every operator (or its customs agent) subject to such a measure is obliged:

- either to deposit a lump sum (which entails necessarily one of the following situations: *either* the sum is ready and available for the operator, in which case it suffers a loss of interests and thus a cost; *or* must borrow the money, in which case it is liable for the payment of the interests for the loan)
- or to deposit a financial guarantee, which the financial institutions deliver only at a cost related to the guaranteed amount.
- or, finally, to commit part of a general security (or continuous bond). If the general security is not sufficient, an additional security is required or an increase of the general security must be provided.

17. The Measure in fact obliged the operators or their customs agents to follow the second or third option described in paragraph 16 (d) above (EC Annex VIII and X). Both options entailed a burden additional to what was required by the US customs authorities in application of ordinary customs duties.

C. The Violation of Article 23 and Article 3 of the DSU.

18. The USTR made clear in a public notice requesting comments on the planned 3 March 1999 action that it was required under Sections 301-310 to implement that action on that date:

> Given that the reasonable period of time for the EC's implementation of the WTO recommendations concerning the EC banana regime expires on January 1, 1999, the USTR *must make the determination* required by section 306(b) no later than January 31, 1999, and, in the event of an affirmative determination, *must implement further action* no later than 30 days thereafter.[7]

19. The USTR thus considered itself bound to take retaliatory action 60 days after the expiry of the implementation period in response to a perceived failure to implement rulings or recommendations of the DSB. The USTR added

> "these time frames permit the USTR to seek recourse to the procedures for compensation and suspension of concessions provided in Article 22 of the DSU"[8].

20. However, when it turned out that the Article 22 procedures were not completed on 3 March 1999 and that the United States could therefore not obtain the necessary DSB authorisation at the time required by its domestic legislation, the USTR nevertheless imposed trade sanctions by "effectively stopping trade". This course of events confirms that the USTR implemented the further action (*unilaterally*) decided upon only on the basis of its domestic legislation and thus *irrespective* of whether that action conformed to the requirements of Article 23; paragraphs 1 *and* 2, of the DSU.

21. Under Article 23 of the DSU, the United States has accepted an unconditional and unqualified obligation to impose suspension of concessions or other obligations only with DSB approval but has applied its domestic legislation in breach of such fundamental obligation under the WTO Agreements.

Moreover, the US measure is at odds with WTO law with regard to its timing, its amount and the total disregard of WTO procedures, thus fundamentally undermining the authority of the WTO bodies dealing with dispute settlement. It also undermines the expectation that WTO Members would ensure the conformity of their domestic administrative procedures with WTO law, in particular with the requirement of the DSU.

As the Panel on "*US-Sections 301-310*"[9] has indicated:

> "Article 23.1 (...) prescribes a general duty of a dual nature. First, it imposes on all Members to "have recourse to" the multilateral process set

---

7 Federal Register, Vol.63. No.204, Thursday, October 22, 1998, pages 56688 and 56689.

8 *Ibid.*, page 56689.

9 Panel Report, *United States – Sections 301-310 of the Trade Act of 1974* ("*US – Section 301*"),WT/DS152/R, adopted 27 January 2000, DSR 2000:II, 815, paras. 7.43-7.45.

out in the DSU when they seek the redress of a WTO inconsistency. In these circumstances, Members have to have recourse to the DSU dispute settlement system to the exclusion of any other system, in particular a system of unilateral enforcement of WTO rights and obligations. This, what one could call "exclusive dispute resolution clause", is an important new element of Members' rights and obligations under the DSU. Second, Article 23.1 also prescribes that Members, when they have recourse to the dispute settlement system in the DSU, have to "abide by" the rules and procedures set out in the DSU. This second obligation under Article 23.1 is of a confirmatory nature: when having recourse to the DSU Members must abide by all DSU rules and procedures.

Turning to the second paragraph under Article 23, Article 23.2 – which, on its face, addresses conduct in specific disputes – starts with the words "[i]n such cases". It is, thus, explicitly linked to, and has to be read together with and subject to, Article 23.1.

Indeed, two of the three prohibitions mentioned in Article 23.2 – Article 23.2(b) and (c) – are but egregious examples of conduct that contradicts the rules and procedures of the DSU which, under the obligation in Article 23.1 to "abide by the rules and procedures" of the DSU, Members are obligated to follow.[10] These rules and procedures clearly cover much more than the ones specifically mentioned in Article 23.2.[11] There is a great deal more State conduct which can violate the general obligation in Article 23.1 to have recourse to, and abide by, the rules and procedures of the DSU than the instances especially singled out in Article 23.2.[12]

22. It finally undermines the achievement of the fundamental objectives under Article 3 of the DSU. Article 3 of the DSU describes the dispute settlement system of the DSU as "a central element in providing security and predictability to the multilateral trading system". As the Appellate Body has indicated in the "*LAN*" report[13], the objective of the "security and predictability of the multilateral trading system" is also an object and purpose of the substantive WTO Agreements themselves. It is the reflection of the general principle of public international law "*pacta sunt servanda*" (Article 26 of the Vienna Convention of the

[10] [original footnote] Article 23.2(a), in contrast, prohibiting Members from making certain determinations, is not covered elsewhere in the DSU.

[11] [original footnote] One could refer, for example, to the requirement to request consultations pursuant to Article 4 of the DSU before requesting a panel under Article 6.

[12] [original footnote] Not notifying mutually agreed solutions to the DSB as required in Article 3.6 of the DSU or not abiding by the requirements for a request for consultations or a panel as elaborated in Articles 4 and 6 are some other examples of conduct that would be contrary to DSU rules and procedures but is not mentioned specifically in Article 23.2.

[13] Appellate Body Report, *European Communities – Customs Classification of Certain Computer Equipment* ("*EC - LAN*"), WT/DS62/AB/R, WT/DS67/AB/R and WT/DS68/AB/R, adopted 22 June 1998, DSR 1998:V,1851.

Law of Treaties), which requires that international agreements be performed in good faith.

D. The Violation of Article 21.5 of the DSU.

23. Article 21.5 of the DSU provides that

> "where there is a disagreement as to the existence or consistency with a covered agreement of measures taken to comply with the recommendations and rulings such dispute shall be decided through recourse to these dispute settlement procedures, including whenever possible resort to the original Panel. The Panel shall circulate its report within 90 days after the date of referral of the matter to it"

24. This provision, and in particular the terms "shall", "Panel" and "these dispute settlement procedures" must be interpreted in accordance with the principles of the Vienna Convention on the Law of Treaties, i.e. it must be interpreted

> "in good faith in accordance with the ordinary meaning to be given to the terms of the treaty in their context and in the light of its object and purpose" (Article 31.1).

25. It is the EC's view that the ordinary meaning of the term "shall" is "expressing a command or duty"[14]. In the WTO context, the term "Panel" is defined in Articles 6, 7 and 8 of the DSU. The terms "these dispute settlement procedures" interpreted in "good faith" in the context of Article 21.5 mean nothing else than a dispute settlement procedure under the DSU, which includes a Panel as defined in Articles, 6, 7 and 8 (and thus *not* just an arbitration procedure whose legal nature, scope of action, procedural and substantial guarantees with respect to the right of defense, access to the Appellate Body, access for third parties is incomparable to a panel procedure).

26. As the Appellate Body stated in the "*India - Mailbox*" case[15], paragraph 45,

> "The duty of a treaty interpreter is to examine the words of the treaty to determine the intentions of the parties. This should be done in accordance with the principles of treaty interpretation set out in Article 31 of the *Vienna Convention*. But these principles of interpretation neither require nor condone the imputation into a treaty of words that are not there or the importation into a treaty of concepts that were not intended."

---

[14] Oxford English Reference Dictionary, 1995.

[15] Appellate Body Report, *India – Patent Protection for Pharmaceutical and Agricultural Chemical Products* ("*India - Mailbox*"), WT/DS50/AB/R, adopted 16 January 1998, DSR 1998:I, 9.

27. Thus, "where there is a disagreement as to the existence or consistency with a covered agreement of measures taken to comply with the recommendations and rulings" there is an *obligation* ("shall") to have recourse to a Panel procedure under Article 21.5 of the DSU (unless the complainant decides not to proceed as it is allowed under Article 3.7, first sentence, of the DSU).

28. The US did nothing of the sort. Well before the conclusion of the 'reasonable period of time' and at a time when not all the EC measures necessary to implement recommendations and rulings of the DSB had yet been adopted by the competent EC Institutions, the US had already unilaterally determined that the EC measures violated the EC's WTO obligations. On the basis of a unilateral determination, driven exclusively by a domestic political agenda prone to intensive lobbying by industry interests, the US has *unilaterally* suspended tariff concessions to the EC for selected products as from 3 March 1999 up to a level that was both legally unjustified and economically unjustifiable.

29. As the Panel report on "*US - Sections 301 - 310*"[16] pointed out at paragraph 7.75:

> "Providing security and predictability to the multilateral trading system is another central object and purpose of the system which could be instrumental to achieving the broad objectives of the Preamble. Of all WTO disciplines, the DSU is one of the most important instruments to protect the security and predictability of the multilateral trading system and through it that of the market-place and its different operators. DSU provisions must, thus, be interpreted in the light of this object and purpose and in a manner which would most effectively enhance it".

Notwithstanding, the US measure ignored completely such *fundamental* reason for the existence, under the WTO Agreements, of a multilateral system for settling disputes and for authorising measures aimed at re-balancing the concessions between Members in case of violation of a WTO obligation.

Conclusions

The EC requests the Panel to find that the US measure under its scrutiny has breached Articles 3, 21.5, 22 and 23 of the DSU and Articles I, II, XI and VIII of the GATT 1994. The US should be urged to take all the necessary measures to comply with such findings.

---

16 Panel Report, *US – Section 301*, *supra*, footnote 9.

Appendix 1.2
The EC oral presentation at the First Substantive Meeting
(16 December 1999)

Mr. Chairman, distinguished Members of the Panel,

1. The European Communities have initiated this procedure with the aim to make the DSB re-affirm, and rule on, some principles of fundamental importance for every system whose functioning is based on law and not on sheer force: nobody can be judge and jury on the same issue, nobody can take justice in their own hands without a prior review by an independent and neutral judge, nobody can disregard the procedures set forth in that legal system, which are aimed at assuring the correct and orderly functioning of that system and, most importantly, the rights of defence.

2. In sum, we are before you to have the principles of a rules based dispute settlement system affirmed against a system of power based bullying.

3. What you, Mr. Chairman and Members of the Panel, are required to do by the terms of reference of this panel is thus to examine and make recommendations on a US measure taken on 3 March 1999 and confirmed on 19 April 1999 which limits the importation of selected products originating in the European Communities. You are not required, because this is in fact completely irrelevant for the resolution of the present dispute, to review the work of other bodies established by the DSB in the context of another dispute settlement procedure or to redraw history, as the US would wish you to do, by qualifying events in a way which simply does not match the reality.

4. In this respect, while the EC is fully prepared at any time - right now, tomorrow or in the next few weeks - to clarify any issue you may deem appropriate, the EC will refrain from analysing in detail all the incorrect presentations concerning the facts which were at the basis of earlier disputes that the US has made in 17 out of 28 pages of its first written submission. The EC believes that such an exercise would amount to a waste of everybody's time.

5. The European Communities considered in its first written submission that the facts of this case were straightforward and did not need much elaboration from our part. The US first written submission confirms the EC's understanding.

6. It may be worth while to recapitulate briefly where we stand on the assessment of the facts as a result of the first exchange of written submissions:

(a) The United States does not contest that the US Measure of 3 March 1999 has an effect on the duties to be paid. At page 16 of its submission, the US affirms that

> 1. "Entry procedures in the United States permit timely or immediate release of goods into the United States. Since liquidation of an entry usually is performed after the goods are in the stream of com-

> merce, *bonding is required in order to guarantee the payment of these additional duties or fees.*"[17] (emphasis added)

Thus, according to the US itself, as soon as the goods were cleared through the US customs on or after 3 March 1999 and a bond amounting to a 100% *ad valorem* duty was submitted or committed, the importer was bound to pay the (prohibitive) increased duty at the time of liquidation of the customs debt. The US confirms moreover that the bonding requirement was essential in order to ensure the collection of the (unauthorised) 100% *ad valorem* duties as from 3 March 1999. It is also confirmed that the bonding requirement was imposed upon a list of products amounting to a trade value of over half a *billion* US$, while, as we all know, the Arbitrator eventually set the level of nullification or impairment of US benefits, and the corresponding equivalent level of suspension of concessions, at 191.4 million US$, a third of the initial amount.

(b) The United States does not contest, and cannot contest, the declaration made by the Deputy USTR attached as Annex X to the EC's first written submission, according to which

> 2. "we retaliated by effectively stopping trade as of March 3 in response to the harm caused by the EC's WTO-inconsistent banana regime".

Thus, it is confirmed that as a result of the imposition by the US customs of the bonding requirements under (1) above, a unilateral disproportionate and unauthorised US retaliatory measure was put in place *effective* as from 3 March 1999, even though the arbitration procedure was still on-going.

(c) In its first written submission, the US attempts to confuse the issue by affirming in paragraph 31, *in fine*, that

> 3. "Th[e requirement of a single transaction bond equal to the entered value of the merchandise, corresponding to 100% *ad valorem*] did not actually assess duties, nor did it prejudge the amount of the total value of the products which would be assessed higher duties."

However, the US is unable to contest not only the affirmation of the Deputy USTR under (2) above, but also that it was *not* possible for any importer *as from 3 March 1999* to import a product included in the unilaterally established retaliation list just by paying a duty not exceeding the tariff bound in the US Schedule of tariff

[17] *Para.* 32, *in fine*.

concessions for that product (i.e. without application of the 100% *ad valorem* duty). Apart from the stopping of the trade, this is the other main consequence *in practice* of the 3 March US measure of "withholding liquidation", which literally prevents the *immediate* liquidation of any customs debt.

(d) While insisting on subjective (and, as a matter of fact, incorrect) descriptions of what happened before and during the arbitration procedure which was concluded on 19 April 1999, the US does not seriously contest, and cannot contest, two important statements of the Arbitrator in the initial decision[18] and in the final decision[19] respectively:

> 4. "(...) we have requested the parties to supply us with additional information. This information should enable us to take a final view on the level of nullification or impairment based on the WTO inconsistency, *if any*, of *the revised EC banana regime*, and, if relevant, to determine the level of suspension of concessions or other obligations equivalent to the level of such nullification or impairment."
>
> 5. "(...) [W]e could resort to the option of measuring the level of nullification or impairment on the basis of our findings in the original dispute, as modified by the Appellate Body and adopted by the DSB. To do that *would mean to ignore altogether the undisputed fact that the European Communities has taken measures to revise its banana import regime*".

Thus, it may well be that an excess of polemics got the US lawyers carried away when they affirmed in the first US submission that

> 6. "(...) the arbitrators thus concluded that what the EC now characterizes as a completely new set of rules for its bananas regime was in great part a repackaging of those very same elements which the panel and Appellate Body originally found inconsistent with the EC's WTO obligations (...)"

Polemics or not, the *fact* remains that the Arbitrator on 2 March 1999 had not yet taken any decision on the level of nullification or impairment, "if any", concerning the "revised" banana import regime that had been "undisputed[ly]" adopted by the EC before the

---

18 WT/DS27/48.

19 Decision by the Arbitrators, *EC - Bananas III (US) (Article 22.6 – EC), supra*, footnote 5, para. 4.7.

end of the reasonable period of time. This is all the more confirmed when considering the following statement of the Arbitrator[20]:

> 7. "We also note that *both parties accept* that it is the consistency or inconsistency with WTO rules of the *new* EC regime - *and not of the previous regime* - that has to be the basis for the assessment of the equivalence between the level of nullification suffered and the level of the proposed suspension."

(e) The United States does not contest, finally, that the requirement to submit or commit bonds beyond the bound rate duty upon importation of selected EC products resulted in increased costs for importers that constitute "other charges" imposed in connection with importation.

7. In the EC's view, therefore, the undisputed facts of this case are confirmed as follows:

The United States did not pursue any prior dispute settlement procedure under Article 21.5 of the DSU, as it should have done, with respect to the revised banana regime that the EC had adopted undisputedly before the end of the reasonable period of time. It undertook on 3 March 1999 to unilaterally impose retaliatory measures on selected products originating from the EC for an amount of over half a billion US$. This action was put in place notwithstanding the fact that an arbitration procedure was still under way and was not concluded before 19 April 1999 when a level of nullification or impairment was set at one third of the level unilaterally determined and imposed by the US. The practical effect of this imposition was (1) to effectively stop the trade on the selected products as from 3 March 1999 and (2) in any case, to deprive as from 3 March 1999 the importers of the their right of importing those products subject to a duty not exceeding the tariff bound under the US Schedule of tariff concessions. Moreover, it triggered additional costs for importers that constitute "other charges" imposed in connection with importation.

8. If we now turn to the legal consequences that should be drawn from the facts as they have just been summarised, the EC considers that the task of the panel has been considerably eased by the presentation made by the United States in its first written submission.

The EC is firmly of the view that the authorisation of suspension of concessions or other obligations by the DSB under Article 22.2 or 22.7 of the DSU can in no case be granted retroactively. The United States claims in its first written submission that the DSU is silent on this question[21], but this is incorrect. In fact, Article

---

20 *Ibid.*, at *para.* 4.5.

21 Cf. para. 39 of the first written submission of the United States.

22.6, last sentence, contains the following rule that limits the right of the complainant to apply the suspension of concessions or other obligations:

> "Concessions or other obligations shall not be suspended during the course of the arbitration."

This provision would become meaningless if the suspension of concessions or other obligations could be applied retrospectively after having been authorised by the DSB. As the present case illustrates, it is in fact impossible in practice to apply the suspension of concessions or other obligations retrospectively *unless* some kind of contingency measure has already been taken which clearly announces the future definitive measure and ensures its enforceability. This contingency measure by itself is however inconsistent with the clear and unqualified obligation not to resort to the suspension of concessions or other obligations during the course of the arbitration procedure, because – as is again illustrated by the present case – such contingency measure will have exactly the same trade effect as the suspension of concessions or other obligations itself. This is because no importer will be prepared to take the risk of being subject to a prohibitive duty after the event, since the importation as such cannot be undone once the product has been put on the market of the importing country.

9. Thus, there is no way in which the US measures in this case could be justified by the alleged silence of the DSU or by referring to a "liability" of the EC as from the end of the reasonable period of time. Any such "liability" presupposes that, before there can be a question about what measures may or may not be justified as a response to an alleged violation of WTO obligations, that this allegation has been confirmed by the appropriate WTO body under the appropriate procedures provided for under the multilateral dispute settlement system. Such "liability" can thus in no case be invoked by any WTO Member before the relevant procedures under the DSU have been completed.

10. We would also like to observe, in this context, that the date chosen by the United States for the retroactive application of the suspension of concessions or other obligations, i.e. 3 March 1999, finds its basis in sections 306(b)(2) and 305(a)(1) of the US Trade Act of 1974 (as amended), because under those provisions the US Trade Representative is required to take action at the latest two times 30 days after the end of the reasonable period of time[22]. This also follows

---

[22] *Section 306(b)(2):* "If the measure [...] concerns the implementation of a recommendation made pursuant to dispute settlement proceedings under the World Trade Organization, and the Trade Representative considers that the foreign country has failed to implement it, the Trade Representative shall make the determination [what further action the Trade Representative shall take under section 301(a)] no later than 30 days after the expiration of the reasonable period of time provided for in such implementation under *para.* [sic!] 21 of the Understanding on Rules and Procedures Governing the Settlement of Disputes [...]".

Section 305(a)(1): "Except as provided in *para.* (2), the Trade Representative shall implement the action the Trade Representative determines [...] to take under section 301, subject to specific direction, if any, by the President regarding such action, by no later than 30 days after the date on which such determination is made."

very clearly, in spite of the US denial in its first written submission, from the notices published in the Federal Register on the subject. One of these notices contains the following official statement by the US authorities:

> "Given that the reasonable period of time for the EC's implementation of the WTO recommendations concerning the EC banana regime expires on January 1, 1999, the USTR *must* make the determination *required* by section 306(b) no later than January 31, 1999, and, in the event of an affirmative determination, *must* implement further action no later than 30 days thereafter"[23] (emphasis added).

The EC would note in this context that it is certainly no coincidence that the time limit of 30 days after 31 January 1999 expired precisely on 2 March 1999 (given that in 1999, February had 28 days).

11. This is confirmed by another Federal Register notice which reads in relevant part as follows:

> "The dates on which the USTR intends to implement action – February 1 or no later than March 3, 1999 – correspond to the *dates contemplated by sections 306(b) and 305(a) of the Trade Act* as well as Article 22 of the DSU"[24] (emphasis added).

Thus, the statement that no action was taken by the USTR under section 301 *et seq.* on 3 March 1999 contained in the first written submission of the United States in the present procedure[25] is in open contradiction with contemporaneous official notices published in the Federal Register which is nothing less than the official gazette of the US government.

12. The legal construction submitted by the US in the present dispute according to which the action taken on 3 March 1999 was based on a so-called "potential liability" of the EC[26] resulting from its alleged failure to implement the recommendations of the DSB in the *Bananas* dispute is thus nothing else than an *ex post facto* attempt to provide a justification to a measure which was taken for reasons related exclusively to domestic political developments in the United States.[27] The EC would like to draw the attention of the Panel to the flagrant contradiction between this action and the explicit, official, repeated and unconditional commitment which the US representatives gave when they appeared before the panel on "*United States - Sections 301-310 of the Trade Act of 1974*" according to which the US Trade Representative would "base any section 301 determi-

---

23 Cf. Federal Register, Thursday October 22, 1998, page 56689/90 (EC Annex I).

24 Cf. Federal Register, Tuesday November 10, 1998, page 63099 (EC Annex II).

25 Cf. para. 49 of the first written submission of the United States.

26 Cf. para. 41 of the first written submission by the United States.

27 Cf. the Bill for a "Uruguay Round Agreements Compliance Act of 1998" (H.R. 4761 dated 9 October 1998, EC Annex V to the its first written submission) pending in the US Congress at the relevant time.

nation that there has been a violation or denial of US rights under the relevant agreement on the panel or Appellate Body findings adopted by the DSB"[28].

13. As we have already explained in detail in our first written submission, the US measures that are the subject matter of the present complaint by the European Communities were taken in flagrant violation of the obligations of all WTO Members to respect the provisions of Article 23 of the DSU which is entitled "*Strengthening of the Multilateral System*". The US claims in its first written submission that "[i]t is difficult to respond to the EC's vague arguments with respect to Article 23 inasmuch as the EC never identifies the precise obligations in question"[29].

14. If the United States has difficulties with the identification of the rules contained in Article 23 of the DSU to which the EC refers in the present case, this only confirms the fundamental disregard of those rules by the United States, since these rules were analysed in great detail in the recent panel report on "*United States – Sections 301-310 of the Trade Act of 1974*". The guiding principle of Article 23 is contained in its paragraph 1 which also governs the more detailed provisions of paragraph 2 since this paragraph starts with the words "In such cases, Members shall" by which paragraph 1 is incorporated into paragraph 2. As the panel on sections 301-310 has stated, Article 23.1 of the DSU prescribes that

> "Members have to have recourse to the DSU dispute settlement system to the exclusion of any other system, *in particular a system of unilateral enforcement of WTO rights and obligations*" [30] (emphasis added).

15. Moreover, Article 23.2(c) clearly requires that Members shall

> "follow the procedures set forth in Article 22 to determine the level of suspension of concessions or other obligations and obtain DSB authorization in accordance with those procedures *before* suspending concessions or other obligations under the covered agreements in response to the failure of the Member concerned to implement the recommendations and rulings within that reasonable period of time" (emphasis added).

The EC submits that the measures complained of in the present case are obviously in breach of this explicit provision concerning the sequence between the procedures under Article 22 of the DSU and the recourse to the suspension of concessions or other obligations.

16. Moreover, in the present case the United States has not followed the correct procedures under the DSU before resorting to a request for authorisation of

---

28 Panel Report, *US – Section 301*, *supra*, footnote 9, para. 7.115

29 Cf. para. 46 of the first written submission of the United States.

30 Panel Report, *US – Section 301*, *supra*, footnote 9, particularly para. 7.4.

the suspension of concessions or other obligations under Article 22.2 and 22.7 of the DSU.

17. While the United States claims in its first written submission that there are no rules governing the sequence between the procedures under these two provisions, the EC would like to recall the mandatory terms of the first sentence of Article 21.5 of the DSU which read as follows

> "Where there is disagreement as to the existence or consistency with a covered agreement of measures taken to comply with the recommendations and rulings such dispute *shall be decided* through recourse to these dispute settlement procedures, including wherever possible resort to the original panel" (emphasis added).

18. The letter of the US Trade Representative Charlene Barshefsky of 13 July 1999, which is contained in Exhibit 1 to the first written submission of the US in the present case, recognises the existence of a disagreement between the parties to the *Bananas* dispute about the measures taken by the EC in order to implement the recommendations and rulings of the DSB of 27 September 1997. The letter further recognises the applicability of Article 21.5 of the DSU to this situation. Thus, it is not even in dispute that the correct multilateral procedure available in this situation is recourse to the procedures under Article 21.5 of the DSU. The US arguments regarding their decision to "economise" the procedures under Article 21.5 in order to be able to have recourse immediately to Article 22.2 of the DSU are simply specious.

19. The request for the EC's "agreement to help ensure that an Article 21.5 procedure [...] will be completed before January 1, 1999"[31] is just another example of bullying tactics by the United States. As is apparent from the description of the sequence of envents given in the first written submission of the United States, the real objective of the United States was to ensure that the schedule of the dispute settlement procedure would conform to the domestic deadlines under sections 306(b) and 305(a) of the US Trade Act of 1974. In fact, this request by the United States to waive the time frames provided for under the DSU demonstrates once again that the United States could not accept a multilateral procedure that was not fully in line with the timetable established under US domestic law.

20. As the evolving practice has meanwhile clearly shown, it is perfectly possible to safeguard the complainants' rights with regard to the suspension of concessions or other obligations in cases where the complainant first requests the establishment of a panel under Article 21.5. There are as of today five cases where the correct sequence between Article 21.5 and 22 has been respected: In the *Bananas* dispute, this has happened in the complaint submitted by Ecuador[32]; in the dispute on *Australia – Measures Affecting Importation of Salmons*, the

---

[31] Cf. the second *para.* of Ms. Barshefsky's letter of 13 July 1999, Exhibit 1 to the first written submission of the United States.

[32] Cf. doc. WT/DS27/41 dated 18 December 1998.

arbitration procedure under Article 22.6 was suspended[33] until such time as the procedure under Article 21.5 will be completed[34]; in the two *Aircraft* disputes between Canada and Brazil, procedures under Article 21.5 were requested[35] before resorting to suspension of concessions; and last, but not least, the United States itself has resorted to Article 21.5 procedures in the *Automotive Leather* dispute[36] with Australia before having recourse to the suspension of concessions. Thus, the mandatory language of Article 21.5 has been respected in *all other cases except* the dispute between the EC and the US on *Bananas*.

21. As is well known to the Panel, in the aftermath of the EC/US dispute on *Bananas*, an attempt has been made to resolve the diverging positions on the sequence between Article 21.5 and Article 22 procedures by negotiations on an amendment of the DSU. However, the perspective for a negotiated solution is presently anything but certain, given the failure of the Ministerial Conference in Seattle to come to a conclusion on the DSU review. These negotiations can thus not serve as an excuse for the United States to oppose a finding by this panel on the present obligations under the DSU as it stands today and as it stood at the time of the relevant facts.

22. The EC therefore maintains its position that the measures taken by the United States that are the subject matter of the present dispute were taken in violation of the procedural obligations of the United States under Article 21.5 of the DSU.

23. Finally, the EC would like to repeat that the application of the measures under dispute also constitutes a violation of the relevant GATT provisions, namely Articles I, II, XI and VIII of GATT 1994. The EC will not elaborate further on this aspect of its complaint unless the panel has questions in this regard.

Mr. Chairman, members of the Panel,

With this I would like to conclude. Thank you for your attention.

---

33 Cf. Canada's request for authorisation of the suspension of concessions or other obligations under Article 22.2 of the DSU, doc. WT/DS18/12 dated 15 July 1999, Australia's request for arbitration under Article 22.6 of the DSU, doc. WT/DS18/13 dated 3 August 1999, and the debate on this subject in the DSB meeting of 28 July 1999, doc. WT/DSB/M/66, page 4 *et seq*.

34 Cf. Canada's request for the establishment of a panel under Article 21.5 of the DSU, doc. WT/DS18/14 dated 3 August 1999.

35 Cf. doc. WT/DS70/9 dated 23 November 1999 (recourse by Brazil to Article 21.5 of the DSU) and doc. WT/DS46/13 dated 26 November 1999 (recourse by Canada to Article 21.5 of the DSU).

36 Cf. doc. WT/DS126/8 dated 4 October 1999.

Appendix 1.3

The EC final statement at the First Substantive Meeting

(17 December 1999)

Mr. Chairman, distinguished Member of the Panel,

As we have explained at the outset of this meeting, the European Communities have initiated this procedure with the aim to make the DSB re-affirm, and rule on, some principles of fundamental importance for every system whose functioning is based on law and not on sheer force

This position is shared by a large majority of WTO Members and the intervening third Parties in this procedure.

The US position is different: it wants to be judge and jury on the question of implementation and take justice in its own hands without a prior review by an independent and neutral Panel.

In order to defend the indefensible, the US tries to hold the EC responsible for its own disregard of the multilateral procedures by alleging inexistent attempts by the EC to prevent, or delay, a 21.5 procedure in the Bananas dispute.

Mr. Chairman, it is still our firm conviction that what was decided by other Bodies of the WTO during the Bananas dispute is not directly relevant for the present case. This case is not limited to a specific trade dispute, it concerns fundamental systemic issues created by the US interpretation of fundamental rules concerning the multilateral functioning of the dispute settlement system, which could arise in other cases. Thus we simply do not wish to follow the US in sterile polemics whose only purpose is to try to re-write history and distract the attention of the Panel.

However, the EC takes note that the Panel has requested some clarification on the EC's position during the Bananas dispute, in particular with regards to the reasonable period of time and the 21.5 procedure. We will obviously answer these questions in detail but we can announce as of today that the US allegations in this context are entirely incorrect.

The United States has raised during this meeting for the first time a question concerning the terms of reference of this Panel. It claims that these terms of reference are limited to what they call the 3 March "action".

As is apparent from EC's request for the establishment of this Panel in document WT/DS165/8 and the 2 annexes thereto, the EC considers that the matter before the Panel pursuant to Article 7 of the DSU is the US measure *effective on* 3 March 1999 on a list of products, contained in Annex 1, and confirmed for "a subset of the products" in a "reduced list" adopted on 19 April 1999, contained in Annex 2.

Appendix 1.4

The EC Responses to Questions of Panel and Parties

(13 January 2000)

Questions from the Panel to Both Parties

1. Is the withholding of the suspension of liquidation (including the bond requirement) a suspension of concessions or other obligations under the DSU?

Reply

The EC reads this question as referring to the withholding *or* suspension of liquidation in the alternative.

In general, to the extent that it prevents the importation of a product against payment of a customs duty not in excess of the bound tariff rate, such a measure is in breach of the tariff binding and therefore of the GATT 1994.

In this particular case, the US measure under dispute was taken without any WTO justification or DSB authorisation and thus without respecting the relevant multilateral procedures. It corresponds therefore to an unauthorised suspension (breach of Articles 3, 21, 22 and 23 of the DSU) of concessions (breach of Article II GATT 1994) *and* other obligations (breach of Articles I, XI and VIII GATT 1994).

2. What is the impact on trade and traders involved in a suspension of liquidation (including the bond requirement)?

Reply

In general, the effect on the trade would depend on the contingent liability imposed on the economic operator by the bonding requirement. For technical reasons, a bonding requirement *must* identify the precise amount to be guaranteed. Moreover, in order to respect WTO law this amount *must* be justified by a cost or charge approximate to the cost of services rendered and/or a duty not exceeding the rate bound in the Member's Schedule of tariff concessions.

3. What is the legal link between the date of assessment of the nullification caused by the EC's non-implementation of the *Bananas III* recommendations and the need to be able to suspend concessions as of 3 March 1999?

Reply

Given that the *DSB* has found on *6 May 1999* that the *revised* EC banana regime was inconsistent with certain WTO obligations of the EC, the only legal link that can be established between the revised EC banana regime and the US measure *effective on 3 March 1999* is the US domestic legislation under Sections 301-310 of the US Trade Act of 1974, as amended[37].

4. Is a new measure (an implementing measure) presumed to be compatible or incompatible with WTO obligations after the reasonable period of time? Which party bears the burden of proof after the reasonable period of time to prove consistency (or lack thereof) with WTO provisions? Is it correct to state that the losing party becomes liable as of the expiry of the reasonable period of time? And liable for what?

Reply

The EC fails to see how the legal status under the WTO of a new measure could be influenced or determined by the status of a measure which was previously in place and that has been withdrawn in accordance with Article 3.7 of the DSU and the recommendations and rulings of the DSB.

For that reason, no presumption of inconsistency is expressly provided for in the DSU. On the contrary, as was confirmed recently by the Appellate Body report on *"Chile – Taxes on Alcoholic Beverages"*[38] at paragraph 74: "Members of the WTO should not be assumed, in any way, to have *continued* previous protection or discrimination through the adoption of a new measure. This would come close to a presumption of bad faith" (emphasis in the original).

Consequently, the burden of proof follows the normal rules as indicated by the Appellate Body in its report on *"United States – Measures Affecting Imports of*

[37] See evidence provided by the EC in its first written submission (Annexes I and II) and the references provided in *paras.* 10 and 11 of the EC's oral statement at the first substantive meeting with the panel on 16 December 1999.

[38] Appellate Body Report, *Chile – Taxes on Alcoholic Beverages* ("*Chile – Alcoholic Beverages*"), WT/DS87/AB/R, WT/DS110/AB/R, adopted 12 January 2000, DSR 2000:I, 281,

Woven Wool Shirts and Blouses from India"[39] and remains with the Member alleging the inconsistency of a measure of another Member.

The very notions of "losing" party and "liability at the end of the reasonable period of time" suggested by the US is entirely inaccurate in this context. On the one hand, if a *new* measure is adopted by the end of the reasonable period of time, the obligation on the respondent in the previous dispute settlement procedure to withdraw its *original* inconsistent measure has been fulfilled. Thus, even referring to the "losing" party in such a case is inappropriate. On the other hand, the notion of "liability" is simply out of context in a procedure covered by the DSU, where the notions of *WTO-consistency* of a given measure and of the *equivalent level of reciprocal concessions* provide the appropriate reference.

5. Who has the responsibility to raise an Article 21.5 case? When should such a request under Article 21.5 take place?

Reply

Article 21.5 does not specifically address the issue of whose responsibility it is to raise a procedure under that provision but declares "these dispute settlement procedures" applicable. Except in the case of the recourse of the EC to Article 21.5 in the Bananas dispute (that will be discussed in response to question 7), all other cases mentioned in the EC's oral statement on 16 December 1999 at paragraph 20 were submitted by the Member alleging the inconsistency.

In case of disagreement as to the consistency with a covered agreement of measures taken to comply with recommendations and rulings of the DSB, an Article 21.5 procedure cannot be requested before the time of the adoption of the implementing measure. Of course, in case of a disagreement on the existence of measures taken to comply with recommendations and rulings of the DSB it is not possible to start a 21.5 procedure before the end of the reasonable period of time.

The DSU does not provide for any statute of limitation or other outer time limit with regard to requests for a procedure under Article 21.5.

[39] Appellate Body Report, *United States – Measure Affecting Imports of Woven Wool Shirts and Blouses from India* ("*US – Shirts and Blouses*"), WT/DS33/AB/R and Corr. 1, adopted 23 May 1997, DSR 1997:I, 323, at 335.

6. What is the consequence of failing to raise an Article 21.5 claim before the end of the reasonable period? If it is not done during this period does the right to an Article 21.5 assessment lapse?

Reply

None.

No. See the EC's response to the previous question.

7. Assuming the US is correct in stating that an Article 21.5 panel should be triggered (by either party) within the reasonable period of time, what is the consequence if this 21.5 panel is never requested or not established? Does the absence of an Article 21.5 assessment result in a presumption that the new measure is compatible or that it is incompatible with WTO obligations? Does the absence of an Article 21.5 panel exclude recourse to Articles 22.6-7?

Reply

The EC considers the US assumption to be entirely incorrect and thus does not wish to elaborate further on what it considers an incorrect interpretation of the DSU.

Consistently with the reply to question 4 the EC submits that in the absence of a decision by the DSB declaring the inconsistency of an implementing measure with a covered agreement, the measure at issue must indeed be presumed compatible. As the EC explained during the procedures before the panel on *European Communities - Regime for the Importation, Sale and Distribution of Bananas - Recourse to Article 21.5 by the European Communities*, "a presumption of *inconsistency* would gravely affect the security and predictability of the international trading system because of the ensuing uncertainty".[40]

The absence of an Article 21.5 ruling or recommendation by the DSB excludes recourse to Article 22.6 and 22.7 of the DSU in all cases *except* where there is no disagreement as to the existence or the consistency of measures taken to comply with recommendations and rulings of the DSB. This latter situation occurred in the *Hormones* dispute between the US, Canada and the EC.

[40] Panel Report, *European Communities – Regime for the Importation, Sale and Distribution of Bananas - Recourse to Article 21.5 of the DSU by the European Communities* ("*EC – Bananas III (Article 21.5 – EC)*"), WT/DS27/RW/EEC and Corr.1, 12 April 1999, DSR 1999:II, 783, para. 2.18 (emphasis in the original).

8. Who determines whether a new measure nullifies WTO benefits?

Reply

In case of disagreement as to the consistency with a covered agreement of measures taken to comply with recommendations and rulings of the DSB, the DSB determines as a result of a procedure under Article 21.5 of the DSU *whether* there is nullification or impairment of the complainant's benefits under the WTO agreement resulting from the new measure.

In the absence of such disagreement, as is illustrated by the *Hormones* case, it is possible to have recourse to Arbitration that will determine the *level* of the nullification or impairment.

9. Is there an implicit assessment of compatibility of any measure that is the object of an Article 22.6-7 Arbitration in view of the Arbitrator mandate to assess whether the level of suspension is equivalent to the level of nullification of benefits?

Reply

The terms of reference of the arbitrator are laid down in Article 22.6 and 22.7 of the DSU. These terms of reference do not extend to findings with regard to the consistency or otherwise of an implementing measure with a covered agreement. In case of disagreement on the consistency of an implementing measure, Article 21.5 of the DSU requires that "such dispute shall be decided through recourse to these dispute settlement procedures, including wherever possible resort to the original panel". An implicit assessment by the arbitrator under Article 22.6 of the compatibility of a measure with a covered agreement would usurp the task of a panel under Article 21.5 of the DSU and thus, if an arbitrator were to make such an assessment, the arbitrator would act *ultra vires*.

10. Please discuss the practice of WTO Members in their use of Articles 21.5 and 22 procedures

Reply

The EC discussed the practice of WTO Members when having recourse to Articles 21.5 and 22 already in para. 20 of its oral statement during the first substantive meeting of the parties with the Panel on 16 December 1999.

Questions from the Panel to the EC

11. Please comment on the US allegations that the EC blocked an Article 21.5 action before the end of the reasonable period of time.

12. If the EC was of the opinion that an Article 21.5 procedure must precede an Article 22 authorization, why did the EC repeatedly refuse to participate in the US Article 21.5 requested before the reasonable period of time?

Common reply to questions 11 and 12

It is incorrect that the EC "blocked an Article 21.5 action before the end of the reasonable period of time" and that it "repeatedly refuse[d] to participate in the US Article 21.5 requested before the reasonable period of time" as alleged by the United States. In fact, under Article 21.5 of the DSU, "[w]here there is disagreement as to the existence or consistency with a covered agreement of measures taken to comply with the recommendations and rulings such dispute shall be decided *through recourse to these dispute settlement procedures*" (emphasis added). Thus, Article 6.1 of the DSU is applicable with regard to the procedure to be followed for the establishment of a panel under Article 21.5 of the DSU. That means that the party complained against is not in a position to "block" the establishment of a panel because the decision is taken by the DSB under the "reversed consensus" rule nor can the party complained against refuse to participate without seriously jeopardising its legal position.

The reference to "these dispute settlement procedures" is of course also relevant with regard to other elements of the procedure to be followed, including consultations under Article 4 of the DSU. The EC therefore expressed the view that such consultations must precede the establishment of a panel under Article 21.5 of the DSU.[41] It is surprising to note in this context that, on the one hand, the United States claimed that the EC's position on the need to hold consultations in the framework of an Article 21.5 procedure leads to "unnecessary, hollow procedural steps"[42], while the United States is complaining in the present dispute, on the other hand, that the EC was unwilling to enter into consultations during the reasonable period of time[43]. This latter complaint is factually simply incorrect, as demonstrated by the statements made by its representatives in the DSB meetings at the relevant time[44].

The EC believes that these statements clearly demonstrate that the EC did not "block" the establishment of a panel under Article 21.5 of the DSU, nor did the EC claim that such a panel could not be established during the reasonable period

41 Cf. the statement made by the EC representative at the DSB meeting on 22 September 1998, DSB/M/48, p. 7 *et seq*.

42 Cf. doc. WT/DS27/18 of 31 August 1998.

43 Cf. first written submission of the United States of 6 December 1999, para. 3.

44 Cf. doc. WT/DSB/M/48, p. 7 *et seq*. (DSB meeting of 22 September 1998); doc. WT/DSB/M/49, p. 4 (DSB meeting of 21 October 1998); doc. WT/DSB/M/51, p. 3 (DSB meeting of 25 November 1998) and doc. WT/DSB/M/51/Add.1, p. 2 (DSB meeting of 21 December 1998).

of time. Rather, the arguments turned around the need to hold consultations under Article 4 of the DSU before resorting to the establishment of a panel under Article 21.5 of the DSU and were also related to the question whether the dispute settlement procedures under Article 21.5 of the DSU could be initiated before the relevant implementing measures had been adopted (*quod non*).

As the events at the end of 1998 and at the beginning of 1999 have shown, the EC tried everything it could in order to convince the United States to engage in Article 21.5 procedures, going as far as taking the unprecedented step of requesting a panel under Art. 21.5 of the DSU at its own initiative[45]. Thus, the record shows that it was not the EC that "blocked" an Article 21.5 panel procedure nor that it refused to participate in such a procedure. Quite on the contrary, it was the United States that had decided to "skip" the procedure under Article 21.5 of the DSU, because the United States wanted to invoke Article 22 of the DSU as soon as the reasonable period of time had ended in order to be able to live up to the requirements of the schedule foreseen under its domestic legislation under sections 306(b) and 305(a) of the Trade Act of 1974, as amended.

Question from the US to the EC

In paragraph 16(d) of the EC's first written submission and paragraph 6(e) of its oral statement, the EC raises several arguments with respect to its claim that the March 3rd action imposed an "other charge" inconsistent with Articles II:2(a) and VIII:1 of the GATT 1994.

(a) Is it the EC's position that this "other charge" arises only in connection with the March 3rd action?

(b) Could the EC confirm that it does not consider surety systems in general, which are contemplated in Article 13 of the Customs Valuation Agreement and maintained by numerous Members (including the EC), as imposing an "other charge"?

(c) If so, how does the EC differentiate the "other charge" it claims is associate with the March 3rd surety requirements from these surety requirements in general?

Reply to the general question by the United States

The question refers to paragraph 16(d) of the EC's first written submission which reads in relevant part:

45 Cf. doc. WT/DS27/40 of 15 December 1998.

"Articles II.2(a) and VIII.1 of the GATT 1994, insofar as the requirement to submit or commit bonds beyond the bound rate duty upon importation of selected EC products results in increased costs for importers that constitute 'other charges' imposed in connection with importation that are prohibited."

As is evident from the context, the reference to Article II.2(a) should in fact read II.2(c).

It is undisputed that the increased charges and costs for importers, because they are calculated on the basis of a duty in excess of the bound rate without any multilateral authorisation or justification, are not limited in amount to the approximate costs in administration in accordance with Article VIII.1(a) and II.2(c) and thus also violate Article II.1(b) of the GATT 1994[46].

Reply to sub-question (a)

It appears that this question is based on an artificial distinction between different "actions", with which the EC does not agree. The EC has demonstrated that the increased costs and charges resulting from the US measure are in violation of Articles II and VIII of the GATT.

Reply to sub-questions (b) and (c)

The EC does not see how the issue of customs valuation is at all relevant in the context of the present case. The EC does not believe that Article 13 of the Customs Valuation Agreement is applicable to the measures under dispute in the present procedure.

Moreover, as the Panel on "*EEC – Programme of Minimum Import Prices, Licences and Surety Deposits for Certain Processed Fruits and Vegetables*" (referred to in footnote 9 to this document) clearly indicated, the increased costs and charges resulting from the imposition of a security imposed in addition to the ordinary customs duties exceed the bound rate and are therefore not covered by the requirements of Article II.1(b) GATT, but by Article II.2(c) GATT to the extent that the amount of the increased charge or cost is limited to the approximate costs of administration in accordance with Article VIII.1(a) GATT.

See therefore what is already mentioned in the reply to the general question.

[46] Cf. panel report on EEC – Programme of Minimum Import Prices, Licences and Surety Deposits for Certain Processed Fruits and Vegetables, BISD 25S/68, *para.* 4.6.

Appendix 1.5

Rebuttal Submission of the European Communities

(21 January 2000)

I. INTRODUCTION

1. The European Communities believe that this second submission serves mainly two functions:

- to recall the main claims and arguments of the EC in this case and
- to rebut certain statements and affirmations by the US which were expressed during the first substantive meeting with the Panel and the US replies to the questions from the Panel and the EC.

Of course, the other points of law and procedure which were advanced by the EC during the first stages of this dispute settlement procedure (including the answers to the questions from the Panel and from the United States) should also be considered entirely confirmed here. This is true in particular for the EC's claims and arguments concerning the violation of Article I and XI of the GATT 1994 and Articles 3 and 23 of the DSU by the US measure.

2. As a brief preliminary point, the EC also submits that the statistical data provided by the US in its Exhibit 5 do not refute Deputy USTR P. Scher's affirmation[47] that "we retaliated by effectively stopping trade as of March 3 in response to the harm caused by the EC's WTO-inconsistent banana regime".

On the one hand, statistical data concerning March 1999 and April 1999 cover periods that precede and follow the entry into force of the 3 March measure and of its 19 April confirmation on a reduced list.

On the other hand, these statistics show for many products a dramatic decrease in imports as from March 1999. This provides confirmation of the point made by the EC that discriminatory suspensions of concessions and other obligations were in force as from 3 March 1999.

Finally, the intention of the US authorities on 3 March 1999 was explicit and is irrefutably demonstrated by their public statements, and the measure made effective as of 3 March 1999 violates in itself the US obligations under the WTO regardless of whether the facts of the trade eventually correspond to the US authorities' initial expectations.

---

[47] The US tries to mislead the Panel when it pretends in its reply to question 21 of the Panel that such assertion comes from the EC.

II. THE SCOPE OF THE PRESENT DISPUTE

3. The US has raised in its answers to the questions from the Panel and from the EC three objections concerning the scope of the present panel procedure. They will be examined in the following sub-chapters.

B. The US Measure Effective on 3 March 1999 and its Confirmation on 19 April 1999.

4. As the EC pointed out in its request for the establishment of this Panel, the measure under dispute "impose[s] a contingent liability for 100% duties" and "has deprived EC imports into the US of the products in question of the right to a duty not in excess of the rate bound in the US Schedule". This request also contains, in the Annex, the product lists published by the United States on 3 March *and* on 19 April 1999, which shows that the EC considers these as being part of one and the same measure. The United States never raised any objection against this request, neither during the DSB meeting where the request was adopted nor at any other time.

5. The issue of the potential duty liability is intimately linked to the question of the scope of the present dispute.

6. Contrary to the position expressed by the United States before the Panel, the EC is of the view that the measure at issue in the present dispute is *not limited* to an increase in surety deposit requirements, but also includes *by necessity* an increase of *duty liability* for imports of the products listed in the instructions addressed to US customs services on 3 March 1999 under the revealing title of "European Sanctions"[48].

In the view of the EC, the increased duty liability was operated on that date and not only on a later date, as the United States would have it now. In the view of the EC, all that happened on 19 April was that the increased duty liability was simply *confirmed* for most of the listed products, while some products were delisted at that time[49]. Thus, the "contingent" duty liability was changed into a "final" one (admittedly with some exceptions)[50].

---

[48] Cf. Annex VIII to the first written submission of the EC dated 10 November 1999.

[49] The EC believes that this understanding of the product lists published on 3 March and 19 April 1999 is corroborated by the United States in para. 35 of its first written submission dated 6 December 1999 where it states that the United States "assess[ed] 100% duties on a *subset* of the products previously indicated on March 3, 1999" and where the list published on 19 April 1999 is called a "*reduced* list". This choice of words indicates that the 19 April publication is a confirmation of the earlier 3 March publication, to the extent that the list contains the same products, and a withdrawal for the remainder of the products which are no longer mentioned in the reduced list.

[50] For obvious reasons, the EC does not complain about the de-listing, but it complains about the increase in duty liability effective as from 3 March and introduced by instructions to customs services on that date. It also complains about the additional costs of the increased surety deposit requirements, which are inconsistent with Article VIII of the GATT 1994.

7. There is no difference, neither in economic terms nor under WTO law, whether a duty beyond the bound rate is called a "potential" or "contingent" duty or a "final" or "definitive" one. What counts is the expected trade effect of the measure. That trade effect is exactly the same, whether the duty is "potential" or "final", not least because the customs procedures of the United States do not allow importers to obtain immediate confirmation of the precise amount of the duty at the time of physical entry of the product.

Moreover, there is no difference, neither in economic terms nor under US domestic law, whether a surety deposit in excess of the approximate costs of the services rendered is "contingent" or "potential" or "final" or "definitive". As the US recognises in its answers to questions 22 and 23 from the Panel, the US customs does not reimburse "any fees which private sureties may have charged US importers" (or, for that matter, EC exporters) or do not pay any interest on an "additional bond requirement or an increased bond amount".

8. The technicalities of how the United States enforced the increased duty liability on or after 3 March 1999 are of limited relevance for the present dispute. The issues concerned with the ancillary nature of the surety deposit and with the date on which a customs debt is incurred are of much greater importance in the context of the present dispute.

1. The Ancillary Nature of the Surety Deposit

9. It is clear that customs surety deposits serve to ensure the payment of the duties and fees owed by the importer. In that sense, customs surety deposits are *ancillary* to the (anticipated) amounts of customs duties and fees the payments of which they serve to guarantee. The amount of any surety deposit is determined by the anticipated duty liability and entirely depends on it.

10. Thus, a self-standing surety deposit could not be justified under WTO law. In fact, it would amount to "a duty or charge of any kind imposed on or in connection with the importation in excess of" the bound rates, which is inconsistent with Articles II and VIII of the GATT 1994[51].

11. The United States accepts this fundamental point of principle. As the US pointed out in its oral statement at the first substantive hearing of the Panel (paragraph 4):

> "the United States Customs Service allows [...] release of merchandise into the United States so long as the importer has provided [...] assurances in the form of a cash deposit or bond that it will pay the *potential duties and fees* owed" (emphasis added).

[51] Panel report on EEC – Programme of Minimum Import Prices, Licences and Surety Deposits for Certain Processed Fruits and Vegetables, adopted on 18 October 1978, BISD 25S/68, para. 4.15.

2. *The Date on Which a Customs Debt is Incurred*

12. Under WTO law, the obligation not to subject imported products to duties and other charges in excess of the bound rates under the relevant Schedule of tariff concessions relates to the time of importation[52].

That means that, in a situation where the duty liability varies over time, the relevant date on which the amount of the duty liability depends is the date of importation of the product in the customs territory of the importing WTO Member, not any other date (in EC customs terminology, this is the date on which the "customs debt is incurred").

13. Thus, assuming that the customs duty for a given product decreases on 1 January of a given year as the result, for example, of a commitment contained in the Schedule of the importing WTO Member, the duty liability for a like product imported on 30 December of the preceding year would not be affected by this decrease. The same is true where the customs duty increases over time[53].

14. There can thus not be a duty which is at the level of X at the time of entry of the product into the customs territory of a WTO Member that decreases to X-1 or that increases to X+1 for the already imported product at some later time.

The argument that the duty liability may change after the entry of the product into the customs territory to which the Schedule relates is simply not in line with existing WTO law (nor would it be in line with current United States customs law and practice, as the US has recognised before this Panel).

It is obvious that, were the customs law of a WTO Member different on this point, this would justify a complaint based on the violation by that WTO Member of Article II of the GATT 1994.

3. *The Application of the Above-Mentioned Principles to the US Measure*

15. It follows that the surety deposit increase for selected products on 3 March 1999 could not have any justification other than the increase of the duty liability that was operated also on 3 March 1999 with immediate effect, and not at any later time. Only in this way could the United States *require* increased surety deposits from importers and justify the confirmation of the increase in duty liability on 19 April to be *effective* as of 3 March. Only in this way could the US collect increased 100% duties on imports of listed products *as from 3 March 1999.*

---

[52] Cf. the wording of Article II.1 (b) and II.1 (c) of GATT 1994 which uses the terminology "on [...] importation into the territory to which the Schedule relates" (Art. II.1 (b)) or "upon importation into the territory to which the Schedule relates" (Art. II.1 (c)). This language clearly refers to the time of importation, not to any other date.

[53] The United States has confirmed, in response to a question from the EC, that this general rule is also applicable in the United States (cf. US answer to question 3, at paras. 6 and 7).

For the reasons already explained, *a duty increase operated on 19 April could not have had any effect on products imported into the customs territory of the United States at any earlier date.*

16. The EC reiterates that both the increase in duty liability, whether potential or definitive, and the corresponding increase in the requirements concerning surety deposits with US customs are inconsistent with the United States' obligations under Articles II.1 (b), II.2 (c) and VIII.1 (a) of the GATT 1994. This is corroborated, in the view of the EC, by the adopted panel report on *EEC – Programme of Minimum Import Prices, Licences and Surety Deposits for Certain Processed Fruits and Vegetables*[54].

17. These claims are explicitly part of the "matter" subject to the scrutiny of this Panel pursuant to Article 7 of the DSU as per the request for the establishment of this Panel[55].

The measure taken by the US on 3 March 1999 contained already both these elements and was merely confirmed on 19 April 1999 (apart from the partial withdrawal, which was operated on that date). There is thus no question of two different measures taken at different dates (except with regard to the partial withdrawal of the 3 March measure on 19 April, which is not under dispute).

18. The EC therefore fundamentally disagrees with the mischaracterization of the measure under dispute contained in the US submissions to date. It also opposes any attempt by the US to the effect of reducing the scope of the present dispute.

B. The Terms of Reference of this Panel Explicitly Cover the Matter that a Member is Obliged to Pursue a Panel Procedure under Article 21.5 of the DSU before Resorting to the Suspension of Concessions or Other Obligations under Article 22 of the DSU in Case of Disagreement on the Consistency with a Covered Agreement of Measures Taken to Implement a Recommendation or Ruling of the DSB

19. The US measure was adopted in the context of an on-going arbitration procedure under Article 22 of the DSU. The EC will summarise below the compelling reasons that justify its claim that the US measure breached Article 22 of the DSU.

However, the EC claims also that the US measure breached Article 21.5 of the DSU.

This claim is explicitly part of the EC's request for the establishment of this Panel contained in the WTO doc. WT/DS165/8 of 11 May 1999. The latter claim is

[54] Report of the Panel adopted on 18 October 1978, BISD 25S/68, *paras.* 4.6 and 4.15.

[55] Cf. WTO doc. WT/DS165/8.

different from the former, since it has more far-reaching implications, as the EC will show below.

20. In the context of the present dispute, the core of the EC's claims is the fact that the US took justice in its own hands and unilaterally decided that the revised EC Banana regime that entered into force on 1 January 1999 breached the EC's WTO obligations.

It must be recalled here that the revised Banana regime repealed and replaced the previous EC regime that had been declared inconsistent with the EC's obligations under the WTO in an adopted panel and Appellate Body report.

The US request for suspension of concessions or other obligations pursuant to Article 22 of the DSU was based on a unilateral determination that the revised EC Banana regime was inconsistent with the EC's WTO obligations[56]. The US measure on 3 March 1999, as confirmed on 19 April 1999, was directly dependent upon this US unilateral determination of non-compliance which was made by the US without an objective verification by a Panel, in application of the provisions of Article 21.5 of the DSU.

21. The EC will discuss further (see chapter No. 4 below) the substantive legal reasons on which its claims on this issue are founded.

However, as a preliminary matter concerning the terms of reference of this Panel, the EC would like to repeat that the issue of the relationship between an arbitration procedure under Article 22 of the DSU and the necessary prior findings of inconsistency under Article 21.5 of the DSU is central in order to correctly resolve the dispute at issue and thus cannot be avoided.

22. Not only should the US not have adopted its 3 March 1999 measure: there was also no justification to confirm it with a reduced list on 19 April 1999. As will be shown below, the WTO-inconsistency of the 3 March measure was not "healed", or in any other way "undone", by the authorisation of the DSB of 19 April 1999 and even less so by the US confirmation of its 3 March measure on that same date.

In the EC's view, the US measure is still inconsistent with the United States' obligations under Articles 21.5, 22 and 23 of the DSU (and several substantive GATT 1994 obligations) and must be withdrawn.

23. The US claims now that "[L]ike the *Section 301* panel, this Panel need not reach the issue of the relationship between Articles 21.5 and 22"[57].

24. The EC responds that, in our view, the Panel has no choice: in order to correctly perform its tasks as described in Article 11 of the DSU, the relationship

[56] Cf. the US answer to question 10 by the Panel, at *para.* 25: "Following the conclusion of the reasonable period of time, the complaining Member is entitled to request DSB-authorization for the suspension of concessions pursuant to Article 22.2 *if it believes* the implementing Member has failed to comply".

[57] US answer to question 9 from the Panel, at para. 23.

between Articles 21.5 and 22 - in the light of Article 23 of the DSU, as interpreted by the *Section 301* panel report - has to be addressed.

25. The panel report on *Section 301* circulated on 22 December 1999 states the following:

> "Whatever the outcome of other pending panel proceedings, on which we have no view, the fact that the USTR did make a determination of non-implementation before the completion of Article 21.5 procedures in Bananas III, even if it turns out eventually that this was illegal, is not, in our view, an act of bad faith."

26. As is apparent from this quotation, the panel on *Section 301* was convinced that this issue was *sub judice* at the time it took its final decision. The EC does not believe it appropriate or necessary to debate here the correctness of this appreciation of the *Section 301* panel on an issue on which it has itself acknowledged it has "no views". The important point here is that the EC, as a WTO Member, has a right under the covered agreements to have this fundamental issue of law resolved *as it stands* within the only correct WTO procedure, i.e. the dispute settlement procedures.

27. A debate *de lege ferenda* cannot and must not have any influence on the duties to be performed by a Panel under Articles 7 and 11 of the DSU in a specific DS procedure. Rather, a consistent practice by the WTO membership can have an influence on the interpretation of existing and applicable WTO provisions such as Articles 21.5 and 22 of the DSU (see, again, chapter No. 4 below).

28. The EC can understand that a panel, such as the *Section 301* panel, may decide that another on-going panel is a better forum to deal with the interpretation of certain WTO provisions, even if those provisions were part of its terms of reference. But it is not ready to accept the line of action suggested by the US according to which, notwithstanding the explicit terms of reference of a panel established by the DSB, *no* panel procedure is the correct forum where *existing* and fully applicable rules of the DSU can be interpreted and applied.

29. The EC urges therefore the Panel to reject this unjustified request by the US that, if granted, would amount to a denial of justice.

C. This Panel's Terms of Reference Include the Question as to which Member Has to Bear the Burden of Proof that a Measure Taken by a Member in order to Comply with Earlier Recommendations and Rulings of the DSB is Incompatible with the WTO Obligations of that Member

30. As was mentioned in the preceding sub-chapter, the core of the EC's claims is the fact that the US took justice in its own hands and unilaterally decided that the revised EC Banana regime that entered into force on 1 January 1999 breached the EC's WTO obligations (after having repealed and replaced the previous EC regime that a Panel report adopted by the DSB had found inconsistent with the EC's obligations under the WTO).

The US request for suspension of concessions or other obligations pursuant to Article 22 of the DSU was based on such unilateral determination[58]. The US measure on 3 March 1999, as confirmed on 19 April 1999, was directly dependent upon the US unilateral determination of non-compliance taken by the US without an objective verification by a Panel, in application of the provisions of Article 21.5 of the DSU.

31. In the EC's view, when dealing with the issue of the interpretation and correct application of Articles 21.5 and 22 of the DSU, the Panel will also have to address another issue which is equally important (and logically and legally connected), namely the question as to which Member has to bear the burden of proof that a new measure adopted by a Member in order to comply with earlier recommendations and rulings of the DSB is incompatible with WTO obligations of that Member.

32. As the EC has already indicated in its reply to the Panel's question No 4 and as will be discussed further in chapter No. 5 of this submission, the burden of proof follows the normal rules as indicated by the Appellate Body in its report on "*United States – Measures Affecting Imports of Woven Wool Shirts and Blouses from India*"[59] and remains with the Member alleging the inconsistency of a measure of another Member. The US has never brought such evidence before a Panel with respect to the revised EC banana regime.

33. The EC therefore urges the Panel to reject the unjustified attempt by the US to reduce the scope of the present procedure by suggesting that "it is not necessary or appropriate to reach in the context of this dispute a conclusion concerning the burden of proof following the reasonable period"[60].

III. THE VIOLATION OF THE PROCEDURAL REQUIREMENTS UNDER ARTICLES 22 AND 23 OF THE DSU

A. *Under no Circumstance is a WTO Member Allowed to Adopt and/or Implement Suspension of Concessions or other Obligations Against Another Member before the Completion of an On-Going Arbitration Procedure and its Authorisation by the DSB*

34. The increase in (potential) duty liability and in surety deposit requirements for the listed products as of 3 March 1999 is clearly in breach of the United States' obligation under Article 22.6, last sentence, of the DSU not to resort to the suspension of concessions or other obligations before the completion of the arbitration procedure and the obligation pursuant to Article 23.2(c) of the DSU to await the authorisation by the DSB before taking such action.

---

58 Cf. the quotation from the US answer to question 10 from the Panel reproduced in footnote 9.

59 Appellate Body Report, *US – Shirts and Blouses*, *supra*, footnote 39, at 335.

60 US answer to question 10 from the Panel, at *para.* 26.

35. On the basis of the panel report on *EEC – Programme of Minimum Import Prices, Licences and Surety Deposits for Certain Processed Fruits and Vegetables*, the increase in surety deposit requirements for duties exceeding the bound duty rates alone is already in breach of Articles II.1 (b), II.2 (c) and VIII.1 of the GATT 1994.

36. The increase in duty liability is even more clearly in breach of Article II.1 (b) of the GATT 1994.

37. Actions of this kind, when taken *on a discriminatory basis*, fall under the definition of "suspension of concessions or other obligations" as contained in Articles 22.6, last sentence, and 23.2(c) of the DSU. This is a broad concept encompassing discriminatory actions taken as a reaction to the breach of WTO obligations by another Member.

38. That the element of discrimination is an integral part of the concept of suspension of concessions and other obligations clearly appears in Article 3.7, last sentence, of the DSU which reads as follows:

> "The last resort which this Understanding provides to the Member invoking the dispute settlement procedures is the possibility of suspending the application of concessions or other obligations under the covered agreements *on a discriminatory basis vis-à-vis the other Member*, subject to authorization by the DSB of such measures" (emphasis added).

39. The US measure on 3 March 1999 corresponds perfectly to the definition of a discriminatory suspension of concessions or other obligations[61]. It was adopted against selected imports from the EC before the arbitration procedure had been completed and obviously when no DSB authorisation had been granted. The disregard by the US of its WTO obligations went as far as adopting the suspension of concessions and other obligations the day after the Arbitrator had issued the following "initial decision"[62]:

> "On 2 March 1999, the Chairman of the Arbitrators informed the Chairman of the DSB as follows (WT/DS27/48):
>
> > "I write to inform you that the Arbitrators have today issued an initial decision to the parties in which we rule on matters related to the scope of our work and to certain aspects of the methodology and calculations of the United States for determining the level of suspension of concessions. In addition, we have requested the parties to supply us with additional in-

---

[61] This is not a surprising conclusion in light of the Deputy USTR's public declaration made on 3 March 1999: "*we retaliated by effectively stopping trade as of March 3* in response to the harm caused by the EC's WTO inconsistent banana regime".

[62] Decision by the Arbitrators, *EC - Bananas III (US) (Article 22.6 – EC), supra*, footnote 5, *para.* 2.10.

> formation. This information should enable us to take a final view on the level of nullification or impairment based on the WTO inconsistency, if any, of the revised EC banana regime, and, if relevant, to determine the level of suspension of concessions or other obligations equivalent to the level of such nullification or impairment. Following our receipt and analysis of that information, we expect to be in a position to issue a final decision in this matter soon thereafter."

40. The EC reiterates that the US 3 March 1999 measure breached Articles 22.6, last sentence, and 23.2(c) of the DSU. There can be no excuse or justification under the covered agreements for such a breach. The only (self-admitted[63]) reason for pursuing such WTO-inconsistent route was that the US decided to grant priority to its domestic law over its WTO obligations, in particular the requirements of Sections 301-310.

B. In Any Case, Article 22.6 does not Warrant the WTO-Compatibility of the Adoption of a Suspension of Concessions or Other Obligations in Presence of Procedural Deficiencies

41. As was indicated in the previous sub-chapter, actions such as the US measure of suspension of concessions and other obligations, when taken *on a discriminatory basis*, fall under the definition of "suspension of concessions or other obligations" as contained in Articles 22.6, last sentence, and 23.2(c) of the DSU.

The EC submits that these actions can be adopted and implemented *only* on the ground of a breach of WTO obligations by another WTO Member positively established by the findings contained in a panel or Appellate Body report adopted by the DSB.

42. Article 22.6 begins with the following words:

> "When the situation described in paragraph 2 occurs, (...)"

Article 22.2 illustrates the "situation" as follows:

> "If the Member concerned fails to bring the measure found to be inconsistent with a covered agreement into compliance therewith or

---

[63] See the notice published in the US federal register, vol. 63, No. 204 of Thursday, 22 October 1998 (EC Annex I): "Section 306(b) [of the Trade Act of 1974, as amended] *requires* the USTR to determine what further action it shall take under section 301(a) of the Trade Act if the USTR considers that a foreign country has failed to implement a recommendation made pursuant to dispute settlement proceedings under WTO. The USTR *shall make* this determination no later than thirty days after the expiration of the reasonable period of time provided for such implementation under Article 21.3 of the DSU. Section 305(a)(1) *requires* the USTR to implement such action by no later than 30 days after the date on which that determination is made."

> otherwise comply with the recommendations and rulings within the reasonable period of time determined pursuant to paragraph 3 of Article 21 (...)".

In addition, Article 23 of the DSU clarifies that:

> "When Members seek the redress of a violation of obligations or other nullification or impairment of benefits under the covered agreements (...)
>
> [I]n such cases, Members shall
>
> (a) not make a determination to the effect that a violation has occurred, that benefits have been nullified or impaired (...) except through recourse to dispute settlement in accordance with the rules and procedures of this Understanding (...)".

Finally, Article 21.5 of the DSU provides that:

> "Where there is disagreement as to (...) the conformity with a covered agreement of measures taken to comply with the recommendations and rulings such dispute shall be decided through recourse to these dispute settlement procedures, including wherever possible resort to the original panel. The panel shall circulate its report within 90 days after the date of referral of the matter to it (...)".

43. In the present case, the revised EC banana regime that entered into force on 1 January 1999 was *never* determined *to be incompatible* with the EC's WTO obligations *in a dispute settlement procedure initiated by the US.*

44. The United States attempts to justify its measure *effective on* 3 March 1999 and confirmed on 19 April 1999 with the claim that the "liability" of a WTO Member for its non-compliance with recommendations and rulings of the DSB "accrues"[64] on the day which follows the end of the "reasonable period of time" referred to in Article 21.3 of the DSU.

45. The EC does not dispute the fact that the end of the reasonable period of time is relevant when examining whether the WTO Member to whom the recommendations and rulings are addressed has implemented them. The EC challenges however the empty notion of "liability" that, it submits, makes no sense in the WTO context. Rather, the examination of the DSU shows a radically different picture.

46. According to Article 3.7 of the DSU, an initial alternative is open:

- either a Member withdraws the measure which was found to be inconsistent with its WTO obligations or
- it does not.

[64] US answer to question No. 9, *para.* 17.

47. *In the case of non-withdrawal*, at the latest at the end of the reasonable period of time, the Member concerned will not have implemented the recommendations and rulings of the DSB at the required time. It will thus have to accept to offer compensation or face the prospect of an authorisation by the DSB for a suspension of concessions or other obligations by the complaining Member(s).

This situation occurred in the "*EC-Hormones*" dispute, where the EC decided for public health reasons not to withdraw the measures that had been found inconsistent with its WTO obligations[65]. It consequently offered compensation. The US rejected the offer and thus the EC faced suspension of concessions or other obligations, after an arbitrator had determined the level of such suspension with respect to the nullification and impairment caused by the EC's inconsistent measure, which was still in place.

48. *In case of withdrawal of the measure*, as was the case for the EC banana regime, according to Article 3.7 of the DSU, the Member concerned has achieved the "first objective of the dispute settlement mechanism [that] is usually to secure the withdrawal of the measures concerned if these are found to be inconsistent with the provisions of any of the covered agreements".

49. However, if the measure that was withdrawn is replaced by *another* measure, as was also the case for the *revised* EC banana regime, *then* the issue can be raised as to whether this *new* measure is compatible with the adopting Member's WTO obligations as spelled out in the earlier recommendations and rulings of the DSB. In case of disagreement and to that effect, the DSU provides for an accelerated procedure under Article 21.5.

50. In no case can the authorisation for the suspension of concessions or other obligations be granted immediately at the end of the reasonable period of time because the DSU clearly foresees some additional procedural steps after the end of the reasonable period of time before the authorisation for the suspension of concessions or other obligations may be granted.

51. In the above legal context, WTO law is thus concerned with a proper procedure to be followed before concessions or other obligations may be suspended.

If the new measure replacing the measure that was withdrawn is found to be inconsistent with the earlier recommendations and rulings of the DSB, and no agreement on compensation can be reached within the schedule foreseen in Article 22.2 of the DSU, the complainant may request authorisation for the suspension of concessions or other obligations.

52. It is however not specified anywhere in the DSU that compensation or the suspension of concessions or other obligations must be effective as of the day immediately following the end of the reasonable period of time. Compensation is a negotiated solution of the dispute, and there is no legal obligation to grant such compensation as from a particular point in time.

---

[65] The mention of this case in the US reply to question 16 from the Panel is therefore irrelevant.

53. The level of suspension of concessions or other obligations may be assessed in the course of an arbitration procedure which may be requested by the Member to whom such suspension would be applied.

As already mentioned, such arbitration implies some further procedural steps which can only be taken after the end of the reasonable period of time and will be completed only at some later time. Since Article 22.6 of the DSU specifically provides that concessions or other obligations may not be suspended during the course of the arbitration procedure, such suspension will necessarily only be available some time after the end of the reasonable period of time.

54. In the present case, apart from the issue of the application of Article 21.5 of the DSU, that will be discussed in the following chapter, the arbitration procedure concerning the US request for authorisation to suspend concessions or other obligations was still ongoing at the time the US adopted *and applied* its 3 March 1999 measure.

55. Moreover, WTO law is concerned with the concept of equivalence between the level of nullification or impairment suffered by the complaining Member and the level of suspension of concessions or other obligations that may be authorised by the DSB (cf. in particular Article 22.4 and 22.7, first sentence, of the DSU).

Again, at the time the US adopted *and applied* its 3 March 1999 measure, the Arbitrator had taken no decision concerning that equivalence and the US had implemented a measure that was almost three times greater than the level that was eventually set by the Arbitrator.

56. Consequently, the concept of immediate "liability for non-compliance" as advocated by the United States in the present dispute has no basis in WTO law. In the EC's view, there can be no doubt that the US measure has breached the provisions of Article 22 of the DSU.

IV. THE OBLIGATION TO RESORT TO THE PROCEDURES UNDER ARTICLE 21.5 OF THE DSU IN CASE OF DISAGREEMENT ABOUT THE CONSISTENCY WITH A COVERED AGREEMENT OF AN IMPLEMENTING MEASURE

57. The United States continues to claim that there is no obligation to have recourse to the procedure under Article 21.5 of the DSU in case of a disagreement about the existence or consistency with a covered agreement of an implementing measure before resorting to a request for the authorisation of the suspension of concessions or other obligations under Article 22.2 of the DSU.

58. This position is not only in flagrant contradiction with the wording of Article 21.5 of the DSU, which contains the auxiliary "shall" by which this procedure is made mandatory. It is also contradicted by the practice of WTO Members as it has developed in the meantime, not least in cases involving the United States itself.

59. The United States omits to mention in its replies to questions by the Panel submitted on 13 January 2000 that it has concluded, in the context of the dispute on *United States - Import Prohibition of Certain Shrimp and Shrimp Products* (WT/DS58), an understanding with Malaysia on 22 December 1999[66]. This understanding contains the following elements (cf. paragraph 2 of the exchange of letters):

> "If Malaysia [...] decides that it may wish to initiate proceedings under Articles 21.5 and 22 of the DSU, Malaysia will initiate proceedings under Article 21.5 prior to any proceedings under Article 22. [...] Malaysia will not request authorization to suspend concessions or other obligations under Article 22 until the adoption of the Article 21.5 panel report. If on the basis of the proceedings under Article 21.5 Malaysia decides to initiate proceedings under Article 22: the United States will not assert that Malaysia is precluded from obtaining DSB authorization because Malaysia's request was made outside the 30-day time period specified in the first sentence of Article 22.6."

60. This is exactly what the EC explained in 1998 and 1999 to be its reading of the relation between Article 21.5 and 22 of the DSU.

61. The EC is not convinced that it is necessary to have this kind of bilateral agreement in order to apply Articles 21.5 and 22 of the DSU correctly. In fact, the EC does not believe that the legal right accruing to any WTO Member, which was a successful complainant in a DS procedure, under the DSU to request and obtain authorisation to suspend concessions or other obligations could be put at risk by the attitude of the defending party in that individual dispute.

The only determinant element in this issue is that the successful complaining party *must* follow *correctly all* the procedures set out in the DSU.

62. The EC would like to draw the attention of the Panel to the following fact.

Assuming *arguendo* that the interpretation on the sequence between Article 21.5 and 22 of the DSU, suggested by the EC, would reduce the "negative consensus rule to a nullity in those cases in which the implementing party does not implement until the completion of the reasonable period"[67], *quod non*, then a bilateral understanding such as the US/Malaysia agreement would be totally insufficient to avoid that risk.

Any Member would in fact be able to prevent the authorisation to suspend concessions or other obligations from being granted by opposing the consensus in the DSB.

63. Under the interpretation suggested by the US, the signature of an understanding (i.e. a bilateral agreement such as the one between the US and Malaysia)

---

[66] Cf. WTO doc. WT/DS58/16 dated 12 January 2000.

[67] See US answer to question No. 12 from the Panel, at *para.* 33.

would be devoid of any real effect in case of opposition of another WTO Member which might even act in the DSB as an ally of the defending Member.

64. The Panel should not condone this scenario, inspired by the US, of tailor-made dispute settlement procedures on a bilateral basis.

There is simply no compelling reason in law why Articles 21.5 and 22 of the DSU should not be implemented in their logical sequence as their terms command (the EC refers the Panel again in particular to text of Articles 21.5 and 22.2, first sentence, of the DSU), thus avoiding useless confusion and unnecessary prolongation of this debate.

A good faith interpretation[68] of Articles 21.5 and 22 in their logical sequence and in the light of the requirements of Article 23 of the DSU does not result in any change in (or loss of) the "reversed consensus" voting rules in the DSB.

Under these Articles, the "reversed consensus" rule is fully justified where the Member concerned follows the dispute settlement procedures correctly. Where these procedures are not followed, the application of the "reversed consensus" rule becomes a tool for imposing unilateral determinations under a multilateral disguise, which conflicts with the fundamental objective of these provisions.

65. The fact that the reading of the above-mentioned provisions of the DSU that was always suggested by the EC has been accepted by both the complainants and the respondents in *all* dispute settlement procedures having reached the implementation stage after the entry into force of the WTO Agreement, with the only exception of the US in the *Bananas* dispute, shows that the DSU procedures are perfectly viable and can be applied correctly as they stand in the interest of all Members concerned.

As the five years experience of the WTO Agreement shows, a good faith performance of the *existing* rules under the DSU is thus the obvious and sufficient recipe to achieve a correct and satisfactory conclusion of the implementation stage of any DS procedure.

66. As was already mentioned in our oral statement at the first substantive meeting with the Panel on 16 December 1999 (paragraph 20), the United States has been able to accept this kind of proceeding in the *Automotive Leather* case against Australia, i.e. even in a situation where it acted as the complainant.

In any case, an agreement of this nature was acceptable to the EC in the context of the *Bananas* dispute, and the EC has reiterated its readiness to follow a similar line throughout the debate with the United States in the second half of 1998 and the beginning of 1999[69].

---

[68] In line with Articles 26 and 31 of the Vienna Convention on the Law of Treaties, applicable as per Article 3.2 of the DSU.

[69] The references to the relevant statements of the EC representatives in the DSB are contained in footnote 8 to the replies of the European Communities to questions from the Panel and the United States dated 13 January 2000.

67. The United States claims that Canada shares its earlier uncompromising position, but this is not borne out by the facts. In the two relevant dispute settlement procedures in which Canada was involved as a complainant, *Australia Salmon* and *Brazil Aircraft*, Canada has allowed the procedure under Article 21.5 of the DSU to be completed *before* resorting to the suspension of concessions or other obligations.

68. In one case (*Australia Salmon*) this was achieved by suspending the procedure under Article 22 of the DSU in order to allow Article 21.5 procedures to follow their course. In the other case, Canada did not yet resort to procedures under Article 22 of the DSU but simply requested Article 21.5 procedures first.

69. In any case, as explained in the opening chapter of this submission, whatever the position of different WTO Members, according to Article 11 of the DSU the Panel must make an objective assessment of the issues before it, without giving too much weight to the tactical positions of individual WTO Members.

70. For the same reason, the discussions on the DSU review are of limited relevance for the present dispute, which is subject to the *existing* provisions of the DSU. Improvements by negotiation are of course always possible and may lead to an amendment of the present rules and procedures. That does not mean that panels are not called upon, as Article 3.2 of the DSU specifically provides, to clarify the rights and obligations of WTO Members under the dispute settlement rules and procedures *as they presently stand*.

71. A denial of justice is no solution and will not help WTO Members to come to grips with the diverging positions that were at the basis of the *Bananas* dispute, which even the United States does not appear to defend anywhere else than in the present proceedings.

72. Finally, the EC believes it appropriate to rebut some statements made by the US while answering question 14 from the Panel. However, it wishes to make clear that it does not accept or share all the other affirmations by the US with respect to the interpretation of Article 21.5 of the DSU as expressed in these panel proceedings.

73. In answering the Panel's question No 14 on "Who determines whether a new measure nullifies WTO benefits", the US stated[70] that

> "As defined in DSU Article 22.7, the Article 22.6 arbitrator's task is to determine 'whether the level of suspension is equivalent to the level of nullification or impairment.' As the *Bananas* arbitrator pointed out, the concept of equivalence between the proposed suspension and the level of nullification or impairment would be 'devoid of meaning' if either of these variables were unknown.[71] Con-

[70] At *para.* 37.

[71] [Original footnote] Decision by the Arbitrators, *EC - Bananas III (US) (Article 22.6 – EC), supra*, footnote 5, para. 4.7."

> sequently, the Article 22.6 arbitrator must examine the new measure to determine the level of nullification or impairment before it can determine whether that level is equivalent to the level of suspension proposed by the complaining party.[72]"

74. The decision by the Arbitrator in the *Bananas* dispute between the US and the EC quoted above, as any other decision adopted in an Arbitration procedure, was *not* adopted by the DSB. Thus, an arbitration decision cannot have the effects that are reserved to adopted panel or Appellate Body reports in accordance with Articles 3.7, 16, 19 and 23 of the DSU.

It is barely necessary to repeat here the obvious: in the WTO DS system, panels and the Appellate Body reports are the basis for the recommendations and rulings of the DSB. The power to adopt and to make recommendations and rulings in an individual DS procedure *binding upon the WTO Members concerned* pertains *exclusively* to the DSB, i.e. the WTO Members collectively.

75. As to the Arbitrator's tasks, they are confined to those set out in Article 22.6 and 22.7 that do not include any of the tasks that are listed in Article 11 of the DSU (whose title is, not surprisingly, "Function of Panels") and are not subject to the provisions of Article 6.2 and 7 of the DSU nor to an appeal under Article 17 of the DSU.

76. Thus, regardless of how the Arbitrator quoted by the US decided to justify its decision concerning the level of suspension or other obligations requested by the US, which is irrelevant in this context[73], its decision is not binding and cannot

---

[72] [Original footnote] "*Ibid.*, paras. 4.7-4.8."

[73] The EC draws the attention of the Panel to the evident *non sequitur* in the US answer to question No. 14. The US affirms, following the Arbitrator, that "the concept of equivalence would be 'devoid of meaning' if either of these variables (i.e. the level of suspension and the level of nullification or impairment) were unknown". It then concludes that "*Consequently*, the Article 22.6 arbitrator must examine the new measure to determine the level of nullification or impairment before it can determine whether the level is equivalent to the level of suspension proposed by the complaining party".

The conclusion suggested by the US is inconsistent with the arbitrator's tasks under Article 22.6 and 22.7 of the DSU. In the EC's view, there are only two alternative consequences that can be drawn under the DSU from the fact that one of the two "variables" is unknown:

(1) *either* the nullification or impairment is not determined "consistent with the findings contained in a panel or Appellate Body report adopted by the DSB" due to the failure of the complaining Member to challenge the compliance with earlier recommendations and rulings of the DSB of the *new* measures taken by the defending Member. A claim of nullification or impairment in this case is thus not compatible with Article 23 of the DSU. In such a case, since that "variable" is missing, the Arbitrators must set the level at zero.

(2) *Or*, a claim that the *new* measures violate a covered agreement is "consistent with the findings contained in a panel or Appellate Body report adopted by the DSB" (and thus with Article 23 DSU) but the complaining Member has failed to indicate correctly the level of the concessions or other obligations which it proposes to be suspended. Here again, since the other "variable" is missing, the level must be set at zero by the Arbitrator, if requested.

The US assertion quoted above refers to the first alternative only. The EC fails to see how it could be justified under the DSU that an arbitrator usurps the task of an Article 21.5 panel.

be binding on any WTO Member outside the scope of its mandate under Article 22.6 and 22.7 of the DSU.

77. The decision as to the consistency with a covered agreement of measures taken by a Member, *in casu* the EC, to comply with earlier recommendations and rulings of the DSB only pertains to the DSB when adopting a report of a panel or the Appellate Body at the conclusion of a procedure under Article 21.5 of the DSU.

78. However, in the case of the US, such a decision by the DSB was missing on 3 March 1999, was also missing on 19 April 1999 and is still missing today.

79. The US cannot rely on the decision taken by the DSB when it adopted on 6 May 1999 the report in the separate panel procedure on "*Bananas - Recourse to Article 21.5 of the DSU by Ecuador*". According to the Appellate Body report on "*Japan - Alcoholic Beverages*"[74],

> "Adopted panel reports are an important part of the GATT *acquis*. They are often considered by subsequent panels. (...) However, they are not binding, except with respect to resolving the particular dispute between the parties to that dispute.[75]

80. Moreover, as the Panel on "*India - Patent Protection - Complaint by the European Communities and their Member States*"[76] stated in paragraph 7.30:

> "[I]t can thus be concluded that panels are not bound by previous decisions of panels or the Appellate Body even if the subject-matter is the same."

81. In conclusion, the EC reiterates that the contested US measure of 3 March 1999, confirmed on 19 April 1999, is inconsistent with Article 21.5 of the DSU.

82. This inconsistency was not healed by the adoption by the DSB of a panel report in the context of a *separate* panel procedure pursued by *another* WTO Member in accordance with Article 21.5 of the DSU.

It was equally not healed by the authorisation to suspend concessions or other obligations benefiting the EC granted by the DSB on 19 April 1999 up to an equivalent of 191.4 million US$. That authorisation is a *necessary* condition but

---

[74] Appellate Body Report, *Japan – Taxes on Alcoholic Beverages* ("*Japan – Alcoholic Beverages*"), WT/DS8/AB/R, WT/DS10/AB/R, WT/DS11/AB/R, adopted 1 November 1996, DSR 1996:I, 97, at 108. In the very recent Panel Report, *Turkey – Restrictions on Imports of Textile and Clothing Products* ("*Turkey - Textiles*"),WT/DS34/R, adopted 19 November 1999, DSR 1999:VI, 2363, para. 9.11), that panel stated that "we recall in this context that Panel and Appellate Body reports are binding on the parties only".

[75] [Original footnote] "It is worth noting that the Statute of the International Court of Justice has an explicit provision, Article 59, to the same effect. This has not inhibited the development by that Court (and its predecessor) of a body of case law in which considerable reliance on the value of previous decisions is readily discernible."

[76] Panel Report, *India – Patent Protection for Pharmaceutical and Agricultural Chemical Products – Complaint by the European Communities* ("*India –Mailbox*"), WT/DS79/R, adopted 22 September 1998, DSR 1998:VI, 2661.

not a *sufficient* condition to warrant the WTO-consistency of a measure of suspension of concessions or other obligations, which was taken by the US in disregard of procedural and substantial rules under the DSU.

V. THE PRESUMPTION OF GOOD FAITH

83. The United States claims in its replies to questions from the Panel[77] that the concept of a "presumption" of compatibility or non-compatibility of a Member's implementation is not provided for in the DSU.

84. This statement is in open contradiction to the recent Appellate Body report on "*Chile – Taxes on Alcoholic Beverages*"[78] which contains the following statement at paragraph 74:

> "Members of the WTO should not be assumed, in any way, to have *continued* previous protection or discrimination through the adoption of a new measure. This would come close to a presumption of bad faith" (emphasis in the original).

85. It is also contradicted by the language of the DSU, particularly Articles 3.7 and 23.

Article 3.7, fourth sentence, of the DSU contains the following guiding principle

> "In the absence of a mutually agreed solution, the first objective of the dispute settlement mechanism is usually to secure the withdrawal of the measures concerned if these *are found* to be inconsistent with the provisions of any of the covered agreements" (emphasis added).

86. Article 23.1 and 23.2(a) of the DSU specify that such a finding (which in the terminology of Article 23 is called a "determination") can only be made under the rules and procedures of the DSU.

87. The only presumption to which the DSU refers is the presumption mentioned in Article 3.8 according to which

> "there is normally a presumption that a breach of the rules has an adverse impact on other Members parties to th[e] covered agreement, and in such case, it shall be up to the Member against which the complaint has been brought to rebut the charge".

88. For the rest, the burden of proof follows the normal rules as indicated by the Appellate Body in its report on "*United States – Measures Affecting Imports of Woven Wool Shirts and Blouses from India*"[79] and remains with the Member

---

77 Cf. US answer to question 10 from the Panel, at *para.* 24.

78 Appellate Body Report, *Chile – Alcoholic Beverages*, *supra*, footnote 38.

79 Appellate Body Report, *US – Shirts and Blouses*, *supra*, footnote 39, at 335.

alleging the inconsistency of a measure of another Member. There is no basis for any other approach in the DSU.

VI. CONCLUSIONS

89. The EC reiterates that the US measure taken on 3 March 1999 and confirmed on 19 April 1999 is inconsistent with Articles 3, 21, 22 and 23 of the DSU and Articles I, II, VIII and XI of the GATT 1994. It respectfully requests the Panel that it recommends the DSB that the US bring the measure under dispute into conformity with its WTO obligations.

Appendix 1.6

The EC letter dated 25 January 2000 concerning the scope of the Panel's terms of reference

(25 January 2000)

Dear Chairman,

The European Communities note with some surprise the request by the United States, contained in the accompanying letter to its second written submission of 21 January 2000, that the Panel clarify "prior to the outset of the second substantive meeting, the measures that it considers to be within the Panel's terms of reference". The Panel should not accede to this request at this late stage of the proceedings before it.

According to paragraph 11 of the working procedures, a request for a preliminary ruling cannot be made at this stage of the proceedings, unless the United States were able to show "good cause" for granting an exception. The United States does not even attempt to show such good cause.

The Panel's terms of reference are contained in document WT/DS165/8 which refers in its main body and in the Annexes to product lists published by the United States on 3 March 1999 and 19 April 1999. There is thus no surprise in the EC's reliance, as from its first written submission, on both these documents, which were the basis of the establishment of the Panel by the DSB. The United States never raised any objection against this request, neither at the DSB meeting where the Panel was established nor at an early stage of the panel procedure. In fact, only in the closing remarks made on 17 December 1999, the US raised a doubt for the first time and stated: "we may need to return to the Panel for a preliminary ruling".

Now that the second written submissions have already been exchanged and more than a month has passed since the US raised a doubt for the first time, the EC cannot see "good cause" to depart from the working procedures for the Panel.

As the EC pointed out in its second written submission of 21 January 2000, the Panel will have to consider the scope of the complaint as a matter of substance. There is no separate procedural matter involved in the United States' request for "clarification of the terms of reference" that the Panel needs to address at this late stage.

Yours sincerely,

Appendix 1.7
The EC Responses to Additional Questions of Panel
(8 February 2000)

Question 48

The United States argues in paragraph 35 of its Rebuttal Submission that "assum[ing] for the sake of argument that ... the March 3 bonding requirements impose a 'charge' under Article II or VIII, these bonding requirements cannot, by definition, be subject to Article XI...." Please further elaborate the distinction between the scope of Article II and VIII, and that of Article XI, keeping in mind the bonding requirements in question.

Reply

1. The legal qualification of the increased bonding requirements in this case depends in the view of the EC on the (self-standing or ancillary) nature of these bonding requirements. As Deputy USTR Peter Scher pointed out in a press conference on 3 March 1999, it was the intention of the United States to "stop all trade" in the listed products from the E[80 1]. To the extent that the increased bonding requirement is of a self-standing nature, as the United States claims in the present dispute, it is in the view of the EC a trade restriction "other than duties, taxes or charges" in the sense of Article XI.1 of the GATT 1994.

2. The EC is aware that the GATT 1994 does not contain a provision dealing with measures "equivalent to quantitative restrictions" that take the form of a duty, tax or charge. The legal qualification of the increased bonding requirement thus depends on the question whether a trade restrictive measure that may be "bought off" by the payment of an amount of money could, for this purely formal reason alone, be considered as a duty, charge or tax.

3. Assuming *arguendo* that in a given WTO Member, customs clearance could only be achieved by paying a bribe to the customs officials, and that the WTO Member in question would tolerate this practice, would that practice qualify as a duty, tax or charge or, in the alternative, as a trade restriction other than a duty, tax or charge? If the former alternative were correct (*quod non* in the view of the EC), any trade restriction the non-observance of which could lead to the imposition of a fine would presumably also qualify as a "duty, tax or charge".

---

[80] Cf. also the quotation in a recent article in the "Time" magazine of 7 February 2000 on "How to Become a Top Banana" (EC Annex XI), according to which an official of the office of the USTR expressed "amazement" about the fact that a US importer was still doing business in one of the listed products because the US authorities were under the impression that the increased tariff had "cut off the industry – shut it down" (at p. 38, top of left column).

The EC therefore considers that it is more appropriate to base the legal qualification on the substance, rather than on the form, of the measure at issue.

4. It follows from these considerations that a trade restriction the prevailing purpose of which is to "stop trade" and that does not provide any revenue for the treasury of the importing WTO Member does not qualify as a "duty, tax or charge", but as a trade restriction of a different nature.

5. However, as the Panel is aware, the EC has qualified the bonding requirements in this case as being ancillary to a simultaneous increase in the (contingent) duty liability for the listed products. The EC's main argument therefore is that the increased bonding requirements should be legally qualified as a charge in close connection with the (increased) customs duty, the payment of which it serves to guarantee, and for which there is no justification under Articles II and VIII of the GATT 1994. Only in the alternative that the Panel considers it established that the United States in the present case introduced an increased bonding requirement without having made the relevant customs tariffs effective at the same time, the line of argument developed in the preceding paragraphs becomes relevant and would lead to the conclusion that the increased bonding requirements constitute a violation of Article XI.1 of the GATT 1994.

6. In any event, both legal qualifications under consideration are meant to complement each other in a seamless manner and would therefore always lead to the finding of a violation of the US obligations under the WTO Agreement.

Question 49

In claiming that the increase in the amount of a required security was to cover 100% tariff which might eventually be due (after the arbitration panel has completed is work), the US appears to assume that the applicable obligation, in the form of tariffs, can change *after* the entry of a listed product into the customs territory of a WTO Member. Is this retroactive change of the applicable law and applicable obligation, acceptable in international law?

Reply

7. As explained in the EC's second written submission of 21 January 2000, the EC is not convinced by the US arguments that the increased customs duties in this case were imposed on 19 April 1999 with retroactive effect as from 3 March 1999. Rather, the EC considers that the duty liability for listed products was in fact increased as from 3 March 1999 and only confirmed on 19 April 1999 on the basis of a reduced list. As the EC has pointed out, the retroactive imposition of increased import duties is at odds with the requirements under US customs law as the US itself has explained them throughout the present dispute, particularly in response to the EC's written questions.

The EC would like to recall that under customs law principles, a bonding requirement may only be justified by a doubt concerning a specific imported product (e.g. correct classification, valuation, origin), but never by a contingency on future changes in law or a doubt on the law itself.

8. Thus, in the view of the EC, the question of the legal restrictions regarding the retroactive imposition of taxes or other financial burdens does not arise in the circumstances of the present case. However, the EC is of course ready to provide its views in the unlikely event that the Panel were to take a different position on this preliminary issue.

9. The restrictions regarding the retroactivity of legal instruments which impose legal obligations or financial burdens on the parties to whom they are applicable are based on the problems created in respect of legal certainty and, where relevant, the legal protection of acquired rights.

10. The achievement of legal certainty is also one of the basic objectives of the WTO and of its dispute settlement system. According to Article 3.2 of the DSU, "the dispute settlement system of the WTO is a central element in providing security and predictability to the multilateral trading system". As the Appellate Body has found: "the security and predictability of 'the reciprocal and mutually advantageous arrangements directed to the substantial reduction of tariffs and other barriers to trade' is an object and purpose of the *WTO Agreement*, generally, as well as of the GATT 1994[81].

11. Legal certainty requires that import charges not be increased retroactively after an item has been lawfully imported into the customs territory of a WTO Member. Such retroactive increase is in open contradiction with the purpose of the WTO to allow international trade to take place on a predictable legal and economic basis. While the imposition of tariffs on imported products is in principle a permissible policy instrument at the disposal of WTO Members, provided that the tariff bindings under the relevant GATT schedule of tariff concessions and the MFN rule are respected, the retroactive increase of a tariff, even in situations where the tariff binding is not breached by such action, is clearly in violation of one of the most basic WTO obligations, namely to permit international trade to take place on a secure and predictable basis.

12. For similar reasons, Article 28 of the Vienna Convention on the Law of Treaties provides for a presumption of non-retroactivity of international treaties. This means that, unless a different intention can be established, an international treaty does not apply to acts or facts that took place or situations that ceased to exist before the entry into force of the treaty. On this basis, it has been ruled that under the European Convention on Human Rights, a claim of violation is not admissible *ratione temporis* with regard to acts that took place before the Convention entered into force for the contracting party concerned, even where the

[81] Cf. Appellate Body Report, *EC - LAN*, *supra*, footnote 13, para. 82. Cf. also the recent Panel Report, *US – Section 301*, *supra*, footnote 9, according to which "[p]roviding security and predictability to the multilateral trading system is another central object and purpose of the system" (at para. 7.75).

consequences of the act complained about remain in place after the entry into force of the Convention (e.g., in case of an expropriation without adequate compensation)[82].

13. Against this legal background, particularly with regard to the requirement to ensure legal certainty, it can be excluded that the suspension of concessions or other obligations could be authorised by the DSB under Article 22.2 or 22.7 of the DSU with retroactive effect. Nor can the suspension of concessions or other obligations be applied retroactively once authorised by the DSB under these provisions. Such retroactive effect of the authorisation is not only without any basis in the relevant provisions of Article 22 of the DSU, it would also be in open conflict with fundamental principles of international law and with the object and purpose of the WTO Agreement in general and the dispute settlement system in particular, as witnessed by Article 3.2 of the DSU and the Appellate Body report in the (already quoted) case on *European Communities - Customs Classification of Certain Computer Equipment*[83].

14. In the present case, there can thus not be the shadow of a doubt that a retroactive increase of tariffs by the United States on listed items imported from the EC would be both in breach of existing tariff bindings and thus in breach of US obligations under GATT, and in breach of the fundamental rule that tariffs may not be increased retroactively for any item once it has been cleared through customs for home use in the importing Member. The United States cannot rely on the DSB decision of 19 April 1999 to justify the retroactive imposition of the customs duties either.

---

[82] The expropriations were considered as instantaneous acts and not as continuing violations, see, e.g., joined applications No. 18890/91, 19048/91, 19342/92 and 19549/92, *Mayer et al v. Germany*, decision of 4 March 1996.

[83] Cf. footnote 2 above.

Appendix 1.8

The EC oral presentation at the Second Substantive Meeting

(9 February 2000)

I. RESPONSE OF THE EC TO THE US STATEMENT ON "MATTERS RELATING TO THE SCOPE OF THIS DISPUTE"

The EC considers the US request for a preliminary ruling for matters relating to the scope of the dispute as untimely. The EC has referred in its request for the establishment of the Panel to two lists of selected products originating in the EC, i.e. a larger list published on 3 March and a reduced list containing a "subset" of products published on 19 April 1999.

It was thus obvious to the United States from the outset that the EC intended to address violations of the WTO provisions identified in the request by making use of both lists.

Moreover, the consultations requested on 4 March 1999 referred to the larger list of products which covered all the products contained in the 19 April list. We cannot see then how the US could claim now that the reference to a reduced list, which contained no addition of products, could enlarge the scope of the present dispute and thus affect its rights of defence.

Finally, the legal qualification of the 3 March 1999 instruction is part of the substance of the present dispute. It cannot be addressed or decided in the context of a preliminary ruling concerning exclusively procedural matters.

II. THE FAILURE BY THE US TO HAVE RECOURSE TO THE MULTILATERAL DISPUTE SETTLEMENT PROCEDURES UNDER ARTICLES 23, 21 AND 22 OF THE DSU BEFORE RESORTING TO SUSPENSION OF CONCESSIONS

After the debate on the procedural issues that we have had at the beginning of today's meeting, we would now like to go into the substance of our case. The substance is of course to a large extent also dependent on the scope of the present dispute, and that is the first matter that we would like to address in our oral statement today.

Mr. Chairman,

Members of the Panel,

You are meanwhile familiar with the basic plea of the EC, namely that the US measures are inconsistent with the fundamental WTO rule according to which no Member can take justice in its own hands. It has to follow the rules and procedures governing the settlement of disputes consigned in the DSU before being able to seek redress for any perceived breach of WTO obligations by another WTO Member. As the Appellate Body has found in the recent report in the case on *Chile – Taxes on Alcoholic Beverages*, there is moreover a presumption of good faith performance of WTO obligations by WTO Members, which is equivalent to the presumption of innocence recognised under criminal law as one of the principles of law recognised by all civilised nations.

It is the breach of this basic prescript of the WTO in general and the DSU in particular that has led the United States in the *Bananas* dispute to have recourse to a request for authorisation of the suspension of concessions or other obligations based on a unilateral determination that the EC failed to honour its WTO obligations.

Thus, it refrained from following the procedures that are foreseen in Article 21.5 of the DSU in case of disagreement about the consistency with a covered agreement of a measure taken to implement the recommendations and rulings of the DSB on the basis of an earlier panel or Appellate Body report.

This has led to the present situation in which the US applies increased tariffs to a number of items imported from the EC without having followed the correct proced ures under the DSU.

In this context, the United States cannot invoke the fact that, on 19 April 1999, the DSB authorised it to suspend concessions or other obligations in the amount established by arbitration under Article 22.6 of the DSU. The DSB authorisation is a necessary, but not a sufficient prerequisite for the lawfulness of the suspension of concessions or other obligations. The United States was also under an obligation to respect the dispute settlement procedures with regard to the disagreement on the consistency with a covered agreement of the implementing measures taken by the EC.

As the Panel is aware, the breach of Articles 21 and 23 of the DSU is specifically mentioned in the EC's request for the establishment of this Panel and is thus part of its terms of reference.

This aspect of the present case has a bearing not only on the legal basis for the violations about which the EC complains, but also on the question whether the violation is of a continuing nature. As the Panel will easily understand, this aspect of the case is therefore of fundamental importance for the EC. If the Panel finds in favour of the EC on this decisive point, the suspension of concessions is and remains inconsistent with the US obligations both for the initial list of 3 March 1999, which constitutes Annex 1 to the EC's request for the establishment of the Panel, and for the reduced list of 19 April 1999 which constitutes Annex 2 to the EC's request for the establishment of the Panel. The EC believes that it is entitled to receive an answer from the Panel with regard to this important claim on which the parties clearly have a disagreement with very important legal and practical consequences in the present case. A denial of justice on this point would necessarily lead to continuing legal uncertainty and more litigation.

The EC has already pointed out in its written submissions that there was no justification to resort to the suspension of concessions or other obligations in the present case, neither on 3 March 1999 nor on 19 April 1999. The WTO-inconsistency of the 3 March measure could not "healed", by the authorisation of the DSB of 19 April 1999 simply because it was legally flawed from the outset. The EC repeats that in this context, the DSB authorisation of 19 April 1999 was a necessary, but not a sufficient prerequisite for the suspension of concessions or other obligations.

III. EXAMINATION OF THE LEGAL CHARACTERISTICS OF THE US MEASURE AND OTHER COMMENTS

Mr. Chairman, Distinguished Members of the Panel

The EC suggests that we start from the beginning, i.e. that we examine once more the US measure at issue. Thanks to your request, the EC is now able to examine the text of the unpublished instructions that the USTR addressed to the US Customs service on 3 March 1999 (US Exhibit 12).

The text is very revealing:

(a) the USTR describes the aim of the instruction as follows: "The USTR *now* seeks to preserve its *right* to impose 100 percent duties *as of March 3*, *pending* the release of the arbitrators' final decision" (emphasis added);

(b) as a consequence the following instruction was given: "Therefore, I am hereby requesting that *until further notice* the Customs Service *withhold liquidation* of entries of all articles identified in the attachment to this letter (...)" (emphasis added);

(c) moreover, as further consequence, the following additional instruction was given: "I further request that the Customs Service *today instruct* port directors to review the *sufficiency of bonds* posted with respect to entries described in the previous sentence, and to take steps to provide adequate *additional security* (...) (emphasis added);

(d) finally, it should be noted that the instruction refers explicitly to "(...) 63 Fed. Reg. *63099* and 63 Fed. Reg. 71665 giving notice of the proposed increase in duties on selected products".

The above confirms therefore that:

(a) On 3 March 1999, the US authorities considered to have the right to impose 100 percent duties on selected products of a total value of 520 million US$ as from that date. However, the US does not indicate, once more, from where it derives this alleged "right". The EC reiterates that this determination of a self-attributed "right" is in open conflict with central provisions of the DSU such as Article 23, 21 and 22.

(b) The US determined that it had the right to the 100 percent increased duties as from 3 March even *pending* the arbitrators' decision. This proves the EC's point that the US measure violates Article 22.6, last sentence, of the DSU which reads as follows: "Concessions or other obligations shall not be suspended during the course of the arbitration".

(c) The text instructs customs to "withhold liquidation". The EC would recall in passing that the US has so far asserted that this expression has no legal meaning and was just for the press release. The EC also notes that this measure is unqualified and gives instruction not to allow customs clearance at the bound MFN rate. What matters for the resolution of this case is the content and the effects of a specific instruction given by the USTR to "withhold liquidation", i.e. not to proceed with the liquidation of customs duties. The effect of this instruction was to prevent as from 3 March 1999 any importer of selected products originating in the EC from clearing those products through customs at a tariff rate not exceeding the rate bound in the US Schedule of tariff concessions as they were entitled under the WTO.

(d) The "withholding" of liquidation was made effective "until further notice", i.e. in a totally open-ended manner. The instruction thus undermines "the security and predictability of 'the reciprocal and mutually advantageous arrangements directed to the substantial reduction of tariffs and other barriers to trade' [which] is an object and purpose of the *WTO Agreement*, generally, as well as of the GATT 1994" as the Appellate Body report on "*European Communities - Customs Classification of Certain Computer Equipment*" indicated (paragraph 82).

(e) The USTR instruction contains also an ancillary order to "review the sufficiency of bonds" and to provide "adequate *additional* security" in order to ensure the implementation of the suspension of tariff concessions as from 3 March 1999.

(f) The USTR instruction cross references to the text of a notice published in the Federal Register of 10 November 1998, at page 63099, which reads as follows: "(...) [T]he dates on which the USTR intends to implement action – February 1 or no later than March 3, 1999 – correspond to the *dates contemplated by sections 306(b) and 305(a) of the Trade Act* as well as Article 22 of the DSU".

As is apparent from the above, the US instruction on 19 April 1999 did not add any further burden upon importation of selected products from the EC. Rather, while confirming the 3 March instruction, it reduced the list of products. The EC does not complain against such reduction.

Mr. Chairman, Members of the Panel,

The US explanations in response to the additional questions of the Panel are simply not credible.

For example, the intention of the US authorities stated in the 3rd March instruction was to make the suspension of concessions effective *immediately* ("now") on 3 March without pursuing the multilateral dispute settlement procedures under Article 21.5 and 23 of the DSU. This is a clear breach of fundamental principles of the WTO that still persists today.

In addition, the US did not bother to await the determination of the *level* of nullification or impairment, if any, before resorting to the application of suspension of concessions, in clear breach of Article 22.6, last sentence, of the DSU. Therefore, any reference to a "particular risk" or any other "risk" evoked by the US in its answers to the Panel's questions amounts to an attempt to mislead the Panel on the reality of the situation.

Moreover, no elaborate explanation concerning the 19 April instruction is capable to dissimulate the events of 3 March.

The sentence in paragraph 18 of the 8 February US document is revealing:

> "[I]n the absence of the April 19 action, each and every entry subject to changed bonding requirements would be liquidated at the entered, MFN rate – precisely because no liability was imposed on March 3".

This flies in the face of the *stated* purpose of the 3 March instructions:

> "the USTR seeks to preserve its right to impose 100 percent duties as of March 3".

The text of the 3 March instruction simply does not permit to assert, as the US does in its 8 February document at paragraph 20, that

> "[T]here was no legal relationship between the March 3 action (changed bonding requirements) and the April 19 action (increasing the duty rate for certain products)".

No more credible is the attempt by the US to rewrite the GATT 1947 adopted panel report on "Minimum Import Prices".

Contrary to the allegations in paragraph 30 of the 8 February document, that panel accepted the *US* argument that

> "these interest charges and costs [in connection with the lodging of the security] were in excess of the bound rate(...)".

The US recognises that there are interest charges and costs associated with the *increased* bonding requirements at a level that the US has identified up to 20 US$ per thousand dollars of bond value (paragraph 12 of the 8 February document).

The cumulative effect of such measure applied to the aggregate value of the selected products worth 520 million US$ reaches approximately 10 million US $, which cannot be reasonably considered as negligible.

According to the 3 March instruction, the increased bonding requirements are a necessary pre-requisite in order to be able to collect (increased) customs duties, the payment of which it serves to guarantee. Such increase should be qualified as a charge in connection with importation in excess of the US bound rate for which there is no justification under Articles II and VIII of the GATT 1994.

As was the case for the "Minimum Import Prices" panel report, in this case surety deposits usually take the form of a bank guarantee. Without providing such guarantee, no import would take place. There again, that panel report is relevant for the solution of the present dispute.

As the Panel will recall, the US stated in paragraph 6 of its 13 January document that

> "[l]iability for payment of duties is incurred at the time the goods arrive on a vessel within a Customs port when there is an intent to unlade (sic) the goods at that port or, if arrival is otherwise than by vessel, at the time of arrival within the Customs territory of the United States".

Thus, according to the US, the liability cannot change after the arrival of the imported good in the customs territory of the Unites States.

The EC agrees with this explanation. As a matter of fact, the EC applies the same rule.

How can the US claim at the same time that "the April 19 action changed this rate for certain products" (paragraph 23 of the 8 February document) although the products had entered the customs territory before that date?

As the Panel is aware the reality is that the duty liability was assessed on the basis of 100 percent ad valorem duty as of 3 March 1999, subject to confirmation at a later date, i.e. 19 April of the same year.

As a matter of principle, upon importing a product into the US, the customs clearance is based on two different types of factors:

- a factor which is related to the assessment of the correct classification, customs valuation and origin of the goods. This depends on the specificities of each individual import operation which must be declared by the importer; and
- a factor which is determined by the relevant customs legislation applicable on the date on which the customs liability is incurred, i.e., in the case of the US, the date of entry into the US customs territory. That legislation sets among other things the applicable duty rate.

A bonding requirement serves the purpose of guaranteeing the correctness of the operators' declarations concerning the *first* factor. However, the US 3 March instruction explicitly imposed a bonding requirement in order to cover the collection of increased duties as a result of a change of the *second* factor. However, WTO law does not allow Members to create or maintain uncertainty with regards to the upper limit of the applicable duty rate, which cannot exceed the bound rate.

The US can point to no other legal basis for its WTO-inconsistent action. The fact that the WTO Agreement on Anti-dumping measures allows retroactive imposition of AD duties under strictly defined circumstances does not prove the US point in *this* case. On the contrary, it is clearly a limited exception to the fundamental principle under Article II of the GATT 1994 and thus applicable only where specifically provided for (General Interpretative Note to Annex 1A of the WTO Agreement).

Moreover, the Kyoto Convention obliges to ("shall")

> "specify the point in time to be taken into consideration for the purpose of determining the rates of import duties and taxes chargeable on goods declared for home use" (Standard 47 of Annex B.1).

As was just mentioned, the US has indeed chosen such a point in time, namely the date of entry of imported goods into the US customs territory. In this context and as a matter of pure logic, a measure of "withholding" of liquidation of a customs debt is not relevant for the determination of the point in time in which that customs debt is incurred.

Consequently, there was no additional "risk" associated with the action of importation of selected products from the EC that could justify the increase of the bonding requirements. No other "risk" could justify "withholding" of liquidation or an increase in duty liability.

The US explanations are thus no more than a smokescreen intended to dissimulate the increase of the duty liability as of 3 March 1999 which was adopted on that date in violation of Articles I, II, VIII and/or XI of GATT and 3, 21, 22 and 23 of the DSU.

This concludes the presentation of the European Communities. Mr Chairman, Distinguished Members of the Panel, thank you for your attention.

Appendix 1.9
The EC Final Statement at the Second Substantive meeting (9 February 2000)

Mr. Chairman,

Distinguished Members of the Panel

the United States appears to have difficulty with the perception of the reality of this case.

The US seems to forget that the Deputy USTR, Mr. P. Scher, has declared on 3 March 1999 to the press that "we retaliated by effectively stopping trade as of March 3 in response to the harm caused by the EC's WTO-inconsistent banana regime". It also disregards quotations from the USTR officials made after 3 March when the affected US industry complained about the effects of the measure. Those USTR officials are quoted in recent US publications as stating that they thought that "the tariff would cut off industry – shut it down".

We now discover that the US representatives in the present procedure are not fully aware of these realities which are part of the unrebutted evidence before this Panel. They have stated this morning that the EC asserts that "the bonding requirements effectively stopped trade. They did not".

The EC has looked once more at Exhibits 5, 7 and 10 submitted by the United States in the present procedure. It has converted the figures submitted by the US into a graph.

Mr. Chairman and Members of the Panel: if the United States' assertions of this morning were correct, i.e. that there was no instruction to customs authorities, no withholding of liquidation, no increase in duty liability, how could these trade effects have occurred?

The EC submits that the text of the USTR notices published in the Federal Register in 1998 and of the USTR 3 March instruction are utterly clear: these trade effects were the direct, intended and unequivocal result of the US measure, by which the duty liability was increased to 100 percent ad valorem as from 3 March in order to stop trade as from that date.

The US described its customs liquidation cycle as allowing immediate release of the imported goods after the provisional assessment of the relevant duty elements. After that provisional assessment, the financial obligations resulting from the importation are liquidated between 314 days and one year after the entry of the imported goods.

The EC operates a similar system, although the periods of financial liquidation are much shorter.

However, as already stated and as a matter of logic, any bond requirement in this context must be related to secure the deferred payment, or to cover possible mistakes in the initial assessment of the duty elements (misclassification, undervaluation, invalid origin claims). All these elements "relate either to credit worthiness of the importer, or to the nature of the merchandise being imported" (US second submission, paragraph 29).

When we compare these principles with the situation in the present case we discover that the financial obligations, for which duty payment was deferred on or after 3 March 1999 for the listed products, were rather based on government action increasing the US duty rates to 100 percent ad valorem, in breach of the US GATT bindings.

Moreover, the Kyoto Convention provides no justification to allow increased sureties to cover changes to the applicable rates of duty *after* the point in time in which the duty liability is incurred. The EC draws the attention of the Panel also to the purpose of the Kyoto Convention which is to facilitate and simplify customs procedures. No good faith interpretation of such Convention could justify measures, such as the US measure, which undermine the security and predictability of the international trading system.

A further point of clarification concerns the scope of the Panel's review of the US measure. The US representative has this morning repeatedly asserted that the EC "is asking the Panel to violate several WTO provisions in order to find that the Article 22.6 arbitral panel in Bananas somehow violated other DSU provisions" (paragraph 12 of US 9 February statement).

The EC submits that it is the US that is confusing procedures here. We confirm that this Panel does not need to even mention the Arbitrators' decision under Article 22.6, since the EC does not request this Panel to review the *level* of nullification or impairment determined under that procedure, regardless of how it was justified.

The EC insists, however, on the fact that *no* panel or Appellate Body report *adopted* by the DSB *and* involving the United States has ever determined that the EC "fail[ed] to bring the measure found to be inconsistent with the covered agreement into compliance therewith or otherwise comply with the recommendations and rulings within the reasonable period of time determined pursuant to paragraph 3 of Article 21 (...)" (Article 22.2 of the DSU).

Thus, the EC repeats that while the authorisation by the DSB under Article 22 of the DSU is a necessary pre-requisite in order to implement a suspension of concessions or other obligations, it is not a sufficient condition where there is a disagreement on the "consistency with a covered agreement of measures taken to comply with the recommendations and rulings" of the DSB (Article 21.5 of the DSU). That necessary condition is only fulfilled once a Panel or Appellate Body report under Article 21.5 of the DSU has been adopted by the DSB.

If the US were to prevail on this central point, this would amount to accepting that a WTO Member can take the law in its own hands. This would undermine the multilateral character of the dispute settlement system and, consequently, of the WTO system as a whole.

US imports of EU products NOT included on final list* - January 1997 until September 1999

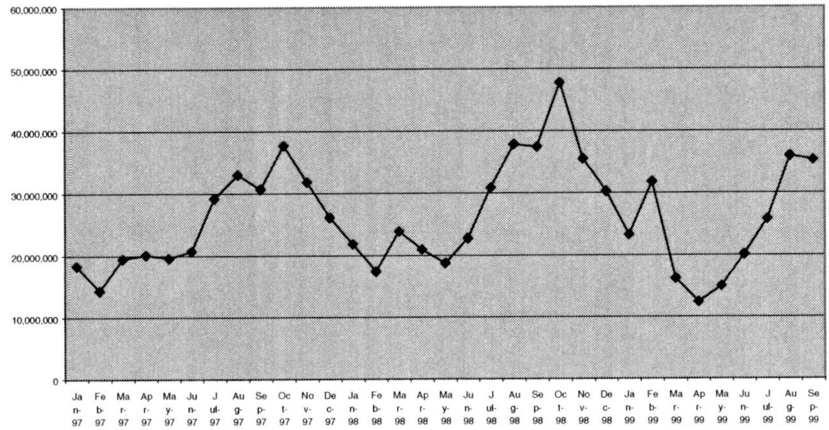

	Jan-97	Feb-97	Apr-97	May-97	Jun-97	Jul-97	Sep-97	Oct-97	Nov-97	Dec-97	Feb-98	Mar-98
Series1	18,34	14,30	20,11	19,60	20,74	29,22	30,70	37,67	31,82	26,13	17,41	23,94

	Apr-98	Jun-98	Jul-98	Aug-98	Sep-98	Nov-98	Dec-98	Jan-99	Feb-99	Apr-99	May-99	Jun-99	Jul-99	Sep-99
Series1	20,95	22,77	30,87	37,81	37,42	35,46	30,27	23,33	31,78	12,40	14,98	20,12	25,85	35,29

* (Prosciutto, pecorino, cookies, candles, plastic film, sweaters, coffee makers). Source: US exhibits 5, 7 and 1C

Appendix 1.10
The EC Responses to Additional Questions of Panel
(10 February 2000)

Question 50

Do parties consider that there is an opportunity cost arising from the bonding requirement, in particular if cash is deposited in lieu of a bond?

Reply

The EC would like to repeat that the financial liquidation process associated with deferred payment of duties is much shorter in the EC system than in the US system.

Under the US system, a cash deposit in lieu of a bond would remain available to the US government until the conclusion of the financial liquidation process in relation to the importation, i.e. not earlier than 314 days. This sum of money, the EC understands, is *additional* to the amount equivalent to the duties due (possibly already deposited in view of final liquidation) for that particular consignment.

Therefore, the US government would benefit from *positive* interests for almost one year for that additional amount of money and, correspondingly, the importer would loose money equivalent to *negative* interests on that sum, increased by the ratio of inflation. Moreover, the importer is restricted in its financial opportunities that the availability of that amount of money would entail since it restricts or makes more expensive its access to credit.

In the case at hand, most of the EC originated products listed in the US measure were subject to 'zero' or marginal duty liability until 2 March 1999. On 3 March 1999, the unilateral US measure increased the duty liability for these products to 100 percent *ad valorem.*

Any operator wishing to utilise the cash deposit in lieu of a bond on or after that date would have been subject to a disproportionate deposit requirement as compared to the negligible or non-existent pre-3 March deposit. This is within a situation where the increase in cash deposit was imposed in order to cover unilaterally increased duties, a governmental measure that has no relation with the purpose of a cash deposit, i.e. to cover uncertainties related to a specific consignment.

In any case, in the scenario described by the Panel's question, the US measure produced a significant increase in "opportunity costs", which finds no justification under the WTO agreements or any other legal instrument.

Appendix 2.1
The First Submission of the United States
(6 December 1999)

I. INTRODUCTION

1. On March 3, 1999, the United States Customs Service began to require that bonds posted on certain imports from the European Communities (EC) cover the potential liability due if the DSB were to authorize the suspension of concessions for the EC's continued non-compliance in the *Bananas* dispute. The sole issue in this dispute is whether, in the specific context of efforts by the European Communities to avoid at all costs complying with its WTO obligations in the *Bananas* dispute, that U.S. response was proper. The EC does not contest that it failed to bring its banana import regime into compliance with its WTO obligations by January 1, 1999, the end of its "reasonable period of time" for doing so. Nor does the EC contest that WTO arbitrators reached this conclusion on April 6, 1999. Nor does the EC contest that the Dispute Settlement Body (DSB) approved a U.S. request for the suspension of concessions in full accordance with the terms of Article 22 of the Understanding on Rules and Procedures Governing the Settlement of Disputes (DSU) on April 19, 1999. Rather, the EC argues that despite confirmation by the arbitrators that the EC has been violating its WTO obligations since January 1, 1999, the United States did not have the right to increase bonding requirements on March 3, 1999 in order to preserve its ability to redress such violations as of that date following DSB approval of the amount of nullification or impairment. As shown in this submission, the March 3 bonding requirements were consistent with the letter and purpose of the DSU.

2. Under the DSU, the EU was liable for its nullification or impairment as of January 2, 1999, one day after the end of the reasonable period of time. The date eventually chosen, March 3, was one day after the date by which Article 22.6 required the WTO arbitrators in the *Bananas* case to have determined the level of nullification or impairment of U.S. benefits resulting from the EC's violation of its WTO obligations.

3. That the arbitral panel was unable to complete its work by March 2, 1999 was in large part due to the efforts of the EC to delay referral of the matter to the panel and to delay the panel's subsequent work. These efforts were but the latest by the EC to delay compliance with its international obligations in connection with its banana import regime. The EC's efforts extended back even to before the 1995 creation of the WTO, to the EC's refusal to bring itself into compliance with two adverse GATT panel rulings on bananas. These efforts continued after the EC's banana import regime was again found in violation of its international obligations by a WTO dispute settlement panel and the WTO Appellate Body. The EC refused to consult with the complaining parties during the reasonable period of time on the EC's revisions to its banana import regime, instead making changes that would again be found inconsistent with EC obligations. Moreover,

during the reasonable period, the EC first repeatedly obstructed the establishment of an Article 21.5 panel on the question of the EC's non-compliance, and then sought to delay until after January 31, 1999 any U.S. request to suspend concessions – which would have denied the United States the benefit of the negative consensus rule under paragraphs 6 or 7 of DSU Article 22. While the EC failed in its effort to prevent the United States from presenting to the DSB its rightful request to suspend concessions, it succeeded in delaying the work of the Article 22.6 arbitrators beyond the DSU-mandated time frame for completion of their work on March 2, 1999. Thus, in the year leading up to March 3, 1999, the EC repeatedly and without exception obstructed the mechanisms provided for in the DSU to address its failure to comply.

4. When the WTO replaced the GATT in 1995, the DSU was expected to be one of the major improvements, in that it was structured so as to ensure prompt settlement of disputes, in particular prompt compliance.[84] The WTO record for the settlement of disputes from 1995 to 1998 was a good one, but the EC's failure to comply in the banana case threatened to change the pattern. The *Bananas* dispute involved the first time a defending party used the reasonable period to make changes that would clearly not involve full compliance by the end of it, and then obstructed DSU procedures for addressing the situation. These actions leading up to March 3, 1999 seriously threatened the credibility of the new dispute settlement system.

5. The U.S. action of March 3, 1999 addressed the threat posed to the credibility of the WTO dispute settlement system by the EC's concerted strategy of delay, and it did so in a manner consistent with U.S. WTO obligations. By requiring importers to post bonds sufficient to cover any duties which the DSB might ultimately authorize as a result of the EC's continued non-compliance with its WTO obligations, the United States preserved its ability to impose DSB-authorized duties and at the same time demonstrated to the EC that it could not hope to benefit from its efforts to undermine DSU rules through delay. This action was consistent with U.S. WTO obligations, and the Panel should reject the EC's claims to the contrary.

II. PROCEDURAL BACKGROUND

6. By letter dated 4 March 1999, the EC requested consultations with the United States regarding the U.S. decision of March 3 to require that bonds posted on certain EC imports to cover the potential liability due if the DSB were to authorize the suspension of concessions with respect to EC imports for the EC's continued non-compliance in the *Bananas* dispute (WT/DS165/1). Consultations were held on 21 April 1999, but failed to resolve the dispute.

[84] *See* DSU Arts. 3.3, 21.1.

7. By letter dated 11 May 1999, the EC requested establishment of a panel with standard terms of reference pursuant to Article 7 of the DSU (WT/DS165/8). On 16 June 1999, the Dispute Settlement Body ("DSB") established a panel pursuant to the EC request (WT/DS165/9).

8. The following terms of reference apply to this proceeding:

> To examine, in the light of the relevant provisions of the covered agreements cited by the European Communities in document WT/DS165/8, the matter referred to the DSB by the European Communities in that document and to make such findings as will assist the DSB in making the recommendations or in giving the rulings provided for in those agreements.

9. On 29 September 1999, the EC requested the Director-General to determine the composition of the Panel pursuant to Article 8.7 of the DSU. On 8 October 1999, the Director-General composed the Panel.

10. Ecuador, India, Jamaica, Japan, St. Lucia and Dominica reserved their rights as third parties to the dispute. (WT/DS165/9, WT/DS165/9/Corr.1).

III. FACTUAL BACKGROUND

11. A full recounting of the EC's actions in the year and a half preceding March 3, 1999 illustrates the threat these actions posed to the DSU's credibility and provides the necessary perspective on U.S. action on that date to address this threat and to preserve its rights under the DSU.

12. On September 25, 1997, the Dispute Settlement Body adopted panel and Appellate Body rulings against the EC in *European Communities - Regime for the Importation, Sale and Distribution of Bananas*, a dispute addressing the complaints of Ecuador, Guatemala, Honduras, Mexico and the United States.[85] These findings were broad and comprehensive, and included findings that the EC's banana import regime (1) wrongly allocated its market as between the access opportunities afforded to Latin American and African, Caribbean and Pacific (ACP) countries, respectively and (2) discriminated in favor of EC banana distribution service suppliers and against U.S. and Latin American service suppliers under the General Agreement on Trade in Services (GATS).

13. At the DSB meeting at which the EC was required to state its intentions concerning implementation, and in subsequent negotiations with the complaining parties under Article 21.3 concerning the "reasonable period of time" for compliance, the EC refused to commit to implement "all" of the DSB recommendations and rulings. The EC spoke only vaguely about meeting its "international obligations" and refused to commit to implement all the rulings and recommendations

---

[85] WT/DSB/M/37.

of the DSB in the reasonable period of time.[86] It eventually recognized its obligations during questioning by the arbitrator appointed pursuant to Article 21.3 of the DSU on the reasonable period of time.[87]

14. As a result of that arbitration, the EC was given a fifteen-month "reasonable period of time" to bring its banana import regime into compliance with the EC's WTO obligations, ending on January 1, 1999.[88] Despite the extent of the WTO findings and the complexity of the EC's measures, however, European Commission officials refused to consult with the United States following the WTO rulings in the fall of 1997. Instead, the Commission began to develop proposed changes to the EC banana regime that ignored the concerns that the complaining parties had expressed.

15. On January 14, 1998 the Commission submitted a proposal to its member States. The inconsistencies of that proposal with the DSB's recommendations were readily apparent. The Commission proposal made only token changes in its allocation of the market, and left open the possibility of maintaining the discrimination against U.S. service suppliers under the GATS. Commission officials simply asserted that their proposal was fully WTO-consistent. During meetings with U.S. officials in early 1998, Commission representatives stressed that they now had no latitude to make any substantive changes to this proposal.

16. Beginning in January 1998, the United States, the four Latin American countries who were complaining parties in the original case, and Panama, a more recent WTO member, also began raising the banana issue on a monthly basis before the DSB.[89] The complaining parties explained to the EC and other WTO Members in great detail the WTO-inconsistencies of the EC proposal and requested negotiations based on a new approach. In response, the EC suggested only that the complaining parties were subverting the DSB process, and it declined to engage in substantive negotiations.

17. During subsequent months, the EC position became even more entrenched, despite U.S. efforts to press for a negotiated resolution. In June 1998, the EC Agriculture Council agreed to the Commission's proposal, on the basis of an agreement, recorded in public minutes, that the licensing regime would be based on the reference period 1994-96, which would have the effect of perpetuating the discriminatory treatment applied to favor European distribution companies receiving licenses.[90] The EC Council adopted the proposal in Regulation

---

86 *See* WT/DSB/M/38.

87 *See* Award of the Arbitrator, *EC - Bananas III*, *supra*, footnote 1, para. 12.

88 *Ibid.*, para. 20.

89 *See* WT/DSB/M/41 (DSB meeting of 22 January); WT/DSB/M/42 (13 February meeting); WT/DSB/M/44 (25 March meeting); WT/DSB/M/45 (22 April meeting); WT/DSB/M/46 (22 June meeting); WT/DSB/M/47 (23 July meeting); WT/DSB/M/48 (22 September meeting); WT/DSB/M/49 (21 October meeting); WT/DSB/M/51 (25 November meeting).

90 *See* report of 2110th Council meeting -Agriculture- Luxembourge, 22/23/24/25 June 1998, 9558/9 (Presse 214-G), page 18 ("The Commission confirms that in managing import licenses in

(EC) 1637/98 of July 20, 1998, which, as the EC explains in its First Submission,[91] entered into force on July 31, 1998 and was applicable from January 1, 1999. The EC provided further implementing rules for licensing - on the basis of the Council-approved 1994-1996 reference period - on October 28, 1998. These entered into force on November 1, 1998 and were applicable in their entirety from January 1, 1999.

18. Beginning in early July 1998, the United States and its co-complainants repeatedly asked the EC to submit to a DSU Article 21.5 panel its claim that its newly adopted measures were, in fact, WTO-consistent. On July 8, U.S. Trade Representative Charlene Barshefsky asked European Commission Vice President Sir Leon Brittan to agree to reconvene the original panel pursuant to DSU Article 21.5 to review the EC measures before the end of the "reasonable period.[92] She indicated that if the EC was not in compliance by the end of the year, the United States would invoke its right to withdraw trade concessions under Article 22 of the DSU. The EC responded at the end of July that it saw "no reason" to reconvene the panel, and stated that "normal procedures" beginning with a request for consultations should be followed.[93] The complaining parties asked the same of the EC at a July 23 meeting of the DSB; the EC representative replied that he was not in a position to respond.[94]

19. In August 1998, the EC insisted on holding formal consultations under DSU Article 4 before it would agree to reconvene the original panel.[95] In response, the complaining parties requested consultations with the EC, while reserving their legal positions that this step was not required. However, the EC's insistence on formal 60-day consultations turned out to be just another tactic for delaying the reconvening of the panel. During the consultations, the EC merely reiterated again its position that the revisions to its banana regime were WTO consistent and declined to agree to re-establish a panel at the next DSB meeting.

20. In September, 1998, the complaining parties requested the intervention of the Chairman of the DSB to help persuade the EC to agree to procedures to reconvene the panel by early November. The EC said that it was only willing to reconvene the panel if its review were limited to violations of the GATT. The EC

accordance with the method of "traditionals/newcomers", it will use the years 1994-96 as the initial reference period for determining operators.") The 1994-96 reference period agreed upon was one in which the GATS-inconsistent regime had been in place, and could accordingly be predicted to perpetuate the inconsistencies previously found by the DSB, as the arbitrators eventually concluded.

91 First Written Submission of the European Communities, para. 3.

92 Letter from Charlene Barshefsky to the Honorable Sir Leon Brittan, July 13, 1998 (U.S. Exhibit 1).

93 Letter from Sir Leon Brittan to Ms. Charlene Barshefsky, 30 July 1998 (U.S. Exhibit 1).

94 *See* WT/DSB/M/47.

95 The EC argued that, with the exception of the 90 day time frame for circulating the report and resort to the original panel, Article 21.5 procedures involved "normal dispute settlement procedures," such as consultations and, presumably, another reasonable period of time for compliance. *See* WT/DSB/M/48 (minutes of DSB meeting of 22 September 1998).

insisted that any panel review under the GATS of its services measures must occur separately at some later unspecified date. The complaining parties could not agree to such a split in the case, which would have been contrary to the manner in which the panel originally considered it. As the original panel noted, the GATT and GATS violations in the case were related. Moreover, there is no basis in the DSU for a defending party to condition its participation in dispute settlement proceedings on the limitation of a complaining party's right to assert any WTO claim. The EC's demand for split proceedings would merely have achieved its goal of delaying panel proceedings.

21. The EC first devoted serious attention to the complaining parties only in November 1998 after the United States began contingency preparations for suspension of concessions. The U.S. preparations were based on the schedule provided for in DSU Article 22. Under Article 22.6, the DSB is required to authorize a request to suspend concessions within 30 days of the end of the reasonable period of time unless there is a consensus not to do so, or unless the Member concerned objects to the level of suspension proposed. In that case, the matter is to be referred to an arbitral panel to determine whether the level of suspension of concessions is equivalent to the level of nullification or impairment. Pursuant to Article 22.6, the arbitrators must complete their work within 60 days of the conclusion of the reasonable period of time, following which the DSB must, under Article 22.7, authorize suspension in the amount found by the arbitrators absent a negative consensus. In order to be placed on the agenda of a DSB meeting to be held on January 31, 1999 – within 30 days of the end of the "reasonable period" – the United States had to request suspension by January 21, 1999.

22. Unfortunately, by the end of November - five months after the original U.S. request - the prospects for completing Article 21.5 panel proceedings by January 21 were becoming increasingly slim. Nonetheless, on November 19, 1998, in meetings with the Chairman of the DSB, the United States made a third proposal to reconvene the panel pursuant to Article 21.5, under an accelerated timetable that would permit a panel report to be issued before January 21.

23. From November 30 to December 3, 1998, the United States and the EC engaged in intensive discussions concerning an expedited panel procedure. These talks did not resolve the outstanding procedural issues for three principal reasons. First, the EC required as a precondition to reconvening the panel that the United States waive its right under the DSU to suspend trade concessions, i.e., forego submitting its request to the DSB between January 21 and 31, the narrow window provided for under Article 22. Second, the EC was unwilling to permit the Latin American co-complainants in the original case - Ecuador, Guatemala, Honduras and Mexico - to participate in the expedited proceeding. Third, the EC's proposed

schedule extended into June of 1999, with no date certain or provisions for the United States to obtain DSB authorization to suspend concessions.[96]

24. On January 14, 1999, the United States requested authorization to suspend concessions in the amount of $520 million under DSU Article 22.2, and placed this request on the agenda of the DSB meeting scheduled to take place on January 25, 1999.[97] Again, Article 22.6 requires that the DSB, upon request, grant authorization to suspend concessions or other obligations within 30 days of the end of the "reasonable period," unless there is a consensus not to do so.

25. Faced with this prospect, the EC responded through the unprecedented step of attempting to block the adoption of the agenda of a meeting of the Dispute Settlement Body.[98] Having delayed and obstructed the establishment of an Article 21.5 panel, the EC now insisted that such a panel process precede any request to suspend concessions under Article 22. The EC therefore demanded that the U.S. Article 22 request be stricken from the agenda before the agenda could be adopted by consensus. In the debate which took place on January 25, 1999 on adoption of the agenda, the Chairman noted,

> "In accordance with past practice and the spirit of the WTO, the consensus rule [for adopting the agenda] had never prevented the right of a government to include issues on the agenda.[99] In arguing for the adjournment of that day's meeting, the Director-General stated that several delegations including Turkey and Mexico had rightly underlined the fundamental systemic issues in the discussion, which not only concerned bananas but the entire system and its functioning. The proposal to adjourn the meeting [rather than close the meeting, the consequence of a failure to adopt the agenda] ... was the best way to oppose the idea that a few delegations could block one item on the agenda or adoption of the agenda. It was correct to oppose this by suspending the meeting ... ."[100]

Upon reconvening on January 28, 1999, the DSB adopted the agenda, and, after lengthy debate and further procedural objections by the EC spanning two days, accepted the EC's request submitted on January 29, 1999 for arbitration of the level of suspension and nullification or impairment pursuant to Article 22.[101]

26. Under Article 22.6, the arbitration panel on the level of suspension was required to complete its work within 60 days of the end of the reasonable period

[96] While the United States and the EC were also far apart on the estimated number of days it would take to complete a proceeding, it was these three EC demands that foreclosed an agreement.

[97] WT/DS27/43.

[98] *See* WT/DSB/M/54, at 3-10.

[99] *Ibid.* at 5.

[100] *Ibid.* at 8.

[101] *Ibid.* at 10-34.

of time, or March 2, 1999.[102] Because of the EC delaying tactics, the arbitrators were unable to do so. The EC hampered the arbitrators' work in several ways. First, the blocking of the DSB agenda delayed referral of the matter to the Article 22.6 arbitrators and the setting of the schedule by a full week in an already tight time frame. Second, in the arbitral proceeding, the EC insisted that the arbitrators accept its compliance as presumed, declared that the arbitrators could not enter into an inquiry on compliance, and refused until the hearing to enter into a comprehensive discussion of the merits of its regime.

27. Accordingly, on March 2, 1999, the arbitrators issued only an initial decision on matters relating to the scope of the arbitration and aspects of the methodology for determining the level of suspension of concessions.[103] The arbitrators rejected EC arguments on the relationship of DSU Articles 21.5 and 22. It also rejected the EC's claim that the Article 22 proceedings must, as a legal matter, be suspended pending completion of Article 21.5 proceedings.[104] The arbitrators stated that contrary to the EC's arguments, they were bound by Article 22 to examine whether the EC's revised regime was consistent with its WTO obligations. However, since the EC had failed to address US arguments on this issue, they stated that they were not in a position at that time to make that determination, and that they required further information from the parties to assist them before they could issue a report.[105]

28. After considering additional information submitted by the parties, the arbitrators issued their final decision on April 6, 1999, determining that the level of nullification or impairment suffered by the United States as a result of the continued EC violations is $191.4 million dollars per year.[106] The arbitrators concluded that the EC's 1998 revisions to its banana import regime continued to violate the General Agreement on Tariffs and Trade 1994 and the General Agreement on Trade in Services.[107] In particular, the arbitrators concluded that the EC's separate tariff rate quota for 857,000 tons of banana imports from ACP States is inconsistent with paragraphs 1 and 2 of GATT 1994 Article XIII, just as had the

[102] Article 22.6 provides that arbitration "*shall* be completed within 60 days after the date of expiry of the reasonable period of time." (Emphasis added.)

[103] *See* WT/DS27/48 (March 2, 1999); Decision by the Arbitrators, *EC - Bananas III (US) (Article 22.6 – EC), supra*, footnote 5, paras. 2.10 - 2.13, Parts III, IV and VI. (April 6, 1999)

[104] Decision by the Arbitrators, *EC - Bananas III (US) (Article 22.6 – EC), supra*, footnote 5, paras. 2.9, 4.11-4.15.

[105] *Ibid.*, paras. 2.11, 5.1.

[106] Decision by the Arbitrators, *EC - Bananas III (US) (Article 22.6 – EC), supra*, footnote 5, para. 8.1. The reports in the two Article 21.5 proceedings were also issued to the parties on April 6, 1999. Panel Report on *European Communities – Regime for the Importation, Sale and Distribution of Bananas - Recourse to Article 21.5 of the DSU by Ecuador* ("*EC – Bananas III (Article 21.5 – Ecuador)*"), WT/DS27/RW/ECU, 12 April 1999, DSR 1999:II, 803; Panel Report, *EC – Bananas III (Article 21.5 – EC), supra,* footnote 40.

[107] The arbitrators concluded that the EC's regime violated *paras.* 1 and 2 of GATT 1994 Article XIII, and GATS Articles II and XVII. Decision by the Arbitrators, *EC - Bananas III (US) (Article 22.6 – EC), supra*, footnote 5, paras. 5.17, 5.33, 5.97.

original combined allocations amounting to 857,000 tons which the revised regime replaced.[108] The arbitrators similarly found that the revised regime's licensing provisions had the effect of carrying over the previous discrimination against U.S. service suppliers originally found to violate the GATS.[109] Thus, U.S. benefits had continued to be nullified and impaired, without interruption.

29. The arbitrators thus concluded that what the EC now characterizes as a "completely new set of rules[110] for its bananas regime was in great part a repackaging of those very same elements which the panel and Appellate Body originally found inconsistent with the EC's WTO obligations, and which the EC had eventually committed to bring into compliance by the end of the reasonable period of time. In fact, comments by senior EC officials after both the initial and final decisions made clear that the EC had long understood that its revisions to the banana import regime continued to violate its WTO obligations. For example, External Relations Commissioner Sir Leon Brittan stated following the March 2 initial decision that the arbitrators' request to the United States for a new damage estimate meant that the WTO arbitrators would likely find that damages amounted to between $200 and $300 million – an apparent acknowledgement that the EC's violation continued.[111] More blunt were the comments of Industry Commissioner Bangemann, who admitted that while he had been forced to defend the EC's position, it was groundless.[112]

30. In light of the schedule provided for in DSU Article 22.6, the United States undertook contingency plans to suspend concessions in early March in accordance with the arbitrators' award and DSU rules. As a legal matter, the DSU envisages redress as of the end of the reasonable period of time.[113] This meant that as of the expiration of the reasonable period of time on January 1, 1999, the EC was no longer permitted to deny U.S. benefits with impunity. U.S. plans were based on this assumption. Nevertheless, the United States intended to apply any authorized suspension only after the date on which the DSU required the arbitrators to complete their work, March 2, 1999.

[108] *Ibid.*, paras. 5.33, 5.97.

[109] In addition, the Panel concluded that the EC's country-specific quota allocations to substantial suppliers is inconsistent with GATT 1994 Article XIII:2, and that the criteria for acquiring "newcomer" status under the EC's revised licensing procedures accord U.S. service suppliers *de facto* less favorable treatment than is accorded to EC service suppliers in violation of Article XVII of GATS Decision by the Arbitrators, *EC - Bananas III (US) (Article 22.6 – EC), supra*, footnote 5, paras. 5.33, 5.95, 5.97. The arbitrators reached the same conclusions in their capacity as Article 21.5 panelists. Panel Report, *EC – Bananas III (Article 21.5 – Ecuador), supra*, footnote 106, paras. 6.160 - 6.163 (12 April 1999).

[110] First Written Submission of the European Communities, para. 4.

[111] *See Inside U.S. Trade*, March 12, 1999, at 3.

[112] A newspaper report indicated that Commissioner Bangemann welcomed the arbitrators' decision against the EC, and quoted him as stating, "As a commissioner, I've had to defend our position. But I can tell you it's bullshit." *The Wall Street Journal Europe*, 22 April 1999, at 1.

[113] This legal issue is discussed further in Section IV.A *infra*.

31. Because EC delaying tactics prevented the arbitrators from completing their work by the March 2, 1999 date called for under the DSU time frame, the United States took steps to preserve its ability to suspend concessions as from that date. Accordingly, the United States announced on March 3, 1999 that the U.S. Customs Service would review the sufficiency of bonds on certain EC merchandise entered on or after March 3, 1999 to ensure that any duties ultimately authorized by the arbitrators could be assessed on those entries. Since any duties which might be assessed would be equal to 100% of the appraised value of the merchandise, the U.S. Customs Service began requiring a single transaction bond equal to the entered value of the merchandise, or a "continuous bond" covering multiple entries equal to 10% of the total entered value of the covered merchandise imported by a particular importer over the previous year.[114] This requirement did not actually assess duties, nor did it prejudge the amount of the total value of the products which would be assessed higher duties.

32. U.S. importers are required to deposit estimated duties at the time of entry; in the event that additional duties or fees are due, Customs is required to collect these on liquidation, that is, when Customs makes the final determination of the rate and amount of duty.[115] Entry procedures in the United States permit timely or immediate release of goods into the United States. Since liquidation of an entry usually is performed after the goods are in the stream of commerce, bonding is required in order to guarantee the payment of these additional duties or fees.

33. The Customs Service requires single transaction bonds or continuous bonds for entries of merchandise as a matter of course. As a rule, all entries must be accompanied by evidence that a bond is posted with Customs to cover any potential duties, taxes, and charges that may accrue. Pursuant to its regulatory authority,[116] a port director may require additional bonding or additional security in order to ensure that the acceptance of an entry will be adequately protected against any duties or other liabilities imposed by law. In this case it was necessary to impose additional bonding requirements to ensure that 100% ad valorem duties would be paid if assessed as a result of DSB authorization. Thus, Customs on March 3 required an increase in the amount of the bond required for the goods that could possibly be subject to the imposition of the 100% tariff rate.

34. The increased bonding requirement constituted the only legal action taken by the United States on March 3, 1999. While press announcements referred to "withholding liquidation," no special legal significance can be attributed to this term. Entries of merchandise are deemed liquidated by law one year from the date of entry unless liquidation is either extended or suspended as required by

---

[114] Memorandum to Customs Area and Port Directors, CMC Directors From Director, Trade Compliance Division, U.S. Customs Service, Regarding European Sanctions (March 3, 1999).

[115] 19 U.S.C. § 1505.

[116] 19 Code of Federal Regulations § 113.13.

statute or court order.[117] Customs may liquidate an entry at any time within that year. However, in order to preserve administrative flexibility and to allow sufficient time for review of entries before the final determination of duties upon liquidation, Customs does not normally initiate the liquidation of an entry until the 314th day after the date of entry.[118] The reference to "withholding liquidation" merely indicated that Customs would not take action outside of its normal administrative procedure, i.e., would not initiate liquidation prior to the 314th day. In fact, no changes were made in Customs procedures as a result of the announced intention to "withhold liquidation."

35. On April 19, 1999, following DSB authorization to suspend concessions in accordance with the Article 22.6 arbitrators award, the United States published notice that it would actually assess 100% duties on a subset of the products previously indicated on March 3, 1999. The reduced list conformed with the level of nullification and impairment which the arbitrators determined, $191.4 million. Duties on the other products on the March 3 list are to be assessed in accordance with the usual, MFN rates set forth in the Harmonized Tariff Schedule of the United States.

IV. LEGAL ARGUMENT

A. *The March 3 Review of Bonding Requirements Was Not Inconsistent With DSU Article 22.6 and GATT Articles I, II, XI and VIII.*

36. The EC asserts that the action taken on March 3, 1999 constitutes a suspension of concessions or other obligations during the pendency of a proceeding under Article 22.6, in violation of that article.[119] The EC also claims that the U.S. action taken on March 3, 1999 is inconsistent with Articles I, II, XI and VIII of the General Agreement on Tariffs and Trade 1994.[120]

37. The Panel should reject these claims because the EC was liable for its nullification or impairment of U.S. benefits immediately after the conclusion of the "reasonable period of time," that is, after January 1, 1999. Because the EC objected to the level of suspension proposed, that level required confirmation by an Article 22.6 arbitral panel. Nevertheless, the liability itself, once confirmed by the DSB, extended from the end of the reasonable period. As a matter of policy, the United States chose to apply duties on entries from March 3, 1999, 60 days later, as this was the date by which the DSU required the Article 22.6 arbitrators

---

[117] 19 U.S.C. § 1504(a).

[118] *See* Memorandum dated May 26, 1997, file number ENT-1 FO:TC:C:E AD to all interested parties, http://www.cebb.customs.treas.gov/public/cgi/cebb.exe?mode=fi&area=13&name=T-ENTRY5.TXT

[119] EC First Written Submission, paras. 13-15.

[120] EC First Written Submission, paras. 16-17.

to complete their work. In reviewing th e sufficiency of bonds posted for entries from March 3, 1999, the Customs Service did no more than preserve the U.S. ability to assess duties in accordance with the determination of the Article 22.6 arbitrators upon authorization of the DSB.

38. That authorization was granted on April 19, 1999. The DSB agreed to grant authorization to suspend the application of concessions to the European Communities and its member States of tariff concessions and related obligations under GATT 1994, consistent with the decision of the arbitrators contained in document WT/DS27/ARB.[121] As the United States noted at the April 19 DSB meeting,[122] the arbitrators were silent with regard to the specific date for the suspension of concessions, referring only to the maximum amount of $191.4 million per year.

39. The provisions of the DSU also are silent on the specific date for the application of the suspension of concessions. DSU Article 22.7 states only that the request for suspension must be consistent with the arbitrators' decision.[123] While the DSU itself is silent on the date on which DSB-authorized suspension may be applied, the context and purpose of the provisions on suspension of concessions make clear that this date may fall at any time after the expiration of the reasonable period.

40. A violation of WTO rules upsets the balance of rights and obligations agreed to by WTO Members. While this effect on the balance of rights and obligations is immediate, WTO dispute settlement procedures permit the resulting nullification or impairment of a Member's benefits to continue until the adoption of DSB rulings and recommendations. Even then, DSU Article 21.3 provides a non-complying party with a further "reasonable period of time" to bring its measure into compliance, *if* immediate compliance is not practicable. Inasmuch as the complaining Member's rights continue to be violated and benefits impaired during the pendency of the "reasonable period," that period is to be the shortest period possible within the non-complying Member's domestic legal system to bring its measure into compliance.[124]

41. Recognizing that governments may in some cases need time to complete domestic processes, the DSU tolerates continued nullification and impairment during the pendency of dispute settlement proceedings and the reasonable period of time which follows. However, that tolerance ends upon the completion of the

---

[121] WT/DSB/M/59.

[122] *Ibid.*

[123] Article 22.7 provides, in relevant part, "The DSB shall be informed promptly of the decision of the arbitrator and shall upon request, grant authorization to suspend concessions or other obligations where the request is consistent with the decision of the arbitrator, unless the DSB decides by consensus to reject the request."

[124] Award of the Arbitrator, *EC Measures Concerning meat and Meat Products (Hormones) - Arbitration under Article 21.3(c) of the DSU* ("*EC – Hormones*"), WT/DS26/15, WT/DS48/13, 29 May 1998, DSR 1998:V, 1833, para. 26.

reasonable period. DSU Article 22.1 explains that the suspension of concessions or other obligations is available "in the event that the recommendations and rulings [of the DSB] are not implemented within a reasonable period of time." A reasonable period of time is available only to Members which commit to implement DSB rulings and recommendations, and a failure to fulfill this commitment compounds the continued impairment of the other Member's benefits inherent in the original violation. At that point, a Member must bear the consequences of its failure to comply, and it becomes potentially liable for its continued impairment, subject only to DSB authorization and the confirmation of the Article 22.6 arbitral panel, if any, to which the matter may have been referred.

42. DSU Article 3.2 provides that the WTO dispute settlement system "serves to preserve the rights and obligations of Members under the covered agreements." The system achieves this purpose in part by ensuring that there are consequences for violations of another Member' s rights, in the form of compensation or suspension of concessions. This purpose would be undermined were a non-complying Member not subject to the consequences of non-compliance at the end of the reasonable period, but instead only from completion of proceedings confirming that it has continued to nullify or impair another Member's benefits. Indeed, the latter interpretation would create a perverse incentive for a non-complying Member to seek to delay completion of those proceedings.

43. This, in fact, is precisely what occurred in the Article 22.6 arbitration in *Bananas*. Beyond delaying the referral of the matter to the arbitral panel,[125] the EC initially refused to address the arguments raised by the United States in its submissions concerning the consistency of the EC's revised regime with the WTO Agreements. This forced the Panel to accompany its initial decision of March 2, 1999 with a request to the EC to respond to the U.S. arguments by March 15, 1999, since this was "necessary for [the panel] to complete [its] task.[126] In its final report, the arbitrators explained, "At our request, the European Communities responded to the US arguments.[127] Thus, the EC sought to exploit for delaying purposes precisely the interpretation it advocates in this case, that any suspension of concessions be applied only following completion of Article 22.6 proceedings.

44. While DSU rules subjected the EC to potential liability for nullification or impairment of U.S. benefits from January 2, 1999, the end of the reasonable period of time, the United States chose as a matter of policy to apply any DSB-authorized duties only from March 3, 1999, one day after the date provided for in DSU rules for the Article 22.6 panel to complete its calculation of the level of nullification or impairment (sixty days following the end of the reasonable period of time). Any further delay in applying duties after March 2 would reward the EC

[125] *See* WT/DSB/M/54, at 3-10; *supra* paras. 24-25.

[126]); Decision by the Arbitrators, *EC - Bananas III (US) (Article 22.6 – EC)*, *supra*, footnote 5, para. 2.11.

[127] *Ibid.*, para. 5.1.

for its efforts to delay the arbitrators' work. It would also contribute to the perception that the WTO dispute settlement system would be plagued by the very same deficiency which ruined the credibility of GATT dispute settlement - namely, that non-complying parties could obstruct multilateral action to impose consequences for non-compliance.

45. When, ultimately, the EC succeeded in delaying the work of the Article 22.6 panel, the U.S. acted only to preserve its ability to apply any duties ultimately authorized by the DSB from March 3, 1999. Again, by increasing bonding requirements for entries on or after March 3, the Customs Service merely placed itself in a position to suspend concessions on these entries upon DSB authorization. It did not actually assess those duties.

B. The EC Has Not Demonstrated that the March 3 Review is Inconsistent With DSU Article 23, and Has Not Asserted a Violation of DSU Article 3.

46. The EC asserts at paragraphs 18-22 of its First Written Submission that the March 3 review of bonding requirements was inconsistent with paragraphs 1 and 2 of Article 23 of the DSU, as well as DSU Article 3. It is difficult to respond to the EC's vague arguments with respect to Article 23 inasmuch as the EC never identifies either the precise obligations in question or how the March 3 review was inconsistent with those obligations.

47. The EC refers to the "timing," "amount" and "total disregard of WTO procedures" which the U.S. measure allegedly involved, but, as explained above, the March 3 review did no more than preserve the ability of the United States to assess duties from that date if, as ultimately occurred, the Article 22.6 arbitrators were to confirm that the EC was continuing to nullify or impair U.S. WTO benefits. As described above, the EC was potentially liable for this continued nullification or impairment from the conclusion of the reasonable period of time on January 1, 1999. The March 3 review of bonding requirements did not actually assess duties, nor did it prejudge the total value of the products which would be assessed duties. These decisions were made in April as a result of, and in accordance with, WTO procedures authorizing the suspension of concessions.

48. Likewise, the EC presents only the vaguest outline of an argument with respect to DSU Article 3. It asserts no violation, but only that the March 3 review undermines the "objectives under Article 3," namely "providing security and predictability." Indeed, no violation of this provision is possible, since it is descriptive, not prescriptive. Inasmuch as the EC asserts no violation, the United States notes only that the U.S. decision on March 3 to preserve its ability to assess duties from that date came in response to an extended series of EC actions which posed a genuine and serious threat to the authority and credibility of the WTO dispute settlement system. In its very first WTO dispute settlement loss, the EC not only refused to comply, but refused to state clearly at the outset that this was in fact the course of action it intended to pursue, as it was required to under DSU Article 21.3. Even now it continues to represent the cosmetic changes it made to

its banana import regime as "a completely new set of rules.[128] Moreover, the EC repeatedly thwarted U.S. efforts to resort to DSU procedures under DSU Articles 21.5 and 22 to address the EC's failure to comply, going so far as to block the adoption of the agenda of the January 25, 1999 DSB meeting in order to avoid the automatic authorization for suspension of concessions which DSU Article 22 guarantees.[129] Far from undermining the authority of the WTO dispute settlement system, as the EC charges, the U.S. response to the EC provided assurances that WTO dispute settlement would not, like the GATT, be hamstrung by the efforts of non-complying parties to avoid the consequences of their non-compliance.

49. Finally, the EC makes the inaccurate and irrelevant claim that the United States was required under Sections 301-310 to implement action on March 3, 1999. The March 3 review of bonding requirements was not made pursuant to Section 301, nor was the United States required under U.S. law to take this step. Rather, as explained above, the U.S. decision to review bonding requirements was undertaken as a matter of policy to preserve the ability of the United States to assess duties from that date if, as ultimately occurred, the Article 22.6 arbitrators were to confirm that the EC's liability for continuing to nullify and impair U.S. WTO benefits.

C. The EC Has Failed to Demonstrate that the March 3 Review Violates DSU Article 21.5.

50. The EC resurrects its argument that DSU Article 21.5 required the United States to first seek a panel under that provision before requesting authorization to suspend concessions pursuant to Article.[130] The Panel should reject the EC's argument for the same reasons that the arbitrators conducting the Article 22.6 proceeding and the Article 21.5 panels brought by Ecuador and the EC rejected the same argument.[131]

51. Article 22 does not by its terms, context or purpose require that a Member first resort to Article 21.5 proceedings. All time frames in Article 22 are measured against the end of the reasonable period of time, and Article 21.5 is not even mentioned once. Likewise, Article 21.5 is not mentioned at all in Article 23.2(c), which only requires that Article 22 proceedings be pursued before suspension of concessions may be undertaken. Article 22 represents a central element in the credibility and effectiveness of WTO dispute settlement, since it provides that non-complying Members may no longer block suspension of concessions against them. However, the EC's claim that Article 21.5 proceedings must first be completed would deprive prevailing parties of this right to suspend concessions since

[128] EC First Written Submission, para. 4.
[129] *See supra* paras. 24-25.
[130] *See* EC First Written Submission, paras. 23-29.
[131] The United States notes that the EC made the same arguments before the panel in Panel Report, *US – Section 301*, *supra*, footnote 9.

Article 22 only applies the negative consensus rule to requests to suspend concessions if such requests are made within 30 days of the conclusion of the reasonable period. Members whose rights have already been found to have been violated, and who have already lived with these violations through the year-and-a-half panel process and additional year of implementation, would find themselves, as they were under the GATT 1947, again at the mercy of the very party that had denied their rights and impaired their trade. The EC argument on "sequencing" was rejected in January 1999 for these reasons and must be rejected again by this Panel.[132]

52. Moreover, in response to the concern that there must first be a multilateral determination of violation, we note that, as the Article 22 arbitrators found, Article 22 proceedings cannot result in suspension of concessions where a Member has in fact brought its measure into compliance, because the level of nullification and impairment in that case would be zero.[133]

53. The EC asserts in paragraph 28 of its submission that the United States had already "unilaterally determined" that the EC violated WTO rules "well before the conclusion of the 'reasonable period of time' and at a time when not all the EC measures necessary to implement recommendations and rulings of the DSB had yet been adopted by the competent EC institutions.[134]

54. These EC arguments ring particularly hollow in light of its efforts to thwart the establishment of an Article 21.5 panel to address its July 1998 revisions to its banana regime. The EC impeded every attempt by the United States and other complaining parties to have the EC 's revised regime reviewed by a multilateral Article 21.5 panel. The United States asked the EC on a monthly basis between July and November 1998 to reconvene the original panel; each time the EC either refused or insisted on conditions that would have required the United States to waive its WTO rights.[135]

55. In response to the EC claim that it had not yet completed implementation, we note that the July 1998 regulation provided for a separate tariff rate quota for 857,000 tons of banana imports from African, Caribbean and Pacific States, a provision which the Article 22 Arbitrators and Article 21.5 panel ultimately con-

---

[132] In addition, the Panel should not reach this issue because doing so would preempt the ongoing DSU review negotiations and encroach upon the rights of *all* WTO Members (not just parties to a single dispute) to negotiate the balance of rights and obligations under the WTO Agreement. Only the Members may amend or adopt interpretations of the DSU (WTO Agreement Arts. IX:2 and X), and Panels cannot add to or diminish the rights and obligations provided in the covered agreements (DSU Arts. 3.2 and 19.2). The results of the Third Ministerial Conference action on the DSU review are likely to lead to amendment of DSU provisions including Article 21.5.

[133] *See* Decision by the Arbitrators, *EC - Bananas III (US) (Article 22.6 – EC)*, *supra*, footnote 5, para. 4.11.

[134] EC First Written Submission, para. 28.

[135] *See supra* paras. 18-23.

cluded is inconsistent with paragraphs 1 and 2 of GATT 1994 Article XIII.[136] As the EC explains,[137] the EC regulation providing for this TRQ "entered into force on July 31, 1998 and was applicable from January 1, 1999." Likewise, the EC's July decision to adopt a reference period of 1994 -1996 was the central element in the arbitrators' conclusion that the revised banana regime continued to violate the GATS.[138] Under well-established GATT and WTO panel precedent, a panel may find a measure inconsistent with GATT or WTO rules if the measure mandates such a violation at some point in the future.[139] An early Article 21.5 review of the July TRQ and choice of reference period would thus have been fully consistent with GATT and WTO jurisprudence, and would also have made clear to the EC that its implementation was deficient before the time to make further adjustments had expired. Instead, the EC sought to delay and to characterize as "unilateral determinations" attempts by the U.S. to resolve this matter through DSU proceedings.

56. The March 3 review of the sufficiency of bonds in no way violates Article 21.5, and the Panel should reject this claim.

V. CONCLUSION

57. For the above reasons, the United States respectfully requests that the Panel reject the EC's claims in their entirety, and find that the action taken by the United States on March 3 is not inconsistent with DSU Articles 3, 21.5, 22.6 or 23, nor with GATT 1994 Articles I, II, XI or VIII. Beyond failing to meet its burden of demonstrating any actual violations, the EC is seeking a result that would reward it for its efforts to deny the United States the possibility of prompt resort to Article 22 procedures, and would inequitably permit the EC to postpone liability for its failure to use the reasonable period of time to come into compliance.

---

[136] Decision by the Arbitrators, *EC - Bananas III (US) (Article 22.6 – EC)*, *supra*, footnote 5, paras. 5.17, 5.96; Panel Report, *EC – Bananas III (Article 21.5 – Ecuador)*, *supra*, footnote 106, para. 6.160.

[137] First Written Submission of the European Communities, para. 3.

[138] Decision by the Arbitrators, *EC - Bananas III (US) (Article 22.6 – EC)*, *supra*, footnote 5, para. 5.78.

[139] Panel Report on United States - Taxes on Petroleum and Certain Imported Substances, adopted 17 June 1987, BISD 34S/136, 159-60, para. 5.2.2 ("U.S. - Superfund").

Appendix 2.2
The US Oral Presentation at the First Substantive Meeting
(16 December 1999)

Introduction

1. Mr. Chairman, members of the Panel, it is my honor to represent the United States before you today. I will keep my remarks brief. Let me start by responding to two gross factual errors by the EC in their statement today. The EC is correct in saying that the facts in this dispute are simple, but they have the wrong so-called "facts." First, contrary to what we just heard, *no* duties were raised on March 3. The EC has provided no evidence to support their claim, nor can they. Second, the March 3rd action was not based on, and had nothing to do with, Section 306. Again, the EC has provided no evidence to show this. I will come back to this briefly at the end of my statement.

2. Mr. Chairman, members of the Panel, we are here now because the European Communities ("EC") found itself in the embarrassing position of failing to comply with its WTO obligations in the *Bananas* dispute, the first WTO Member to do so (a dubious accomplishment which the EC has since repeated in another dispute). The EC's embarrassment was compounded by its very vocal protestations of having complied, and of being the victim of improper accusations of non-compliance, protestations found baseless by the Article 22 arbitrator and Article 21.5 panel in *Bananas*. The EC's response to this situation has been to bring this case in order to continue to portray itself as a victim, and as the defender of dispute settlement procedures. This position is remarkable, in that it was the EC's refusal to abide by those DSU procedures and their attempt to "game" them for the purpose of delay which created the crisis that confronted WTO Members earlier this year. And now the EC has invoked those same dispute settlement procedures to challenge the United States March 3rd action in an effort to seek approval of the EC's own delaying tactics.

3. The U.S. March 3rd action consisted of reviewing the sufficiency of importer bonds for certain EC imports. The review was intended to ensure that the United States would be in a position to collect duties which might be authorized by the DSB, in accordance with DSU rules and time frames. The U.S. March 3rd action was consistent with U.S. rights and obligations, and enhanced, rather than undermined, the credibility of WTO dispute settlement procedures in light of the EC's obligation to have brought its measures into compliance as of January 1, 1999, and in light of the U.S. right under the DSU to a decision by the Article 22 arbitrator no later than March 2, 1999.

The Entry System of the United States and the Risk Created by the EC's Non-Compliance

4. I would first like to review the operation of the U.S. system for entering merchandise. It is our understanding that the EC is not challenging this system.

As contemplated by Article 13 of the *Agreement on Implementation of Article VII of the General Agreement on Tariffs and Trade 1994* – the "Customs Valuation Agreement" – the United States has long employed a surety system which allows for the early release of merchandise into the United States. Rather than holding merchandise for the days, weeks or months which might be required to confirm a product's proper valuation or classification, or an importer's compliance with all administrative formalities, the United States Customs Service allows virtually immediate release of merchandise into the United States – often in a matter of hours – so long as the importer has provided minimal information on the entry, as well as assurances in the form of a cash deposit or bond that it will pay the potential duties and fees owed. Those assurances are necessary to address the risks assumed by Customs, which no longer controls the merchandise and thus has no recourse against it, that the full amount of duties and fees owed might not ultimately be paid.

5. The EC's persistent breach of its WTO obligations in the *Bananas* dispute and its failure to provide adequate compensation meant that EC imports would, upon DSB authorization, be subject to suspension of tariff concessions in the amount of the nullification or impairment of U.S. benefits, and existing bonds therefore might not prove adequate. The EC thus created a new risk for the United States concerning its ability to collect the full amount of duties which might be due.

6. The March 3 review of bond sufficiency addressed this risk. In increasing the bonding levels, the United States did not suspend any concessions – it did not assess duties, nor did it pre-judge the total value of imports which might be assessed higher duties as a result of DSB authorization. The United States did not decide to assess higher duties, and did not decide which imports would be assessed these duties, until DSB authorization on April 19, 1999. We note that these April 19 decisions are not within the terms of reference of this Panel, however. The Panel's terms of reference examine the action taken on one day, March 3, 1999.

The EC's Liability for Its Non-Compliance

7. The United States decision to increase bonding levels on March 3 reflected its attempt to preserve its ability to apply any DSB-authorized suspension of concessions from that date. The choice of that date was made based on the schedule provided for in the DSU. March 3 fell 61 days after the EC's "reasonable period of time" for compliance expired, and is the day after an Article 22.6 arbitral panel was required under that provision to complete its work on whether the proposed level of suspension was equivalent to the level of nullification or impairment to U.S. benefits.

8. While the United States had decided not to apply any DSB-authorized suspension prior to March 3, the EC's liability for its continued nullification or impairment of U.S. benefits in fact accrued from January 2, the day after the reasonable period of time expired. As explained in the U.S. submission, the DSU

tolerates the ongoing nullification or impairment by one Member of another Member's benefits through the initial panel proceedings and adoption of DSB rulings and recommendations, as well as through a "reasonable period of time" for compliance when a Member is unable to comply immediately. However, this tolerance ends at the conclusion of the reasonable period of time. As Article 22.1 explains, suspension of concessions is then available. Indeed, there would be little logic to designating a "reasonable period of time" for compliance – and little meaning to the requirement that the Member be in compliance by the end of the period – if a Member were entitled to continue its breach well beyond the reasonable period without consequences. The absence of such consequences would invite the very delaying tactics the EC employed to such effect in the *Bananas* dispute.

9. As outlined in detail in the U.S. submission, the EC record of non-compliance and delay in connection with its banana import regime extends back for years, and continued through the reasonable period (and in fact persists even now, almost 8 months after the arbitrator's conclusions). The EC refused to consult with the United States and other complaining parties before deciding on revisions to its banana regime, ignored explanations from the complaining parties as to how the revisions would remain inconsistent with EC obligations and prevented the early formation of an Article 21.5 panel to confirm this non-compliance. The EC next took the extraordinary step of seeking to block adoption of the agenda of the January 1999 DSB meeting at which the U.S. request to suspend concessions was to be considered. After delaying adoption of the agenda and referral of the question of the level of suspension to an Article 22.6 arbitrator, it then refused to engage U.S. arguments on its continued nullification and impairment of U.S. benefits. As a result, the panel was unable to complete its work by its DSU-mandated March 2 deadline.

10. The EC's concerted effort at delay demonstrated its lack of respect for DSU procedures and the DSU admonition to seek mutually satisfactory solutions, and threatened to undermine the very authority and credibility of the DSU itself. The EC's actions recalled its efforts under the GATT 1947 to obstruct adverse panel proceedings, and raised doubts among many that WTO dispute settlement procedures would live up to their initial promise. The United States action of March 3 was a measured response intended to make clear that the EC's efforts at delay would not be rewarded. By ensuring that the U.S. Customs Service would be in a position to collect DSB-authorized duties from March 3, it reaffirmed that the new WTO dispute settlement system, unlike the old GATT system, could not be gamed to avoid compliance or the consequences of non-compliance.

11. I would now like to further address several errors in the EC's oral statement. First, as discussed earlier, the March 3rd action did not increase duties on EC products. The EC states at paragraph 6(a) of its oral statement that, as a result of the March 3rd action, "the importer was bound to pay the (prohibitive) increased duty at the time of liquidation of the customs debt." This is simply incorrect. The United States did not require additional duties on any entries until April 19, following DSB authorization. Likewise, in paragraph 6(c), the EC incorrectly

states that the March 3rd action prevented the immediate liquidation of any customs debt. The March 3rd action had no impact on the timing of liquidation. Under U.S. law, there is no right to immediate liquidation. Customs' normal liquidation cycle is 314 days, and importers would not have received liquidation before then.

12. The EC also at various points in its statement raises arguments with respect to the relationship between Articles 21.5 and 22 of the DSU. I ask that this Panel decline, as have all prior panels and arbitrators and the General Council, to endorse the EC's erroneous view of the relationship between DSU Articles 21.5 and 22. I would be happy to address any questions the Panel may have with respect to the specific examples cited in the EC submission. Finally, with respect to Section 301, I would like to reiterate the point made earlier that neither this provision nor others in the related legislation served as the basis for the March 3rd action. I am surprised that the EC appears to be saying that it knows better than the United States the legal basis for U.S. domestic legal action. Further, the EC persists in several misunderstandings concerning the Section 301 statute, which is surprising in light of the fact that we have just completed a lengthy panel process in which the details of the operation of this statute were addressed at length. The report of that panel will be issued shortly.

Conclusion

13. The EC is correct in asserting that this dispute involves the authority and credibility of the WTO dispute settlement system, and the actions of one Member which undermined that authority. That Member is the EC. The Panel should reject the EC's attempt to seek approval through this proceeding for its efforts to delay and obstruct the operations of the DSU.

Appendix 2.3

The US closing remarks at the First Substantive Meeting (17 December 1999)

1. Mr. Chairman, members of the Panel, I will not recount here again the long series of actions by the EC which have shown their disrespect for WTO dispute settlement procedures, except to note that it is at odds with their current claims to be the defender of the DSU.

2. Having said that, I would like to clarify again the precise nature of the action taken on March 3, 1999. That action consisted solely of reviewing the bonding requirements on certain EC imports. Nothing more. That action did not itself assess duties on these entries. No action was taken in that regard until April 19.

3. We note that the EC in its closing statement just now has for the first time raised this matter relating to the terms of reference of this Panel. I am reading the EC's panel request and that request indicated that the measure was the decision, effective March 3, concerning withholding liquidation, contingent liabilities and bonding. In other words, this is what it understood to be the actions taken on March 3, 1999. Given that the EC is raising this issue relating to the terms of reference at this late stage in the proceeding, we may need to return to the Panel for a preliminary ruling.

4. Thank you very much.

Appendix 2.4
The US Responses to Questions of Panel and Parties
(13 January 2000)

Q1: Assuming that an importer wished to clear through the US customs on 4 March 1999 a tonne of "Uncoated felt paper and paperboard in rolls or sheets" (US HTS 4805 50 00) originating in Switzerland, what would have been the duty liability for such import on that date? What would be the answer if such a product originated in the EC?

1. The duty liability would have been based on a "free" rate of duty, regardless of whether the product originated in Switzerland or an EC Member State.

Q2: Assuming that an importer wished to clear through the US customs on 4 March 1999 a tonne of "Sweet biscuits, waffles and wafers" (US HTS 1905 30 00) originating in Switzerland, what would have been the requirements on that date (in particular with regard to the amount to be guaranteed) with regard to the posting of a security (bond) for an individual importation or concerning the commitment of a general security (continuous bond)? What would be the answer had this situation occurred concerning such a product originating in the EC?

2. Assuming a commercial formal entry was filed, a bond would have been required. The bond could have been guaranteed by a surety or by a deposit of cash in lieu of a surety. The bond could have been a continuous entry bond or a single entry bond.

3. An importer of the Swiss-origin product would have been required to post either:

(a) a single transaction bond in the amount of three times the entered value of the merchandise, or

(b) a continuous bond in the amount of 10% of the duties, taxes and fees paid by the importer of record for all products during the calendar year preceding the date of the bond application, but in no case less than $50,000.

4. An importer of such goods originating in a Member State of the European Communities not listed in the Customs instruction[140] would have been subject to the requirements listed above. An importer of such listed goods would have been required to post either:

(a) a single transaction bond in the amount of three times the entered value of the merchandise; or

[140] *See* U.S. Exhibit 7 and EC Annex VIII.

(b) a continuous bond in the amount of 10% of the entered value of the covered merchandise which the importer imported during the previous year.

5. The amount of the single transaction bond for the above product was three times the entered value because it was subject to additional requirements of the U.S. Food and Drug Administration relating to public health or safety. Merchandise not subject to such other agency requirements would have been subject to the following single transaction bond requirements:

Product not on list: a single transaction bond in the amount of the entered value of the merchandise plus any duties, taxes and fees for the entry;

Product on list: a single transaction bond in the amount of the entered value of the merchandise.

Q3: What is the relevant date under US customs law on which the customs debt is incurred (in order to determine the duty applicable to imports of a product):

- **the date of physical importation or**
- **the date of the final liquidation of the customs debt or**
- **any other date?**

6. Liability for payment of duties is incurred at the time the goods arrive on a vessel within a Customs port when there is an intent to unlade the goods at that port, or, if arrival is otherwise than by vessel, at the time of arrival within the Customs territory of the United States. The applicable rate of duty is the rate for the date the merchandise was entered for consumption or for immediate transportation of goods from one U.S. port to another (so that Customs documentation can be submitted at the latter port).

Q4: What is the US customs practice in this regard in case of a duty decreasing over time as a result, for example, of the US obligations under a WTO Agreement? Does the US customs practice differ in case of a duty increasing over time as a result, for example, of a US action in application of a trade defence instrument?

7. As indicated in the previous paragraph, the duty ultimately paid is that applicable for the date of entry. Hence, it would not be relevant that a duty might decrease at some point after that date - unless the decrease were made effective from that date or earlier. The practice would not differ for a duty increase.

Q5: In the light of the answers to the previous questions, can the US explain what is the meaning of its statement made in the oral submission of 16 December 1999 (paragraphs 3, 4 and 5) where it refers initially to "potential duties ... owed" as a result of the "risk created by the EC's non-compliance" and then that "the March 3 review of bond sufficiency addressed this risk"? What was this "potential risk" on 3 March 1999?

8. As explained in the U.S. First Submission at paragraphs 37-42 and the U.S. Oral Statement at paragraphs 7-8, the EC's liability for its failure to bring its measure into compliance by the conclusion of the reasonable period of time extended from that date. The EC's failure to comply with the DSB's rulings and recommendations meant that EC Members' imports into the United States after that date would potentially be subject to the application of duties in excess of bound rates, subject to confirmation by the Article 22 arbitrator and authorization by the DSB. There was a risk that the arbitrator would, as turned out to be the case, confirm that the level of nullification or impairment was above zero (that the EC was failing to comply) and that the DSB would accordingly authorize the suspension of concessions. From the perspective of the United States Customs Service, the resulting risk was that bonds on entries from March 3 would not be sufficient to cover the higher duties (100% *ad valorem*) which would be due if the suspension were authorized, in the event that the importers would not pay the additional duties at liquidation. The United States increased bonding levels to ensure that such duties, if any, could be collected.

Q6: Assuming *arguendo* the existence of such a risk, what was the basis for the US to take action as from 3 March 1999 in the absence of a multilateral determination on the EC revised banana regime?

9. The basis for action was the need to ensure that all duties could be collected on entries of goods released into the United States, and thus beyond Customs' control. The EC presumably would not have had Customs hold the merchandise until completion of the Article 22 proceedings it was working to delay.

10. As noted previously,[141] the revised bonding requirements did not actually impose higher duties. The U.S. action imposing higher duties came on April 19, 1999, following the arbitrator's multilateral determination and the DSB's multilateral authorization. In the absence of the arbitrator's determination, DSB authorization and the U.S. April 19 action, the duties payable on each and every entry subject to the revised bonding requirements would have been at the applied, MFN rate. Thus, the EC incorrectly asserts that the March 3 action deprived importers of the right to import products at bound rates.[142]

Q7: Is the withholding of the suspension of liquidation (including the bond requirement) a suspension of concessions or other obligations under the DSU?

11. We wish to emphasize again that the only action taken on March 3 was the change of bonding requirements on certain entries. As we noted at paragraph 34 of the U.S. First Submission, no action was taken with respect to "withholding" or "suspending" liquidation, notwithstanding press statements on this point. En-

[141] *See* U.S. First Submission, paras. 31, 45; U.S. Oral Statement, paras. 6.

[142] *See* EC Oral Statement, para. 7.

tries on and after March 3 were subject to precisely the same liquidation cycle as those prior to March 3, that is, they were scheduled for liquidation between 314 days and one year following entry.[143] The normal 314-day liquidation cycle allows adequate time for all information relating to entries (testing analysis and results, submission by importers of corrected or supplemental information, verification of information) to be collected and to allow the proper ascertainment of the value and classification of entered merchandise. The normal 314-day liquidation cycle employed in the United States is not within the terms of reference of this dispute.[144]

12. Likewise the ordinary bonding requirements associated with surety systems are not within the terms of reference of this dispute. Such bonding requirements applied to entries both before and after March 3, 1999. They were, and continue to be, applicable to *every* commercial formal entry of merchandise into the United States, regardless of origin. Article 13 of the *Agreement on Implementation of Article VII of the General Agreement on Tariffs and Trade 1994* - the "Customs Valuation Agreement" - specifically contemplates the use of surety systems which allow for the early release of merchandise.[145] The alternative to the U.S. surety system would be the far more trade-restrictive approach of holding the merchandise for the days, weeks or months necessary to confirm a product's proper valuation or classification, or an importer's compliance with all administrative formalities.

13. At the first substantive meeting of the Panel, the EC for the first time raised questions about the scope of the Panel's terms of reference. The United States noted this, and noted that the only action within the terms of reference of this dispute is that taken on March 3, 1999[146]: the change in bonding requirements for certain products originating in EC Member States. As described in the U.S. First Submission and the U.S. Oral Statement, the EC has failed to meet its burden of demonstrating that this action represents a suspension of concessions or other obligations under the DSU.

---

[143] *See* Memorandum dated May 26, 1997, file number ENT-1 FO:TC:C:E AD to all interested parties, http://www.cebb.customs.treas.gov/public/cgi/cebb.exe?mode=fi&area=13&name=T-ENTRY5.TXT (U.S. Exhibit 2).

[144] While "withholding liquidation" has no legal significance under U.S. law, "suspension of liquidation" is a statutory term of art referring to delaying liquidation beyond one year based on a statute or court order. U.S. law also provides for "extension of liquidation" beyond one year, by Customs on its own initiative or in response to a request by the importer, in order to obtain missing information on appraisement or classification or to ensure the importer's compliance with applicable law. The U.S. March 3 action involved neither "extension" or "suspension."

[145] Likewise, the Kyoto Convention on the Simplification and Harmonization of Customs Procedures provides that Customs authorities may require importers to furnish security to ensure compliance with undertakings to Customs, and may condition release on condition that security is furnished to ensure collection of any additional import duties and taxes that might become chargeable. Kyoto Convention on the Simplification and Harmonization of Customs Procedures, (done at Kyoto on 18 May 1973 and entered into force on 25 September 1974), Annex B.1, 59-61(on the release of goods).

[146] Customs made this action effective as of March 4, 1999.

Q8: What is the impact on trade and traders involved in a suspension of liquidation (including the bond requirement)?

14. Again, no "suspension of liquidation" took place on March 3, 1999. In further clarification of the U.S. system, entries are normally liquidated no earlier than 314 days after entry, but are required by law to be liquidated within one year of entry, unless liquidation is "extended" or "suspended." A suspension of liquidation would occur, for example, if an antidumping proceeding were under way in which final antidumping duties could not be calculated and assessed within one year of entry. An extension would occur, for example, to obtain necessary information on classification or appraisement.

15. Accordingly, since there was no "suspension of liquidation," there was no impact on trade and traders from such a suspension. However, the United States would note that, for the claims at issue in this dispute, the impact on trade and traders is not a consideration in determining whether there has been a violation. The United States would further note that, as described in response to the previous question, the use of a surety and bonding system is trade-facilitating, inasmuch as it allows for the early release of merchandise into the United States.

Q9: What is the legal link between the date of assessment of the nullification caused by the EC's non-implementation of the *Bananas III* recommendations and the need to be able to suspend concessions as of 3 March 1999?

16. As explained at paragraphs 39-42 of the U.S. First Submission, a Member's liability for failing to comply with DSB rulings and recommendations within the "reasonable period of time" accrues from that date. DSU Article 22.1 is clear. It makes the suspension of concessions or other obligations available "in the event that the recommendations and rulings [of the DSB] are not implemented within a reasonable period of time." The purpose of the reasonable period of time - to provide a grace period for a Member to bring itself into compliance without consequences - in its very enunciation implies that the consequences of non-compliance accrue from the conclusion of that period. To deny a Member recourse once another Member has failed to come into compliance by the end of the reasonable period of time would be to alter the balance of rights and obligations under the WTO. Further, the requirement that a Member bring its measure into compliance by the conclusion of the reasonable period would be drained of meaning if, in fact, a Member were entitled to continue its breach without consequences. Such an interpretation of DSU requirements would be at odds with the purpose of the DSU itself, "to preserve the rights and obligations of Members under the covered agreements,"[147] since Members would be encouraged to follow the lead of the EC in delaying DSU procedures for DSB authorization of suspension of concessions.[148]

---

147 DSU Art. 3.2.

148 *See* U.S. First Submission at paras. 24-27, 43; WT/DSB/M/54, at 3-10.

17. A further contextual element supporting the conclusion that a Member's liability for non-compliance accrues from the end of the reasonable period is the fact that compensation under Article 22.2 is available immediately upon expiration of the reasonable period. Article 22.2 provides that compensation negotiations must begin *no later than* the conclusion of the reasonable period. There would be little logic to providing for immediate liability for non-compliance in the case of compensation but not suspension of concessions. Moreover, such a distinction in the timing of the liability would create a strong disincentive for pursuing the mutually agreed remedy of compensation - and another incentive for delay.
18. The United States' intention to apply any DSB-authorized suspension of concessions from March 3, 1999 must be understood in light of the EC's legal liability for its non-compliance in *Bananas* which accrued as from January 2, 1999. Notwithstanding this legal liability, the United States intended to apply the suspension only after the date by which the DSU required the Article 22 arbitrator to complete its work, March 2, 1999.[149] The March 3 action of reviewing bonding levels was a response to the EC's long record of delay, including delay of the Article 22 proceedings, and enabled the United States to suspend concessions from that date in accordance with its rights upon DSB authorization.

General response to Questions 10 - 16:

19. Questions 10-16 deal generally with procedures applicable in the context of DSU Articles 21.5 and 22. These issues are not directly relevant to this dispute, since it has already been determined pursuant to these provisions that the EC did, in fact, fail to comply with the DSB's rulings and recommendations, just as it has already been decided by the arbitrator whether the level of suspension proposed by the United States in response was equivalent to the level of nullification or impairment. Put in these terms, the EC's goal with respect to its Article 21.5 claim is apparent: to relitigate an issue it lost before other panels; namely, whether those panels had jurisdiction under the DSU to consider issues relating to the level of suspension of concessions without the convening of an Article 21.5 panel.
20. The Panel must recognize that the consequence of accepting the EC argument that an Article 21.5 panel is a prerequisite to a request for suspension of concessions under Article 22 would be to find that the Article 22.6 proceeding conducted in *Bananas,* and the suspension of concessions authorized by the DSB in that case, was illegitimate and illegal, a violation of DSU rules. The EC in its oral statement expresses the view that the Panel is not required "to review the work of other bodies established by the DSB in the context of another dispute

[149] *See* U.S. First Submission at paras. 37, 44. The United States is of course entitled to delay the application of the suspension of concessions to a later date better suited, for example, to providing advance notification to its importers of the potential change.

settlement procedure."[150] The EC is thus encouraging the Panel to ignore the reasoning and conclusions of the *Bananas* arbitrator/panelists, and to unnecessarily and incorrectly make findings at odds with those panelists. In other words, the EC is asking the Panel to join it in expressing the EC's lack of respect for the *Bananas* arbitral panel and its decisions, and for the DSB-approved suspension of concessions based on those decisions. This attitude exemplifies the EC's disregard for the impact of its actions and positions on the integrity of the dispute settlement system throughout proceedings relating to *Bananas*, an attitude reflected in the EC's refusal to consult the complaining parties, its refusal to reconvene an Article 21.5 panel and its efforts to block the agenda of a DSB meeting.[151]

21. The extreme sensitivity of the relationship between DSU Articles 21.5 and 22 is apparent both from record of DSB discussions on this issue over the course of the reasonable period and in the context of the DSU review.[152] The confusion arising from the impossibility of conducting a 90-day Article 21.5 proceeding[153] within the time frames for requesting suspension (30 days from the end of the reasonable period) and for arbitration on the level of suspension (60 days from the end of the reasonable period), has led the Members to conclude that Article 21.5 itself should be deleted and completely rewritten.[154]

---

[150] EC Oral Statement, para. 3.

[151] *See* U.S. First Submission, paras. 18-27.

[152] The relationship between Articles 21.5 and 22 has been the subject of extensive discussion among WTO Members. The Members broadly recognize that the relationship between Articles 21 and 22 requires additional clarification. *See. e.g.*, DSU Review, Discussion Paper from the European Communities (30 June 1999), Document No. 3864 (acknowledging that "some other Members have interpreted" Articles 21, 22 and 23 differently than the EC, and proposing principles to clarify and elaborate these Articles); Review of the DSU, Note by the Secretariat, Compilation of Comments Submitted by Members – Rev. 3 (12 December 1998) (Para. 296 – Australia noting that implementation procedures lack clarity; Para. 298 – Guatemala suggesting that Article 21.5 proceedings should include authorization to apply countermeasures, to make clear that two proceedings are unnecessary; Paras. 306-316 – expressing various views on Article 22; Para. 316 - Singapore notes that Article 21.5 does not include a moratorium on suspension of concessions pending conclusion of the proceedings like that found in Article 22.6, and suggesting that such a moratorium be included); Review of the DSU, Chairman's Summary of Informal Meeting of 16 March 1999 (22 March 1999), Doc. No. 1660 (summarizing discussion of issues relating to Articles 21, 22 and presumptions in Article 21.5 and 22 proceedings, including statements by Members that Article 22 should be amended to refer to the end of Article 21.5 proceedings instead of the reasonable period of time (para. 19)); Review of the DSU, Chairman's Summary of Informal Meeting of 19 May 1999 (25 May 1999), Doc. No. 2957 (noting that "[s]ome Members were of the view that recent difficulties in regard to implementation and suspension of concessions were due in part to lack of clarity of current DSU language", and that proposals had been made to delete Article 21.5 and replace it); Review of the DSU, Draft Proposal on Implementation (June 8, 1999), Doc. No. 3276 (compilation of formal and informal proposals related to implementation provisions). *See, also,* Minutes of the General Counsel Meeting Held on 8 March 1999 (WT/GC/M/37)(the Director-General stated that "there were different interpretations of the assumptions which had to be taken into account in applying compensatory measures - the question of Articles 21.5 and 22...").

[153] The EC would add to this 90 days a further 60 days for consultations.

[154] *See* Proposed Amendment of the Dispute Settlement Understanding, WT/MIN(99)/8 (22 November 1999) (U.S. Exhibit 3).

22. As the United States noted at footnote 49 of its First Submission, the Panel may not reach the issue of the relationship between Articles 21.5 and 22 because doing so would preempt the ongoing DSU review negotiations and encroach upon the rights of *all* WTO Members (not just parties to a single dispute) to negotiate the balance of rights and obligations under the WTO Agreement. Only the Members may amend or adopt interpretations of the DSU (WTO Agreement Arts. IX:2 and X), and Panels cannot add to or diminish the rights and obligations provided in the covered agreements (DSU Arts. 3.2 and 19.2). To adopt the EC position in this dispute would effectively amend DSU Article 22 by reading out the application of the negative consensus rule to requests for suspension of concessions, and would diminish the Members' rights under the current text of DSU Article 22 both to receive the benefit of the negative consensus rule and to receive a decision on the level of suspension as early as 60 days following the expiry of the reasonable period of time. The Members may yet agree to extend the time frames for arbitral decisions on the level of suspension and for the authorization of suspension, but that must take place through amendment of the DSU by all Members, and not through a panel proceeding brought by one.

23. Not only the *Bananas* arbitrator and Article 21.5 panels, but the panel in *Sections 301-310,* recognized that the DSU review is addressing the issue of the relationship of Articles 21.5 and 22.[155] Like the *Section 301* panel, this Panel need not reach the issue of the relationship between Articles 21.5 and 22. The EC is claiming that the March 3 action is inconsistent with Article 21.5. It has failed to explain, however, how changing bonding requirements can be inconsistent with a provision relating to dispute settlement procedures available when there is a disagreement on implementation. The EC has not shown, nor can it show, that the measure at issue (changed bonding requirements) is inconsistent with an obligation provided for in Article 21.5. There is simply no tenable link to be drawn.

Q10: Is a new measure (an implementing measure) presumed to be compatible or incompatible with WTO obligations after the reasonable period of time? Which party bears the burden of proof after the reasonable period of time to prove consistency (or lack thereof) with WTO provisions? Is it correct to state that the losing party becomes liable as of the expiry of the reasonable period of time? And liable for what?

24. For the reasons described in response to question 9 and in the U.S. First Submission, it is correct to state that the losing party is liable at the conclusion of the reasonable period of time if it has failed to comply with the rulings and rec-

155 See Panel Report, *EC – Bananas III (Article 21.5 – EC), supra*, footnote 40, para. 4.17 (12 April 1999) (the Panel stated, "in respect of the EC arguments concerning Articles 21, 22 and 23 of the DSU, we are well aware of the controversy in the DSB over the interpretation of these Articles and their relationship, but we view that question as one best resolved by Members in the context of the on-going DSU review . . ."); Decision by the Arbitrators, *EC - Bananas III (US) (Article 22.6 – EC), supra*, footnote 5, para. 4.11, note 11; Panel Report, *US – Section 301*, *supra*, footnote 9, para. 7.154 (22 December 1999).

ommendations of the DSB. It is liable for its continued nullification or impairment of the benefits of the complaining party under the covered agreements. Article 22 provides for compensation or suspension of concessions in the amount of this liability.

25. The concept of a "presumption" of compatibility or non-compatibility of a Member's implementation is not provided for in the DSU, and is unnecessary to the resolution of questions relating to the suspension of concessions following the reasonable period. Following the conclusion of the reasonable period of time, the complaining Member is entitled to request DSB-authorization for the suspension of concessions pursuant to Article 22.2 if it believes the implementing Member has failed to comply. If the implementing Member chooses not to contest the level of the suspension, it has effectively assented to the conclusion that it has failed to comply. On the other hand, if the implementing Member believes it has complied, it is likewise entitled under Article 22.6 to request arbitration of the level of the suspension, and argue that the level is zero because of its compliance. This in fact occurred in the *Bananas* dispute. (By contrast, in *Hormones*, the EC only contested the level of suspension, and did not claim it had complied.) As the Article 22.6 arbitrator in *Bananas* noted, "any assessment of the level of nullification or impairment presupposes an evaluation of consistency or inconsistency with WTO rules of the implementation measures taken by the European Communities."[156]

26. Just as it is not necessary or appropriate to for this Panel to address whether there is a presumption of compliance or non-compliance, it is not necessary or appropriate to reach in the context of this dispute a conclusion concerning the burden of proof following the reasonable period. In the Article 22.6 proceeding in *Bananas*, the arbitrator did not make an explicit ruling on this issue. On the other hand, in *Hormones*, the arbitrator concluded that the burden of proving that a proposed level of suspension is inconsistent with the Article 22.4 requirement that this level be equivalent to the level of nullification or impairment lies with the party challenging the proposed level of suspension, namely, the implementing party.[157]

27. Regardless of where presumptions or burdens may or may not lie in a proceeding dealing with the issue of compliance, any conclusion resulting from that proceeding that the implementing Member has failed to comply necessarily means that the Member has not been complying - and has nullified and impaired the complaining Member's benefits – since the adoption of the DSB recommendations and rulings, *and since the end of the reasonable period of time*. For the

[156] Decision by the Arbitrators, *EC - Bananas III (US) (Article 22.6 – EC)*, *supra*, footnote 5, para. 4.3.

[157] Decision by the Arbitrators, *EC - Bananas III (US) (Article 22.6 – EC)*, *supra*, footnote 5, para. 4.13; Decision by the Arbitrators, *European Communities – Measures Concerning Meat and Meat Products (Hormones) – Original Complaint by the United States - Recourse to Arbitration by the European Communities under Article 22.6 of the DSU*, ("*EC – Hormones (US) (Article 22.6 – EC)*"), WT/DS26/ARB, 12 July 1999, DSR 1999:III, 1105, para. 9.

reasons set forth in response to question 9, the non-complying Member is liable for that nullification or impairment from the end of the reasonable period.

Q11: Who has the responsibility to raise an Article 21.5 case? When should such a request under Article 21.5 take place?

28. The complaining party may (but need not) request an Article 21.5 review of the implementing party's measures. The DSU does not provide a time limitation on when an Article 21.5 review may be requested. The Article 22.6 arbitrator in *Bananas* observed, "The express wording of Article 21.5 of the DSU does not exclude the possibility of initiating such a proceeding *before* or *after* the expiry of the reasonable period of time."[158]

29. The United States sought to undertake an Article 21.5 proceeding prior to the conclusion of the reasonable period of time in *Bananas* because it was apparent that the implementation measures that the EC had already taken failed to comply with the EC's WTO obligations. By requesting an early Article 21.5 panel ruling prior to the conclusion of the reasonable period, the United States hoped to avoid the need to suspend concessions by making clear to the EC *before* its reasonable period for compliance expired that its violations had not been corrected, and that other measures would therefore be necessary, and thus permit the EC to promptly adopt those other measures. The EC chose instead to delay.

30. Thus, the United States request for an Article 21.5 panel was not, as the EC would have it,[159] an admission that a complaining party *must* resort to Article 21.5 proceedings before proceeding to Article 22. The United States strongly disputes the EC assertion that this or other points are "not even in dispute."[160]

31. Further, as noted in the U.S. First Submission,[161] the Article 22.6 arbitrator rejected the EC position that a complaining party must resort to Article 21.5 proceedings before making an Article 22 request to suspend concessions.[162] The EC has failed to address the logic of either the arbitrator or the United States on this point.

Q12: What is the consequence of failing to raise an Article 21.5 claim before the end of the reasonable period? If it is not done during this period does the right to an Article 21.5 assessment lapse?

32. As noted in response to question 11, the Article 22.6 arbitrator in *Bananas* explained, "The express wording of Article 21.5 of the DSU does not exclude the possibility of initiating such a proceeding *before* or *after* the expiry of the rea-

---

158 Decision by the Arbitrators, *EC - Bananas III (US) (Article 22.6 – EC), supra*, footnote 5, n.11.

159 EC Oral Statement, para. 18.

160 *See id.*, para. 18; *see, also, id.*, para. 6 (the United States contests each and every point the EC argues is uncontested).

161 *See* U.S. First Submission, para. 50.

162 Decision by the Arbitrators, *EC - Bananas III (US) (Article 22.6 – EC), supra*, footnote 5, paras. 4.10-4.15.

sonable period of time."[163] Thus, the right to pursue an Article 21.5 panel would not lapse if no request were made during the reasonable period, and there are no consequences for failing to raise an Article 21.5 claim before the end of the reasonable period.

33. The Article 22.6 arbitrator emphasized the importance of giving effect to both Article 21.5 and Article 22. While Article 21.5 proceedings may be requested at any time, including after the reasonable period of time, an Article 22 request for suspension may only occur within the terms specified in that article – within 30 days of the end of the reasonable period of time – if the negative consensus rule is to be given effect.[164] Because an Article 21.5 proceeding by its terms requires 90 days, the conclusion that an Article 21.5 proceeding must precede an Article 22 request would thus render the Article 22 right to DSB authorization with the negative consensus rule a nullity in those cases in which the implementing party does not implement until the completion of the reasonable period. On the other hand, concluding that an Article 22 request need not be preceded by an Article 21.5 proceeding would not deny effect to Article 21.5, since that proceeding would still remain available to complaining parties not wishing to suspend concessions, and to those willing to have the DSB decide by positive consensus whether to authorize the suspension of concessions.[165]

34. Further, as explained in the U.S. First Submission at paragraph 51, neither Articles 22.2 and 22.6 nor Article 23.2(c) make any reference to Article 21.5 proceedings as a prerequisite to a request for, DSB authorization of, or implementation of, a suspension of concessions. Rather, Article 22 provides time frames measured from the end of the reasonable period, and Article 23.2(c) requires that Article 22 procedures be followed before suspending concessions. The EC is thus incorrect in suggesting that there is an obligation to pursue Article 21.5 proceedings before pursuing a suspension of concessions under Article 22.

Q13: Assuming the US is correct in stating that an Article 21.5 panel should be triggered (by either party) within the reasonable period of time, what is the consequence if this 21.5 panel is never requested or not established? Does the absence of an Article 21.5 assessment result in a presumption that the new measure is compatible or that it is incompatible with WTO obligations? Does the absence of an Article 21.5 panel exclude recourse to Articles 22.6-7?

[163] Decision by the Arbitrators, *EC - Bananas III (US) (Article 22.6 – EC), supra*, footnote 5, n.11.

[164] *Ibid.*, para. 4.11. The arbitrator explained,

For those Members that for whatever reasons do not wish to suspend concessions, Article 21.5 will remain the prime vehicle for challenging implementation measures. However, if we accepted the EC's argument, we would in fact read the time-limit foreseen in Article 22.6 out of the DSU since an Article 21.5 proceeding, which in the EC view includes consultations and an appeal, would seldom, if ever, be completed before the end of the time-limit specified within Article 22.6 (i.e., thirty days of the expiry of the reasonable period of time).

[165] See id.

35. The United States does not take the position that an Article 21.5 panel *should* be requested during the reasonable period. As described in response to question 11, the United States attempted to avail itself of Article 21.5 procedures during the reasonable period in *Bananas* in order to demonstrate to the EC, while the EC still had time to revise its measure, that this measure would have to be changed in order to comply with the DSB's rulings and recommendations. The possibility of requesting an Article 21.5 panel before the end of the reasonable period presented itself in *Bananas* because the EC did, in fact, put into effect changes to its regime well before the end of the reasonable period, even if these changes were not to be applied before the end of the reasonable period.[166] Had the EC not taken steps until the expiry of the reasonable period, this option would not have been available.[167]

36. As noted in response to questions 10 and 12, there are no consequences if an Article 21.5 panel has not been requested or constituted, and there is no need to consider whether there is a presumption of compliance or non-compliance at the conclusion of the reasonable period. Further, as noted in response to question 11, the absence of an Article 21.5 panel does not preclude resort to Article 22.6-22.7, as the Article 22.6 arbitrator concluded in *Bananas.*

Q14: Who determines whether a new measure nullifies WTO benefits?

37. As defined in DSU Article 22.7, the Article 22.6 arbitrator's task is to determine "whether the level of suspension is equivalent to the level of nullification or impairment." As the *Bananas* arbitrator pointed out, the concept of equivalence between the proposed suspension and the level of nullification or impairment would be "devoid of meaning" if either of these variables were unknown.[168] Consequently, the Article 22.6 arbitrator must examine the new measure to determine the level of nullification or impairment before it can determine whether that level is equivalent to the level of suspension proposed by the complaining party.[169]

38. As described in response to question 10, following the conclusion of the reasonable period of time, the complaining Member is entitled to request DSB-authorization for the suspension of concessions pursuant to Article 22.2 if it believes the implementing Member's measure nullifies its agreement benefits. If the implementing Member chooses not to contest the level of the suspension, it has effectively assented to the conclusion that its new measure nullifies WTO

---

[166] *See* U.S. First Submission, para. 55.

[167] Thus, in *Australia Salmon,* Canada could not attempt to request an Article 21.5 panel before the expiry of the reasonable period because Australia had not implemented any measure. Canada therefore had to request suspension under Article 22 within 30 days of the expiry of the reasonable period to preserve its right to DSB authorization with the benefit of the negative-consensus rule. *See* WT/DSB/M/66, at 5-6; *supra* response to Question 16.

[168] Decision by the Arbitrators, *EC - Bananas III (US) (Article 22.6 – EC), supra,* footnote 5, para. 4.7.

[169] *Ibid.*, paras. 4.7-4.8.

benefits. On the other hand, if the implementing Member believes its measure does not nullify benefits, it is likewise entitled under Article 22.6 to request arbitration of the level of the suspension, and argue that the level is zero because its measure does not nullify WTO benefits. This in fact occurred in the *Bananas* dispute. (By contrast, in *Hormones*, the EC only contested the level of suspension, and did not claim the level of nullification was zero.)

Q15: Is there an implicit assessment of compatibility of any measure that is the object of an Article 22.6-7 Arbitration in view of the Arbitrator mandate to assess whether the level of suspension is equivalent to the level of nullification of benefits?

39. This is indeed the conclusion of the Article 22.6 arbitrator in *Bananas,* a conclusion with which the United States concurs. As the arbitrator noted, "we cannot fulfill our task to assess the *equivalence* between the two levels before we have reached a view on whether the revised EC regime is . . . fully WTO consistent."[170] The arbitrator also noted, "any assessment of the level of nullification or impairment presupposes an evaluation of consistency or inconsistency with WTO rules of the implementation measures taken by the European Communities."[171]

Q16: Please discuss the practice of WTO Members in their use of Articles 21.5 and 22 procedures.

40. The practice of WTO Members supports the interpretation of the United States and the *Bananas* arbitrator that Article 21.5 proceedings need not be undertaken as a condition for suspending concessions under Article 22. The EC description of this practice at paragraph 20 of its oral statement is highly misleading in this regard.

41. For example, the EC fails to point out with respect to the *Automotive Leather* dispute that the United States and Australia agreed to extend DSU Article 22.6 deadlines in that case pursuant to specific authority to do so in the Agreement on Subsidies and Countervailing Measures.[172] Footnote 6 to the SCM Agreement explicitly authorizes parties to a dispute under the SCM agreement to agree to extend the deadlines provided for in SCM Agreement Article 4, which include those in DSU Article 22.6. It was only because of footnote 6 that this procedure was possible, as reflected in the points made by the United States at the DSB meeting of October 14, 1999. At that meeting, the United States said:

- "I know, Mr. Chairman, that many delegations may be somewhat surprised to see that the United States has agreed with Australia to pursue

---

[170] Decision by the Arbitrators, *EC - Bananas III (US) (Article 22.6 – EC), supra*, footnote 5, para. 4.8.

[171] Decision by the Arbitrators, *EC - Bananas III (US) (Article 22.6 – EC), supra*, footnote 5, para. 4.3.

[172] *See* WT/DS126/8, p.2, point 6.

Article 21.5 now and only later pursue DSU Article 22 and/or SCM Article 4.10 proceedings.

- "This is not a fundamental change in the U.S. position on the applicability of those articles. This dispute, since it is under Article 4 of the SCM Agreement, presents special circumstances and unique opportunities. In particular, unlike in normal dispute settlement proceedings, here the parties may agree to extend the deadline for exercising the right to request Article 22 procedures. We and Australia have so agreed. This permits the parties additional time to resort to Article 21.5 proceedings, and we have been willing to accommodate the other party's desires in this respect.
- "The approach we have agreed to follow here is not required under the DSU. It is a special agreement for this dispute only. But it does reflect a process which many Members are supporting in the current discussions on the DSU, and we hope that it will demonstrate that such a process – and timetable – is workable, efficient and prompt."[173]

42. As in the *Leather* dispute, the two *Aircraft* disputes between Brazil and Canada involved the SCM Agreement. As did the parties in the *Leather* dispute, Brazil and Canada explicitly relied on Article 4 and footnote 6 of the SCM Agreement in agreeing to extend the Article 22.6 deadlines to permit prior completion of Article 21.5 panels without waiving the benefit of the negative-consensus rule in the DSB's authorization of suspension of concessions.[174]

43. With respect to *Australia Salmon*, Canada did *not* first resort to Article 21.5 procedures before requesting suspension under Article 22. It first preserved its rights under Article 22 by requesting suspension within 30 days of the expiry of the reasonable period, without any request for an Article 21.5 panel.[175] At the DSB meeting held on July 27-28, 1999, Canada did, ultimately, agree to pursue an Article 21.5 proceeding, but it insisted on the need to also form an Article 22 panel (since Australia disagreed with the proposed level of suspension), which it would agree to suspend pending the outcome of the Article 21.5 panel. Canada noted that while it had tabled a proposal at the DSU Review requiring an Article 21.5 panel before a suspension request could be made under Article 22, no agreement had yet been reached on the proposal. Absent such an agreement,

> Canada had to pursue its rights in accordance with the *existing provisions* of the DSU. At this stage, it was not possible for Canada to proceed with the Article 21.5 panel proceedings only, because such proceedings would be concluded after the expiry of the

---

173 Statement of the United States at DSB Meeting of 14 October 1999; *see* WT/DSB/M/69.

174 *See* WT/DS70/9, dated 23 November 1999, Annex at point 5; WT/DS46/13, dated 26 November 1999, Annex at point 5.

175 Canada requested a special meeting of the DSB to seek authorization to suspend concessions in a communication dated 15 July 1999. The communication made no mention of Article 21.5. *See* WT/DS18/12, dated 15 July 1999.

> 30-day period provided for in Article 22, within which Canada had the right to request suspension of concessions by negative consensus. Canada could have initiated such proceedings during the compliance period, if Australia had put in place its implementing measures, which it had not done.[176]

44. Canada thus concurred with the U.S. interpretation that Article 22 *requires* a request for suspension within 30 days of the expiry of the reasonable period, regardless of whether Article 21.5 proceedings have been conducted, and that Article 21.5 proceedings can be conducted during the reasonable period only if a measure has been implemented during that period. Canada did choose to accommodate Australia's desire for an Article 21.5 panel by consenting to waive its right under Article 22 to have the arbitrator complete its work within 60 days of the end of the reasonable period of time. However, Canada's decision to waive this Article 22 right cannot be read to mean that these rights do not exist.

45. Likewise, in pursuing an Article 21.5 panel in *Bananas* without requesting suspension within 30 days of the expiry of the reasonable period, Ecuador waived its right to receive DSB authorization to suspend concessions with the benefit of the negative consensus rule. Although the EC has purportedly agreed not to oppose Ecuador's request for suspension, Ecuador cannot be assured that a third party will not. Ecuador's decision to waive its rights in its case cannot be read as waiving the rights of other Members in other disputes. Further, Ecuador's pursuit of an Article 21.5 panel merely confirms the point made by the *Bananas* arbitrator that Article 21.5 is always available to parties not wishing to suspend concessions with the benefit of the negative consensus rule, and that pursuit of suspension pursuant to Article 22 without an Article 21.5 panel would not deny effect to Article 21.[177]

46. Finally, the EC neglects to mention its own decision in the *EC - Hormones* dispute to participate in Article 22.6 proceedings on the level of suspension proposed by the United States, and *without* insisting on Article 21.5 proceedings to confirm its non-compliance.

47. Thus, the *Aircraft* and *Leather* examples are inapplicable because the SCM Agreement provided authority to extend deadlines, while the *Salmon* and *Ecuador Bananas* examples merely stand for the proposition that Members may waive their rights in a particular dispute. As noted, Canada's actions in *Salmon* in fact support the U.S. position that Article 21.5 is not a prerequisite to a request for suspension, and that such a request must be made within 30 days of the expiry of the reasonable period in order to preserve one's rights to suspend concessions with the benefit of the negative consensus rule.

---

[176] WT/DSB/M/66, at 4-5 (emphasis added).

[177] *See* Decision by the Arbitrators, *EC - Bananas III (US) (Article 22.6 – EC), supra*, footnote 5, para. 4.11; discussion *supra* at paras. 30-31.

Q19: What exactly is involved from an administrative perspective in the withholding of liquidation and the related requirements for bonds? What alternative types of instruments does Customs accept for the posting of bonds?

48. Again, the term "withholding liquidation" has no legal significance under U.S. law, and no such action was taken in this regard on, or effective on, March 3, 1999. The normal liquidation cycle for the U.S. Customs Service is between 314 days and one year. This merely means that Customs makes its final determination of duties and other fees during that period, and bills or refunds importers (or liquidates their entries as entered) accordingly. The alternatives to surety bonds are set forth in 19 CFR § 113.40. Essentially, in lieu of surety bonds, the port director may accept U.S. money, U.S. bonds (other than U.S. savings bonds), U.S. certificates of indebtedness, Treasury notes or Treasury bills, in an amount equal to the amount of the bond.

Q20: How many of such bonds (and for how much and for which products) were posted during the period between 3 March and 19 April 1999?

49. As previously described, such bonds were required for 100% of formal entries of all goods from commercial sources, regardless of country of origin, both before, during and after the period 3 March to 19 April 1999. Normal bonding levels are set forth in the 1991 Customs Directive provided at U.S. Exhibit 4, and are described in response to question 2. The requirements applicable for most of the EC products listed in the Customs instructions (see U.S. Exhibit 7) announcement were as follows: a single transaction bond in the amount of the entered value of the merchandise,[178] or a continuous entry bond in the amount of 10% of the entered value of the merchandise which the importer imported during the previous year. The value of imports of all listed products for the months of March and April (including March 1-2 and April 20-30) was approximately 42 million dollars. The value of the products subject to the changed bonding requirements was the fraction of those imports entered between March 3 and April 19.

Q21: Please provide statistics on the level of trade between the EC and US by each listed product in 1997, 1998 and 1999 on a monthly and calendar year basis.

50. Please see U.S. Exhibit 5. As is clear from those figures, the additional bonding requirements did not, as the EC asserts, "effectively stop the trade in the affected products as from 3 March 1999."[179]

---

[178] Described in response to Question 2, certain products are subject to single transaction bond levels of three times the entered value of the merchandise because they are subject to requirements of other agencies, such as the public health and safety requirements of the Food and Drug Administration. For such products, the March 3 action did not change single transaction bond levels.

[179] *E.g.*, EC Oral Statement, para. 7.

Q22: If a bond is required and then duties are never assessed or assessed at a lower level, what level of interest does the Customs Service pay to the importer?

51. Customs is authorized and required to pay interest on excess duties, fees and taxes deposited by an importer. No interest would be paid on an additional bond requirement or an increased bond amount.

Q23: Following the reduction in the authorized level of suspension of concessions on 19 April 1999, were the EC importers reimbursed for any additional costs? If so, how? How, if at all, did you compensate importers/exporters that were inhibited from trading prior to 19 April?

52. There was no government reimbursement for any fees which private sureties may have charged U.S. importers of the listed products as a result of the additional bonding requirements. The additional bonding requirements did not result in additional payments to the government.

Q24: What is the average period of delay for liquidation for these types of products?

53. Liquidation of these products was based on the normal liquidation schedule applicable to all commercial goods entering the United States, between 314 days and one year.

Q25: What are the exact differences in US internal law between the ordinary and standard customs practice for imports and what was decided on 3 March 1999 with regard to those listed imports? Please elaborate on every single difference.

54. As described in response to question 2, for entries of the listed goods entered or withdrawn from warehouse for consumption on or after March 3, U.S. Customs reviewed the sufficiency of the bond and required a single transaction bond in the amount of the entered value of the merchandise,[180] or a continuous entry bond in the amount of 10% of the entered value of the merchandise which the importer imported during the previous year. These amounts differed slightly from the bonding levels applicable to other entries, a typical example of which is provided in response to question 2. All bonding levels are set forth in the Customs Directive provided in U.S. Exhibit 4.

55. Apart from this change in the bonding levels, no other changes were made in the ordinary procedures applied to imported goods. All goods were subject to the normal liquidation period (i.e., between 314 days and one year).

[180] As described in response to Question 2, certain products are subject to single transaction bond levels of three times the entered value of the merchandise because they are subject to requirements of other agencies, such as the public health and safety requirements of the Food and Drug Administration. For such products, the March 3 action did not change single transaction bond levels.

Q26: On what domestic legal authority did the USTR rely to require the Customs Service to begin the suspension of liquidation? Was this an administrative action that could be done at any time?

56. As described earlier, no suspension of liquidation was required or occurred as a result of the March 3 action. With respect to the revision of bonding levels, as described at paragraph 33 and note 33 of the U.S. First Submission, 19 CFR § 113.13 provides port directors with authority to require additional bonding or additional security to ensure that the acceptance of an entry will be adequately protected against any duties or other liabilities imposed by law. This discretionary authority may be exercised at any time when Customs becomes aware of a risk that normal bonding requirements will be inadequate.[181] The March 3 bonding review was implemented by Customs in response to the fact that the goods in question might, upon DSB authorization, be subject to a substantially higher rate of duty. USTR had informed Customs of this risk.

Q27: Please provide copies of the legislative authority and related regulations upon which USTR and the Customs Service relied.

57. 19 CFR § 113.13 is provided at U.S. Exhibit 6.

Q28: Did the US really need to be able to calculate the level of duties between 3 March and 19 April in order to preserve its rights to eventually impose suspension of concessions or other obligations? How exactly was the ability of the US to suspend concessions or other obligations impaired by not withholding liquidation on 3 March?

58. Again, the United States did not take action on March 3 to "withhold" or "suspend" liquidation. The only action taken was to revise bonding levels for certain imports. In the absence of these changes in bonding levels on entries between March 3 and April 19, this merchandise would have been released into the United States with bonds inadequate to cover the full amount of duties that might ultimately be authorized by the DSB. Because of this, and because estimated duty payments during the period March 3 to April 19 were made at the MFN rates normally in effect, Customs would not have had adequate recourse against either the surety or the merchandise in the event that the importer failed to pay the difference between the estimated duties and the duties ultimately authorized by the DSB.

Q29: On what products did the US begin suspension of liquidation as of 3 March 1999? On what principles were the listed products selected? Which were the products that were dropped after 19 April 1999 and on what basis?

[181] The 1991 Customs Directive provided in U.S. Exhibit 4 also discusses the role of risk evaluation in setting bonding levels.

59. The United States did not "suspend" or "withhold" liquidation on any products as of March 3, 1999. The United States revised bonding requirements. The list of products subject to the revised bonding requirements is set forth at U.S. Exhibit 7. The products were selected based on the principles set forth in DSU Article 22.3. Products were dropped from the final list in order to ensure that duties would be assessed at a level equivalent to the level of nullification or impairment calculated by the Article 22.6 arbitrator and authorized by the DSB. The items dropped from the final list are indicated in U.S. Exhibit 7.

Q30: What is the total annual level of EC exports to the US for 1997, 1998 and 1999 calendar years?

60. The total annual level of U.S. imports from EC member States was as follows:

1997: 157.5 billion dollars

1998: 176.4 billion dollars

1999 (first ten months): 159.8 billion dollars.

Q31: What were/are the tariff bindings and the applied rates on the listed imports in the absence of the 3 March decision?

61. The applied rates on the listed imports (which are also the bound rates) are provided in U.S. Exhibit 7. These rates were not changed by the March 3 decision. Had no further action been taken on April 19, 1999, each and every entry of a product subject to the revised bonding requirements would have been liquidated at these rates.

Appendix 2.5

Rebuttal Submission of the United States (including its cover letter)

(21 January 2000)

Dear Chairman:

Attached is the second submission of the United States in the dispute United States - Import Measures on Certain Products from the European Communities.

Part II of this submission addresses the issue of the scope of the Panel's term of reference. This issue, which was only identified at the first substantive meeting of the Panel, is of great significance. Accordingly, the United States respectfully requests the Panel to clarify, prior to the outset of the second substantive meeting, the measures that it considers to be within the Panel's terms of reference so that the United States may, in accordance with basic due process concerns, have full knowledge of the measures at issue and an adequate opportunity to respond to all of the claims made against all U.S. measures that may be the subject of the Panel's report. Had this issue been identified at the outset, the United States would have requested a preliminary ruling pursuant to paragraph 11 of the Panel's working procedures. It is no less important now that this issue be clarified promptly.

A copy of this submission and request for a preliminary ruling has been provided directly to the European Communities.

Sincerely,

Rebuttal Submission of the United States

I. INTRODUCTION

1. While the EC is correct that the facts of this case are straightforward, it is incorrect as to the facts. On March 3, 1999, the day after the Article 22.6 arbitrator in *Bananas* was required by the DSU to complete its work, the United States decided to modify bonding requirements on certain EC entries. The United States took this step to preserve its ability to collect any duties which might ultimately be authorized by the DSB as a result of the EC's failure to comply with the DSB's rulings and recommendations in *Bananas*. The bonding requirements did not increase the duty liability on those entries. The EC on March 4 requested consultations on the March 3 decision, and ultimately requested the establishment of this Panel based on those consultations, thereby limiting the measure under dispute to the March 3 bonding requirements. The Panel's task in this proceeding is to make findings on whether the EC has met its burden of demonstrating that the March 3 bonding requirements are inconsistent with GATT 1994 Articles I, II, VIII and XI. Because the EC has failed to meet this burden, the Panel must find

that the March 3 bonding requirements are not inconsistent with these articles, nor with DSU Articles 22.6 and 23.2(c).

2. The Panel should also reject the EC's DSU Article 3 and 21.5 claims. In this dispute, the EC seeks to have the Panel declare *ultra vires* the work of the Article 22.6 arbitrator in *Bananas* based on arguments on the relationship between DSU Articles 21.5 and 22 it has presented in four prior proceedings. Time after time, panels and arbitrators have turned down or rejected these EC arguments. This Panel should as well.

II. THE ONLY MEASURE WITHIN THE TERMS OF REFERENCE IS THE U.S. DECISION TO INCREASE BONDING REQUIREMENTS.

3. The EC has attempted throughout this proceeding to avoid identification of the specific U.S. measure it is challenging. Its reasons are easily understood: it has based its arguments on an erroneous understanding of what actions the United States actually took on March 3, and any recognition of this on its part would undermine its claims. Further, the EC hopes to obtain Panel findings on measures which are not part of the terms of reference of this dispute. The Panel must reject these EC efforts at obfuscation, confirm that the only measure within the terms of reference of this dispute is the U.S. modification to bonding requirements, and base its findings on a determination of whether the EC has met its burden of demonstrating that this measure is inconsistent with the WTO provisions identified in the EC's panel request.

4. The terms of reference provide for this Panel to examine "the matter referred to the DSB by the European Communities in" document WT/DS165/8.[182] That document is the EC's 11 May 1999 request for the establishment of this Panel. There, the EC identified the measure as

> the U.S. decision, effective as of 3 March 1999, to withhold liquidation on imports from the EC of a list of products, together valued at $520 million on an annual basis, and to impose a contingent liability for 100% duties on each individual importation of affected products as of this date .... This measure includes administrative provisions that foresee, among other things, the posting of a bond to cover the full potential liability.[183]

5. The EC panel request followed its request for consultations of 4 March 1999, which described the measure using similar language:

> the U.S. decision, effective as of 3 March 1999, to withhold liquidation on imports from the EC of a series of products ..., together valued at over $500 million on an annual basis, and to impose a

---

[182] WT/DS165/9.

[183] *See* WT/DS165/8.

> contingent liability for 100% duties on each individual importation of affected products as of this date .... According to information provided by the United States Trade Representative (USTR), this measure includes administrative provisions which foresee, among other things, the posting of a bond to cover the full potential liability.[184]

6. As described in the U.S. First Submission, Oral Statement and Responses to Panel and EC Questions,[185] the EC's reference to "withhold[ing] liquidation" does not describe any U.S. "decision, effective as of 3 March 1999." The term "withhold liquidation" has no legal significance in U.S. law, and the United States neither "suspended" nor "extended" liquidation with respect to entries of any of the listed products referenced in the EC's panel request.[186] The United States continued to apply its normal 314-day liquidation cycle with respect to these products. Inasmuch as that 314-day liquidation cycle is not a "decision, effective 3 March 1999,"[187] it cannot, under any interpretation, be considered to fall within the terms of reference of this dispute.

7. Likewise, the bonding requirements normally imposed by the U.S. Customs Service cannot be considered part of the measure subject to this dispute. The requirement that importers post bonds has been part of Customs practice for decades, and the specific bonding requirements now in force were established in 1991.[188] They did not result from any "decision, effective 3 March 1999." In its submissions, the EC appears to recognize that the normal bonding requirements of the United States are not part of this dispute, and at times does not appear to be challenging them. For example, the EC at paragraph 16(d) of its first written submission purports to set forth the bonding requirements imposed by the measure at issue, then states in paragraph 17 that these requirements "entailed a burden *additional* to what was required by the US customs authorities in application of ordinary customs duties."[189] Likewise, in its replies to Panel and US questions, the EC in its clarification of paragraph 16(d) refers to the "*increased* charges and costs for importers ... calculated on the basis of a duty in excess of the bound rate,"[190] suggesting that it is not challenging any charges and costs it claims might exist with respect to bonding requirements normally in effect. For the reasons

---

[184] *See* WT/DS165/1.

[185] *See* U.S. First Submission, para. 34; U.S. Oral Statement, para. 11; U.S. Responses to Panel and EC Questions, responses to questions 7, 8, 19, 25, 28, 29.

[186] The terms "extend liquidation" or "suspend liquidation" are explained in *para.* 14 and note 5 of the U.S. Responses to Panel and EC Questions.

[187] The 314-day liquidation cycle was instituted on May 26, 1997. *See* Memorandum dated May 26, 1997, file number ENT-1 FO:TC:C:E AD to all interested parties, http://www.cebb.customs.treas.gov/public/cgi/cebb.exe?mode=fi&area=13&name=T-ENTRY5.TXT(U.S. Exhibit 2).

[188] *See* Customs Directive Regarding Monetary Guidelines for Setting Bond Amounts (U.S. Exhibit 4).

[189] EC First Submission, para. 16(d), 17 (emphasis added).

[190] EC Replies to Panel and US Questions, at 6-7 (reply to U.S. question) (emphasis added).

described below in Section III.B, the United States denies that there are charges or costs within the meaning of GATT 1994 Articles II:2(c) and VIII:1 associated with either normal bonding requirements or those additional requirements nominally imposed on March.[191] Nevertheless, the distinction the EC appears to be drawing is evidence that it does not consider the normal bonding requirements of the United States to be part of the measure in dispute.

8. On the other hand, the EC has refused to respond to the invitation in the U.S. question to the EC to draw a tenable distinction between the changed bonding requirements of March 3 and the normal bonding requirements in the United States, since its arguments would implicate both.[192] The U.S. question was directed at the fact that the EC's argument that bonding requirements are a prohibited "other charge" would, if accepted, render all such bonding systems, in the United States and elsewhere (including the EC), a WTO violation. Instead of addressing this issue, the EC vaguely responded, "this question is based on an artificial distinction between different 'actions', with which the EC does not agree." Given the possible implication that the EC believes that the normal bonding requirements of the United States are subject to this dispute, the Panel should clarify that this is not the case, and base its analysis on the fact that only the additional bonding requirements imposed on March 3 are within the terms of reference.

9. The Panel should also reject the EC's attempt to ascribe to the March 3 bonding requirements legal or practical impacts they simply did not have. Thus, the Panel must reject the EC's unsupported assertions that the measure "effectively already imposed 100% duties on each individual importation as of 3 March 1999, the return of which was uncertain, depending on future US decisions"[193] or that the effect of the measure was "to deprive as from 3 March 1999 the importers of their right of importing those products subject to a duty not exceeding the tariff bound under the US Schedule of tariff concessions."[194] As the United States has explained from the outset of this dispute,[195] the March 3 bonding requirements did not create any additional duty liability. Had the United States taken no further action on April 19 following DSB authorization, each and every entry subject to the changed bonding requirements would have been liquidated at the MFN, entered rate.

---

[191] By way of clarification, while the United States announced the increased bonding requirements on March 3, the Customs instructions to increase bonding requirements were actually issued on March 4, and were effective for entries from that date.

[192] *See* U.S. Question to the EC; EC Responses to Panel and US Questions, at 6-7.

[193] WT/DS165/8.

[194] EC Oral Statement, para. 7. Similarly, and equally incorrectly, the EC asserts that as a result of the March 3 bonding requirements, "the importer was bound to pay the (prohibitive) increased duty at the time of liquidation of the customs debt." EC Oral Statement, para. 6(a).

[195] U.S. First Submission, paras. 31, 45; U.S. Oral Statement, para. 6; U.S. Responses to Panel Questions, paras. 10, 60.

10. An important element of the entry process is the deposit of estimated duties, which must occur at the time of entry or shortly thereafter.[196] A bond provides assurances to U.S. authorities that, upon liquidation, any duty not covered by those estimated duties can be collected if the importer fails to pay. This is necessary precisely because the bonding requirement itself does *not* impose any additional liability. Had any such additional liability existed at the time of entry, Customs would have required higher deposits of *estimated duties.*

11. Estimated duty deposits on entries from March 3 to April 19 were only in the amount of the MFN duties, because this was the only duty liability these entries were subject to. However, it was known that, as a result of DSB authorization, the duties on these entries might ultimately be higher. As a consequence, in the absence of increased bonding requirements, Customs could not have been assured that importers would pay the difference between the MFN duty deposits and any higher duties which might ultimately be authorized by the DSB. When that authorization came on April 19, the duty liability increased to 100%, and Customs began to require higher deposits of estimated duties. With such higher deposits in hand, there was no longer a gap between the estimated duty deposits and the known potential duty liability. The risk that Customs would not be able to collect the full amount of duties owed returned to normal levels,[197] and normal bonding requirements applied.

12. The EC confuses the effect of the U.S. March 3 action with that of action taken on April 19. However the April 19 action is not at issue in this proceeding because that measure could not have been the subject of a consultation request made on March 4. A Member may request the establishment of a Panel with respect to a measure only if it has first requested consultations on that measure.[198] On March 4, the measures taken on April 19 did not exist. The EC was free, after April 19, to request consultations on the April 19 measures, but chose not to. It must not now be permitted to circumvent the rules of the DSU by mischaracterizing the March 3 measures to encompass those on April 19.

13. The EC itself has long recognized and relied on the principle that dispute settlement proceedings cannot be undertaken before the measure in question has been taken. For example, the EC was insistent over the course of U.S. efforts to form an Article 21.5 panel that such a panel could not be formed because one point of its implementation, the licensing regime, had allegedly not been under-

---

196 Details on this and other aspects of the entry process are described at the web-site of the U.S. Customs Service at http://www.customs.ustreas.gov/imp-exp2/pubform/import/index.htm Excerpts from this site are provided in U.S. Exhibit 8.

197 The risk under normal circumstances, after deposit of estimated duties, would be covered by the normal bonding requirements for such goods and relates to the possibility, for example, that the merchandise is misclassified or misvalued, or that the goods are found to be inadmissible because they fail to comply with U.S. health or safety requirements.

198 *See* DSU Arts. 4.2-4.5, 4.7. Article 4.2 provides for consultations on "measures ... taken within the territory" of a Member. The EC's consultation request thus could not have been made for a measure which had not been "taken" as of March 4, namely, the April 19 actions.

taken until late October 1998. The EC stated at the September 22, 1998 DSB meeting,

> The Community was therefore not in a position to accept this point since no measures had yet been taken. Although this issue had also been subject to consultations, the Community could not accept the position of the complaining parties since legally the measures had not been taken and there was no decision on the import licensing regime.[199]

14. The EC went so far as to threaten to block the agenda of the September 1998 DSB meeting until it received assurances that the DSB would not act on the request of the *Bananas* complaining parties for the establishment of an Article 21.5 panel.[200] This is how the EC managed to circumvent the DSU rule that the DSB must establish a panel in the absence of a negative consensus, a rule the EC cites in denying that it could have "blocked" the establishment of an Article 21.5 panel.[201] The EC is technically correct: it did not block panel establishment; instead, it threatened to block *all* work at the September DSB meeting, *including* panel establishment. (Its willingness to carry out such a threat was confirmed by the events of the January 27, 1999 DSB meeting.[202])

15. Unlike the EC, the United States would not have claimed any right to block the formation of this Panel had it believed the EC would attempt to litigate measures not subject to a consultation request. A ruling on such issues is the responsibility of the Panel formed under multilateral rules, and not the unilateral decision of one party. Leaving aside the accuracy of the EC's claims as to whether part of its implementation measure was ripe for Article 21.5 review, or its position that the party complained against, rather than a panel, should decide that question, the EC's explanation of when a measure is ripe for panel review is accurate: if a measure has not yet been taken, it cannot be the subject of dispute settlement proceedings, including the consultations which are a prerequisite to panel establishment. The EC six years earlier also enunciated this principle, when it explained that a December 1992 meeting of the EC Council

> did not in fact result in a formal decision on [its banana import] regime: the result of the debate was limited to a political orientation about some of the features of the future common market organiza-

---

199 WT/DSB/M/48 (Minutes of DSB Meeting of 22 September 1999).

200 *See id.* at 1-2 ("Prior to the adoption of the agenda, the representative of the European Communities ... inquired whether ... item [4 of the agenda entitled "Recourse to Article 21.5 of the DSU by Ecuador, Guatemala, Honduras, Mexico and the United States"] had been included on the agenda for information only. *Depending on the answer he would indicate whether he could accept item 4 to remain on the agenda.*" (Emphasis added)).

201 In its response to the Panel's question concerning the EC's repeated refusal to participate in an Article 21.5 proceeding, the EC stated that it was incorrect to assert that it blocked an Article 21.5 action. The EC explained: "the party complained against is not in a position to 'block' establishment of a panel because the decision is taken by the DSB under the 'reversed consensus' rule." EC Responses to Panel and US Questions, at 5-6 (Replies 11, 12).

202 *See* WT/DSB/M/54, at 3-10; U.S. First Submission, para. 25.

> tion for bananas which still need to be formalized in the internal decision-making process of the Community institutions. The present preparatory works cannot therefore be considered as a measure under Article XXII:1 or XXIII:1 of the General Agreement allowing for formal consultations under one of these provisions."[203]

The April 19 measures increasing duty liability had not been taken as of the EC's March 4 consultation request, and therefore could neither have been the measure provided for in that request or in the panel establishment request which subsequently followed.

16. In its closing statement at the first substantive meeting of the Panel, the EC attempted to recast its description of its measure in the hope of drawing into this proceeding the actions taken on April 19. It stated that the matter before the Panel is "the US measure effective on 3 March 1999 on a list of products, contained in Annex 1, and confirmed for 'a subset of the products' in a 'reduced list' adopted on 19 April 1999, contained in Annex 2."[204] This reformulation of the measure does not correspond to that in the EC's Panel or consultation requests. The EC's consultation request obviously does not reference the April 19 action, both because it had not yet been taken, and because it was not then clear how much longer the EC would succeed in delaying the Article 22 panel. Furthermore, while the EC panel request does reference the April 19 action, it describes it only as having "confirmed" the liability imposed by the March 3 decision. None of these formulations would permit the April 19 actions to be drawn into this dispute. The April 19 actions were not part of the EC's consultation request, and the March 3 action created *no* duty liability that could be "confirmed" on April 19. The Panel must reject the EC's attempt to redefine the terms of reference in this dispute.

17. The Appellate Body in *Shirts and Blouses* stated with respect to the burden of proof, "we find it difficult, indeed, to see how any system of judicial settlement could work if it incorporated the proposition that the mere assertion of a claim might amount to proof ... [T]he party who asserts a fact ... is responsible for providing proof thereof."[205] In this proceeding, the EC has attempted, through mere assertions, to argue that the United States on March 3 took action it did not take. The United States has responded to the EC with *facts* concerning what action it did, and did not, take on March 3. The only measure at issue in this dispute is the March 3 modification to bonding requirements on certain products from the EC. The Panel should consider arguments with respect to that action only. For the reasons set forth in the U.S. First Submission and the following sections of this submission, the EC has failed to demonstrate that the March 3 bonding requirements are inconsistent with U.S. WTO obligations.

---

[203] DS38/4, cited in Analytical Index (6th ed.), at 570.

[204] EC Closing Statement at the First Substantive Meeting of the Panel (17 December 1999).

[205] Appellate Body Report, *US – Shirts and Blouses*, *supra*, footnote 39, at 335.

III. THE EC HAS FAILED TO MEET ITS BURDEN OF DEMONSTRATING THAT THE MARCH 3 ACTION WAS INCONSISTENT WITH GATT 1994 ARTICLES I, II, VIII AND XI

18. The burden is on the EC, as the complaining party in this dispute, to present arguments and evidence sufficient to establish a *prima facie* case in respect of the various elements of its claims. The Panel's task is to balance all evidence on the record and decide whether the EC, as the party bearing the original burden of proof, has convinced the Panel of the validity of its claims. In cases of uncertainty, i.e., when the evidence and arguments remain in equipoise, the Panel must give the benefit of the doubt to the United States as the defending party.[206] The EC has failed to meet its burden in this dispute with respect to any of its claims.

A. *The EC Has Failed to Demonstrate That the March 3 Action Was Inconsistent With GATT 1994 Article I*

19. The EC has asserted that the March 3 bonding requirements are inconsistent with Article I because they allegedly discriminate between products originating in the EC and products originating in other countries.[207] This assertion is incorrect, because the U.S. action of increasing bonding requirements merely addressed the particular risks associated with these entries, risks not present with respect to entries of other products from other countries.

20. The particular risks associated with these EC entries were the result of the EC's failure to bring its banana import regime into compliance with the DSB's rulings and recommendations by the end of the reasonable period. As a result, upon confirmation by the Article 22.6 arbitrator of the nullification of U.S. benefits and DSB authorization to suspend concessions, these EC entries would be subject to higher duties. In the absence of higher deposits of estimated duties (which Customs did not collect because the liability on these entries remained at MFN rates), Customs faced the risk that existing bonds would not provide sufficient recourse if importers refused to pay the difference between estimated duties and the higher duties which might ultimately be assessed. Thus, in imposing different bonding requirements on these entries, the United States did no more than respond to the special risks associated with these entries.

21. Finally, the United States notes that, even if the Panel were to consider the March 3 bonding requirements to provide different treatment to entries of certain

---

[206] Appellate Body Report, *EC - Measures Concerning Meat and Meat Products (Hormones)* ("*EC – Hormones*"), WT/DS26/AB/R, WT/DS48/AB/R, adopted 13 February 1998, DSR 1998:I, 135, para. 109; *see, also*, Appellate Body Report, *US – Shirts and Blouses, supra*, footnote 39, at 337 ("a party claiming a violation of a provision of the WTO Agreement by another Member must assert and prove its claim"); and Appellate Body Report, *India – Mailbox, supra*, footnote 15, para. 74 (noting that the Panel had "properly requir[ed] the [complaining party] to establish a *prima facie* case" before proceeding to the next step of its evaluation of the claim at issue); Panel Report on *US – Section 301, supra*, footnote 9, para. 7.14 (22 December 1999).

[207] EC First Submission, para. 16(a).

products from the EC than those of other Members, notwithstanding the particular risks associated with these EC entries, only the requirements applied to continuous entry bonds could even arguably be viewed as less favorable. As described in response to EC question 2 and panel question 20, the single transaction bond requirements applied to the listed products were actually *lower* than those applied to normal entries for most of the products, and the same for others.[208]

22. However, the Panel should, together with the EC's other claims, reject the EC's argument that the March 3 bonding requirements provided EC entries with treatment different and less favorable than that accorded product of other Members. The March 3 bonding requirements were consistent with GATT 1994 Article I.

B. The EC Has Failed to Demonstrate That the March 3 Action Was Inconsistent With GATT 1994 Articles II and VIII

23. The March 3 bonding requirements either do not impose an "other charge" within the meaning of GATT 1994 Articles II:1(b) and VIII:1, or, if they do, these charges are "commensurate with the cost of services rendered," and thereby permitted under Articles II.2(c) and VIII:1. Under either interpretation, the March 3 bonding requirements are not inconsistent with these provisions.

24. As described above, the only measure within the terms of reference of this dispute is the March 3 change in bonding requirements. The normal bonding requirements of the United States are neither within the terms of reference of this dispute, nor does it appear that the EC is challenging these requirements.[209] Nevertheless, the EC has failed to draw a tenable distinction between the changed bonding requirements of March 3 and the normal bonding requirements in the United States and numerous WTO Members, including several EC member States.[210] In simply arguing that such bonding systems impose "other charges" inconsistent with Articles II and VIII because there may be costs associated with

---

[208] As described in response to questions 2 and 20, products subject to requirements of agencies such as the Food and Drug Administration were subject to a single transaction bond rate of three times the entered value of the merchandise, regardless of whether it was a listed product. Products not subject to such other agency requirements are normally subject to a single transaction bond requirement of the entered value of the merchandise plus any duties, taxes and fees for the entry, while single transaction bonds for listed products from the EC had only to be in the amount of the entered value of the merchandise.

[209] See discussion in Section II at paras. 7-8 regarding the terms of reference, and the EC's argument that it is challenging the "additional" burden allegedly created by the March 3 action and the "increased" charges allegedly imposed by that action.

[210] It is our understanding that at least several EC member State customs administrations (e.g., those of the United Kingdom and Germany) provide for a surety system allowing the early release of goods without final payment of duties. It is also our understanding that such systems can differ among member States (e.g., for some, a surety may only be required for goods considered to be "high risk" for compliance purposes, such as liquor and cigarettes), and that not every member State (e.g., Italy) provides for a surety system.

obtaining the bonds,[211] the EC would, presumably unintentionally, implicate all bonding systems.

25. The problem is highlighted by the U.S. question to the EC, and the EC's failure to respond. The U.S. explicitly asked the EC whether surety systems in general impose "other charges" within the meaning of Articles II and VIII, and, if so, how the EC would distinguish these from any "other charges" associated with the March 3 action. The EC refused to answer the question, merely reiterating its argument that the March 3 action imposed an "other charge" not limited to the approximate costs of administration.[212]

26. The U.S. question pointed out that surety systems are explicitly contemplated in Article 13 of the Customs Valuation Agreement, to which the EC responded that valuation issues are not relevant to this dispute.[213] The EC response misses the point: the EC cannot propose a definition of "other charges" under Article II which would lead to the conclusion that surety systems in general violate Article II, since such systems are explicitly contemplated in Article 13 of the Customs Valuation Agreement. An agreement provision must not be interpreted so as to create a conflict with another provision.[214] If, merely because there may be costs associated with bonding requirements, all surety systems would impose prohibited "other charges," then the EC's interpretation of "other charges" is creating precisely such a conflict.

27. In addition to Article 13 of the Customs Valuation Agreement, surety systems are explicitly provided for in the Kyoto Convention on the Simplification and Harmonization of Customs Procedures.[215] The Convention, like the Customs Valuation Agreement, encourages the early release of merchandise, and permits the adoption of surety systems to ensure compliance with regulatory undertakings, as well as to ensure collection of any *additional* import duties and taxes that

---

[211] EC First Submission, para. 16(d).

[212] EC First Submission, para. 16(d); EC Response to Panel and US Questions, at 6-7 (Reply to U.S. question).

[213] EC Responses to Panel and US Questions, at 6-7.

[214] *See, e.g.*, Panel Report, *Indonesia – Certain Measures Affecting the Automotive Industry* ("*Indonesia – Autos*"), WT/DS54/R and Corr. 1,2,3,4, WT/DS55/R and Corr. 1,2,3,4, WT/DS64/R and Corr. 1,2,3,4, WT/DS69/R and Corr. 1,2,3,4, adopted 23 July 1998, DSR 1998, DSR 1998:VI, 2201, para. 14.28 (the panel stated, "we recall first that in public international law there is a presumption against conflict.[footnote omitted] This presumption is especially relevant in the WTO context [footnote omitted] since all WTO agreements, including GATT 1994 which was modified by Understandings when judged necessary, were negotiated at the same time, by the same Members and in the same forum.").

[215] Kyoto Convention on the Simplification and Harmonization of Customs Procedures, (done at Kyoto on 18 May 1973 and entered into force on 25 September 1974), Annex B.1, 59-61 (on the release of goods) (*Kyoto Convention*) (U.S. Exhibit 9). The Convention Members include [virtually all] WTO Members. The Convention is a relevant rule of international law applicable in the relations between the Members, and is therefore relevant to the interpretation of a WTO Agreement provision, such as the meaning of "other charges" under GATT 1994 Articles II and VIII. Vienna Convention on the Law of Treaties, Art. 31.3(c).

might become chargeable.[216] Thus, the Convention explicitly contemplates that, as a necessary consequence of the early release of merchandise, it might become necessary to impose bonding requirements to ensure collection of duties beyond those for which an importer might be liable based on information at the time of entry, and which might become due as a result of events subsequent to entry.[217]

28. In light of the specific provision for surety systems both in the Customs Valuation Agreement and the Kyoto Convention, this Panel should find that surety systems used by customs authorities to ensure collection of duties, taxes and fees and compliance with other importer undertakings following the release of merchandise are not "other charges" within the meaning of GATT Articles II and VIII. The facts concerning the full range of surety systems employed by Members in connection with the early release of goods is not before the Panel, and the Panel should avoid findings which could have unintended consequences on these trade-enhancing measures. The Customs Valuation Agreement and Kyoto Convention provide for surety systems precisely because these are acknowledged to be a necessary component of customs systems which allow release of merchandise in the shortest possible time.

29. The bonding requirements imposed by the United States do not entail any payments to the United States Government. Rather, importers must provide evidence that they have obtained either single transaction bonds or continuous entry bonds (or cash in lieu of surety on a bond) for the entry or entries in question. These bonds are obtained from private surety companies, who charge the importers based on the risk involved with the transaction. That risk can relate either to the credit-worthiness of the importer, or to the nature of the merchandise being imported. While the actual costs charged by surety companies will vary for these and other commercial reasons, the typical cost for a single transaction bond would be $3.50 per thousand dollars of bond value (0.35%), while the typical cost for a continuous entry bond would be $10-20 per thousand dollars of bond value.[218]

30. If, on the other hand, the Panel concludes that surety systems providing for the early release of merchandise impose an "other charge," the Panel must also conclude that costs associated with the March 3 bonding requirements are "commensurate with the cost of services rendered" and "limited in amount to the approximate cost of services rendered,[219] and thus justified under Article II:2(c)

---

216 *Kyoto Convention*, Annex B.1, 59-61.

217 Similarly, the International Chamber of Commerce International Customs Guidelines provide in Guideline 19 that a modern, efficient and effective customs administration: "19. operates a corporate surety bonding system, or other appropriate means, such as a duty- and tax-deferral system, to protect the revenue and ensure compliance with customs laws without unnecessarily delaying the release of goods." ICC International Customs Guidelines, www.iccwbo.org/home/statements_rules/rules/1997/customsdoc.asp (10 July 1997).

218 These costs are only approximate values based on informal inquiries and could vary widely depending on the parties to the transaction.

219 The panel in *Customs User Fee* concluded that differences in wording between Article II:2(c) and VIII:1 were not intended to have a different meaning, but merely resulted from the different

and Article VIII:1.[220] Again, the Panel must not make findings which would render Article II violations the surety systems contemplated in the Valuation Agreement and the Kyoto Convention.

31. Nevertheless, as the United States has demonstrated, the Panel should find that surety systems used in connection with the early release of merchandise are not "other charges" within the meaning of Articles II and VIII, or should decline to make findings with respect to these claims if not necessary to resolve this dispute.

B. *The EC Has Failed to Demonstrate That the March 3 Action Was Inconsistent With GATT 1994 Article XI*

32. The EC merely asserts that the effect of the March 3 bonding requirements was to "effectively stop trade in the affected products as from 3 March 1999,"[221] and on this basis asks the Panel to find that the requirements are inconsistent with Article XI.[222] The EC argument with respect to GATT Article XI

paths by which the provisions entered the GATT 1947. Panel Report on *United States – Customs User Fee*, adopted 2 February 1988, BISD 35S/245, 275, para. 75.

220 The service in question is the early release of merchandise into the United States. As indicated in the U.S. First Submission, such early release of the merchandise can come within hours of its arrival, whereas estimated duties are not routinely deposited until 10 working days (or two weeks) later. Prior to the widespread use of early release, U.S. importers frequently paid dock storage charges, had higher administrative costs for obtaining release of their goods and other increased costs associated with their inability to use "just-in-time" inventorying.

The cost to Customs of early release is the risk that duties, taxes and fees will not be paid, or that the entries violate quota or other regulatory requirements. In part, this risk relates to the total value of the potential liability in the transaction (e.g., duties, other fees, or liquidated damages.) It also relates to the credit-worthiness of the importer. For example, continuous entry bonds will, by definition, be used by importers with a history of importations establishing a credit history. By tying bonding requirements to the level of risk associated with the entries, Customs is "charging" importers based on the cost of early release.

The March 3 action responded to the higher level of risk associated with imports of listed products from the EC. The particular risks associated with these EC entries, were, as described in earlier submissions (*See* U.S. Responses to Panel and EC Questions, para. 8; U.S. Oral Statement, paras. 4-6), the result of the EC's failure to bring its banana import regime into compliance with the DSB's rulings and recommendations by the end of the reasonable period. As a result, upon confirmation by the Article 22.6 arbitrator of the nullification of U.S. benefits and DSB authorization to suspend concessions, these EC entries would be subject to higher duties. In the absence of higher deposits of estimated duties (which Customs did not collect because the liability on these entries remained at MFN rates), Customs faced the risk that existing bonds would not provide sufficient recourse if importers refused to pay the difference between estimated duties and the higher duties which might ultimately be assessed. Thus, in imposing different bonding requirements on these entries, the United States did no more than respond to the special risks associated with these entries, and the additional bonding requirements were an appropriate "charge" commensurate with this cost to Customs.

221 EC Oral Statement, para. 7.

222 *E.g.*, EC First Submission, para. 16(c); EC Oral Statement, para. 23.

constitutes "mere assertion,"[223] and falls woefully short of meeting the EC's burden with respect to this claim.

33. Even were the Panel to conclude that the March 3 action is not an "other charge," the EC has failed to meet its burden of demonstrating that the action is inconsistent with Article XI. The EC's sole argument in this connection is its assertion that the March 3 action "effectively stopped trade." As a factual matter, this is simply incorrect, as the United States explained in response to question.[224] U.S. Exhibit 5 demonstrates that a substantial trade in listed products continued after March 3. In particular, if the impact of the March 3 action is segregated from that of the April 19 action, the figures indicate there was little if any impact from the March 3 action. This is clear from an examination of the nine-month import values for products not included on the final list (see U.S. Exhibit 10). The 1998 total imports of these products totaled $213,991,343, while the 1999 figure was $212,574,917.

34. The EC's argument with respect to Article XI thus consists of a single, inaccurate assertion. For this reason, the Panel should find that the EC has failed to meet its burden with respect to this claim, if the Panel concludes that the March 3 action falls within the scope of Article XI and is not excluded because it is an "other charge."

35. As a technical matter, if one were to assume for the sake of argument that the EC were correct that the March 3 bonding requirements impose a "charge" under Article II or VIII, then these bonding requirements cannot, by definition, be subject to Article XI, which explicitly only covers prohibitions or restrictions "other than duties, taxes or other charges." To the extent this Panel were to find that the March 3 action constitutes an "other charge" - whether or not within the meaning of Articles II and VIII, and whether or not meeting the requirements of Article II:2(c) - the March 3 action cannot fall within the scope of Article XI.

IV. THE EC HAS FAILED TO MEET ITS BURDEN OF DEMONSTRATING THAT THE MARCH 3 ACTION WAS INCONSISTENT WITH DSU ARTICLES 23.2(c) AND 22.6

36. In its oral statement at the first panel meeting, the EC for the first time identifies the provision of DSU Article 23 it claims the U.S. has violated, Article 23.2(c).[225] DSU Article 23.2(c) requires that a complaining party follow Article 22 procedures and obtain DSB authorization before suspending concessions or other obligations. Similarly, DSU Article 22.6, last sentence, requires that con-

[223] The Appellate Body in *Shirts and Blouses* stated with respect to the burden of proof, "we find it difficult, indeed, to see how any system of judicial settlement could work if it incorporated the proposition that the mere assertion of a claim might amount to proof ... [T]he party who asserts a fact ... is responsible for providing proof thereof." Appellate Body Report, *US – Shirts and Blouses*, *supra*, footnote 39, at 335.

[224] *See* U.S. Responses to Panel and EC Questions, para. 50.

[225] EC Oral Statement, para. 15.

cessions or other obligations not be suspended during the course of the arbitration. Inasmuch as the EC has failed to demonstrate that the March 3 bonding requirements are inconsistent with GATT 1994 Articles I, II, VIII or XI, it has failed to demonstrate that these requirements involved a U.S. suspension of concessions or other obligations. Thus, the EC has failed to meet its burden of demonstrating that the March 3 bonding requirements were inconsistent with either DSU Article 23.2(c) or DSU Article 22.6, last sentence.

V. THE EC HAS FAILED TO MEET ITS BURDEN OF DEMONSTRATING THAT THE MARCH 3 ACTION WAS INCONSISTENT WITH DSU ARTICLE 21.5

37. The EC is asking this Panel to make findings it should not and need not make: that Article 21.5 proceedings must precede an Article 22 request for suspension of concessions. This is now the fifth time the EC is seeking to have a panel legislate on this point, to "add to" *and* "diminish" the rights and obligations of Members in violation of DSU Article 3.2. No previous panel has accepted the EC's invitation to legislate, and this Panel must decline to do so as well.

38. The EC in its January 13 answers makes explicit that, as the United States pointed out in its January 13 submission,[226] the EC's goal is to have this Panel declare the work of the *Bananas* Article 22.6 arbitrator, and the DSB-authorized suspension of concessions which followed, illegitimate and illegal, a violation of DSU rules. According to the EC,

> An implicit assessment by the arbitrator under Article 22.6 of the compatibility of a measure with a covered agreement would usurp the task of a panel under Article 21.5 of the DSU and thus, if an arbitrator were to make such an assessment, the arbitrator would act *ultra vires.*[227]

Yet the Article 22.6 arbitrator in *Bananas* concluded that such an implicit assessment of compatibility *was*, necessarily, part of its task, and undertook such an assessment.[228]

39. The aim of the dispute settlement mechanism is "to secure a positive solution" to a dispute;[229] it is not to seek repeated justification for a Member's efforts to delay and obstruct the consequences of its non-compliance with DSB rulings and recommendations, nor to seek the condemnation by one panel for the work of another for the political benefits this might offer. Having failed before the two

---

[226] U.S. Responses to Panel and EC Questions, paras. 19-20.

[227] EC Replies to Panel and US Questions, at 4 (Reply 9).

[228] The arbitrator stated: "we cannot fulfill our task to assess the *equivalence* between the two levels [of nullification or impairment and of the proposed suspension] before we have reached a view on whether the revised EC regime is ... fully WTO consistent." Decision by the Arbitrators, *EC - Bananas III (US) (Article 22.6 – EC), supra*, footnote 5, para.4.8.

[229] DSU Art. 3.7.

Bananas Article 21.5 panels, the *Bananas* Article 22.6 arbitral panel, and the *Section 301* panel to justify its position on the relationship between Article 21.5 and 22, the EC now comes before this Panel. Presumably, if this Panel as well does not accept the EC's reasoning, the EC will ask yet another panel to ignore or reject *this* Panel's work. One hopes for early agreement on appropriate amendments to the DSU considered in the DSU Review last year, which would completely rewrite Article 21.5 procedures, so that the Members can formally declare this issue moot and put behind them once and for all the EC's seemingly unending attempts to justify its delaying tactics in *Bananas.*

40. The United States will not repeat in full its arguments on why this Panel must not make findings with respect to Article 21.5 which would preempt the DSU Review negotiations, amend or adopt an interpretation (functions which may be performed only by the Members), or add to or diminish the rights and obligations of Members. Instead it refers the Panel to note 49 of the U.S. First Submission and paragraphs 19-23 of the U.S. Responses to Panel and EC Questions.

41. Nor will the United States fully recount again the reasoning of the Article 22.6 arbitrator on this relationship, with which the United States concurs. This reasoning can be found at paragraphs 4.10-4.15 of the *Article 22.6 Arbitration*, and is discussed at paragraphs 51-52 of the U.S. First Submission and paragraphs 32-34 and 37-39 of the U.S. Responses to Panel and EC Questions. In summary: (1) neither Article 22 nor Article 23.2(c) reference Article 21.5 proceedings at all, let alone as a prerequisite for request for, DSB authorization of, or implementation of, a suspension of concessions; (2) the EC interpretation would deny effect to the Article 22.6 right to DSB-authorization to suspend concessions with the benefit of the negative consensus rule, while the Article 22.6 arbitrator's interpretation would give effect to both Articles 21.5 and 22; and (3) the goal of multilateral determination of non-compliance is met through an examination of this question by an Article 22.6 arbitrator of whether the level of nullification or impairment is above zero.

42. Further, as discussed in response to Panel questions 9, 10 and 14, it is not necessary or appropriate in this proceeding to address the existence or non-existence of presumptions or burdens in Article 21.5 or Article 22.6 proceedings, since this proceeding is neither. The panel in the EC's Article 21.5 proceeding in *Bananas* noted, "the issue of whether a claim may be made in a particular dispute is best left for determination in that procedure."[230] Likewise, the issue of burdens or presumptions in Article 21.5 and Article 22 proceedings should be left to those proceedings (or to the Members acting in the DSU Review). Moreover, as described in response to Question 10, DSU procedures are adequate to resolve questions relating to suspension of concessions following the reasonable period, without need for the concept of a "presumption" of compatibility or incompatibility.

---

[230] Panel Report, *EC – Bananas III (Article 21.5 – EC), supra*, footnote 40, para. 4.16.

43. For the above reasons, the Panel should not make findings on the relationship between Articles 21.5 and Article 22, nor accept the EC's interpretation of that relationship. Beyond that, however, there is no need for this Panel to make such a ruling because the EC has done no more than assert that there has been a violation of Article 21.5, without drawing any tenable link between the measure - increased bonding requirements - and any obligation allegedly found in Article 21.5 to resort (exclusively) to Article 21.5 proceedings in the event of a disagreement. Even under the EC's reading of Article 21.5, the measure that would presumably implicate Article 21.5 would be a decision not to resort to Article 21.5 proceedings in the event of a disagreement on compliance. However, the measure in this dispute is increased bonding requirements relating to a customs-related risk, not a decision not to pursue Article 21.5 proceedings. The EC appears to suggest that *anything* a complaining Member does while an implementation issue is pending violates Article 21.5 if that Member has not requested and completed Article 21.5 proceedings. However, the purpose of Article 21.5 is not to provide a club to a non-complying Member to distract attention from its non-compliance, it is to provide procedures to help resolve disputes.

44. The self-serving manner in which the EC has attempted to wield Article 21.5 is further highlighted by its response to the Panel's question regarding when an Article 21.5 proceeding should be requested. The EC states,

> an Article 21.5 procedure cannot be requested before the time of the adoption of the implementing measure. Of course, in case of a disagreement on the existence of measures taken to comply with recommendations and rulings of the DSB it is not possible to start a 21.5 procedure before the end of the reasonable period of time.[231]

45. Thus, according to the EC, the complaining party must resort to Article 21.5 procedures if there is a disagreement over implementation, and can be found in violation of Article 21.5 (at the discretion of the (non-)implementing Member if it desires to assert this claim), *unless* the (non-)implementing Member unilaterally determines that the measure does not exist, in which case it may veto the Article 21.5 procedure. Hence, the EC considered itself entitled to threaten to block the adoption of the agenda at the September 1999 DSB meeting at which a request by the complaining parties for an Article 21.5 panel was to be considered, because the EC considered it appropriate for it, and not the Article 21.5 panel, to decide whether the EC's implementation was ripe for review.[232] Article 21.5 makes the procedure under that article available "when there is disagreement as to the existence or consistency with a covered agreement of measures taken to

[231] EC Replies to Panel and US Questions, at 3 (Reply 5).

[232] *See* WT/DSB/M/48 (Minutes of DSB Meeting of 22 September 1999), at 1-2 ("Prior to adoption of the agenda, the representative of the European Communities ... inquired whether ... item [4 of the agenda entitled "Recourse to Article 21.5 of the DSU by Ecuador, Guatemala, Honduras, Mexico and the United States"] had been included on the agenda for information only. *Depending on the answer he would indicate whether he could accept item 4 to remain on the agenda.*" (Emphasis added)).

comply with the recommendations and ruling."[233] The EC would have the Panel create a one-sided obligation applicable only to challenging parties and not implementing parties.

46. The Panel should decline to create any such obligation, applicable to either party. It is simply not relevant to this dispute given that the measure in question is a decision to increase bonding requirements, and nothing in Article 21.5 relates to this. The EC argues that the March 3 action suspended concessions or other obligations. Issues relating to the conditions for suspension of concessions or other obligations are found in Article 23.2(c), and not in Article 21.5. The Panel must reject the EC's attempt to have this Panel condemn the work of the Article 22.6 arbitrator in *Bananas*.

VI. THE PANEL SHOULD REJECT THE EC'S UNSUPPORTED ASSERTIONS THAT THE MARCH 3 ACTION WAS UNDERTAKEN PURSUANT TO SECTIONS 305 OR 306 OF THE TRADE ACT OF 1974

47. Just as the EC is attempting to relitigate issues it lost in connection with the *Bananas* panels and arbitration, it is also seeking to relitigate issues it lost in the panel on *Sections 301-310 of the Trade Act of 1974*. The EC attempts to attribute to Section 305 and 306 responsibility for the March 3 bonding requirements, in disregard for the conclusions of the *Section 301* panel. The Panel must reject the EC's groundless assertions, which only serve to further highlight the EC's political goals in this case.

48. As described in paragraph 33 and note 33 of the U.S. First Submission and in paragraph 55 of the U.S. Responses to Panel and EC Questions, the authority for the March 3 modification to bonding requirements is found in 19 CFR § 113.13. This provision provides Customs with authority to increase bonding requirements to address risks associated with particular entries. The EC provides no evidence of any U.S. determination or action indicating that the March 3 bonding requirements were based on or compelled by Sections 305 and 306.

49. The EC argues that October and November 1998 Federal Register notices indicate that Sections 305-306 somehow forced the United States to adopt the March 3, 1999 bonding requirements, or that these provisions provided the authority for the requirements.[234] However, the EC raised the very same arguments concerning the 1998 Federal Register notices in the *Section 301* panel proceeding, and the panel rejected them.[235] The *Section 301* panel concluded as a factual matter that Sections 305 and 306 provide the U.S. government with discretion to await the completion of WTO proceedings on implementation, even if these pro-

---

[233] DSU Art. 21.5 (emphasis added).

[234] *E.g.*, EC Oral Statement, para. 10.

[235] *See Panel Report, US - Section 301*, *supra*, footnote 9, paras. 4.949-4.950.

ceedings extend well beyond 60 days after the expiry of the reasonable period.[236] In other words, Sections 305 and 306 did not force the United States to adopt the March 3 bonding requirements, and even this indirect a connection between Sections 305 and 306 and those requirements cannot be drawn. The *Section 301* panel examined the factual issues in that dispute in great detail before reaching its conclusions, and this Panel should reject the EC's attempt to have this Panel summarily reject those conclusions for the purpose of advancing the EC's political goals for this dispute. The March 3 action was not taken pursuant to Sections 305 and 306, nor was it compelled by these provisions.

VII. CONCLUSION

50. For the above reasons, the United States respectfully requests that the Panel reject the EC's claims in their entirety, and find that the action taken by the United States on March 3 is not inconsistent with DSU Articles 3, 21.5, 22.6 or 23, nor with GATT 1994 Articles I, II, XI or VIII.

[236] *Panel Report, US - Section 301*, *supra*, footnote 9, paras. 7.147, 7.175, 7.181, nn.721, 722, 724. Among other conclusions, the *Section 301* panel noted its agreement with the United States that the U.S. government had discretion to delay any action decided upon for a total of 240 days following the expiry of the reasonable period, and that this "should be sufficient for the USTR to await in all cases the completion of both Article 21.5 and Article 22.6 procedures as well as DSB authorization to suspend concessions." *Ibid.*, n.724.

Appendix 2.6
The US Responses to Additional Questions of Panel
(8 February 2000)

Q32. The following five legal documents seem to be relevant to the Panel's examination:

- **relevant statutory provisions providing for the normal procedures for the early release of merchandise into the US, including those authorizing the director of the customs office to release merchandise into the United States in advance of liquidation, on the condition of the lodging of a bond;**
- **the federal regulation concerning the amount of bonds (US Exhibit 6);**
- **the Directive Concerning Monetary Guidelines for Setting Bond Amounts (the "Directive") (US Exhibit 4);**
- **the Memorandum to Customs Area and Port Directors, CMC Directors from Director, Trade Compliance Division, US Customs Service, Regarding European Sanction, dated 3 March 1999 (the "Memorandum") (EC Exhibit VIII); and**
- **the USTR's notification and request, as referred to in the Memorandum.**

  (a) Please provide the text of the relevant statutory provisions, and the USTR's notification and request.

  (b) Please explain the relationship between the legal documents enumerated above. For example, please explain the legal basis on which the Director of the Trade Compliance Division issued the Memorandum to the customs area and port directors, and the Memorandum overrode the Directive in respect of the amount of bonds required for EC products on list, thus binding on the customs area and port directors.

  (c) Please briefly explain the ordinary bonding mechanism to help the Panel better understand what happened as of 3 March 1999.

1. The relevant statutory and regulatory sections are provided in U.S. Exhibit 11, and the USTR letter to Customs in U.S. Exhibit 12. The statutory provisions include 19 U.S.C. §§ 1484, 1504 and 1623. The regulatory sections include 19 CFR §§ 142.4 and 142.12.

2. The statute and regulations do not refer to "early release" as such. Rather, they provide for release of merchandise upon filing of a bond and proper documentation, and for liquidation within a year of entry for consumption (19 CFR § 142.4(a) & 19 U.S.C. § 1504). Thus, the importer can obtain early release by Customs merely by submitting a bond and filing proper documentation. By way

of comparison, a system not providing for "early release" would condition release upon final determination and payment of all duties, taxes and charges. This can takes weeks or months, which is why obtaining the release of imported goods in many countries which do not have a surety system or similar type of procedure can often be a lengthy process.

3. The legal basis on which the Memorandum was issued was 19 CFR § 113.13. This regulation provides port directors with authority to require additional bonding or additional security to ensure that the acceptance of an entry will be adequately protected against any duties or other liabilities imposed by law. This discretionary authority may be exercised at any time when Customs becomes aware of a risk that normal bonding requirements will be inadequate. USTR had informed Customs of this risk, and the Memorandum then conveyed this information to the port directors.

4. It is not accurate to describe the Memorandum as "overriding" the Directive in U.S. Exhibit 4 in respect to the amount of bonds. To the contrary, the Directive itself explains on page 3 that standard bonding amounts are to apply to entries,

> unless any district director is aware that either extraordinary circumstances *or a greater risk to the government* is involved. When such extenuating circumstances are involved, the district director with such knowledge shall contact the district where the bond is filed and convey the supporting facts so that appropriate action, if required, can be taken. For example: when the amount of a continuous bond does not cover the duty on a particular shipment and the district director suspects that *a greater risk to the government is involved*, the district director shall:
>
> 1. secure, at the time of release, deposit of the estimated duty due on the shipment, or,
> 2. request a single entry bond for that shipment, or
> 3. request that a new continuous bond in a higher amount be filed.[237]

5. The Directive thus makes clear that, in the ordinary course of Customs operations, and in the exercise of its regulatory authority under 19 CFR § 113.13,[238] it may be necessary for Customs to adjust the bonding requirements for particular entries because of particular risks associated with those entries. The particular risk associated with the entries affected by the Memorandum was that the DSB might authorize higher duties with respect to those entries, and Customs might be unable to collect such duties from importers. The letter from USTR and

[237] U.S. Exhibit 4, page 3 (emphasis added).

[238] *See* U.S. Exhibit 4, page 1, 3.A ("The amount of the bond shall be set by utilizing information on the bond application prescribed in Section 113.12, Customs Regulations (CR), in conjunction with the criteria set forth in Section 113.13 CR, and the guidelines attached to this Directive.").

the Memorandum respectively informed Customs and its port directors of the risk, and indicated that the appropriate response would be changed bonding requirements (options 2 and 3 above).

6. With respect to the operation of the ordinary bonding mechanism, as discussed in previous submissions, importers obtain bonds from private surety companies. The importer presents the bond at the time of formal entry for consumption in order to obtain Customs' release of the merchandise. Importers using a continuous bond which has already been filed with Customs merely refer to the bond in their Customs documentation. On March 4, as a result of the modified bonding requirements, importers wishing to use their continuous bonds had to provide a statement to the port director that these continuous bonds were sufficient to meet the modified requirements. Some importers chose to provide the statement. Others chose to employ single transaction bonds for entries of listed products, rather than reviewing the adequacy of their continuous bonds. Customs did not undertake an entry-by-entry review of continuous bonds to ensure that they met the new requirements.

Q33. The Directive indicates that "[t]he purpose of the bond is to protect the revenue and ensure compliance". (para. 3.B) The "Guidelines for Determining Amounts of Bonds" (the "Guidelines") attached to the Directive indicates that the amount of a continuous bond shall be determined on the basis of not only applicable tariffs, but also "taxes and fees". (Section "Activity 1 – Importer or Broker - Continuous," paragraph a, page 4)

(a) Please explain whether it is possible to legally distinguish part of a continuous bond that is to guarantee the payment of tariffs, from the remaining part which is to cover "taxes and fees" and to "ensure compliance" with applicable laws and regulations. For example, can the whole amount of a bond required for the early release of a given import be forfeited in order to cover fees (if the actual amount of fees exceeds its amount estimated at the time of determination of the amount of the bond) or any penalty or financial obligations arising from a violation of relevant laws or regulations? If not distinguishable, please explain whether such covered fees (or any other financial obligations than tariffs and taxes) are to be collected in return for "services rendered to imports" within the meaning of GATT Article VIII (assuming for the sake of argument that the bonding requirements are deemed to impose "charges" on imports within the meaning of Articles II and VIII).

7. It is not possible to legally distinguish part of a continuous bond that is to guarantee payment of tariffs from that covering taxes and fees and ensuring compliance with applicable laws and regulations. In the event of non-payment of either duties, taxes or fees, or in the event of non-compliance with laws and regulations giving rise to liquidated damages, Customs would have recourse against the bond up to the amount owed for the non-payment or non-compliance, or the full

amount of the bond, whichever is less. Recourse would not be limited to some percentage of the bond amount.

8. While we do not agree that bonding requirements are charges, if, for the sake of argument, they were, they would be commensurate with the cost of services rendered, regardless of the fact that they are intended to cover financial obligations other than tariffs and taxes. As explained in the U.S. Second Submission,[239] the service rendered to the importer is the early release of the merchandise, without delaying release until the amount of duties, taxes or fees are finally determined and paid, and until it has been definitively determined that other obligations have been met. The cost to Customs is the risk that it will be unable to collect any amounts owed by importers if they do not deposit estimated duties, taxes and fees, if finally assessed duties, taxes and fees differ from those deposited, or if the imported goods do not meet other agency requirements. This risk is present because the merchandise will already have been released before estimated duties, taxes and fees have been deposited, and before the full amounts owed are finally determined; there is thus no recourse against the merchandise if the importer refuses to pay. The amount of the risk (the cost to Customs) relates to the full amount which might be due, which includes more than just duties. Thus, the EC is incorrect when it asserts, "The amount of any surety deposit is determined by the anticipated duty liability and *entirely* depends on it."[240] The amount of the surety deposit is in fact determined by the level of risk, which depends not only on the anticipated duty liability but on the full amount of all liabilities (taxes, fees, liquidated damages) which might accrue.[241]

9. The question asks whether "covered fees" or other financial obligations are collected in return for "services rendered to imports." This would depend on the fees in question, and cannot be answered in the abstract. With respect to financial obligations in connection with other agency obligations, this too would depend on the specific obligation. Such fees and other obligations are not themselves at issue in this dispute. Nor are the normal bonding requirements which ensure payment of these fees and other obligations.[242] The measure in question only includes the changes to bonding requirements made on March 3 in connection with the possibility that higher duties might be assessed on certain products from EC countries. The Panel's findings on Articles II and VIII should be limited to this measure, and made only if necessary to resolve this dispute. Our view, again, is that bonding requirements are not "other charges."

---

239 U.S. Second Submission, n.39.

240 EC Second Submission, para. 9 (emphasis added).

241 Likewise, as described in note 29 of the U.S. Second Submission, it is our understanding that the United Kingdom employs a surety system with respect to "high risk" merchandise such as tobacco and alcohol. This provides a good example of the fact that the risk extends beyond the mere duty owed.

242 While not at issue in this dispute, we note that the Kyoto Convention provides that the importer may be required to furnish security to ensure compliance with undertakings to Customs. See U.S. Exhibit 9, Kyoto Convention, Annex B.1, 59-62.

(b) Can the same apply to a single transaction bond, in particular, that in case where the bond in the amount of three times the entered value of imports, for example, because they are subject to any administrative requirements imposed by the Food and Drug Administration?

10. Again, neither the penalties imposed for failure to comply with health and safety laws nor the bonding requirements normally in place to ensure compliance are within the terms of reference of this dispute. Only the *changes* to bonding requirements made on March 3 are within the terms of reference. Single transaction bond requirements applicable to products subject to other agency requirements, such as those of the FDA, did not change as a result of the March 3 action. Having said that, we note that the Kyoto Convention provides for customs authorities to require security to ensure compliance with undertakings and the payment of penalties for non-compliance, in order that merchandise may be released early.[243]

Q34. Can importers normally choose between a continuous bond and a single transaction bond for a given entry, at their discretion? Please provide your statistics or estimate on the percentage of imports (those from the EC and all imports) which were covered by continuous bonds rather than single transaction bonds before 3 March 1999.

11. Importers may normally choose between continuous bonds and single transaction bonds, at their discretion. It has not been possible in the time provided to collect data on the percentage of imports covered by continuous and single transaction bonds. We hope to have this data shortly.

Q35. Paragraphs 3 and 4 of the US Responses to Panel and EC Question, dated 13 January 2000 indicates that the amount of a continuous bond for non-EC products on list was "10% of the duties, taxes and fees paid by the importer of record for all products during the calendar year preceding the date of the bond application," while that for EC products on list was "10% of the entered value of the covered merchandise which the importer imported during the previous year." Please confirm whether the total amount of "the duties, taxes and fees paid by the importer ¼ for all products ¼" is smaller than "the entered value of the covered merchandise".

12. This would depend on the circumstances of the particular importer. For example, if the covered merchandise represented only a small proportion of the products imported during the previous year, it is possible that the duties, taxes and fees on all products might exceed the entered value of the covered merchandise included among those products. To clarify further, with respect to continuous bonds Customs gave importers of the covered merchandise the option of providing a statement that their existing continuous bonds met the new requirements,

[243] U.S. Exhibit 9, Kyoto Convention, Annex B.1, 60, n.2, 62.

or employing single transaction bonds for the covered merchandise. Importers choosing to supplement their existing bonds to meet the new requirements did so by increasing the bond value by an amount equal to 10% of the entered value of covered merchandise included in the merchandise for which the bond was originally calculated. In other words, if the continuous bond had been calculated based on entries during the previous year valued at $1,000,000, and $50,000 of this was covered merchandise, the continuous bond would be supplemented by $5,000 (10% of $50,000). A typical amount which a private surety might charge for this additional coverage would be approximately $50 - $100 (based on a rate of $10-20 per thousand dollars of bond value, as described in paragraph 29 of the U.S. Second Submission).

Q36. Please provide the Panel with the *bindings* (you provided the Panel with only the applied tariffs) of all listed products on 3 March.

13. The rates provided in U.S. Exhibit 7 are the bound, as well as applied, rates.

Q37. To the EC's question "Assuming that an importer wished to clear through the US customs on 4 March 1999 a tonne of 'Uncoated felt paper and paperboard in rolls or sheets' (US HTS 4805 50 00) originating in Switzerland, what would have been the duty liability for such import on that date? What would be the answer if such a product originated in the EC?," the US answer was that the duty liability would have been *based* on a "free" rate of duty. Please provide the Panel with an intelligent explanation of the consequences of the 3 March decision on EC imports of listed products, such as the "Uncoated felt paper and paperboard in rolls or sheets" in comparison with a situation where the same imported products would come from Switzerland.

14. The duty liability as of March 3 would have been zero, regardless of whether the product originated in Switzerland or an EC member State. The March 3 decision had absolutely no consequences for the duty liability; it only affected the bonding requirements. As noted in the U.S. Answers to Panel and EC Questions,[244] with respect to all products listed on March 3, in the absence of further action on April 19, each and every product would have been liquidated at the MFN, applied (and bound) rate. Because the April 19 action specified that duties were to increase for "uncoated felt paper and paperboard in rolls or sheets," entries of this product from EC countries are being liquidated at the rate of 100%.

---

[244] *See* U.S. Answers to Panel and EC Questions, paras. 10, 60; *see, also,* U.S. Second Submission, para. 9.

Q38. In paragraph 5 to the US Responses, the US seems to conclude that products on the list could be imported into the US only upon the submission of a "single transaction bond" in the amount of "the entered value of the merchandises", while the products not on the list could be imported subject to more requirements, i.e. upon the submission of a single transaction bond in the amount of "the entered value of the merchandise plus any duties, taxes and fees for the entry". Is the US stating that as of 3 March 1999 the EC listed products benefitted from positive discrimination *vis-à-vis* other imports of like products from other WTO Members?

15. The single transaction bond amount for listed products was, in fact, less than that for non-listed products. This was intended to minimize the burden on importers wishing to employ single transaction bonds rather than amending their continuous bonds. Importers which normally would have employed single transaction bonds were, in fact, subject to lower bonding requirements, except for importers of listed products subject to other agency requirements, for whom the bonding requirement was three times the entered value. This requirement was unchanged by the March 3 action.

Q39. The official USTR notification (EC Annex VII) entitled "UNITED STATES TAKES CUSTOMS ACTION ON EUROPEAN IMPORTS" provides that "¼effective today, the US Customs Service will begin 'withholding liquidation' on imports valued at over $500 million of selected products from the European Union (EU), consistent with US rights under the WTO Agreements. Withholding liquidation imposes contingent liability for 100% duties on affected products as of March 3, 1999"

Throughout its answers to the Panel's questions the US repeated that on 3 March 1999, no action with regard to "withholding or suspension of liquidation" took place. Does the US imply that as of 3 March duties on imports of listed products were indeed "liquidated" and that duties were effectively collected as of 3 March?

16. The United States wishes to clarify that Exhibit 7 is a press release, with no legal status under U.S. law. The press release's reference to "withholding liquidation" in fact is a non-technical or colloquial reference to the understanding that these entries would not be liquidated outside the normal 314-day liquidation cycle. This does not mean that duties were either "liquidated" or "effectively collected" on March 3. As explained in prior submissions, liquidation (the final determination of duties, taxes and fees) takes place between 314 days and one year after entry. At the time of liquidation, Customs has completed the process of confirming the correct amount of the duties, taxes and fees due for a given entry (including analysis of matters relating to this such as classification and valuation). If there is a difference between the estimated duties, taxes and fees deposited at entry and the finally determined duties, taxes and fees, the difference is either collected or refunded.

17. For entries between March 3 and April 19, Customs would, at liquidation, review the entries of the listed products. For products not listed on April 19, liquidation has and will occur at the entered (MFN) rate, and no further collections or refunds are necessary to supplement the MFN duty deposits provided at entry. For products listed on April 19, the correct duty rate for the entry would have been 100% of the entered value, based on the DSB authorization and the April 19 action, and the difference between estimated duty deposits at the MFN rate and the higher duty amount would be collected. Customs would have recourse against bonds for those importers not paying the difference.

18. The March 3 bonding requirements imposed no liability, effective or otherwise. They merely reduced the risk that Customs would not be able to collect additional duties *if* any such duties were imposed as a result of – and after – DSB authorization. In the absence of the April 19 action, each and every entry subject to changed bonding requirements would be liquidated at the entered, MFN rate – precisely because no liability was imposed on March 3.

Q40. USTR official notification of its 3 March decision anticipates a future event, the arbitrators decision, that would then lead to the US collecting 100% duties on selected EC products: "The United States will refrain from collecting higher duties *until* the release of the arbitrators' final decision. *When the arbitration is complete*, the US will *assess 100% duties on selected products imported as of 3 March* as necessary to offset the harm to the US interests as determined by the arbitrators". How does the US assess the legal relationship between the 3 March decision and the eventual decision of the arbitrators?

19. As explained in response to question 39, EC Annex VII is a press release with no legal status under U.S. law. It is not an "official notification." Its statement that the United States would assess 100% duties as determined by the arbitrators was merely descriptive of the arbitral process and the intentions of the United States in response to that process. If the arbitrators had determined that the appropriate level of suspension was zero, the United States would have taken no action on April 19 to assess 100% duties on any entries. In the absence of such action, each and every entry between March 3 and April 19 would have been liquidated at the entered, MFN rate. In the actual event, the arbitrators determined a level of suspension which the United States implemented through the April 19 action. As described in response to previous questions, the March 3 action did not assess any additional duty liability, nor did it result in the collection of higher duty deposits. It only changed the bonding requirements on certain entries in response to the risk that DSB-authorized higher duties might not be paid for these entries.

Q41. In paragraph 60 the US Responses, the US states *"Had no further action been taken on 19 April 1999*, each and every entry of a product subject to the revised bonding requirements would have been liquidated at

these rates" (see also paragraph 9 of the US Rebuttal Submission). What action exactly was taken on 19 April and what is the legal relationship, if any, between the 3 March decision and the 19 April action referred to by the US and what are the legal consequences of the 19 April 1999 decision?

20. On April 19, following DSB authorization to suspend concessions, the port directors were instructed to assess 100% duties on products included in a list issued on that date. As a result, for entries from April 19, 100% duty deposits were required at the time of entry. At liquidation, such duties would be assessed. For entries between March 3 and April 19 of products listed on April 19, Customs would, at liquidation, collect the difference between MFN duty deposits and the 100% duties assessed. Entries between March 3 and April 19 of products not listed on April 19 were unaffected by the April 19 action. They would be liquidated at the entered, MFN rate. There was no legal relationship between the March 3 action (changed bonding requirements) and the April 19 action (increasing the duty rate for certain products).

Q42. If the 19 April action had not taken place, or if for the sake of arguments, the decision of the arbitrator had been that the EC new Bananas measure did not nullify nor impair the US rights, when would the importer of listed products get their bonding requirements reduced? When did the importers of products included on the 3 March list but not on the 19 April list, get their bonding requirement reduced? were they offered any compensation for the increased bonding requirement?

21. In fact, the United States restored bonding requirements to normal levels for products not included on the final list on April 14, shortly after the arbitrators completed their work and a revised list was prepared. The arbitrator's decision eliminated the additional risk that higher duties would be applicable to these particular products (and that importers might not pay). From April 19, the bonding requirements returned to normal levels for the remaining products, since entries of these products from that date were subject to 100% duty deposits, thereby reducing to normal levels the risk that these deposits would be inadequate.[245] Thus, regardless of the decision which the arbitrators might have reached, bonding requirements would have changed to normal levels following that decision. Inasmuch as importers made no additional payments to the government in connection with the changed bonding requirements, there were no refunds to be made. We are unaware of what arrangements might have been made between the importers and the private surety companies.

Q43. What happened exactly to the importers of cookies (EU 13 HS 34060000) as of 3 March 1999 and as of 20 April 1999 with regard to all entry requirements into the United States? Have duties on imports of cook-

[245] *See* U.S. Second Submission, para. 11.

ies in March been liquidated? And if so how much duty was collected on such items?

22. Importers of cookies, HS19053000, (and candles, HS3406000) were, from March 4, subject to the bonding requirements described in response to question 2.[246] For cookies, the single transaction bonding requirement was unaffected by the March 3 action since this product was subject to health and safety requirements. The bonding requirement remained unchanged at three times the entered value of the product. (For candles, the single entry bonding requirement changed from the entered value plus duties, taxes and fees, to the entered value.) On April 14, the bonding levels for cookies (and candles) returned to normal levels. No other entry requirements changed for these products as a result of either the March 3 or April 19 actions.

23. Attached at U.S. Exhibit 13 is a copy of Customs form 7501, the entry summary. This document is completed by importers and submitted with the estimated duties at, or shortly after, the time of entry. The importer indicates in column 34 the applicable duty rate. An importer of cookies or candles, regardless of source, would have indicated "zero" in this column. Customs would have accepted this document as accurate, and, because the rate of duty was zero, would not have required the deposit of estimated duties. Further, Customs would have liquidated the entries of these products at the entered rate of zero because nothing would have occurred between the time of entry and liquidation to indicate that this rate should be other than zero. The April 19 action changed this rate for certain products - but not for cookies or candles and the other products omitted from the April 19 list.

24. Data on liquidated duties collected for products on the March 3 list is provided in Exhibit 14. Some liquidations have occurred. An explanation of Exhibit 14 is provided in response to question 45. For cookies and candles, any such liquidations would have been, and will be, at the MFN, entered rate – zero.

Q44. Have the tariffs on "Hand Bags (HS 42023210)" imported into the US in March 1999 been liquidated? And if so what is the value of the duties so far collected on these items? Is the collection of duties for these product dating back to 3 March?

25. Data on liquidated duties collected for products on the March 3 list is provided in Exhibit 14. Some liquidations have occurred. An explanation of Exhibit 14 is provided in response to question 45. The duties assessed would be 100% for this product, including entries dating back to March 3, as a result of the actions taken on April 19.

---

246 *See* U.S. Responses to Panel and EC Questions, paras. 3-5.

Q45. Could the US provide the Panel with the product-by-product data on the amount of duties collected on all listed imports as of 3 March for which duties have been liquidated?

26. Data on duties collected is provided in U.S. Exhibit 14. Customs records data for liquidated duties for entries, rather than products included on those entries. An entry may have included one or more listed products; it may also have included one or more *non*-listed products. As a result, it is not possible to provide the precise amount of liquidated duties collected for the products in question. Rather, Exhibit 14 provides information on the estimated duties collected for each product at, or shortly after, the time of entry. These estimated duties were at the MFN rate for all products on the March 3 list, since the March 3 action did not affect duty liability. Exhibit 14 also includes the *total* estimated duties collected for *entries* which included the listed products. Because these entries included other products, the total estimated duties collected for the entries which included the listed products is higher than the estimated duties collected for the listed product. Finally, Exhibit 14 includes the liquidated duties collected for entries which included the listed products. Where the liquidated duties for the entry precisely equals the estimated duties collected for the entry, this confirms that the liquidation occurred at the entered, MFN rates. Where these amounts are different, this may be attributable either to the fact that the entry included other products for which the duty changed as a result of the April 19 action, or it may, for example, be attributable to the fact that other products included in the entry were misclassified or misvalued. Thus, for the products omitted from the April 19 list, the total liquidated duties for the entries equaled the total estimated duty deposits for entries including pork and cheese, were slightly higher or lower for entries including plates and sweaters, and were higher by varying degrees for entries including sweet biscuits and candles. Products included on the final list indicate liquidated duties by entry higher than the estimated duties by entry in all cases.

Q46. Why was the "risk" - to which the US refers as a justification for its 3 March increased bonding requirement and which relates to the possibility of an arbitration award that would conclude that the new EC measure still nullifies and impairs the US WTO, different on 2 March than on 3 or 4 March?

27. In fact, the risk that existing bonds would be inadequate to ensure payment of DSB-authorized higher duties existed from the conclusion of the reasonable period of time, since the EC would be liable from that point for its failure to comply with its WTO obligations, subject to DSB authorization. This risk heightened from March 3 because the Article 22.6 arbitrator in *Bananas* rejected the EC's argument that the arbitrator lacked jurisdiction to proceed with its examination of the level of nullification or impairment, reached decisions on certain

methodological issues, and indicated that it would focus more intensively on determining the level of nullification or impairment (once the EC provided information it had previously refused to submit).[247] Moreover, the EC's own statements confirm that it anticipated that this level would be above zero, i.e., that it knew its allegedly "new" measure would continue to violate the EC's WTO obligations. As described at paragraph 29 of the U.S. First Submission, External Relations Commissioner Sir Leon Brittan stated following the March 2 initial decision that the arbitrators' request to the United States for a new damage estimate meant that the WTO arbitrators would likely find that damages amounted to between $200 and $300 million.[248] More blunt were the comments of Industry Commissioner Bangemann, who admitted that while he had been forced to defend the EC's position, it was groundless.[249] These factors, in combination, indicated an increased risk that the DSB would, ultimately, authorize higher duties.

Q47. In paragraph 55 of the US Rebuttal Submission, the US wrote that "USTR informed Customs of this risk". Can the US provide the Panel with a copy of such communication between USTR and Customs identifying and defining such risk and any other relevant instruction.

28. Please see U.S. Exhibit 12.

Q48. The United States argues in paragraph 35 of its Rebuttal Submission that "assum[ing] for the sake of argument that ¼ the March 3 bonding requirements impose a 'charge' under Article II or VIII, these bonding requirements cannot, by definition, be subject to Article XI¼." Please further elaborate the distinction between the scope of Article II and VIII, and that of Article XI, keeping in mind the bonding requirements in question.

29. Beyond the explanation provided in paragraph 35 of the U.S. Second Submission, the United States notes again that the March 3 bonding requirements did not involve any payments to or charges by the United States government. Importers were required to provide evidence that they obtained either single transaction bonds or continuous entry bonds (or provide a guarantee through a cash deposit in lieu of surety on a bond) for the entry or entries in question. Such bonds are obtained from private surety companies. Customs authorities typically impose several documentation and other requirements. Such requirements do not become "charges" merely because there may be costs associated with them.

---

[247] Decision by the Arbitrators, *EC - Bananas III (US) (Article 22.6 – EC)*, *supra*, footnote 5, paras. 2.11, 3.1-4.15, 6.27.

[248] *See Inside U.S. Trade,* March 12, 1999, at 3.

[249] *See* U.S. First Submission, para. 29 & n.29.

30. The EC has cited the GATT dispute on *Minimum Import Prices (MIPs)*[250] as supporting its view that the March 3 changes to bonding requirements should be considered "other charges."[251] The *MIPs* dispute involved the lodging of two separate securities which guaranteed that importations would be made in accordance with importer undertakings and that importations of tomato concentrate would be made at, or above, a minimum import price. The securities would be forfeit if the importations were not effected or if the prices for tomato concentrate were below the minimum import price.[252] The EC fails to mention the *MIPs* panel's conclusion that the provisions providing for forfeiture of these securities were *not* considered other charges subject to Articles II and VIII, since they were either a penalty for not fulfilling obligations or a mechanism for enforcing the minimum import price system.[253] The sureties at issue in this dispute are enforcing the importer's obligation to pay duties, and thus should not be considered "other charges" under Articles II and VIII. In addition, the *MIPs* panel examined interest charges and costs in connection with the securities at issue in that dispute. It is not clear from the *MIPs* report whether these charges were collected by governmental authorities. If so, the *MIPs* conclusions would not be applicable here, since the U.S. government charges nothing for the bonds it requires. Moreover, the EC fails to mention the *MIPs* panel's findings that even though these interest charges and costs were "other charges," for one of the securities they were quite small, and "commensurate with the cost of services rendered."[254] To the extent that the Panel considers that charges by *private* sureties would be "other charges," they too are quite small, and should be considered commensurate with the cost of services rendered. As described in paragraph 29 of the U.S. Second Submission, a typical charge by a private surety would be $3.50 per thousand dollars of bond value for single transaction bonds and $10-20 dollars per thousand dollars of bond value for continuous bonds. However, it would be troubling precedent for a panel to review the price charged by private entities for the services rendered by those entities.

Q49. In claiming that the increase in the amount of a required security was to cover 100% tariff which might eventually be due (after the arbitration panel has completed is work), the US appears to assume that the applicable obligation, in the form of tariffs, can change *after* the entry of a listed product into the customs territory of a WTO Member. Is this retroactive change of the applicable law and applicable obligation, acceptable in international law?

---

250 GATT Panel Report on EEC – Programme of Minimum Import Prices. Licenses and Surety Deposits for Certain Processed Fruits and Vegetables (MIPS), adopted 18 October 1978, BISD 25S/68.

251 *E.g.*, EC Second Written Submission, para. 16.

252 *MIPs*, para. 2.6.

253 *MIPs,* paras. 4.7 and 4.16.

254 *MIPs*, paras. 4.2, 4.6.

31. As an initial matter, we note that the March 3 action did not itself change the duty rate applicable to entries from March 3. It merely changed bonding requirements for these entries.

32. As the EC observes in its second submission, the duty liability for a given product is that on the date of importation.[255] However, it is not always the case that the duty applicable *for* the date of importation is that anticipated *on* that date. For example, if an importer misclassifies a product on importation, it may be some time after importation that customs authorities or the importer recognize the misclassification, and change the duty rate accordingly.[256] Likewise, an error in valuation of a product could result in a higher duty liability than that anticipated at the time of entry, and this might not be discovered, and changed, until sometime after entry. An importer is thus not always entitled to pay the duties it thought were due at the time of entry.

33. Likewise, in antidumping investigations, there may be instances in which duties might be applied to past entries based on a decision made some time after entry. Article 10 of the Agreement on Implementation of Article VI of the General Agreement on Tariffs and Trade 1994 (the Antidumping Agreement) provides for the imposition of duties from the date of imposition of provisional measures following final determinations of dumping and injury (Article 10.2). Further, antidumping duties may be imposed on entries made even prior to the application of provisional measures (that is, before even preliminary determinations of dumping and injury have been made) under specified circumstances (Article 10.6).

34. As discussed at paragraph 38-42 of the U.S. First Submission and paragraphs 16-18 of the U.S. Answers to Panel and EC Questions, the context and purpose of the provisions on suspension of concessions make clear that this date may fall at any time after the expiration of the reasonable period. DSU Article 22.7 states only that the request for suspension must be consistent with the arbitrators' decision.[257] Article 22.1 is clear that the suspension of concessions or other obligations is available "in the event that the recommendations and rulings [of the DSB] are not implemented within a reasonable period of time." The purpose of the reasonable period of time - to provide a grace period for a Member to bring itself into compliance without consequences - in its very enunciation implies that the consequences of non-compliance accrue from the conclusion of that period. Likewise, compensation under Article 22.2 is available from the end of the reasonable period, and it would only encourage delay, and discourage agree-

---

[255] EC Second Submission, para. 12.

[256] In fact, it is our understanding that customs authorities of EC member States can reclassify and thereby apply higher duty rates to goods for up to three years after such goods have been entered.

[257] Article 22.7 provides, in relevant part, "The DSB shall be informed promptly of the decision of the arbitrator and shall upon request, grant authorization to suspend concessions or other obligations where the request is consistent with the decision of the arbitrator, unless the DSB decides by consensus to reject the request."

ments on compensation, if liability for suspension of concessions were delayed after that point.

35. Thus, WTO rules provide both in the context of suspension of concessions and otherwise that the duty applicable on the date of entry may not be that anticipated on that date. Looking beyond WTO rules, as noted in paragraph 27 of the U.S. Second Submission, the Kyoto Convention, like the WTO Customs Valuation Agreement, encourages the early release of merchandise, and permits the adoption of surety systems to ensure compliance with regulatory undertakings, as well as to ensure collection of any *additional* import duties and taxes that might become chargeable.[258] Thus, the Convention explicitly contemplates that, as a necessary consequence of the early release of merchandise, it might become necessary to impose bonding requirements to ensure collection of duties beyond those for which an importer might be liable based on information at the time of entry, and which might become due as a result of events subsequent to entry. In this way, the Kyoto Convention as well makes clear that the duties ultimately assessed may exceed those anticipated at the time of entry.

[258] *Kyoto Convention*, Annex B.1, 59-61.

Appendix 2.7
The US oral presentation on matters relating to the scope of this dispute at the Second Substantive Meeting (9 February 2000)

1. Mr. Chairman, Members of the Panel, the United States appreciates this opportunity to address the EC's attempt to mischaracterize the measure in question and the terms of reference of this dispute. Mr. Chairman, the United States has asked the Panel for a preliminary ruling on this issue. A preliminary ruling is important for the United States – as well as the EC – to know what measures are at issue in this Panel proceeding so that the parties can direct their evidence and arguments to claims within the Panel's terms of reference, and not burden the Panel with material that goes to claims outside those terms of reference. We are now at the second meeting of the Panel. The written submissions have all been filed, the oral statements all prepared. This is the last opportunity to respond to arguments. If the United States does not know at this meeting which measures the Panel considers to be before it in this proceeding, how can the United States be expected to have an opportunity to respond?

2. In its January 24 letter, the EC asserts that the U.S. request for a preliminary ruling on the measure at issue is untimely. However, the timing of the U.S. request has been a function of the timing of the EC's own attempt to expand the terms of reference. Recognizing that the actions taken on March 3 were limited to bonding, the EC for the first time in its statement at the first substantive meeting attempted to recast the scope of this proceeding. It would be unfair and a denial of due process to preclude the United States from responding and seeking clarification as to the measures at issue. Beyond this, questions concerning the terms of reference can, and should, be raised at any time in the dispute settlement process, since they are jurisdictional in nature and relate to a Panel's competence to consider a measure. In India - Patent Protection for Pharmaceutical and Agricultural Chemical Products (19 December 1997, WT/DS50/AB/R, para. 92), the Appellate Body found that the parties could not agree to jurisdiction over a claim that was not in the panel request. The Appellate Body stated:

> The jurisdiction of a panel is established by that panel's terms of reference, which are governed by Article 7 of the DSU. A panel may consider only those claims that it has the authority to consider under its terms of reference. A panel cannot assume jurisdiction that it does not have.

3. Mr. Chairman, DSU Article 4.2 provides for consultations on "measures . . . taken," while DSU Article 4.7 provides that a complaining party may request the establishment of a panel if the consultations on that measure fail to resolve the dispute. The basic principle that a measure must have been taken before it may be subject to a consultation request and subsequent panel proceedings is fundamental to the WTO dispute settlement process. We do not think the EC disputes this, particularly in light of the vehemence with which it refused the re-

quest by the complaining parties in Bananas to convene an Article 21.5 panel on this basis. As we have noted elsewhere, the EC went so far as to threaten to block the agenda of the September 1998 DSB meeting rather than see the DSB authorize the formation of a panel on what the EC considered a measure not yet taken.

4. The EC submitted its consultation request on March 4, 1999, the day following the U.S. announcement of its decision to change bonding requirements. Obviously, the consultation request could not, and so did not, include any measures taken on April 19. Moreover, at the consultations the United States made clear that the April 19 actions were not within the scope of the consultations, and there were no consultations on them. We assume that the EC officials at the consultations informed their counterparts responsible for this Panel proceeding as to what transpired at the consultations. As the U.S. actions taken on April 19 following DSB authorization to suspend concessions were not subject to a consultation request or consultations, the EC's panel request could not have covered them. Nevertheless, the EC is attempting to draw the actions of April 19 into the scope of this proceeding, based on its late appreciation that the March 3 action involved nothing more than changes to U.S. bonding requirements.

5. The March 3 action in no way affected duty liabilities. Any duty deposits for products imported from March 3 to April 19 were made at the MFN, bound rates. The only change in the entry procedures for these importers was the modified bonding requirements. As with normal bonding requirements, the changed bonding requirements did not entail any payment to the government. Nor did these bonding requirements alter in any way the ultimate duty liability, notwithstanding the mere assertions to the contrary by the EC. In the absence of the April 19 action, each and every entry subject to increased bonding requirements would have been liquidated at the entered, MFN rate.

6. The EC asserts in paragraph 7 of yesterday's responses to questions that it "is not convinced" that the March 3 action did not increase any duty liability. However, as explained by the Appellate Body in Shirts and Blouses, the burden of demonstrating a fact lies with the party asserting it. Mere assertions do not suffice. The EC has merely asserted that the bonding requirements increased duty liability, with no explanation of how this would be the case under U.S. law. The United States is confident that it has a better grasp than does the EC regarding the operation of U.S. law, and the EC is simply wrong.

7. The EC incorrectly theorizes that it could draw into the scope of this dispute actions of April 19, even though they could not have been subject to a March 4 consultation request, by claiming that its panel request refers to the April 19 action as confirming the duty liability imposed on March 3. Again, however, there was no duty liability imposed on March 3, and so it could not have been "confirmed." Even this theory fails.

8. In its January 24 letter, the EC also argues that because it included the list issued on April 19 as an attachment to its panel request, the April 19 actions are within the terms of reference. However, the inclusion of this list cannot cure the fact that the EC's March 4 consultation request could not have included measures

not yet taken. Moreover, the inclusion of this list cannot cure the fact that in the EC's panel request, the only reference to the April 19 action is that just mentioned – namely, that this action allegedly confirmed a non-existent liability said to have been imposed on March 3. The list included with the panel request can be viewed as no more than informational.

9. The terms of reference of this dispute do not provide jurisdiction to address the actions taken on April 19, and we urge the Panel to reject the EC's attempts to draw these actions into the scope of this dispute. We look forward to your decision.

Appendix 2.8

The US oral presentation at the Second Substantive Meeting

(9 February 2000)

Introduction

1. Mr. Chairman, thank you for your preliminary ruling that the April 19 actions are not within the scope of this proceeding. At the same time, we appreciate the panel's recognition that it is important that we understand these actions. This importance will become clearer in a few moments.

2. Mr. Chairman, distinguished members of the Panel, it is again my honor to represent the United States before you today. It is now the second meeting of this Panel, and the issues in this dispute have become clearer. For example, it is now clear that the only measure taken on March 3 was the modification of bonding requirements with respect to certain merchandise from EC countries, and that this change in bonding requirements did not impose any duty liability beyond the MFN, bound rates applicable to all imports from all sources. It is also clear that this action came in the context of EC efforts to delay the completion of Article 22.6 proceedings required, under DSU rules, to finish by March 2. Further, it is clear that the EC's efforts at delay were but the most recent of its attempts to undermine the operation of the WTO dispute settlement system in order to escape the consequences of its failure to comply with DSB rulings and recommendations in *Bananas*.

3. Unfortunately, the EC's argumentation in this dispute has shown its continued desire to obfuscate the issues and its lack of regard for the consequences of its actions on the dispute settlement and international trading system. The EC has explicitly asked this Panel to find the work of another panel *ultra vires*, and has implicitly asked this Panel to violate WTO rules which reserve to the Members the right to amend WTO provisions. Moreover, the EC has conveniently put aside its insistence during the reasonable period that only a measure actually taken may be subject to dispute settlement procedures, and instead has sought to have this Panel consider actions not taken on March 3 which are not within the Panel's terms of reference. Further, the EC has shown itself willing to make overly broad arguments which would undermine trade-enhancing early-release bonding systems in its single-minded effort to receive Panel sanction for its delaying tactics in *Bananas*.

4. Mr. Chairman, this Panel must focus not on what the EC asserts to have occurred on March 3, but on the actions actually taken on that date. Moreover, this Panel should analyze those actions for their consistency with U.S. WTO obligations with a sober eye, making only those findings necessary to complete its task. It should refuse the EC's invitation to legislate, to exceed the terms of reference, and to make sweeping pronunciations of law with uncertain consequences for international trade. When the actions actually taken on March 3 are examined

against applicable U.S. obligations, it is clear that they were consistent with those obligations.

The Measure

5. I would first like to briefly address some of the points which the EC raised today. Regarding the USTR letter to the U.S. Customs Service, it is important to recognize that, as is clear from the language used in the letter, this was a request, not an "instruction." The only authority for action cited in the letter is that which Customs employed to undertake the changed bonding requirements, 19 CFR § 113.13. The letter resulted from an interagency process, and reflected that process, but the only legal authority under which action was taken was that of Customs. With respect to "withholding liquidation," it must be recognized that there is no right to immediate liquidation. Customs procedures already called for a 314-day to one-year liquidation period. Thus, the first request in the USTR letter regarding "withholding liquidation" could not be honored, since Customs was already employing a 314 liquidation cycle, and this was not changed.

6. Regarding the April 19 actions, notwithstanding the EC's arguments, these actions did make duties retroactive to entries from March 3. All that the United States did on March 3 was to change bonding requirements so that Customs would have a better chance of collecting duties *if* the DSB authorized suspension of concessions and *if* the United States acted to increase duties. That action came on April 19.

7. I would like to review again how the U.S. system works for imports. When an import arrives in the United States, the importer provides cursory documentation regarding the import, along with evidence of a bond. Upon presentation of this documentation and evidence of a bond, the merchandise is immediately released. At or shortly after release, the importer deposits estimated duties. Yesterday we submitted Exhibit 14, which provided data on duties for listed products. That exhibit includes a column for estimated duties paid. For every item on that list the estimated duties paid were at the MFN rate. Customs accepted the deposits as accurate because this was the only duty liability at that time. There was no instruction to port directors to increase duties, and therefore the ports did not collect higher duty deposits. At liquidation, Customs finalizes its determination of the duty liability. It looks at the classification and valuation, for example, to confirm that they are correct. Once it has confirmed the liability, it sends a notice to the importer. If there is a difference between the duty deposits and the actual duty liability, the difference is either collected or refunded. A short time after liquidation has occurred, the door is closed for Customs to review the duty liability. Customs can't go back, except in cases of fraud, and reliquidate the entry. It is our understanding that the U.S. system is different from others in this regard. In other systems, the statute of limitations permits customs authorities to go back and correct duty liabilities up to the statute of limitations of around three years. In the United States this is capped at one year. Customs must liquidate between 314 days and one year.

8. I would like to reiterate that the only measure within the terms of reference of this dispute is the March 3 change in bonding requirements on certain products from EC countries. The March 3 press release is not itself a measure, nor is the USTR letter to Customs. The EC requested consultations on March 4 with reference to actions taken on March 3, and only those actions may properly be the subject of these dispute settlement proceedings. Nothing the United States did on March 3 affected duty liabilities, nor did it delay liquidation. Any deposits for products imported from March 3 to April 19 were made at the MFN, bound rates. The only change in the entry procedures for these importers was the modified bonding requirements. As with normal bonding requirements, the changed bonding requirements did not entail any payment to the government. Nor did these bonding requirements alter in any way the ultimate duty liability, notwithstanding mere assertions to the contrary by the EC. In the absence of the April 19 action, each and every entry subject to increased bonding requirements would have been liquidated at the entered, MFN rate.

GATT Articles, and DSU Articles 22.6 and 23.2(c)

9. The EC added little new in its answers to panel questions or second submission on issues relating to GATT Articles I, II, VIII or XI. As described in the U.S. submissions, the EC has failed to meet its burden of demonstrating that the March 3 action is inconsistent with any of these provisions. In particular, the United States wishes to draw attention to the EC's arguments concerning Articles II and VIII. The EC appears to argue that only the changes to bonding requirements instituted on March 3 should be considered prohibited other charges, but its arguments would implicate all bonding systems. In its determination to obtain findings against the March 3 action, the EC would have the Panel undermine a trade-facilitating mechanism which speeds the early release of goods by customs authorities, and which is contemplated – and encouraged – by the WTO Customs Valuation Agreement and the Kyoto Convention. Many WTO Members employ surety systems to guarantee the collection of customs duties and to address risks relating to specific imports of merchandise.

10. When customs authorities release goods into their territories before duties and other fees have been deposited or finally determined, and before it has been possible to definitively confirm compliance with all relevant importer undertakings, this obviously involves an assumption of risk by those customs authorities. The risk directly relates to the total liabilities which might be due, including not only duties, but also other taxes and fees, as well as liquidated damages for failure to comply with other undertakings to Customs. Should importers choose not to pay their customs debts, customs authorities could find themselves without the ability to collect these debts. Faced with this risk, customs authorities may choose to hold the merchandise until the importer's total liabilities have been finally determined and paid, and until it has been definitively determined that the importer has met other requirements. However, as contemplated in the Customs Valuation Agreement and the Kyoto Convention (as well as the International Chamber of

Commerce International Customs Guidelines), early release of merchandise is still possible, and should be undertaken, if customs authorities employ surety systems to address the risks inherent in that practice.

11. The EC's arguments on Articles II and VIII would implicate all bonding systems, and create conflicts both with the Customs Valuation Agreement and the Kyoto Convention. Such interpretations are unnecessary, and should be avoided. The U.S. bonding requirements in connection with early release of goods do not require a payment to the government, and do not impose an "other charge" within the meaning of Articles II and VIII. This includes the revised bonding requirements of March 3. The government collected no fees in connection with the bonds for entries subject to the revised bonding requirements. Obviously, this case is not about the fee structure of *private* banks for providing sureties, a normal financial service. We want to note that the EC on page 4 of its statement today suggests that the fees charged by these private sureties would total $10 million dollars on $520 million in trade. This figure is pure fantasy. The EC ignores the fact that the continuous bond amount is only 10% of the entered value, and that these bonding requirements were in place for only about a month. We believe private sureties typically charge about $10-20 per thousand dollars of bond amount for continuous bonds, so the numbers these private sureties would charge bear no resemblance to the EC figure.

12. The EC in paragraph 4 of yesterday's answers appears to acknowledge that a measure which "does not provide any revenue for the treasury of the importing WTO Member does not qualify as a 'duty, tax or other charge.'" The EC made this statement in the context of its discussion of Article XI, regarding which the EC has failed to demonstrate a violation. Nevertheless, the EC cannot argue that if the bonding requirements do not qualify as a "charge" for purposes of Article XI, they may still be a "charge" purposes of Article II. There is no basis for drawing this distinction. Beyond the fact that the government received no payment or revenue in connection with the bonding requirement, the bonding requirement is not an "other charge" because the bonds are merely enforcing the obligation to pay duties, and such sureties as enforcement mechanisms are not an other charge under the *MIPs* precedent, which we note was followed in the *Bananas II* GATT panel (DS38/R, 11 February 1994).

13. However, even if the Panel were to conclude that the bonding requirements were an "other charge" covered by Articles II and VIII, any such "charges" must be considered commensurate with the cost of services rendered, namely, the risk that importers may not pay their duty and other liabilities. Should the Panel consider it necessary to reach the question of whether any "charges" specifically associated with the March 3 bonding requirements are consistent with Articles II and VIII, it should find that such "charges" are commensurate with the additional "cost" associated with early release of the affected entries, that is, the risk that additional duties authorized by the DSB would be imposed on these entries, and that importers might choose not to pay them.

14. With regard to Article XI, and its relationship to Articles II and VIII, we would like to note that the EC yesterday stated in paragraph 5 that its Article XI arguments would only be relevant if the bonding requirements did not also increase the customs tariffs. Since the bonding requirements did not, the EC is admitting that Articles II and VIII are not implicated. However, the EC argument with respect to Article XI fails on its own. As noted in our submissions, the EC's Article XI argument has rested solely on the incorrect assertion that the bonding requirements effectively stopped trade. They did not. Further, in yesterday's submission, the EC suggests at paragraph 4 that the "purpose" to stop trade also creates an Article XI violation. However, the purpose of a measure is not relevant to whether it violates Article XI. In *Bananas II*, the Panel considered the argument of the complaining parties that a high over-quota rate was inconsistent with Article XI:1 because it adversely affected trade. At paragraph 139 of its report the panel agreed with the *EEC Oilseeds* and *Japan Leather* panels that the actual impact of a measure is irrelevant to an Article XI analysis, and noted that commercial impact is nowhere mentioned in Article XI. Likewise, allegations concerning the "purpose" of a measure are nowhere mentioned in Article XI, and are irrelevant to that analysis.

15. For this reason, and for the reasons discussed in our submissions, the EC has failed to demonstrate that the March 3 bonding requirements were inconsistent with GATT Articles I, II, VIII and XI. In light of this, the EC has also failed to demonstrate that the March 3 action involved a suspension of concessions or other obligations. Therefore, the EC has also failed to demonstrate that the March 3 actions were inconsistent with Articles 22.6 or 23.2(c), which set forth conditions for the suspension of concessions or other obligations.

Article 21.5

16. I would now like to address the EC's arguments with respect to Article 21.5. I would like to begin by quoting DSU Article 22.7: "The parties shall accept the arbitrator's decision as final and the parties concerned shall not seek a second arbitration." This is a firm obligation. And yet this seems very much at odds with the EC's request to find the Article 22.6 arbitrator's decision *ultra vires*, as well as with the statement made this morning by the EC that if the Panel agrees with the EC on Article 21.5, the suspension of concessions determined by the arbitrators and authorized by the DSB "is and remains" inconsistent with U.S. obligations - and that includes both after March 3 and after April 19. This is anything but acceptance, and by its very asking calls into question the EC's compliance with Article 22.7

17. It is now clear that the EC's arguments on Article 21.5 have nothing to do with the measure at issue in this dispute, increased bonding requirements. The EC itself has been unable to draw any connection between the bonding requirements and Article 21.5 beyond the tenuous and unsustainable argument that the March 3 measure "was directly dependent upon" actions which allegedly violate Article 21.5 (actions not within the terms of reference of this dispute), rather than that

the March 3 measure itself violates Article 21.5 (see EC Second Written Submission, para. 20).

18. The EC is asking this Panel to violate several WTO provisions in order to find that the Article 22.6 arbitral panel in *Bananas* somehow violated other DSU provisions. This transparently political exercise has nothing to do with resolving the issues in this dispute concerning increased bonding requirements, but is instead merely an attempt to circumvent the DSU review process and violate the exclusive right of all WTO Members to amend the DSU. Moreover, we do not see how the EC reconciles asking this Panel to declare the work of the *Bananas* arbitrator *ultra vires* with the EC's obligation under DSU Article 22.7 to "accept the arbitrator's decision as final." We are particularly troubled by the EC's implication that the arbitrator's report is "not binding" or can otherwise be disregarded with respect to the right of the United States to suspend concessions (EC Second Submission, paragraphs 74-76). The EC's direct challenge to the validity of the Article 22.6 arbitrator's decision represents anything but the acceptance of the arbitrator's report required by Article 22.7.

19. The simple consideration that bonding requirements have nothing to do with a DSU article providing for a mechanism to settle disputes on implementation exposes the utter lack of foundation of the EC's Article 21.5 claim. The EC purports to find in Article 21.5 a firm obligation on the part of complaining parties (but, of course, not the party accused of non-implementation) to resort to Article 21.5 procedures, to the exclusion of Article 22 procedures explicitly provided for in the DSU and which, by their terms, do not so much as reference Article 21.5. Neither the *Bananas* arbitrators nor the *Section 301* panel found such an obligation to exist, and we agree that it does not. However, even if there were such an obligation, the EC has offered no credible explanation of how increased bonding requirements violate such an obligation. Instead, the EC believes it may infer actions which violate Article 21.5, just as it believes it may, through mere assertion, include within the scope of this dispute actions not taken on March 3, or actions not within the terms of reference. According to the EC, if a non-implementing party believes it has implemented DSB rulings and recommendations, and a complaining party has not requested Article 21.5 proceedings, then *anything* the complaining party does violates Article 21.5. Requesting multilateral proceedings under Article 22 violates Article 21.5, providing evidence to an Article 22 arbitrator violates Article 21.5, increasing bonding requirements violates Article 21.5 – virtually anything that highlights the EC's non-compliance in *Bananas* violates Article 21.5. This is simply not a tenable interpretation.

20. Let us step back for a second and recall that the purpose of Article 21.5 is to provide a multilateral, expedited mechanism to resolve disputes on implementation. It is not intended to serve as a justification for delaying multilateral consequences for non-compliance. Nor is it intended to nullify multilateral rights to have the DSB authorize suspension of concessions under the negative consensus rule within 30 days of the end of the reasonable period, or to have an Article 22 arbitrator complete its work within 60 days. And Article 21.5 is not intended to provide non-implementing parties with a club to deter complaining parties from

pursuing their WTO rights to request DSB-authorized suspension. The EC's reading of Article 21.5 would turn the purpose of Article 21.5 on its head and make it a tool to undermine WTO provisions central to ensuring that Members comply with their WTO obligations.

21. The EC argues that it is entitled to a ruling from this Panel on the relationship between Article 21.5 and Article 22, that failure to make such a ruling would be a denial of "justice." However, the Panel may rule on the EC's Article 21.5 claim without implicating or nullifying Article 22 by simply rejecting the Article 21.5 claim on the grounds that the bonding requirements do not implicate any conceivable obligation under Article 21.5. Should the Panel reach this conclusion, or choose not to reach the EC's Article 21.5 claim, justice would indeed be well-served. There would be no justice in findings that another WTO panel has acted *ultra vires*, that rights under Article 22 on the negative consensus rule and on the timing of Article 22.6 proceedings should be nullified, that the DSU Article 3.2 requirement that Panels neither add to or diminish rights should be ignored, or that Panels may exercise the right to amend the DSU granted exclusively to Members under WTO Agreement Article X. Such findings might serve the EC's political goals, but they would not serve justice.

22. I would like to briefly respond to several matters relating to the EC's Article 21.5 arguments from its second submission. The first is the EC's claim that its implementation was a "new" measure. As we have explained, the novelty of a member's implementation actions is irrelevant to this dispute. However, we do not wish the Panel to be left with a misleading impression concerning the EC's changes to its bananas import regime. The elements of the so-called "new" banana import regime which violated the EC's obligations were virtually identical to the old regime, and violated it for the same reasons – it provided for separate, discriminatory banana regimes in violation of GATT 1994 Article XIII and assigned licenses based on a reference period which guaranteed discriminatory results in violation of GATS Articles II and XVII. The *Bananas* complaining parties pointed this out to the EC from as early as January 1998, but the EC ignored them, considering that it had the right to continue to nullify and impair the WTO benefits of the complaining parties through the expedient of repackaging its old regime. This has been the EC's practice throughout the nearly ten years of the *Bananas* dispute. In part this has made the various panels' work easier – when the WTO *Bananas* panel examined an earlier example of the EC's repackaging efforts, the panel was able to complete its analysis by merely quoting several pages from the report of its GATT predecessor, and add "we agree." (*Bananas* Panel Report, paras. 7.179-7.180.) Just as the continued violation of the EC's repackaged regime was apparent to the complaining parties and to the *Bananas* arbitrator/panelists, it was apparent to EC officials. I refer the Panel to paragraph 29 of the U.S. First Submission, which quotes EC officials acknowledging that the EC's claim to have instituted a WTO-consistent "new" regime were groundless.

23. Another point from the EC's second submission which the United States would like to address relates to U.S. actions with respect to Article 21.5 in *Shrimp Turtle*. The U.S. agreement with Malaysia only reinforces the fact that

DSU rules as they now stand compel parties to undertake such agreements if they wish to delay Article 22 proceedings without opening the door to the possibility of a defending party blocking authorization to suspend concessions. The EC at paragraphs 62-63 of its Second Submission points out that such agreements do not prevent third parties from still blocking consensus, and this is true. However, the EC does not explain how its interpretation of Articles 21.5 or Article 22 would overcome this deficiency. In fact it would heighten it. As these provisions are currently drafted, if Article 21.5 proceedings were required prior to Article 22 proceedings, then not only third parties, but also non-implementing parties, could deny complaining parties the benefit of the negative consensus rule under Article 22, and complaining parties would also be denied the right under Article 22 to have the arbitrators complete their work within 60 days of the end of the reasonable period. In other words, entire provisions of Article 22 would be denied legal effect. Avoiding such a result is the "compelling reason in law" not to adopt the EC interpretation, notwithstanding the EC's difficulty in understanding this (EC Second Submission, paragraph 64).

24. However much the WTO Members may or may not agree that procedures similar to Article 21.5 should or should not precede a request for suspension, DSU rules as they now stand do not provide for this. The Members of the WTO have been working on *amendments* to the DSU that would provide for this, and would cure the problems relating to the negative consensus rule which exist in the current DSU text. However, only the Members can amend the DSU. A single member cannot ask a single panel to *legislate* such changes by fiat, in violation of DSU Article 3.2 and in the exercise of the Member's exclusive rights under WTO Agreement Article X.

25. That the EC is asking the Panel to do just this is even clearer in the EC's demand that the Panel legislate the creation of burdens and presumptions applicable in Article 21.5 and Article 22 proceedings. There is no possible basis for the EC to demand that this Panel dictate to *other panels* how they must conduct their proceedings, on the basis of new rights and obligations pulled out of thin air. As the EC notes at paragraph 87 of its second submission, the *only* presumption referred to in the DSU is that in DSU Article 3.8, that a breach of the rules is presumed to have an adverse effect. The EC refers to the statement of the Appellate Body in *Chile Liquors* that there is *no* presumption of bad faith - not that there *is* a presumption of good faith, as the EC asserted this morning - but this only reinforces the point that panels should not engage in the wholesale creation of presumptions not found in the WTO Agreements. The issue of burdens and presumptions in Article 21.5 proceedings is irrelevant to this dispute, and there is no need to make findings on this topic to resolve it.

26. The March 3 bonding requirements simply do not relate to Article 21.5. We urge the Panel to reject the EC's flexible and self-serving approach to defining the measure in this dispute so as to achieve improper legislative pronouncements, just as we urged the Panel to reject the EC's flexible interpretation of the terms of reference to cover measures outside the scope of the EC's consultation request.

Conclusion

27. As the complaining party in this dispute, the EC has the burden of demonstrating that the March 3 bonding requirements were inconsistent with U.S. WTO obligations. It has failed to meet this burden, and the Panel should reject the EC's claims in their entirety. Thank you very much.

Appendix 2.9

The US closing statement at the Second Substantive Meeting

(9 February 2000)

1. Mr. Chairman, members of the Panel, I want to begin this statement by thanking you both for your efforts to date in sifting through the various arguments of the parties, and for the efforts you will now undertake in reaching your decision. As the parties are now concluding their arguments both on what happened on March 3 and on whether this complied with U.S. WTO obligations, I think it is important to step back and ask how we got here today, and to summarize where we are. Simply put, we are here because, at the same time that the EC continues to deny the United States over $191 million per year in negotiated and agreed WTO benefits, the EC is complaining about less than seven weeks of changed bonding requirements.

2. Since the beginning of the WTO, the EC has maintained a banana regime in breach of its WTO obligations. It is now firmly established that this regime nullifies and impairs U.S. benefits under the WTO in an amount of $191.4 million per year. This multimillion dollar nullification and impairment persisted, without any compensation for the United States, through consultations, over a year of panel proceedings, then Appellate Body proceedings, then a reasonable period of time of over 15 months. Finally, when all other avenues of redress failed, the United States sought and was granted authorization by the DSB to suspend concessions. Even that authorization was delayed beyond the date promised the United States under the DSU by the failure of the EC to provide the arbitrator with the necessary information.

3. No sooner did it become apparent that the United States was going to be provided some redress than the EC immediately challenged the small step the United States took to try to preserve its ability to put the DSB authorized suspension of concessions into effect. The EC is complaining about less than seven weeks of changed bonding requirements, even though it has not yet seen fit to remedy years of multimillion dollar nullification and impairment.

4. Which brings us to exactly what did and did not happen on March 3. The EC relies on press statements and requests – not instructions – from USTR to argue that Customs began to withhold liquidation. We have provided and referenced official Customs statutes, notices and regulations concerning their pre-existing policy of liquidating entries between 314 days and one year. We have pointed out that the March 3 actions had no effect on the implementation of this policy, and that there is no such measure under U.S. law as "withholding liquidation." The EC argues that the United States revised bonding requirements, and we did – continuous bonds were increased by 10% (not 100%) of the value of covered merchandise previously imported. This entailed no payment to the government. Further, as the example in our response to question 35 makes clear, there were at most negligible payments to private sureties associated with the bonds.

5. Which brings us to the heart of the matter. The bonding requirements – the only action taken on March 3 and the only measure in existence at the time this dispute was commenced – did not impose any duty liability. The EC's argument that the United States "effectively increased" duty liability is made without reference to a single U.S. law allegedly imposing such a liability. There is no such thing as an "effectively increased" duty liability. There is either a duty liability or there is not. Had there been a duty liability the instructions to port directors on March 3 would have indicated that they should collect such duties, and these port directors would have required deposits of estimated duties to match such higher liability. This did not happen on March 3. Only on April 19 was a higher duty assessed, and higher duty deposits collected. The EC claims that the U.S. could not under U.S. law retroactively increase duties on April 19. This is simply not true. Our response to question 4 makes clear that duty increases or decreases may be made effective retroactively under U.S. law. Without such authority, there would be no way to implement, for example, antidumping duties under the circumstances specified in Article 10.6 of the Antidumping Agreement, or, for that matter, duty decreases made retroactively in accordance with the Generalized System of Preferences. And such authority is necessary when implementing DSB-authorized suspension of concessions. However, while the April 19 action applied duties to entries commencing from March 3, that action is not within the terms of reference of this dispute. It could not have been, since it had not taken place on March 4, the date of the EC's consultation request.

6. All that a bond provides is assurances that *if* a duty liability is later found to be higher than at importation, the *risk* that Customs will not be paid is reduced. The United States made changes to its bonding requirements to ensure that *if* the DSB authorized concessions, the U.S. would be in a better position to collect them from March 3. It must be remembered that the *Bananas* arbitrator/panel's decisions made clear that the measure the EC had in place from January 2 was inconsistent with WTO obligations, and continued the nullification or impairment of U.S. benefits from that date. For the reasons described in the U.S. submissions, the U.S. had the right, upon DSB authorization, to suspend concessions from January 2. The March 3 bonding requirements helped to preserve this right.

7. But since the March 3 measure consisted only of revised bonding requirements, which imposed no duty liability, where does this leave the EC's claims? As an initial matter, it is clear that bonding requirements have nothing to do with Article 21.5, and that claim can be dismissed, without undertaking the condemnation of the work of another WTO dispute proceeding requested by the EC. With respect to GATT 1994 Article I, the March 3 bonding requirements, like all bonding requirements, were addressed to risks associated with particular entries. Numerous WTO Members provide their customs authorities with the ability to address specific risks through changed bonding requirements. With regard to Articles II and VIII, the March 3 bonding requirements imposed no additional duty liability, and provided no additional revenue to the U.S. Treasury. Under the EC's own construction, the bonding requirements are therefore not subject to Article II and VIII, as they are not a "charge." This is not a dispute

about whether private banks' fees for sureties are set too high. Moreover, the EC has failed to make any substantive case that the changed bonding requirements were inconsistent with Article XI.

8. Mr. Chairman, let me now turn briefly to the chart just distributed. I would first like to point out that it indicates that trade was *not* stopped. There was a big surge in imports before March 1999, so it should be no surprise that there was no need to import as much after that, since there was so much inventory on hand. Furthermore, imports continued even after April 19. This suggests that the United States has not, in fact, suspended the full amount of concessions authorized by the DSB.

9. Mr. Chairman, members of the Panel, we ask you now to address your findings to what actually happened on March 3 – a change in bonding requirements – and to find that these bonding requirements did not violate the U.S. WTO obligations asserted by the EC. I want to thank you again for your work to date, and from now until the end of this case.

Appendix 2.10
The US Responses to Additional Questions of Panel
(10 February 2000)

Q50. Do parties consider that there is an opportunity cost arising from the bonding requirement, in particular if cash is deposited in lieu of a bond?

1. "Opportunity cost" is not a WTO legal term, and is found nowhere in the text of the WTO Agreement.[259] As an economic concept, it is irrelevant to a consideration of the claims in this dispute. Moreover, as a factual matter, the opportunity costs associated with delayed release of goods until duties have been paid (inventory carrying expenses, delayed sales, dock storage charges, higher administrative costs) far exceed any opportunity costs associated with bonding systems allowing for early release of goods. This is why such systems are encouraged. We reiterate that the U.S. government receives no revenue from its bonding requirement, and is not a "charge" within the meaning of Articles II and VIII.

Q51. Please provide copies of any Customs' advisory notices concerning the 3 March measure.

2. Apart from the March 4 instructions, the only Customs advisory notice in connection with the March 3 measure was a March 16 document clarifying the bonding requirements set forth in the March 4 instructions. It is provided in U.S. Exhibit 15.

Q52. Please provide the data contained in US Exhibits 5 and 10, in an Excel format.

3. Excel file copies of U.S. Exhibits 5 and 10 are attached to the electronic version of this response.

Q53. Please inform us whether any importer of listed products chose to deposit money in lieu of a bond, as permitted under Section 1623(e) of the Tariff Act of 1930 (US Exhibit 11), during the period from 3 March 1999 to 19 April. Further, in general, in what circumstances do importers choose to deposit money in lieu of a bond?

4. It is our understanding based on a review of relevant import records that no importer chose to deposit cash in lieu of a bond for entries of the listed prod-

[259] *C.f.*, the Appellate Body's caution against reliance on terms not found in the WTO Agreement. Appellate Body Report, *EC – Hormones*, *supra*, footnote 206, para. 181.

ucts during the period from March 3 to April 19, 1999. It is also our understanding that, in general, it is rare for importers to avail themselves of this option. While we do not have information on the situations in which an importer would choose to deposit cash, it is conceivable that this might occur if the credit history of an importer were to lead surety companies to refuse to provide a bond to the importer.

Q54. What is the basis for the US statement that the costs incurred on a bonding requirement are small? To what extent, if any, did the costs change following the 3 March measure?

5. This statement is based on our understanding of typical fees charged by private sureties, as described in paragraph 29 of the U.S. Second Submission.[260] It is our understanding that a typical amount charged for a single transaction bond is $3.50 for thousand dollars of bond value (0.35%). It is our understanding that the fees for continuous bonds are typically between $10 - 20 per thousand dollars of bond value (1-2%). The typical continuous bond requirement is 10% of the duties, taxes and fees incurred by the importer in the previous year. As a rough estimate, duties, taxes and fees are typically around 5% of the entered value for imports into the United States. Thus, the typical continuous bond amount would be 10% of 5% of the entered value, or 0.5% of entered value, and the amount paid for the bond would be 1-2% of this, or 0.005-0.01% of entered value. This is subject to the caveat that the minimum continuous bond amount is $50,000, which would cost between $500 - $1000, assuming a rate of $10-20 per thousand dollars of bond value.

6. The March 3 bonding requirements increased the continuous bond requirements for listed products to 10% of the entered value of these products in the previous year. Thus, the amount paid for the bond would be 1-2% of 10% of the entered value, or 0.1-0.2% of entered value. Our response to question 35 illustrates the impact on an importer. To repeat that example, if the normal continuous bond had been calculated based on entries during the previous year valued at $1,000,000, and $50,000 of this was covered merchandise, the continuous bond would be supplemented by $5,000 (10% of $50,000) to meet the revised bonding requirements. A typical amount which a private surety might charge for this additional coverage would be approximately *$50 - $100*, based on a rate of $10-20 per thousand dollars of bond value.

[260] Also as described in *para.* 29, these can vary.

Q55. In what respects did the duty deposit requirements for the listed products imported between 3 March 1999 and 19 April change after 19 April 1999?

7. Duty deposit requirements for listed products imported between March 3 and April 19, and for which duty deposits were made before April 19, 1999, did not change after April 19, 1999. If the duty deposits were not made until on or after April 19,[261] *and* the product was on the April 19 list, a 100% duty deposit would have been required.

Q56. To what extent did the US Customs have to have recourse against the bond for those importers not paying the difference between the estimated duty deposit at the MFN rate and the higher duty amount following the 19 April action?

8. It is not possible to make this determination at this time. To the extent estimated duties are not sufficient to cover a duty liability, importers have six months following liquidation to pay the difference before Customs would make a claim against the bond. Thus, it is not yet clear how often it will be necessary to make claims against bonds.

Q57. What happens, if anything, to the bond when the estimated duty deposits are paid? Is it reduced by the amount paid? If the bond is not reduced by such payments, why would the importer choose to pay the increased estimated duty deposits rather than allow Customs to have recourse against the bond?

9. It is important to recall that a bond is nothing more than a guarantee, backed by a private surety company. The importer pays a minimal fee for the bond, as described in response to question 54.

10. Nothing happens to the bond itself once estimated duties are deposited. Most fundamentally, the deposit of estimated duties is only one of the conditions which must be satisfied under a bond. The bond guarantees that duties, taxes and fees will be paid, and that the laws and regulations relating to the merchandise will be satisfied. Therefore, the bond amount is not modified or reduced when one of the conditions, deposit of estimated duties, has been satisfied. Of course, Customs would not have recourse against the bond to cover any liabilities accounted for by the duty deposit.

[261] As described in the U.S. Second Submission at footnote 39 and in yesterday's oral statement, the importer may deposit estimated duties up to ten working days (two weeks) after entry. Thus, for example, an importer which entered merchandise on April 18 could have deposited estimated duties on that date, or could have chosen to wait for up to ten working days to do so.

11. Again, the bond is nothing more than a guarantee that if the importer refuses to pay any liability relating to the merchandise, Customs can collect from the third-party surety providing the bond. The importer purchases the bond for a fixed amount from the private surety. Even were it theoretically possible to reduce the bonding amount upon satisfaction of one bond condition, it would not make economic sense for an importer to obtain a separate bond at a lower level. An importer would not want to return to a surety to obtain another bond in the lower amount, since this would typically entail an additional cost, however small. The existing bond would be sufficient to meet even a lower bonding level. The Customs bond may be analogized to an insurance policy. If a consumer purchases auto insurance on January 1 for a non-refundable fee of $200 covering accidents in that year for up to $500,000, he or she would not purchase for $100 a second policy on July 1 to cover $250,000 in accidents for the remainder of the year, even if the risk were reduced to that level.

12. With regard to payments of estimated duty deposits, as described in response to question 55, importers were not required after April 19 to deposit increased estimated duties if they had already deposited estimated duties at the MFN rate prior to that date. With respect to estimated duty deposits made from April 19, an importer would likely choose to pay the higher duty deposits rather than allowing Customs to have recourse against the bond in order to maintain its credit rating. Moreover, failure to pay the estimated duty deposits at all could expose the importer to liquidated damages. Given that the private surety would have to pay the liability, it is quite possible the surety would not be willing to provide bonds in the future to that importer, or would raise its premiums for the bond. It is worth recalling that the surety is typically only being paid well under 1% of the entered value of the goods for the bond (see response 54), as opposed to the duty deposits of 100% being collected after April 19. If the importer were unable to obtain a bond because it had failed to fulfill an earlier obligation, it would have to provide a cash deposit in lieu of surety.

Supplemental Responses to Earlier Questions

Question 34, use of single transaction and continuous bonds

13. Based on data for February 1999, continuous bonds were used for approximately 97% of all entries made in that month, versus 3% use of single transaction bonds. For entries from EC countries, approximately 94% of entries in February 1999 were made using continuous bonds, versus 6% use of single transaction.

Question 45, data on duties for listed products

14. In our response to this question, we explained that, with respect to the data in U.S. Exhibit 14, where liquidated duties for an entry differ from the estimated duties for the entry, this could be because the entry included products on the

April 19 list, or because products on the entry were misclassified or misvalued. We also noted that the liquidated duties for entries which included candles (a product not on the April 19 list) were higher than the estimated duties for these entries. Upon further investigation, we determined that several entries which included candles also included bath preparations, folding cartons or both. Both bath preparations and folding cartons were on the April 19 list, and were thus subject to 100% duties, thus explaining the difference between estimated and liquidated duties for entries which included candles.

Appendix 3

Oral presentation of Dominica and St. Lucia at Third Party session (17 December 1999)

The interest of the Commonwealth of Dominica and St Lucia in this case derives from the continuing effect of the illegal trade measure imposed by the US on March 3, 1999. These measures were so excessive as to have frightened economic actors and the public so as to influence and pressure governments to conform to a US vision of WTO compatibility without the sanction of the multilateral trading system. This was its tactical and strategic purpose - to secure a wrongful trade advantage with continuing legal, political and psychological impact.

The issue in this case is whether the measures taken by the US on March 3, 1999 limiting the importation of selected EC products is WTO incompatible. We are not going to recap the events surrounding the legitimate exercise of DSU rights by the EC in the year and a half preceding March 3rd. Suffice it to say that the account provided in the Respondent's First Written Submission does not address the issue the way African, Caribbean & Pacific (ACP) countries see it. Our intervention is focussed on the matter before this Panel.

The US measure of March 3,1999 is a violation of basic GATT norms

The mere US announcement of its intention of withholding liquidation on $520 million worth of targeted EC products subject to a contingent duty liability of 100% directly impacted trade flows. To appropriate the words of Deputy USTR Peter Scher, the US "retaliated by effectively stopping trade as of March 3".[262]

The illegal March 3rd measure resulted in severe competitive disadvantages for the selected list of EC products. The equal treatment principle was not applied to targeted EC exports. These products faced discriminatory duties in excess of US tariff bindings. Importation of targeted EC goods entailed increased risks, costs, fees and other charges. We submit that the *de jure* and *de facto* discrimination against EC products in this regard constitutes a breach of GATT rules as advanced in the First Written Submission of the Complainant. We further support the assertion of the Complainant that the US measure is a restriction "other than duties, taxes or other charges" within the meaning of Article XI:1 of the GATT 1994.

We ask - would an importer of targeted EC products, aware of the risk of having to pay 100% *ad valorem* duties, continue to purchase such goods? He is placed in a quandary - If he puts the goods up for sale he might attempt to pass on the contingent liability - though 100% duties might make the product unsaleable. But if

[262] Press conference held on March 3rd 1999; see First Written Submission of the European Communities, EC Annex XI.

he does not pass on the duty once the goods have already been sold he will not be able to recoup the duty if it subsequently becomes payable. So why would he handle the goods at all given the significant losses he could face? He won't. *Peter Scher was right.*

GATT Article XI, "General Elimination of Quantitative Restrictions", provides that

> XI.1 No prohibitions or restrictions other than duties, taxes or other charges, whether made effective through quotas, import or export licences or other measures, shall be instituted or maintained by any contracting party on the importation of any product of the territory of any other contracting party ...

This wording indicates clearly that any measure instituted or maintained by a Member which restricts the importation of products is covered by this provision, irrespective of the legal status of the measure. The language used is comprehensive.[263]

The March 3rd measure is a fundamental violation of the DSU

The abuse of process demonstrated in the March 3rd illegal measure undermines the strengthened multilateral system and the rule of law. It subjects the international rule of law to power-oriented theories of 'justified unilateralism'.

On 19 April 1999, the US confirmed the retroactive imposition of 100% duties on a reduced category of EC products under the ostensible cover of the arbitrators' ruling. The initial figure of $520 million was scaled back to $191.4 million. This underscoring the maxim, *nemo debet esse judex in propria causa* - no man ought to be a judge in his own cause. A Member cannot be relied upon to objectively determine the level of concessions to be suspended in such circumstances.

The Respondent in its submission states: "Because EC delaying tactics prevented the arbitrators from completing their work by the March 2, 1999 date called for under the DSU time frame, the United States took steps to preserve its ability to suspend concessions as from that date."[264] The Respondent further states "The EC hampered the arbitrators' work in several ways. First, the blocking of the DSB agenda delayed referral of the matter to the Article 22.6 arbitrators and the setting of the schedule by a full week in an already tight time frame."[265]

The importance of a rules-based system is that everyone has a voice. What the record actually shows is that it was two small Member states, Dominica and St Lucia, which objected to the adoption of the DSB agenda. DSB proceedings were thereby temporarily delayed out of respect for the rule of law - there was no at-

---

[263] See Report of panel on *Japan - trade in semi-conductors*, BISD 35S/116 (1989), paras 106 *et seq.*

[264] First Written Submission of the United States, para. 31.

[265] *Ibid.*, para. 26.

tempt to obstruct due process. Our concern was that the US request was untimely. What we sought to uphold concerned fundamental rules of procedural justice.[266]

The DSU provides that a Member may request authorization to suspend concessions or other obligations in certain limited circumstances, that is, where another Member has failed to bring the measure found to be inconsistent with a covered agreement into compliance therewith or otherwise comply with the recommendations and rulings of the DSB within a reasonable period of time.[267] No Member shall make a determination to the effect that a violation has occurred except through recourse to dispute settlement in accordance with the rules and procedures of the DSU.[268] Moreover, Members shall obtain DSB authorization in accordance with the rules of the DSU before suspending concessions or other obligations under the covered agreements in response to the failure of the Member concerned to implement the recommendations and rulings within that reasonable period of time.[269]

The language of the DSU is prospective. The suggestion that a Member is entitled to suspend concessions from the end of the reasonable period is counter to basic principles of interpretation. There is a presumption in international law that treaties do not permit retroactive measures where these measures limit or deprive Members of their rights or privileges and effectively confiscate the property of economic actors.[270] To suggest otherwise, to permit the retroactive withdrawal of concessions or other obligations would bring about an unacceptable level of uncertainty in trade. It would undermine the predictability and security of the multilateral trading system.

An Effective Remedy

Article 3.7 of the DSU provides that "the first objective of the dispute settlement mechanism is usually to secure the withdrawal of the measures concerned if these are found to be inconsistent with the provision of any of the covered agreements." However, situations arise where mere withdrawal is inadequate. International obligations do not come to an end simply because they are infringed. Some wrongs have a continuing character. In such cases the process of recommencing compliance with a continuing obligation may be little different from that of providing a remedy for having broken it, i.e, reparation. Some violations of the DSU, for example, as instanced in this case, undermine the fundamental basis of the rules-based system which poses a continuing threat to us all. The mere with-

---

[266] See WT/DSB/M/54, esp pp 3-6.

[267] DSU, Article 22.2.

[268] DSU, Article 23.2(a).

[269] DSU, Article 23.2(c).

[270] E.g. Report of Appellate Body, *US - Restrictions on Imports of Cotton and Man-made Fibre Underwear* ("*US – Underwear*"), WT/DS24/AB/R, adopted 25 February 1997, DSR 1997:I, 11, at 21-22.

drawal of such measure without further action would leave the dispute settlement system fundamentally impaired.

The only legal option open to the US with respect to the measures imposed on March 3rd was, in relation to the targeted EC exports, to terminate the bonding requirement, release any bonds, refund any cash deposits and terminate the suspension of liquidation of entries made during the period of application of the inconsistent measures. Instead, on April 19th the US confirmed the retroactive application of 100% duties on a subset of these products. The duties levied on these products retroactively to March 3rd should have been reimbursed. These duties should not have been levied at all.

Some who now argue for the right to retroactively impose duties, have in the past denied the right of panels to suggest retroactive remedies.[271] Thus it is said that "no GATT 1947 or WTO panel ever has awarded monetary compensation to an exporting country for lost trade, even when blatantly-illegal quantitative restrictions had been imposed."[272] The issue here is not merely blatantly illegal trade measures but unbridled unilateralism that undercuts the very foundation of the rules-based system.

An effective remedy is one which preserves the stability and predictability of the multilateral trading system. It must provide assurance to all Members, including the poorest and most vulnerable - those without the capacity to effectively retaliate.

If a Member can unilaterally withdraw concessions without prior DSB authorization, and flout the explicit provision that "[c]oncessions or other obligations shall not be suspended during the course of the arbitration"[273], without facing effective multilateral sanctions, we will witness the increasing use of unilateral reprisals. The WTO will simply be a cloak for "power politics in disguise". Power-oriented theories of "justified disobedience" and unilateralism have no place in the strengthened rules-based system which provides protection for all Members and the transnational exercise of rights.

Let me Chairman take this opportunity to make a comment of a general nature.

We commend the advances made within recent months both in recognising the serious constraints facing small vulnerable developing countries and the commitment to adopting tangible measures to address them. Also, worthy of acknowledgement are the initiatives such as the recent "Geneva week" which sought to enhance and facilitate the functioning of the non-Geneva based missions such as my own.

---

[271] E.g. US in Panel Report, *Guatemala - Anti-Dumping Investigation Regarding Portland Cement from Mexico* ("*Guatemala – Cement I*"), WT/DS60/R, adopted 25 November 1998, DSR 1998:IX, 3797, paras 5.61 et seq.

[272] *Ibid.*, para 5.64.

[273] DSU, Article 22.6.

I must assure you that it is not due to any lack of vital trading interests to be protected that we are not resident in Geneva. We want to contribute in whatever modest way we can to the regulation of the global trading system. We do not have a resident mission here simply because we cannot afford one. But this should not negate our rights as a WTO Member.

With this in mind I thought it necessary to draw to your attention the additional impediments which we faced in preparing for this meeting. Although we are third parties, we did not receive the submission of the US until the afternoon of Tuesday this week leaving us precious little time to analyse it and prepare our intervention, effectively precluding any prospect of a written submission. I expect that the US would have made its submission on schedule which means that, unlike ourselves, parties resident in Geneva would have had sufficient time for study.

It is regrettable that, often our constraints are not taken into account but we are obliged to operate under more demanding conditions than others who are already better endowed.

In closing, Dominica and St Lucia insist that this Panel establish the rules on this matter so as to ensure that the US measure of March 3,1999 is no more than an aberration in WTO practice and does not establish a precedent for the conduct of future trading relations and will not be emulated.

Appendix 4

Oral presentation of Ecuador at Third Party session

(17 December 1999)

(Spanish original)

Ecuador is closely following this case as an interested third party. The delegation of Ecuador would like to take this opportunity to make the following two remarks, bearing in mind that its interest in the case is based on systemic considerations and on the fact that it involves the subject of bananas:

- Almost a year after the events which gave rise to this dispute, the European Communities has still not fulfilled its obligation to implement the recommendations adopted by the Dispute Settlement Body in the banana case.
- In the banana case, Ecuador has shown that the multilateral procedures can indeed move forward in spite of any contradictions or gaps in the interpretation of Articles 21 and 22 of the Dispute Settlement Understanding. However, as regards the multilateral implementation of these procedures, Ecuador has had to show considerable good faith. And it is probably the absence of good faith they can give rise to situations such as the one which has arisen in this dispute.

Ecuador repeats its interest in this case and has decided to continue to seek a rapid solution to this dispute.

Thank you.

Appendix 5
Third Party Submission of India
(10 December 1999)

Introduction

India has a strong systemic interest in this dispute. The fundamental question is whether a prevailing Member in a dispute can unilaterally determine the compliance or non-compliance of the measures taken by the implementing Member pursuant to the recommendations and rulings of the Dispute Settlement Body (DSB) and based on this determination take unilateral measures suspending the concession of the implementing Member without formal authorization for such suspension of concessions by the DSB. At the heart of this matter are issues such as sequencing of multilateral determination of compliance and suspension of concessions or the relationship between Article 21 and 22 of the DSU.

Facts of the Dispute

In the EC – Banana dispute, the reasonable period of time (RPT) for compliance with the DSB rulings by the EC was to expire on 1.1.99 as per the arbitration held under Article 21.5 of the Understanding on Rules and Procedures Governing the Settlement of Disputes (DSU). Pursuant to these DSB rulings, EC claimed to have amended or revised in July and November 1998 its banana importation regime, which was to be applicable from 1.1.99 onwards i.e., at the end of RPT.

In the period between October – December 1998, i.e., before the expiry of RPT, the US had published three notices in its Federal Registry proposing to impose 100% ad valorem duties on imports of certain products of EC from 3.3.99 onwards. Accordingly, the US Customs Service had required importers of the EC products to post bonds to cover the contingent duty liability, which could be realized if the DSB authorized suspension of concessions.

The US did not request the DSB to refer to the original panel under Article 21.5 for determination on the compliance of EC measures with the DSB rulings. Instead it sought on 14.1.99 the DSB authorisation to suspend the tariff concessions and related GATT obligations under the DSU Article 22. When EC objected to the level of concessions sought to be suspended by the US and requested for arbitration, the DSB referred the matter to arbitration under the DSU Article 22.6 on 29.1.99. The arbitrator issued his final decision on 9.4.99 and the DSB authorised US for suspension of concessions *at* a reduced level of US $ 191.4 million (from $ 520 million) on 19.4.99. On the same date the US confirmed the application of 100% ad velorem duty on the EC products retroactively from 3.3.99 onwards.

Aggrieved by the US Customs Service decision requiring importers of EC products to post 100% duty bonds, the EC requested consultations with the US on that decision. The consultations were held on 21.4.99, but failed to resolve the dispute. By a letter dated 11.5.99 EC requested for a panel, which was established by the DSB on 16.6.99 with standard terms of reference.

LEGAL ARGUMENT

In the light of the above factual background, the main issue of systemic concern to India in this dispute is: whether the US decision, made on a unilateral basis, that the EC's measures were not in conformity with the DSB rulings is permissible under the DSU. Further, pending a decision by Article 22.6 arbitrator on the level of suspension of concessions and formal authorization by the DSB for such suspension of concession under Article 22.7, can the US proceed with its so-called contingency measures of requiring bonds from the importers of the EC products.

Articles 3, 21.5 and 23 of the DSU

Article 3 is a general provision. It states that the dispute settlement system as provided in the WTO "is a central element in providing security and predictability to the multilateral trading system". Article 23 obligates the Members of the WTO to ("shall") "have recourse to, and abide by, the rules and procedures" of the DSU in resolving their disputes. By doing so and by not resorting to unilateral measures, the Members, as indicated by the title of the Article, are expected to 'strengthen the multilateral system' as established *by* the DSU/WTO.

US argued in its first written submission that EC had failed to show that its March 3 review of bonding requirements were violation of its obligations under Article 23. Further it dismissed Article 3 as only a "descriptive, not prescriptive" provision (at para 48 of the submission. However, it cited the same Article 3.2 at para 42 in support of its action violating the DSU Article 22.6. It asserted there that the purpose of the WTO dispute settlement system – i.e., to preserve the rights and obligations of Members – would be undermined if suspension of concessions was to await completion of arbitral proceedings under Article 22.6).

It may, however, be noted that these two articles stress the importance of multilateral decision making and dispute settlement system in the international trading system. And they are part of an international treaty, to which the US, as an important trading State, has subscribed and become a party. One of the general principles of International Law is that treaty provisions shall be observed in good faith by the parties. This is codified in the Article 26 of the Vienna Convention on the Law of Treaties.

The March 3 decision by US regarding bonding requirements was clearly without the DSB authorisation; furthermore, the requirement was imposed, pending the completion of Article 22.6 arbitration. Also, this requirement was not based on any multilateral decision of the DSB but based on a unilateral decision by the US that the EC measures were not in conformity with the DSB recommendations and rulings. Thus US actions, which were clearly unilateral in nature, were contrary to the letter and spirit of Articles 3 and 23 of the DSU.

Further, if there is any disagreement on the conformity of measures of a Member with the DSB rulings, the Members are required by the DSU Article 21.5 to follow dispute settlement procedures, including resorting to the original panel to decide upon compliance or otherwise of those measures. However, as outlined above, the US chose not to invoke this provision; rather, it unilaterally decided that EC measures were not in compliance with the DSB rulings and recommendations.

India strongly rejects the US assertion that the DSU allows a Member to proceed to Article 22 without first traversing Article 21.5. It is India's view that the only possible interpretation of the DSU procedures is that it is obligatory to go through Article 21.5 before resorting to Article 22.

Article 22.6 of the DSU

The last sentence of Article 22.6 lays down that "Concessions and other obligations shall not be suspended during the course of arbitration". Despite this clear provision, the US decided to take so-called contingency measures on 3.3.99, before the decision by the arbitrator on 9.4.99. This was in clear violation of Article 22.6 of the DSU.

We do not agree with the US assertion that the DSU is silent as to the date of the suspension of concessions. We believe that any measures suspending the concessions of a Member can be taken only after completion of dispute settlement proceedings under the DSU. Otherwise it would undermine the multilateral system of dispute settlement, as established by the DSU and would set a bad precedent of far reaching consequences for the whole WTO system. If a Member is free to determine and suspend unilaterally the trade concessions to another Member, there is nothing in DSU requiring it to adhere to any maximum level of suspension of concessions. Members would normally tend to resort to suspension at a higher level than their actual loss. This could result in enormous loss to the traders.

In the present case, while the arbitrator had decided the level of nullification/impairment of benefits to the US due to non-compliance of DSB rulings by the EC at $191.4 million, the US had in advance determined that level at $520 million, and went ahead of enforcing it by requiring the importers of the EC products to deposit the enhanced duty-bonds. This unilateral action of US had done enough damage by imposing additional financial burden on the trade operators as explained by EC at paras 16(d) & 17 of its first submission.

Conclusion

In conclusion, it is India's view that the US violated key provisions of the DSU such as Articles 3, 21, 22 and 23 by taking arbitrary and unilateral measures with regard to imports of certain products from the European Communities.

Appendix 6
Third Party Submission of Jamaica
(8 December 1999)

Jamaica has sought third party participation in the present dispute hearing between the European Communities and the United States of America as it believes that the action taken by the United States of America on the 3rd March 1999, which is the subject of the present dispute, was contrary to the WTO rules and if not determined to be illegal by way of a Panel's ruling, will have a fundamental impact on the future of the Dispute Settlement Mechanism (DSM).

The multilateral trading system as defined by the WTO agreements creates rights and obligations for all participating members countries. The maintenance of the balance between these rights and obligations is crucial to the success of this global trading system. The Dispute Settlement Mechanism with its accompanying rules and procedures, plays a fundamental role in the maintenance of the balance within the WTO and therefore is "*a central element in providing security and predictability to the multilateral trading system*" (Article 3:1 , Dispute Settlement Understanding [DSU]).

In this respect, Jamaica , as a developing country member of the WTO is concerned about any threat to the functioning of the DSM and has thus chosen to exercise its right to participate in this dispute as a means of seeking to preserve the integrity of the DSM .

The Dispute Settlement Understanding (DSU) requires parties to "*seek the redress of a violation of obligations* [by way of] *the rules and procedures of* [the DSU]" (Article 23:1)

Furthermore, parties are not to make a "*determination to the effect that a violation has occurred... except through recourse to dispute settlement in accordance with the rules and procedures of this Understanding"* (Article 23:2(a))

According to Jamaica's understanding of the rules in this present matter, where a party is seeking to enforce sanctions such as suspension of concessions against another Member, Article 21:2 requires firstly that authorisation must be sought from the Dispute Settlement Body (DSB) to suspend concessions. Additionally, where the level of suspension is being determined by way of arbitration, Article 21:6 states that *concessions or other obligations shall* ***not*** *be suspended during the course of arbitration* ".

The United States of America , like members of the European Communities and any other WTO Member, has agreed to be bound by the rules and procedures of the DSU. As such, the United States like every other WTO Member has the right to seek judicial determination of, and remedy for, an alleged injury by another WTO Member. However, the United States, and every other WTO Member must exercise this right within the prescribed boundaries of the DSU.

The voluntary disregard of DSU provisions, in favour of a unilateral determination of injury and subsequent enforcement of remedial action unauthorized by the

DSB, such as those put into effect by the United States of America, is clearly a breach of the multilaterally agreed rules and procedures; rules and procedures which the United States of America itself helped to design and adopt in 1994.

This breach by the United States of America sets a dangerous precedent. If the illegality of this measure is not determined through the available avenues under the WTO such as this Panel process and is subsequently relied upon by other WTO members, it would have the effect of undermining the whole purpose of the WTO , that of providing a reliable rules-based global trading system.

Jamaica, therefore, calls on the Panel to uphold the WTO rules by finding that the United States of America acted contrary to its obligations under the DSU.

Appendix 7
Oral presentation of Japan at Third Party session
(17 December 1999)

Mr. Chairman,

(SUPREMACY OF A MULTILATERAL DECISION OVER A UNILATERAL DECISION)

1. At the DSB meeting in April of this year, Japan, as a third party to the EC-Banana case, registered its view on the importance of multilateral determination over unilateral determination. We emphasised that the maintenance of a sequence between Articles 21.5, and 22.6 or 22.7, is one of the key elements in safeguarding the multilateral character of the Dispute Settlement Mechanism, and more broadly of the organisation of the WTO.

2. While the EC deserves condemnation for the fact that it failed to fully implement the rulings and recommendations of the Panel and Appellate Body within the reasonable period of time, Japan cannot but register its concern at the actions taken by the United States on 3 March, 1999.

(ARTICLE 22.6 OF THE DSU)

3. No matter how the United States characterises its action taken on 3 March, be it "contingency plans" or "preservation of its ability to suspend concessions", the fact remains that the action "effectively stopped trade" and thus had an effect equivalent to the suspension of concessions. This constitutes a violation of Article 22.6. We therefore fully support the EC's argument in paragraph 14 of its submission.

4. The counter-argument presented in the US submission in this regard, that the *"withholding of liquidation" was undertaken to "preserve administrative flexibility" and has no special legal significance*, runs counter to the basic tenet of WTO law, i.e., ensuring predictability and stability in trade. The US argument should therefore be rejected.

(ARTICLES 23 AND 3.7 OF THE DSU)

5. We cannot but also register our grave concern at the argument of the United States that it may start suspending the concessions anytime after the end of RPT regardless of the whether the DSB has authorised the suspension. Such an argument is inconsistent with the objectives of Articles 23 and 3.7 of the DSU and has no basis in any of the DSU provisions.

6. The United States also argues that the EC has not demonstrated that the action of 3 March is inconsistent with DSU Article 23 and has not asserted a violation of DSU Article 3, and that the US did no more than preserve the ability of the United States to assess duties from 3 March. This argument of the US does not stand the test of scrutiny against the specific provisions of Article 23. Article 23.2(a) clearly states that "Members shall not make a determination *to the effect*

that a violation has occurred, that benefits have been nullified or impaired". The US action on 3 March to "preserve the ability to assess duties from 3 March", directly contradicts the provision of Article 23.2, because the US action was indeed based on the determination to the effect that the violation has occurred.

7. The Arbitrators also noted in paragraph 4.14 of its report that "the DSB has the ability to reject its decision on the level of suspension as it does to reject panel and Appellate Body reports". The language contained in Article 23.2(c) of the DSU is unequivocal to the effect that a DSB authorisation is a prerequisite for suspending concessions or other obligations. Thus, the justification advanced by the US in its submission for the US action taken on March 3, 1999 falls short of fulfilling the provision of Article 23.2.

(ARTICLES I, II, XI, AND VIII OF THE GATT 1994)

8. In addition to the observation above, we also support the EC's argument that the measure taken by the United States violates Articles I, II, XI, and VIII of the GATT 1994 as is established in the First Submission of the EC.

(ARTICLE 21.5 OF THE DSU)

9. As the EC clearly demonstrates in paragraphs 23, 24 and 27 of their First Submission, it is the obligation of the parties to have recourse to a Panel established under Article 21.5, where there is a disagreement as to the consistency with a covered agreement of measures taken to comply with the recommendations and rulings. This provision of Article 21.5 is an expression of supremacy of multilateral decision over unilateral decision, and is the bedrock of the multilateral trading system upon which the WTO was founded.

10. We hereby request that the Panel conduct its analysis in a way that preserves such foundation of the multilateral trading system and declare that the US measure has breached Articles 3, 21.5. 22 and 23 of the DSU and Articles I, II, XI and VIII of the GATT 1994.

Thank you.

UNITED STATES – SECTION 110(5) OF THE US COPYRIGHT ACT

Arbitration under Article 21.3(c) of the Understanding on Rules and Procedures Governing the Settlement of Disputes

WT/DS160/12

I. INTRODUCTION

1. On 27 July 2000, the Dispute Settlement Body (the "DSB") adopted the Panel Report[1] in *United States – Section 110(5) of the US Copyright Act* ("*United States – Section 110(5)*"). On 24 August 2000, the United States informed the DSB, pursuant to Article 21.3 of the *Understanding on Rules and Procedures Governing the Settlement of Disputes* (the "DSU"), that it would implement the recommendations and rulings of the DSB in this dispute.[2] At the DSB meeting of 11 September 2000, the United States said that it would require a "reasonable period of time" to do so, under the terms of Article 21.3 of the DSU.[3]

2. In view of the impossibility to reach an agreement with the United States on the period of time required for the implementation of those recommendations and rulings, the European Communities and their member States (hereinafter referred to as the "European Communities") requested that such period be determined by binding arbitration pursuant to Article 21.3(c) of the DSU.[4]

3. By joint letter of 22 November 2000, the European Communities and the United States notified the DSB that they had agreed that the duration of the "reasonable period of time" for implementation should be determined through binding arbitration, under the terms of Article 21.3(c) of the DSU, and that I should act as Arbitrator. The parties also indicated in that letter that they had agreed to extend the time-period for the arbitration, fixed at 90 days from the date of adoption by the DSB by Article 21.3(c) of the DSU, until 26 January 2001.[5] Notwithstanding this extension of the time-period, the parties stated that the arbitration award would be deemed to be an award made under Article 21.3(c) of the DSU. My acceptance of this designation as Arbitrator was conveyed to the parties by letter of 23 November 2000.

---

1 Panel Report, *United States – Section 110(5) of the US Copyright Act* ("*United States – Section 110(5)*"), WT/DS160/R, adopted 27 July 2000.

2 Communication from the United States, WT/DS160/9.

3 WT/DSB/M/88, para. 2.

4 WT/DS160/10.

5 WT/DS160/11.

4. Written submissions were received from the European Communities and the United States on 1 December 2000, and an oral hearing was held on 7 December 2000.

II. ARGUMENTS OF THE PARTIES

A. European Communities

5. In the view of the European Communities, implementation in this dispute requires a "repeal" of Section 110(5)(B) of the Copyright Act, as well as a "modest adaptation" to Section 110(5)(A) of that Act. The European Communities considers that given the "simplicity" of these legislative measures and the "potential" of the United States legislative system to enact legislation expeditiously, implementation can be achieved in a period of time significantly shorter than the indicative period of 15 months set out in Article 21.3(c) of the DSU. The European Communities argues that the reasonable period of time for implementation of the DSB's recommendations and rulings in this dispute is 10 months from the date of adoption of the Panel Report on 27 July 2000, which concludes on 27 May 2001.

6. According to the European Communities, past arbitration awards under Article 21.3(c) make clear that the "reasonable period of time" for implementation is the shortest period possible within the legal system of the Member to implement the recommendations and rulings of the DSB. As implementation in this dispute will be done by legislative means, it is therefore "instructive" to note that the "reasonable periods of time" for implementation in other disputes involving legislative action range from 11 months and two weeks to 15 months and one week.

7. With regard to the United States legislative process, the European Communities notes the following. First, there exists no specific structural time-frame in the United States legislative system. In the United States House of Representatives (the "House"), a draft bill on the subject of copyright would normally be examined by the Judiciary Committee. There is no minimum time limit for this examination, nor any constitutional or regulatory obligation to consult certain parties within a predetermined time-frame. The only fixed time-frame in the House is the rule according to which a draft bill may not be considered in the House until the third calendar day on which the committee report has been available to the Members of the House. In the United States Senate, the time-frame at the similar stage of the procedure is even shorter. Thus, as there are no constitutionally fixed time-frames for initiating and completing each stage of the legislative process, there is no limit on the speed at which a legislative action to comply with WTO obligations can be undertaken.

8. The European Communities refers to a number of recent examples of intellectual property legislation under the United States legislative process, as an indication of the normal time-period in which this type of legislation is enacted.

In particular, the European Communities cites three examples of legislation that was enacted in less than two months.

9. The European Communities also emphasizes that implementation of the recommendations and rulings in this dispute is "rather straight forward". The European Communities notes that "highly complex" pieces of legislation have been enacted under the United States legislative process in very short periods of time, ranging from 28 to 113 days.

10. In conclusion, the European Communities considers that the reasonable period of time for implementation in this dispute should not exceed 10 months from the date of adoption of the Panel Report, which would be 27 May 2001.

B. United States

11. The United States submits that the reasonable period of time for implementation of the recommendations and rulings of the DSB in this dispute is a period of "at least 15 months", and that a period that concludes upon the adjournment of the first session of the 107th Congress would be "even more prudent".

12. The United States bases its proposal on the language of Article 21.3(c) as well as past arbitration awards under this provision. Article 21.3(c) states that the "reasonable period of time" "should not exceed 15 months from the date of the adoption of a panel or Appellate Body report." However, "that time may be shorter or longer, depending upon the particular circumstances." The relevant "particular circumstances" are: the legal form of implementation (legislative or regulatory), the technical complexity of the necessary measures the Member must draft, adopt and implement, and the period of time in which the implementing Member can achieve the proposed form of implementation in accordance with its system of government. With regard to the last point, past arbitrators have stressed that the "reasonable period of time" for implementation is the shortest period possible within the normal law-making procedures of the implementing Member.

13. The United States submits that the "particular circumstances" of this dispute require that the "reasonable period of time" be "at least 15 months", or until the adjournment of the first session of the 107th Congress. In support of its proposal, the United States explains, as set out in the paragraphs below, why this period is the shortest period possible within its normal law-making procedures, based on the legislative process as described by the United States and the schedule under which the next Congress will be operating.

14. With regard to its legislative process, the United States notes that securing the enactment of legislation is a "complex and lengthy" process. The power to legislate is vested in the United States Congress, which has two chambers, the House and the Senate. The first step in the legislative process is for a bill to be introduced in the House or the Senate by a member of Congress. This introduction may be initiated by the Executive Branch.

15. After introduction, as a general rule, a bill is referred to a standing committee or committees having jurisdiction over the subject matter of that bill. In the House, a bill may be referred to a number of committees simultaneously, while in the Senate a bill is more commonly referred to the committee with primary subject matter jurisdiction and then may be sequentially referred to other committees. Most bills are referred by the committee with jurisdiction to a subcommittee for consideration.

16. In the House, the subcommittee normally schedules public hearings to obtain the views of proponents and opponents of a bill, including government agencies, experts, interested organizations and individuals. There is no specified time-frame for committee consideration. When the hearings are completed, the subcommittee usually meets to "mark-up" the bill, i.e., to make changes and amendments prior to deciding whether to recommend the bill to the full committee. If the subcommittee votes to recommend, it is called "reporting". The subcommittee may also suggest that a bill be "tabled" (postponed indefinitely).

17. After receiving the subcommittee's report (recommendation), the full committee may conduct further study and hearings. There will again be a mark-up process. The full committee then votes whether to report the bill, either as originally introduced without amendment, or as revised, to the full House. If the full committee votes to report a bill to the House, a committee report is written by the committee's staff. An approved bill is "reported back" to the House.

18. The timing of consideration of legislation on the House floor is determined as a general rule by the Speaker of the House and the majority political party leader, who may place the bill on the calendar for House debate. The House Rules Committee generally recommends the amount of time that will be allocated for debate and whether amendments may be offered. During the debate process, the bill is read in detail and there is opportunity for members of Congress to offer further amendments. After voting on amendments, the House immediately votes on the bill itself with any adopted amendments. The bill can also be returned to the committee that reported it. If passed, the bill must be referred to the Senate, which may or may not have concurrent pending legislation.

19. While the Senate has similar procedures for consideration of legislation by relevant committees, there are significant differences in the way the Senate considers proposed legislation. The Senate functions in a less rule-driven manner than the House, and scheduling and floor consideration is generally decided by consensus. Unlike the House, where debate is strictly controlled, in the Senate debate is rarely restricted. The Senate does not have a Rules Committee to govern floor consideration. Rather, there are complex rules mandating unanimous consent for Senate floor consideration.

20. Most bills are unlikely to be passed by the Senate exactly as referred by the House. The Senate may amend a bill or pass its own similar legislation. Therefore, a conference committee is organized to reconcile differences between the House and Senate versions. Conference committee members are appointed by each chamber and given specific instructions, which may be revised every 21

days. If the conference committee cannot reach agreement, the bill dies. If the conference committee reaches agreement on a single bill, a conference report is prepared describing the committee members' rationale for changes. The conference report must be approved by both chambers, in identical form, or the revised legislation dies.

21. After the bill proposed by the conference committee is approved by both chambers, it is sent to the President for approval. Only after presidential approval does proposed legislation become law.

22. The United States also emphasizes the importance of the Congressional schedule for the process. The Constitution mandates only that Congress meet "at least once in every year" and that it convene on 3 January, unless another date is chosen. A Congress lasts two years, and meets in two sessions of one year each, beginning in January. Accordingly, the earliest date a bill can be introduced is January. The adjournment date varies, largely depending on whether it is an election year. In an election year, Congress may adjourn in October, but in a non-election year it is typical for Congress to adjourn in November or December.

23. With regard to the Congressional schedule for 2001, the United States makes the following points. As a result of the 7 November 2000 elections, a new President and executive administration and a new Congress will have to address this issue. The new President will be sworn in on 20 January 2001. Since any legislation proposed by the Executive Branch will have to be approved by a new administration prior to its transmittal to Congress, it is unreasonable to expect that legislation would be transmitted to Congress before March or April 2001 at the earliest.

24. In any event, while the new Congress will officially be in session on 3 January, the usual business during at least the first month of Congress is to choose committee chairpersons and members, fill leadership posts, and address other administrative concerns. The new Congress is not likely to even begin serious consideration of legislation until mid to late February or early March of 2001.

25. In addition, the United States notes that other factors, such as the large volume of legislation introduced at the beginning of every Congress, and the inherent "myriad opportunities" for delay, create complexity and uncertainty in the United States legislative process.

26. For these reasons, the United States requests that it be given "at least 15 months" from the date of adoption of the Panel Report on 27 July 2000, and preferably until the adjournment of the first session of the 107th Congress, as a "reasonable period of time" for implementation. In the view of the United States, a period of "at least 15 months" is also consistent with previous arbitration awards under Article 21.3(c) involving implementation through legislative means.

III. REASONABLE PERIOD OF TIME

27. The United States has said that it will comply with the recommendations and rulings of the DSB in *United States – Section 110(5)*, but has requested a "reasonable period of time" under Article 21.3 of the DSU in which to do so. As the duration of the "reasonable period of time" in this case has not been agreed by the parties, they have requested that I determine this period of time through binding arbitration under Article 21.3(c) of the DSU. Thus, the issue to be resolved in this arbitration is the following: what is the "reasonable period of time" for implementation of the recommendations and rulings of the DSB in *United States – Section 110(5)*?

28. My mandate in this arbitration is governed by Article 21.3(c) of the DSU. Article 21.3(c) provides that when the "reasonable period of time" is determined through arbitration:

> ... a guideline for the arbitrator should be that the reasonable period of time to implement panel or Appellate Body recommendations should not exceed 15 months from the date of adoption of a panel or Appellate Body report. However, that time may be shorter or longer, depending upon the particular circumstances.

29. Thus, when the "reasonable period of time" is determined through arbitration, the guideline for the arbitrator is that this period should not exceed 15 months from the date of adoption of the panel report and/or the Appellate Body report. This does not mean, however, that the arbitrator is obliged to grant 15 months in all cases. Article 21.3(c) makes clear that the "reasonable period of time" may be shorter or longer, depending upon the "particular circumstances". The applicable "particular circumstances" thus influence the determination of what is a "reasonable period of time" for implementation, as has been stated by previous arbitrators.[6]

30. The meaning of Article 21.3(c) is elucidated by its context. Paragraph 1 of Article 21 provides:

> *Prompt* compliance with recommendations or rulings of the DSB is essential in order to ensure effective resolution of disputes to the benefit of all Members. (emphasis added)

31. Thus, the DSU explicitly emphasizes the importance of "prompt" compliance. In recognition of this principle, previous arbitrators have established that

---

[6] See, e.g., Award of the Arbitrator, *Chile – Taxes on Alcoholic Beverages – Arbitration under Article 21.3(c) of the DSU*, ("*Chile- Alcoholic Beverages*"), WT/DS87/15, WT/DS110/14, 23 May 2000, DSR 2000:V, 2589, paras. 39, 41-45; Award of the Arbitrator, *Canada – Certain Measures Affecting the Automotive Industry - Arbitration under Article 21.3(c) of the DSU* ("*Canada – Autos*"), WT/DS139/12, WT/DS142/12, 4 October 2000, para. 39; Award of the Arbitrator, *Canada – Patent Protection of Pharmaceutical Products - Arbitration under Article 21.3(c) of the DSU* ("*Canada – Pharmaceutical Patents*"), WT/DS114/13, 18 August 2000, para. 48.

the most important factor in establishing the length of the "reasonable period of time" is the following:

> ... it is clear that the reasonable period of time, as determined under Article 21.3(c), should be the *shortest period possible within the legal system of the Member* to implement the recommendations and rulings of the DSB.[7] (emphasis added)

32. The "shortest period possible within the legal system of the Member" generally refers to the "normal legislative procedures", and does not require a Member to utilize an "*extraordinary* legislative procedure" in every case.[8]

33. With these principles in mind, I now turn to an examination of the arguments made by the European Communities and the United States in order to determine what would be a "reasonable period of time" in the "particular circumstances" of this dispute.

34. At the outset, I note that the parties agree that the means of implementation in this dispute is legislative, rather than administrative. I recall the statement of a past arbitrator that a legislative change is likely, absent evidence to the contrary, to be more time-consuming than an administrative change.[9]

35. In this arbitration, the United States originally proposed, in a communication to the DSB dated 24 August 2000, 15 months from the date of adoption of the Panel Report as a "reasonable period of time" for implementation.[10] However, in these proceedings, the United States states that it is asking for "a period of time of at least 15 months or until the adjournment of the next session of Congress"[11] for implementation. The United States explains that implementation will likely not be completed until the end of the first session of the 107th Congress, which could end "as late as December 2001".[12] By my calculation, the United States appears to be asking for between 15 months and 17 months and four days, the latter period being the time between 27 July 2000, the date of adoption of the Panel Report, and the last day of December 2001, 31 December.

36. The United States emphasizes the following factors as relevant in support of its request for a reasonable period of time of "at least 15 months or until the adjournment of the next session of Congress": the "complexity" of the United States legislative procedure[13]; the Congressional schedule for 2001, including the

---

7 Award of the Arbitrator, *EC Measures Concerning Meat and Meat Products (Hormones) - Arbitration under Article 21.3(c) of the DSU ("EC – Homones")*, WT/DS26/15, WT/DS48/13, 29 May 1998, DSR 1998:V, 1833, para. 26; quoted with approval in Award of the Arbitrator, *Korea – Taxes on Alcoholic Beverages - Arbitration under Article 21.3(c) of the DSU* ("*Korea – Alcoholic Beverages*"), WT/DS75/16, WT/DS84/14, 4 June 1999, DSR 1999:II, 937, para. 37.

8 Award of the Arbitrator, *Korea – Alcoholic Beverages, supra*, footnote 7, para. 42.

9 Award of the Arbitrator, *Canada – Pharmaceutical Patents, supra*, footnote 6, para. 49.

10 Communication from the United States, WT/DS160/9.

11 United States' submission, para. 40.

12 *Ibid.*, para. 2.

13 *Ibid.*, paras. 7-15, 34.

fact that the new President and executive administration and the new Congress are not yet in place[14]; the "controversy" surrounding this legislation[15]; and the enormous volume of legislation introduced into each new Congress and the small percentage of legislation that is actually passed.[16] The United States also notes the "myriad opportunities for delay inherent in the U.S. legislative process" as a factor that creates uncertainty as to the timing of any proposed legislation.[17]

37. The European Communities proposes that the "reasonable period of time" be set at 10 months from the date of adoption of the Panel Report. If this proposal were accepted, the "reasonable period of time" would conclude on 27 May 2001.[18] In support of its proposal, the European Communities emphasizes the flexibility inherent in the United States legislative system, as evidenced by the absence of any mandatory time-frames in the system, and by the time-periods that have actually been utilized by the United States Congress in enacting other legislation.[19] In addition, the European Communities contends that the legislative changes required to bring the United States measure into conformity will be relatively simple.[20]

38. With regard to the specific proposal of the United States, it seems to me that the United States has proposed a longer period of time than is reasonable for implementation in this case. In this regard, I note that the United States Congress appears to have flexibility with regard to the amount of time it takes to enact legislation. In response to questioning at the oral hearing, the United States acknowledged that Congress has "a fair amount of flexibility" in the scheduling of its work. Furthermore, the "vast majority" of steps in the legislative process, according to the United States, are not subject to mandatory time-frames. Thus, when the United States Congress wants to act promptly on a matter, its normal legislative procedures allow it the flexibility to do so. In my view, the time-period proposed by the United States does not take sufficient account of this flexibility.

39. As stated above, in implementing the DSB's recommendations and rulings, the implementing Member should act "promptly". For the legislation at issue here, Congress will be acting to bring the United States into compliance with its international obligations under the *WTO Agreement*. It seems to me that this is the type of matter for which Congress would try to comply with the international obligations of the United States as soon as possible, taking advantage of the flexibility that it has within its normal legislative procedures.

---

14 *Ibid.*, paras. 16-25, 32-33.
15 *Ibid.*, para. 32.
16 *Ibid.*, para. 21.
17 *Ibid.*, para. 34.
18 European Communities' submission, para. 39.
19 European Communities' submission, paras. 26-38.
20 *Ibid.*, para. 5.

40. The United States emphasizes the enormous volume of legislation introduced every year and the small percentage of legislation that is actually passed.[21] It may be true that a great deal of legislation is introduced every year, and that only a small percentage of it becomes law. However, I do not see how this should affect, in any substantial way, the obligations of the United States to implement the recommendations and rulings of the DSB in a particular dispute.

41. Furthermore, in my view, one of the factors listed by the United States as support for the period it has proposed is not relevant for the determination of a "reasonable period of time" for implementation. The United States refers to the "controversy" surrounding the legislation, and the "divergent views of stakeholders".[22] However, as a past arbitrator has stated clearly:

> I see nothing in Article 21.3 to indicate that the supposed domestic "contentiousness" of a measure taken to comply with a WTO ruling should in any way be a factor to be considered in determining a "reasonable period of time" for implementation.[23]

42. I agree. Thus, any argument as to the "controversy", in the sense of domestic "contentiousness", regarding the measure at issue is not relevant. In the oral hearing, the United States conceded that "controversy", in this sense, is not relevant, and stated that the "controversy" to which it referred was related to the *content* of the legislation to be enacted to effect implementation, that is, whether the legislation would simply repeal Section 110(5)(B) of the Copyright Act or whether some other approach would be utilized. While I agree that this is an important issue, I do not see how it will add any *additional* time to the legislative process, as the *content* of the legislation effecting implementation is precisely the issue that Congress will decide through its normal procedures.

43. For all of these reasons, it is my view that the period of time proposed by the United States, that is, "at least 15 months" or until the end of the next legislative session of the United States Congress, is not justified by the "particular circumstances" of this case.

44. The European Communities argues that 10 months is a "reasonable period of time" for implementation. The European Communities emphasized at the oral hearing that the United States Congress can act "extremely quickly" if it so chooses.

45. I have no doubt that it is true that the United States Congress can act quickly. However, I recall the statement by the arbitrator in *Korea – Alcoholic Beverages* that an implementing Member should not be forced to utilize "extraordinary legislative procedures" in every case. Rather, the Member's "normal legislative procedures" are, generally, to be used.[24] In this arbitration, while it is

---

21 United States' submission, para. 21.

22 *Ibid.*, para. 32, footnote 37.

23 Award of the Arbitrator, *Canada – Pharmaceutical Patents*, *supra*, footnote 6, para. 60.

24 Award of the Arbitrator, *Korea – Alcoholic Beverages*, *supra*, footnote 7, para. 42.

true that the United States Congress has flexibility in the timing and management of its legislative procedures, it is clear that the process involves a number of time-consuming and complex steps. Given that the Congressional schedule for 2001 begins, at the earliest, in January, a "reasonable period of time" of 10 months, ending on 27 May 2001, does not seem sufficient in the particular circumstances of this case.

46. Finally, I would like to conclude by making the following general observation regarding implementation of recommendations and rulings of the DSB. Article 21.3(c) makes clear that the "reasonable period of time" for implementation is measured as from the "date of adoption of a panel or Appellate Body report". I recall that Article 21.1 establishes that "prompt compliance" is essential in order to ensure effective resolution of disputes to the benefit of all Members. Clearly, timeliness is of the essence. Thus, an implementing Member must use the time after adoption of a panel and/or Appellate Body report to begin to implement the recommendations and rulings of the DSB. Arbitrators will scrutinize very carefully the actions an implementing Member takes in respect of implementation during the period after adoption of a panel and/or Appellate Body report and prior to any arbitration proceeding. If it is perceived by an arbitrator that an implementing Member has not adequately begun implementation after adoption so as to effect "prompt compliance", it is to be expected that the arbitrator will take this into account in determining the "reasonable period of time".

IV. THE AWARD

47. I determine that the "reasonable period of time" for the United States to implement the recommendations and rulings of the DSB in this case is *12 months* from the date of adoption of the Panel Report by the DSB on 27 July 2000. The "reasonable period of time" will thus expire on *27 July 2001*.

UNITED STATES – SECTION 110(5) OF THE US COPYRIGHT ACT

Recourse to Arbitration under Article 25 of the DSU

Award of the Arbitrators

WT/DS160/ARB25/1

TABLE OF CONTENTS

I. INTRODUCTION

A. *Proceedings*

1.1 On 23 July 2001, the European Communities (EC)[1] and the United States (hereinafter also the "parties") notified to the Dispute Settlement Body (DSB) their mutual agreement to resort to arbitration pursuant to Article 25 of the Understanding on Rules and Procedures Governing the Settlement of Disputes (hereafter the "DSU").[2] The stated object of the arbitration was to determine the

---

[1] For the purpose of these proceedings, references to the "European Communities" shall be deemed, wherever applicable, to refer to the European Communities and their Member States.

[2] See WT/DS160/15. Article 25 of the DSU reads as follows:

> "1. Expeditious arbitration within the WTO as an alternative means of dispute settlement can facilitate the solution of certain disputes that concern issues that are clearly defined by both parties.
>
> 2. Except as otherwise provided in this Understanding, resort to arbitration shall be subject to mutual agreement of the parties which shall agree on the procedures to be followed. Agreements to resort to arbitration shall be notified to all Members sufficiently in advance of the actual commencement of the arbitration process.
>
> 3. Other Members may become party to an arbitration proceeding only upon the agreement of the parties which have agreed to have recourse to arbitration. The parties to the proceeding shall agree to abide by the arbitration award. Arbitration awards shall be notified to the DSB and the Council or Committee of any relevant agreement where any Member may raise any point relating thereto.

level of nullification or impairment of benefits to the European Communities as a result of the operation of Section 110(5)(B) of the US Copyright Act.

1.2 The parties have resorted to this arbitration further to the adoption by the DSB of the report of the panel which, at the request of the European Communities, reviewed the compatibility of Section 110(5) of the US Copyright Act,[3] as amended by the Fairness in Music Licensing Act of 1998,[4] with the Agreement on Trade-Related Aspects of Intellectual Property Rights.[5] The conclusions and recommendations of the panel[6] read as follows:

> "7.1 In the light of the findings in paragraphs 6.92-6.95, 6.133, 6.159, 6.211, 6.219, 6.266 and 6.272 above, the Panel concludes that:
>
> (a) Subparagraph (A) of Section 110(5) of the US Copyright Act meets the requirements of Article 13 of the TRIPS Agreement and is thus consistent with Articles 11*bis*(1)(iii) and 11(1)(ii) of the Berne Convention (1971) as incorporated into the TRIPS Agreement by Article 9.1 of that Agreement.
>
> (b) Subparagraph (B) of Section 110(5) of the US Copyright Act does not meet the requirements of Article 13 of the TRIPS Agreement and is thus inconsistent with Articles 11*bis*(1)(iii) and 11(1)(ii) of the Berne Convention (1971) as incorporated into the TRIPS Agreement by Article 9.1 of that Agreement.
>
> 7.2 The Panel *recommends* that the Dispute Settlement Body request the United States to bring subparagraph (B) of Section 110(5) into conformity with its obligations under the TRIPS Agreement."[7]

1.3 The parties requested the Chairman of the DSB to contact the original panelists in the dispute, to determine their availability to serve as arbitrators.[8] The Chairperson of the original panel, Mrs. Carmen Luz Guarda and one Member, Mr. A. V. Ganesan, were no longer available. In accordance with the agreed

4. Articles 21 and 22 of this Understanding shall apply *mutatis mutandis* to arbitration awards."

[3] United States Copyright Act of 1976, Act of 19 October 1976, Pub.L. 94-553, 90 Stat. 2541 (as amended).

[4] Fairness in Music Licensing Act of 27 October 1998, Pub.L. 105-298, 112 Stat. 2830, 105th Cong., 2nd Session (1998), hereinafter the "1998 Amendment".

[5] Hereafter the "TRIPS Agreement".

[6] See the Panel Report on *United States – Section 110(5) of the US Copyright Act* ("*United States – Section 110(5)*"), WT/DS160/R, adopted 27 July 2000. The original panel will be hereafter referred to as the "Panel".

[7] *Ibid.*, paras. 7.1 and 7.2.

[8] See WT/DS160/15.

procedures for the selection of the arbitrators contained in document WT/DS160/15, the Director-General appointed two arbitrators[9] to replace them.

1.4 On 13 August 2001, the Members were informed that the names of the Arbitrators were the following[10]:

Chairman: Mr. Ian F. Sheppard

Members: Mrs. Margaret Liang

Mr. David Vivas-Eugui.

1.5 Following an organizational meeting with the parties on 13 August 2001, the Arbitrators developed their Working Procedures and timetable on the basis of the agreed procedures and timetable for Article 25 arbitration annexed to the parties' communication to the Chairman of the DSB on their recourse to Article 25 of the DSU.[11]

1.6 The jurisdiction of the Arbitrators is contained in document WT/DS160/15 which reads, in relevant parts, as follows:

> "The United States and the European Communities (EC), having mutually agreed pursuant to Article 25.2 of the Understanding on Rules and Procedures for the Settlement of Disputes (DSU) to enter into arbitration to determine the level of nullification or impairment of benefits to the EC as a result of Section 110(5)(B) of the US Copyright Act, respectfully request that you contact the original panelists in the dispute "United States – Section 110(5) of the US Copyright Act" (WT/DS160), to determine their availability to serve as arbitrators in this proceeding. [...]
>
> The parties agree that the award of the arbitrator shall be final, and they shall accept it as the level of nullification or impairment for purposes of any future proceedings under Article 22 of the DSU related to this dispute."

1.7 In accordance with the timetable, the European Communities submitted a methodology paper on 14 August 2001. Both parties made concurrent written submissions on 21 August 2001. They submitted concurrent written rebuttals on 28 August 2001. The Arbitrators met with the parties on 5 September 2001. Replies to questions of the Arbitrators were received on 11 September. Parties were allowed to comment on each other's replies by 14 September 2001.[12]

---

9 The group of three arbitrators will be hereafter referred to as the "Arbitrators".

10 See WT/DS160/16.

11 See WT/DS160/15.

12 The United States submitted comments on that date. The European Communities did not, but later contested the admissibility of certain pieces of evidence submitted by the United States. Regarding subsequent procedural issues, see Section I.B.1. below.

1.8 The Arbitrators issued their award to the parties on 12 October 2001. The award was notified to the DSB and the TRIPS Council in application of Article 25.3 of the DSU on 9 November 2001.

B. Procedural Issues which Arose in the Course of the Proceedings

1. Treatment of Replies to Questions Asked by the Arbitrators to some US Collective Management Organizations

1.9 On 5 September 2001, the **Arbitrators** decided to seek additional information from two of the US collective management organizations[13]: the American Society of Authors, Composers and Publishers (ASCAP) and Broadcast Music Inc. (BMI).[14] The Arbitrators consulted the parties on the questions asked to those CMOs. The parties did not object to the Arbitrators seeking such information.[15] The Arbitrators agreed that the parties might comment on any information submitted by the US CMOs. ASCAP and BMI were given until 14 September to reply. However, no reply was received on that date.

1.10 The Arbitrators were mindful of the particular circumstances which may have delayed any reply and considered that, should ASCAP and/or BMI provide at a later stage any information likely to influence significantly the calculations to be performed, the Arbitrators would seek comments from the parties on such information before finalizing their award. BMI submitted some information on 25 September 2001. However, BMI attached a number of conditions to the use of that information, in particular the obligation for the Arbitrators to submit "any proposed public document" to BMI's counsel in order for it to confirm that the confidentiality of the information submitted by BMI was effectively protected. The Arbitrators understood that the term "any proposed public document" could apply to their award. Having regard to their Working Procedures and to general practice under public international law, they considered that such a condition was incompatible with the confidentiality of their deliberations, which extends to the content of their report until it is made public. The Arbitrators also feared that such conditions, if they were accepted, could make access to evidence more dif-

---

[13] Hereafter referred to as "CMOs".

[14] A third CMO is involved in this sector: the Society of European Stage Authors and Composers (SESAC). However, for reasons explained *infra*, the parties did not include SESAC's activities in their calculations. SESAC itself did not cooperate in the proceedings before the Panel. Having regard to the explanations given by the parties, the Arbitrators did not find it necessary to request information from SESAC.

[15] The request for information was conveyed in a letter addressed to the President and Chairman of the Board of ASCAP and to the President and Chief Executive Officer of BMI. For the text of the letter, see Annex I to this award.

ficult in future cases under the DSU. As a result, they decided not to use the information submitted by BMI on 25 September 2001.

1.11 ASCAP submitted its responses on 3 October 2001. On 4 October, the Arbitrators sought the views of the parties as to whether the information submitted should be taken into consideration. The **European Communities** considered that the information received from ASCAP did no more than repeat and confirm information already submitted by the parties to the Arbitrators and the Panel and did not justify delaying the issue of the award. The **United States** said that it would not object if the Arbitrators were to take into account the information from ASCAP but also stated that the new information merely confirmed the reasonableness of the US calculations.

1.12 BMI informed the Arbitrators on 10 October 2001 that it would submit additional information, without imposing the conditions which had lead the Arbitrators to disregard its previous submission of information.[16] The Arbitrators sought the views of the parties on the advisability of taking BMI new information into account. The **European Communities** stated that this information should not be taken into account if this further delayed the issue of the award. **The United States** considered that the Arbitrators possessed sufficient information to render a fair decision on the level of nullification or impairment of benefits caused by Section 110(5)(B). Nevertheless, if the Arbitrators preferred to await the information that BMI may submit, the United States had no objection. The United States nonetheless recalled that the "reasonable period of time" for implementation in this case expires on the earlier of the date on which the current session of the US Congress adjourns or 31 December 2001. In light of this time constraint and the parties' ongoing efforts to reach a consensual resolution of the dispute, the United States was interested in obtaining a fair decision expeditiously.

1.13 The **Arbitrators** recall that one of the main concerns expressed by the parties when this matter was referred to arbitration was that we proceed expeditiously. We note that, had we taken into account the information supplied by ASCAP and BMI, we would have had to delay considerably the date of the issue of our award. We emphasize in this regard that the European Communities has expressed the opinion that the information provided by ASCAP and BMI does not warrant any delay. We also note that the United States has not specifically requested us to consider ASCAP or BMI figures. We are, therefore, reluctant to postpone the issue of our award. We note in this respect that any delay in issuing our report shortens the time-period available to both parties to reach a mutually satisfactory solution before the end of the reasonable period of time agreed to by the DSB.

1.14 In the light of this procedural consideration, we conclude that we should not take account of the information made available by ASCAP and BMI.

---

16 The information was received on 11 October 2001.

2. *Admissibility of Some Pieces of Evidence Submitted by the United States*

1.15 On 17 September 2001, the European Communities sent a letter to the Chairman of the Arbitrators objecting to the submission of certain pieces of evidence by the United States in its comments of 14 September 2001 on the replies of the parties to the questions of the Arbitrators. On 19 September, the Chairman of the Arbitrators sent a letter to the parties, the relevant parts of which read as follows:

> "I refer to the letter of the European Communities (EC), dated 17 September 2001, addressed to me as Chairman of the Arbitrators in the above-mentioned case. In that letter, the EC refers to paragraph (f) of our Working Procedures of 16 August 2001 and claims that exhibits US ARB-25 and US ARB-26, attached by the United States to its comments of 14 September 2001, have been submitted belatedly and that "no showing of good cause" for granting an exception has been made. The European Communities concludes that the exhibits in question should be disregarded by the Arbitrators. In addition, the EC offers some comments on the substance of exhibit US ARB-26.
>
> The Arbitrators recall that paragraph (f) provides as follows:
>
>> '(f) the parties shall submit all factual evidence to the Arbitrators no later than the first written submissions to the Arbitrators, except with respect to evidence necessary for purposes of rebuttal submissions. Exceptions to this procedure will be granted upon a showing of good cause. In such cases, the other party shall be accorded a period of time for comments, as appropriate;'
>
> The Arbitrators note that the United States has submitted new materials in the form of exhibits US ARB-25 and US ARB-26, as part of the comments which the parties were allowed to make on each other's replies to the questions of the Arbitrators. The Arbitrators also note that the EC has submitted comments both on the admissibility and on the substance of these exhibits. The Arbitrators conclude that, without prejudice to any ultimate decision they may take regarding the EC request, the EC has not been deprived of the possibility to comment under paragraph (f) of our Working Procedures.
>
> Under those circumstances, the Arbitrators deem it appropriate to address the issues raised by the EC claims contained in the letter of 17 September 2001 in the arbitration award."

1.16 On 20 September 2001, the United States commented on the EC letter of 17 September, stating that it had good cause to submit the exhibits at issue, since they were intended to rebut statements made by the European Communities in its response to the written questions of the Arbitrators. In the opinion of the United States, these EC statements introduced new factual issues. The United States also contested the right of the European Communities to submit new arguments which did not respond to the rebuttals.

1.17 The Arbitrators note that the United States did not try to justify the submission of exhibits US ARB-25 and US ARB-26 in terms of paragraph (f) requirements when it submitted them. The United States claimed that it had good cause to submit those exhibits only in a subsequent letter of 20 September 2001. The Arbitrators are of the view that paragraph (f) should normally be interpreted to require the showing of good cause before or at the moment new evidence is presented, at the time or after the rebuttal submission. However, the circumstances of this case, the conditions under which the exhibits were submitted and the European Communities' reaction are special and justify that paragraph (f) be interpreted with some limited flexibility.

1.18 First, in a case where relevant information was scarce, and given the timeframe within which the Arbitrators were supposed to complete their work, any additional information was welcome at any time and *a priori* important in the light of the Arbitrators' duty to provide an objective assessment of the facts.

1.19 Second, the additional information was adduced by the United States as part of a rebuttal of EC arguments contained in its reply to questions of the Arbitrators, as agreed with the Arbitrators at the hearing. The Arbitrators note that the EC did not claim that the exhibits were not related to the rebuttal of EC arguments contained in its reply to questions from the Arbitrators.

1.20 Finally, whilst the US justification for its production of exhibits US ARB-25 and US ARB-26 was belated, in its response the European Communities did in fact deal with the substance of these exhibits. As the Chairman noted in his letter of 19 September 2001 to the parties, the EC has thus not been deprived of the opportunity to comment on the US exhibits.

1.21 Given these special circumstances, the Arbitrators hold that exhibits US ARB-25 and US ARB-26 are admitted in the procedure. As far as the substance of these pieces of evidence is concerned, the Arbitrators will revert to it as necessary in the course of this award.

3. *Treatment of Business Confidential Information Submitted by the Parties*

1.22 Both parties have submitted some information on a confidential basis which they requested should not be communicated to private parties.[17]

1.23 The Arbitrators recall that the Panel agreed to treat some information from the European Communities and the United States as confidential, while also re-

[17] US first and second written submissions, exhibits US ARB-5, 7, 8, 9, 10, 12.

calling that the designation of information as confidential did not assist the Panel in its responsibility to make findings that will best enable the DSB to perform its dispute settlement functions.[18]

1.24 In the absence of specific requests from the parties as to how confidentiality of business confidential information should be preserved, the Arbitrators will rely generally on the practice of the Appellate Body on this matter.[19] To the extent that confidential information may appear as such in the award in order to support the findings of the Arbitrators, the Arbitrators decided that two versions of the award would be prepared. One, for the parties, would contain all the information used in support of the determinations of the Arbitrators. The other, which would be circulated to all Members, would be edited so as not to include the information for which, after consultation with the parties, the Arbitrators would conclude that confidentiality for business reasons was sufficiently warranted. The information which the Arbitrators would consider to be business confidential would be replaced by "x".[20]

II. SCOPE OF THE MANDATE OF THE ARBITRATORS

A. *Jurisdiction under Article 25 of the DSU to Address the Issue Referred to the Arbitrators by the Parties*

2.1 The Arbitrators note that this is the first time since the establishment of the WTO that Members have had recourse to arbitration pursuant to Article 25 of the DSU.[21] Whereas the DSB establishes panels or refers matters to other arbitration bodies, Article 25 provides for a different procedure. The parties to this dispute only had to *notify* the DSB of their recourse to arbitration. No decision is required from the DSB for a matter to be referred to arbitration under Article 25. In the absence of a multilateral control over recourse to that provision, it is incumbent on the Arbitrators themselves to ensure that it is applied in accordance with the rules and principles governing the WTO system.[22] As recalled by the

18 See the Panel Report, *United States – Section 110(5")*, *supra*, footnote 6, para. 6.208 and footnote 192, and para. 6.233 and footnote 209.

19 See, in particular, the Appellate Body Report, *Canada – Measures Affecting the Export of Civilian Aircraft ("Canada – Aircraft")*, WT/DS70/AB/R, adopted 20 August 1999, DSR 1999:III, 1377, paras. 141-147.

20 This approach was used in one Article 22.6 arbitration and does not seem to have met with objections in the DSB. See the Decision by the Arbitrators, *Brazil – Export Financing Programme for Aircraft – Recourse to Arbitration by Brazil under Article 22.6 of the DSU and Article 4.11 of the SCM Agreement ("Brazil – Aircraft (Article 22.6 - Brazil)")*, WT/DS46/ARB, 28 August 2000, para. 2.14.

21 The Arbitrators recall that arbitration was seldom used under GATT 1947.

22 In particular, the Arbitrators believe that this arbitration should not be applied so as to circumvent the provisions of Article 22.6 of the DSU (See Article 23.2(c) of the DSU).

Appellate Body in *United States – Anti-Dumping Act of 1916*[23], it is a widely accepted rule that an international tribunal is entitled to consider the issue of its own jurisdiction on its own initiative. The Arbitrators believe that this principle applies also to arbitration bodies.[24] In case there be any question as to the jurisdiction of the Arbitrators to deal with this dispute, we provide brief reasons for our conclusion that we do have the necessary jurisdiction.

2.2 The Arbitrators recall that this arbitration has been called upon to address a particular issue resulting from the implementation of the DSB rulings and recommendations on the basis of the Panel Report on *US – Section 110(5) Copyright Act*. In that context, our mandate is to "determine the level of nullification or impairment of benefits to the European Communities as a result of Section 110(5)(B) of the US Copyright Act".[25]

2.3 The Arbitrators first note that, pursuant to the text of Article 25.1, arbitration under Article 25 is an "*alternative* means of dispute settlement".[26] The term "dispute settlement" is generally used in the WTO Agreement to refer to the complete process of dispute[27] resolution under the DSU, not to one aspect of it, such as the determination of the level of benefits nullified or impaired as a result of a violation. It may be argued that the procedure provided for in Article 25 is actually an alternative to a panel procedure. This would seem to be confirmed by the terms of Article 25.4, which provides that "Articles 21 and 22 of this Understanding shall apply *mutatis mutandis* to arbitration awards."[28] Article 22.2 itself, unlike Article 21.3(c), does not refer to arbitration as an alternative to the negotiation of mutually acceptable compensation. It could then be argued that arbitration under Article 25 is not intended for "determin[ing] the level of nullification or impairment of benefits to the European Communities as a result of Section 110(5)(B) of the US Copyright Act."

---

23 See the Appellate Body Report, *United States - Anti-Dumping Act of 1916* ("*US – 1916 Act*"), WT/DS136/AB/R and WT/DS162/AB/R, adopted 26 September 2000, para. 54, footnote 30.

24 This is evidenced by Article 21 of the Optional Rules of the Permanent Court of Arbitration for arbitrations involving international organizations and States. See, Permanent Court of Arbitration: Optional Rules for Arbitration involving International Organizations and States, effective 1 July 1996, International Bureau of the Permanent Court of Arbitration, The Hague, The Netherlands.

25 WT/DS160/15.

26 Emphasis added.

27 In a note by the GATT Secretariat on Concept, Forms and Effects of Arbitration (MTN.GNG/NG13/W/20, 22 February 1988), the term "dispute" is defined as a specific disagreement concerning a matter of fact, law or policy in which a claim or assertion by one party is met with refusal, counter-claim or denial by another.

28 The text of Article 25 of the DSU is essentially identical to that of *paras.* 1, 2 and 3 of Section E of the 1989 Decision on improvements to the GATT dispute settlement procedures (BISD 36S/63). It is worth noting that, in that Decision, Section E follows other sections on means of resolution of disputes, such as consultations (Section C) and good offices, conciliation and mediation (Section D). Moreover, GATT 1947 did not provide for the sophisticated means of enforcement found in the DSU. The note MTN.GNG/NG13/W/20 of 22 February 1988, referred to above, also presents arbitration "as an alternative to the normal dispute settlement process" (para. 12) or "as an alternative to panel proceedings" (para. 17).

2.4 While being mindful of these elements of interpretation, the Arbitrators are of the view that they are outweighed by other elements, based on the fact that none of the provisions concerned expressly excludes recourse to arbitration under Article 25 in the particular context in which they apply. Article 25.2 itself provides that resort to arbitration shall be subject to mutual agreement of the parties which shall agree on the procedures to be followed "except as otherwise provided in this Understanding". Article 25 itself does not specify that recourse to Article 25 arbitration should be excluded when determining the level of nullification or impairment suffered by a Member. On the contrary, the terms of Article 25.1 referring to "the solution of certain disputes that concern issues that are clearly defined by the parties" may support the view that Article 25 should be understood as an arbitration mechanism to which Members may have recourse whenever necessary within the WTO framework. We also note that Article 22.2 refers to "negotiations [...] with a view to developing mutually acceptable compensation." There is no language in that provision which would make it impossible to consider arbitration as a means of reaching a mutually acceptable compensation.

2.5 Moreover, recourse to Article 25 arbitration in the present situation is fully consistent with the object and purpose of the DSU. Arbitration is likely to contribute to the prompt settlement of a dispute between Members, as commanded by Article 3.3 of the DSU. Indeed, it may facilitate the resolution of a divergence in the context of a negotiation of compensations, thus paving the way to implementation without suspension of concessions or other obligations.

2.6 In general, recourse to arbitration under Article 25 strengthens the dispute resolution system by complementing negotiation under Article 22.2. The possibility for the parties to a dispute to seek arbitration in relation to the negotiation of compensation operates to increase the effectiveness of that option under Article 22.2. Incidentally, the Arbitrators note that compensation, in their opinion, is always to be preferred to countermeasures of any sort, since it enhances trade instead of restricting or diverting it. Finally, such an application of Article 25 does not, at least in the case at hand, affect the rights of other Members under the DSU.[29]

2.7 Having regard to the object of the arbitration requested by the parties and the fact that the rights of other Members under the DSU are not affected by the decision of the European Communities and the United States to seek arbitration under Article 25, the Arbitrators are of the view that, pending further interpretation by the Members, they should declare that they have jurisdiction under Article 25 to determine the level of EC benefits which are being nullified or impaired in this case.[30]

---

[29] As a matter of fact, it may affect them positively, given the *erga omnes* character of compensation.

[30] The Arbitrators' recognition of their jurisdiction in this case is not a unilateral extension of WTO jurisdiction, since it is dependent on the agreement of the parties to a dispute to have recourse to

III. CONCEPTUAL ISSUES

3.1 Since the present arbitration proceedings are the first ones in which a WTO adjudicating body is entrusted with the task of determining the level of benefits nullified or impaired as a consequence of an infringement of obligations under the TRIPS Agreement, it is necessary to address at some length two conceptual issues before undertaking any actual calculations of the level of nullification or impairment suffered by the European Communities in this case.

A. *Nature and Level of Benefits Nullified or Impaired*

3.2 The first issue which the Arbitrators turn to examine concerns the nature and level of the benefits which are being nullified or impaired in the present case.

3.3 The **European Communities** submits that this case is special in that it involves the denial by the United States of exclusive rights which the United States is required under the TRIPS Agreement to grant to nationals of other WTO Members. The European Communities notes that, in contrast, in none of the past arbitration proceedings under Article 22.6 of the DSU did any of the entities affected by the relevant WTO-inconsistent measures enjoy any exclusive rights. Instead, they only enjoyed expectations as to the legal framework and factual conditions in which they could pursue their economic activities. The European Communities considers that, because the TRIPS Agreement guarantees specific exclusive rights rather than merely expectations, the proper way of measuring nullification or impairment of benefits in this case is by assessing the economic value of the denied exclusive rights.

3.4 With reference to the present dispute, the European Communities argues that a correct assessment of the value of the exclusive copyrights which are being denied to EC right holders as a consequence of Section 110(5)(B) cannot be made, unless it is assumed that all those establishments which use copyright works of EC right holders are licensed. The European Communities notes that, otherwise, those establishments would engage in acts of piracy. The European Communities therefore is of the view that the economic value of the copyrights at issue in the present dispute corresponds to the licensing revenue *potentially* foregone by EC right holders as a result of Section 110(5)(B).

3.5 The **United States** considers that the level of nullification or impairment of benefits caused to the European Communities is equal to the annual benefits lost by EC right holders as a result of Section 110(5)(B). Like the European Communities, the United States believes that the level of nullification or impair-

---

Article 25 of the DSU. This decision is without prejudice to the DSU compatibility of the decision of the parties to accept this award as the level of nullification or impairment for the purpose of any further proceedings under Article 22 of the DSU in relation to this case. It is also without prejudice to any interpretation of the provisions of Articles 22 and 25 of the DSU by the Ministerial Conference or the General Council.

ment should be measured by reference to the licensing royalties lost by EC right holders. However, the United States disagrees with the European Communities' contention that it has lost benefits equal to the total licensing royalties that hypothetically could be collected. In the view of the United States, the most accurate and factually grounded way to quantify the lost benefits is to determine the benefits that EC right holders were receiving prior to the enactment of Section 110(5)(B).

3.6 According to the United States, the European Communities' proposed methodology should be rejected because it calculates foregone licensing royalties as though copyright holders would receive royalties from *every* user of radio or television music that is affected by Section 110(5)(B). The United States maintains that prior to the enactment of Section 110(5)(B) many bars, restaurants and retail establishments in the United States that could have played radio or television music were not licensed to do so. The United States submits that this absence of 100% licensing is to be expected, as the US CMOs which administer the rights of the copyright holders face substantial costs in licensing bars, restaurants and retail establishments. The United States argues that, given the geographically dispersed user base in the United States, it is not economically rational for US CMOs to locate and attempt to obtain and administer licenses for every establishment that plays radio or television music. The United States is therefore of the view that, because it disregards the cost of collecting and distributing royalties, the European Communities' proposed methodology produces a windfall for itself, which would be contrary to WTO rules and would unfairly penalize the United States.

3.7 The **European Communities** rejects the United States' argument that it would be "too costly" to license certain categories of businesses or businesses in certain areas of the United States. The European Communities submits that this is tantamount to suggesting that a WTO Member in which piracy rates are very high or where the enforcement of intellectual property is particularly difficult or costly is, for all practical purposes, released from its substantive obligations under the TRIPS Agreement.

3.8 The **Arbitrators** note that they are called on, in this case, to determine the level of nullification or impairment of benefits accruing to the European Communities as a result of the continued application of Section 110(5)(B). In respect of Section 110(5)(B), the Panel reached the conclusion that it was "[...] inconsistent with Articles 11*bis*(1)(iii) and 11(1)(ii) of the Berne Convention (1971) as incorporated into the TRIPS Agreement by Article 9.1 of that Agreement."[31] Neither party to this dispute contests that Section 110(5)(B), as currently in force, continues to be inconsistent with the provisions of the aforementioned articles.

3.9 It is clear, therefore, that the benefits which Section 110(5)(B) is impairing or nullifying are those which should accrue to the European Communities and

[31] Panel Report, *United States – Section 110(5")*, *supra*, footnote 6, para. 7.1(b).

other Members under the provisions of Articles 11*bis*(1)(iii) and 11(1)(ii) of the Berne Convention (1971)[32] as incorporated into the TRIPS Agreement by Article 9.1 of that Agreement.

3.10 It is apparent from the submissions of the parties that they do not so much differ regarding the *nature* of the benefits which should accrue to the European Communities under the provisions of Articles 11*bis*(1)(iii) and 11(1)(ii), but rather regarding the *level* of benefits which the European Communities could expect to accrue to it under those provisions. The Arbitrators will address these issues in turn.[33]

3.11 As concerns, first, the *nature* of the benefits which would accrue to the European Communities if Section 110(5)(B) were brought into conformity with Articles 11*bis*(1)(iii) and 11(1)(ii), it is well to recall at the outset what those Articles actually provide.

3.12 Article 11*bis*(1)(iii) reads:

> Authors of literary and artistic works shall enjoy the exclusive right of authorizing:
>
> [...]
>
> (iii) the public communication by loudspeaker or any other analogous instrument transmitting, by signs, sounds or images, the broadcast of the work.

3.13 Article 11(1)(ii) states:

> Authors of dramatic, dramatico-musical and musical works shall enjoy the exclusive right of authorizing:
>
> [...]
>
> (ii) any communication to the public of the performance of their works.

3.14 By virtue of Article 9.1 of the TRIPS Agreement[34], the provisions of Articles 11*bis*(1)(iii) and 11(1)(ii) "[...] have become part of the TRIPS Agreement and as provisions of that Agreement have to be read as applying to WTO Members."[35]

---

[32] Articles 11*bis*(1)(iii) and 11(1)(ii) of the Berne Convention (1971) will hereafter be referred to as "Articles 11*bis*(1)(iii) and 11(1)(ii)".

[33] The Arbitrators note that, in those cases where users of copyright works are covered by Section 110(5)(B), the European Communities does not currently derive *any* benefits from the provisions of Articles 11*bis*(1)(iii) and 11(1)(ii). It is, therefore, of no account whether the question before the Arbitrators is framed as "What is the level of EC benefits which are being nullified or impaired as a result of Section 110(5)(B)?" or as "What is the level of benefits which would accrue to the European Communities if Section 110(5)(B) were brought into conformity with Articles 11*bis*(1)(iii) and 11(1)(ii)?".

[34] Article 9.1 of the TRIPS Agreement provides in pertinent part that "Members shall comply with Articles 1 through 21 of the Berne Convention (1971) and the Appendix thereto."

[35] Panel Report, *United States – Section 110(5")*, *supra*, footnote 6, para. 6.18.

3.15 For purposes of the present dispute, this means that the United States is under an obligation to make available to EC right holders the exclusive rights set forth in Articles 11*bis*(1)(iii) and 11(1)(ii).[36] It is important to bear in mind, however, that, while it is for the *United States* to *provide* EC right holders with the exclusive rights set forth in Articles 11*bis*(1)(iii) and 11(1)(ii), it is for *EC right holders* to determine whether and how to *exercise* or *exploit* those rights.

3.16 Although there may be a variety of ways in which EC right holders could exercise or exploit the exclusive rights which the United States must make available to them, the parties are in agreement that, in practice, such exclusive rights are and would be exploited through licensing. The Arbitrators see no reason to differ from the parties in this regard.[37]

3.17 If it is assumed, then, that copyright holders exploit their exclusive rights by granting licences for the use of their works, one of the benefits which arises from those rights consists of the licensing royalties which right holders would receive. Thus, exclusive rights such as those set forth in Articles 11*bis*(1)(iii) and 11(1)(ii) will normally translate into economic benefits for copyright holders.

3.18 In their submissions to the Arbitrators, the parties have focused on this type of benefit accruing to copyright holders. The Arbitrators concur with the parties that, for purposes of these arbitration proceedings, the relevant benefits are those which are economic in nature.[38] This is consistent with previous decisions of arbitrators acting under Article 22.6 of the DSU.[39] Moreover, like the

---

[36] Article 1.1 of the TRIPS Agreement makes clear that "Members shall give effect to the provisions of the [TRIPS] Agreement." Members must, therefore, implement in their domestic law the protection required by the TRIPS Agreement. Moreover, Article 1.3 of the TRIPS Agreement provides in relevant part that "Members shall accord the treatment provided for in this Agreement to the nationals of other Members." (footnote omitted) This confirms that the exclusive rights conferred by Articles 11*bis*(1)(iii) and 11(1)(ii) must be granted to EC right holders.

[37] The assumption that the exclusive rights at issue in this dispute are exploited through licensing is, of course, without prejudice to any assumptions that may appropriately be made in other cases involving other exclusive rights guaranteed by the TRIPS Agreement.

[38] This view is based on the object of the present proceedings, which is to quantify the economic harm suffered by the European Communities as a consequence of the continued application of Section 110(5)(B). It does not necessarily follow that Members having recourse to Article 64 of the TRIPS Agreement need to establish nullification or impairment of *economic* benefits accruing to them under the TRIPS Agreement. The Arbitrators find support for their view in the following statement by the arbitrators in *European Communities – Regime for the Importation, Sale and Distribution of Bananas – Recourse to Arbitration by the European Communities under Article 22.6 of the DSU*: "[A] Member's potential interests in trade in goods or services and its interest in a determination of rights and obligations under the WTO Agreements are each sufficient to establish a right to pursue a WTO dispute settlement proceeding. However, a Member's legal interest in compliance by other Members does not, in our view, automatically imply that it is entitled to obtain authorization to suspend concessions under Article 22 of the DSU." See the Decision by the Arbitrators, *European Communities – Regime for the Importation, Sale and Distribution of Bananas – Recourse to Arbitration by the European Communities under Article 22.6 of the DSU* ("*EC - Bananas III (US) (Article 22.6 - EC)*"), WT/DS27/ARB, 9 April 1999, DSR 1999:II, 725, para. 6.10.

[39] See, e.g., the Decision by the Arbitrators, *EC – Bananas III (US) (Article 22.6 – EC), supra*, footnote 38, para. 6.12 (benefits nullified or impaired: losses in US exports of goods and losses by

parties to this dispute, the Arbitrators will proceed on the assumption that the licensing royalties realizable by copyright holders constitute an adequate measure of the economic benefits arising from Articles 11*bis*(1)(iii) and 11(1)(ii).

3.19 Accordingly, the Arbitrators will, in this case, assess the level of EC benefits which Section 110(5)(B) is nullifying or impairing in terms of the royalty income foregone by EC right holders. In making this observation, the Arbitrators are aware that their task in this case is to determine the benefits which are denied to the *European Communities* rather than determining the benefits which are denied to *EC right holders*. However, there can be no question that the benefits which are denied to the European Communities include the benefits which are denied to EC right holders.[40] What is more, the European Communities has not made out a claim to the effect that Section 110(5)(B) is nullifying or impairing benefits additional to those which EC right holders could otherwise derive from Articles 11*bis*(1)(iii) and 11(1)(ii). As a result, it is appropriate, for the purposes of these proceedings, to determine the level of EC benefits which Section 110(5)(B) is nullifying or impairing in terms of the benefits foregone by EC right holders.

3.20 Having addressed the nature of the benefits which should accrue to the European Communities under Articles 11*bis*(1)(iii) and 11(1)(ii), the Arbitrators next turn to the issue of the *level* of benefits which the European Communities could expect to accrue to it under those Articles. Put in another way, the next issue confronting the Arbitrators relates to the level of royalty income which EC right holders could expect to receive if the United States were to comply with its obligations under Articles 11*bis*(1)(iii) and 11(1)(ii).[41]

US service suppliers in services supply); Decision by the Arbitrators, *European Communities – Regime for the Importation, Sale and Distribution of Bananas – Recourse to Arbitration by the European Communities under Article 22.6 of the DSU*, ("*EC – Bananas III (Ecuador) (Article 22.6 – EC)*"), WT/DS27/ARB/ECU, 24 March 2000, DSR 2000:V, 2243, footnote 52 (benefits nullified or impaired: losses by Ecuador of actual trade and of potential trade opportunities in bananas and the loss of actual and potential distribution service supply);); Decision by the Arbitrators, *European Communities - Measures Concerning Meat and Meat Products (Hormones) - Original Complaint by the United States - Recourse to Arbitration by the European Communities under Article 22.6 of the DSU* ("*EC - Hormones (US) (Article 22.6 - EC)* "), WT/DS26/ARB, 12 July 1999, DSR 1999:III, 1105, para. 41 (benefits nullified or impaired: foregone US exports of hormone-treated beef and beef products); Decision by the Arbitrators, *European Communities - Measures Concerning Meat and Meat Products (Hormones) - Original Complaint by Canada - Recourse to Arbitration by the European Communities under Article 22.6 of the DSU* ("*EC - Hormones (Canada) (Article 22.6 – EC)*"), WT/DS48/ARB, 12 July 1999, DSR 1999:III, 1135, para. 40 (benefits nullified or impaired: foregone Canadian exports of hormone-treated beef and beef products).

40 Indeed, as already pointed out, the rights set forth in Articles 11*bis*(1)(iii) and 11(1)(ii) must, in conformity with the provisions of Article 1.3 of the TRIPS Agreement, be granted to EC right holders.

41 It should be noted that it is not in dispute that the level of benefits which EC right holders could expect to accrue to them if Section 110(5)(B) were brought into conformity with the TRIPS Agreement would depend, first and foremost, on the competitive position of EC right holders in the US market. As a matter of fact, both parties have attempted to estimate what percentage of total royalty

3.21 The European Communities considers that, because this dispute involves exclusive rights, the level of benefits which EC right holders could expect to obtain should be assessed by reference to the economic value of the exclusive rights conferred on them by Articles 11*bis*(1)(iii) and 11(1)(ii). The European Communities argues that the economic value of those rights corresponds to the royalty income *potentially* realizable by EC right holders. The European Communities recalls, in this regard, that all US bars, restaurants and retail establishments which play radio or television music would have to pay licensing fees and that any unauthorized use of copyrighted musical works by such establishments would be illegal.

3.22 The Arbitrators are cognizant of the fact that the rights set forth in Articles 11*bis*(1)(iii) and 11(1)(ii) are in the nature of exclusive rights. If granted by the United States, those rights would provide EC right holders with the assurance that any unauthorized use of those works would be illegal as a matter of US law. It is also true, as the European Communities suggests, that any unauthorized use of copyright works, quite apart from being illegal, would deprive EC right holders of royalty income. However, the question is whether the level of royalty income which EC right holders could expect to receive *includes* the royalty income of which they would be deprived by all unauthorized users of their works.

3.23 The European Communities answers this question in the affirmative. In essence, it argues that because EC right holders *should* receive licensing royalties from *all* users of their copyright works - i.e., legal and illegal users - the benefits which the European Communities can expect to accrue to it are equal to the royalty income which EC right holders *should* receive.[42]

3.24 The Arbitrators consider that the benefits which they should take into account in this case are those which the European Communities could reasonably expect to accrue to it under Articles 11*bis*(1)(iii) and 11(1)(ii).[43] In this regard, the Arbitrators certainly appreciate the European Communities' point that, as a

---

income generated in the United States would accrue to EC right holders if Section 110(5)(B) were made to conform to Articles 11*bis*(1)(iii) and 11(1)(ii).

[42] In the European Communities' view, the royalty income which EC right holders *should* receive - i.e., the royalty income potentially realizable by EC right holders - represents the economic value of the exclusive rights at issue in this dispute. Even assuming that were correct (a question which the Arbitrators do not here decide), the Arbitrators note that they are not called on, in this case, to assess the economic value of the *rights* set forth in Articles 11*bis*(1)(iii) and 11(1)(ii). Rather, the mandate of the Arbitrators is to determine the economic value of the *benefits* which would arise from those rights on an annual basis. See document WT/DS160/15. Therefore, the Arbitrators do not find it appropriate, in the context of the present proceedings, to speak of the "economic value of the rights set forth in Articles 11*bis*(1)(iii) and 11(1)(ii)".

[43] It should be recalled, in this context, that the inquiry into the level of benefits which the European Communities could expect to accrue to it *if* Section 110(5)(B) were brought into conformity with the TRIPS Agreement is hypothetical in nature. The Arbitrators consider that, in such a situation, it is necessary to proceed with caution, such that only those benefits which the European Communities could, in good faith and taking account of all relevant circumstances, expect to derive from Articles 11*bis*(1)(iii) and 11(1)(ii) are found to be nullified or impaired.

matter of US law, all users of copyright works by EC right holders *should* be licensed and *should* pay licensing fees. But is it reasonable, in the circumstances of the present dispute, for the European Communities to expect that all users of the works of EC right holders *would* be licensed and *would* pay licensing fees?

3.25 In considering this issue, it is important to recall that the rights set forth in Articles 11*bis*(1)(iii) and 11(1)(ii) do not exercise or enforce themselves. In this connection, the Arbitrators note that neither party to this dispute has suggested that, in the event those rights were available under US law, the United States would have any role to play in how those rights would be exercised. Nor has it been asserted that it would be the duty of the United States to enforce those rights on behalf of EC right holders. In the view of the Arbitrators, it is clear that the exercise and enforcement of the rights conferred by Articles 11*bis*(1)(iii) and 11(1)(ii) would not be the responsibility of the United States but of EC right holders.[44]

3.26 Indeed, it is common ground that, in practice, copyright holders entrust CMOs with the exercise and enforcement of the exclusive rights at issue in this dispute.[45] Such CMOs are authorized by copyright holders to identify users of their rights, grant licences for the use of those rights and take legal action to enforce licences or pursue users who fail to seek licences.

3.27 The United States submits that, in performing the aforementioned tasks, US CMOs incur substantial costs. The United States recalls in this respect that, in the United States, the potential base of users of copyrighted musical works - i.e., bars, restaurants and retail establishments - is wide, geographically dispersed and in almost constant change, as users continually leave and enter the market. From these considerations, the United States infers that it is not economically rational for US CMOs - which the United States says generally seek to maximize profits

---

[44] It should be mentioned, however, that the TRIPS Agreement does lay on the United States certain obligations in respect of the enforcement of intellectual property rights in its territory. Those obligations are laid down in Articles 41 *et seq.* of the TRIPS Agreement. The general obligation is set out in Article 41, which provides in relevant part that "Members shall ensure that enforcement procedures [...] are available under their law so as to permit effective action against any act of infringement of intellectual property rights covered by this Agreement [...]". Before the Panel, the European Communities did not raise a claim of violation in respect of any of the enforcement provisions of the TRIPS Agreement. See the Panel Report, *United States – Section 110(5")*, *supra*, footnote 6, para. 3.2. The Arbitrators must therefore assume that the United States is acting consistently with the enforcement obligations contained in the TRIPS Agreement.

[45] See the Panel Report *United States – Section 110(5")*, *supra*, footnote 6, para. 2.17. EC right holders could theoretically attempt to license users of their copyright works directly, i.e., with no involvement of US CMOs. The Arbitrators consider, however, that it is justifiable, for purposes of the present proceedings, to leave out of account the possibility of direct licensing by EC right holders. From the evidence on record, it appears to the Arbitrators that, because of the very high transaction costs associated with direct licensing, it is unlikely that EC right holders would license their rights directly to a significant extent. At any rate, neither party has specifically requested that royalty income stemming from direct licensing be factored into the Arbitrators' calculation.

for the right holders they represent[46] - to attempt to identify and obtain licences from *every* user of copyright works.[47] According to the United States, estimates relating to the time before Section 110(5)(B) was enacted in fact bear out its view that right holders do not license *all* of the potential users of their works.[48]

3.28 The European Communities does not deny that the exercise of the exclusive rights of right holders entails costs. Nor has the European Communities specifically contested the United States' argument that it might not be economically rational for US CMOs to attempt to license each and every user of copyright works. The European Communities nevertheless considers that the costs of the administration and enforcement of exclusive rights should not be factored into the calculation of the level of EC benefits which are being nullified or impaired as a result of Section 110(5)(B). The European Communities submits that to do so would mean that, notwithstanding the TRIPS Agreement, EC right holders would have to accept a certain level of what the European Communities terms as "piracy".

3.29 The Arbitrators see force in the United States' argument that the number of users whom US CMOs will seek to license is a function of the expected cost and revenue per licence. The Arbitrators also find persuasive the suggestion that the cost and revenue per licence vary according to the characteristics of the user base, including such factors as the number, size and location of the users that play broadcast music as well as the extent to which users play such music.[49]

---

[46] The United States also points out, however, that US CMOs themselves may, in some cases, be organised as non-profit organizations. The United States notes that this is true, for example, of ASCAP.

[47] The United States notes that US CMOs are, in practice, most interested in licensing users from which expected revenue is greatest and expected cost of collection is least. According to the United States, US CMOs would, for example, be more likely to incur the cost of licensing a large department store in New York City than to incur the likely higher cost of identifying and licensing a small bar in rural Kansas.

[48] The United States estimates that before Section 110(5)(B) was enacted, between xx% (estimate for 1996) and 19% (estimate for 1997) of restaurants in the United States were licensed to play music. On the other hand, the United States has indicated before the Panel that approximately 74% of all restaurants in the United States play music. See Panel Report, *United States – Section 110(5*"), *supra*, footnote 6, Attachment 2.3 (US response to question 11(b) by the Panel to United States).

[49] Unlike the European Communities, the Arbitrators see nothing in *para.* 6.247 of the Panel report which would suggest that it would be inappropriate, in the circumstances and for purposes of *this* dispute, to take into consideration such factors as the transaction costs associated with licensing and the characteristics of the user base. Nor is it clear to the Arbitrators how taking account of those factors could "undermine the scope and binding effect" of the TRIPS Agreement. *Para.* 6.247 addresses the issue of whether a Member could justifiably limit the exclusive rights set forth in Articles 11*bis*(1)(iii) and 11(1)(ii) on the basis that right holders would, in terms of actual rather than potential losses, be no worse off after the introduction of the limitation than before its introduction. See Panel Report, *United States – Section 110(5*"), *supra*, footnote 6, para. 6.247. This is an issue which is quite different from the ones confronting the Arbitrators in this case.

Similarly, the Panel's statement in *para.* 6.196 of its report that the licensing practices of CMOs cannot necessarily be fully indicative of "normal exploitation" of exclusive rights in no way runs counter to the view of the Arbitrators that the level of licensing which US CMOs aim to achieve is a

3.30 Moreover, it is clear from the information supplied by the parties on the characteristics of the US user base that US CMOs would incur very significant costs if they were to attempt to achieve licensing levels of 100%. It is quite reasonable, therefore, that US CMOs could generate greater net licensing revenues for themselves at lower levels of licensing. Indeed, the evidence on record supports the United States' claim that, in practice, US CMOs collect only a proportion of the royalty income potentially realizable by right holders and that they do not license all users of copyright works.[50]

3.31 Contrary to the European Communities' view, taking account of the transaction costs incurred by US CMOs and of the bearing those costs have on the level of licensing does not carry the implication that right holders "have to" accept a certain level of "piracy". Right holders, or the CMOs representing them, are at liberty to seek to license all users of their works. As should be clear from the preceding paragraphs, however, were CMOs to do so, they would not necessarily maximize the royalty income of the right holders they represent.

3.32 In response to the European Communities' "piracy" argument the Arbitrators further wish to note that "piracy" is of course an emotive word when used in the context of the infringement of copyright. In areas of copyright use not covered by the exemptions provided for in Section 110(5), it would be surprising if there were now 100% collection of royalties potentially due. Before the enactment of the 1998 Amendment, it was most unlikely that all the enterprises now entitled to the benefit of the exemptions there provided for would either have been licensed or, if licensed, would have actually paid all the licensing fees which were due. But, as previously indicated, the European Communities has not formally made a claim of violation in respect of any of the enforcement provisions of the TRIPS Agreement. If the 1998 Amendment had not been passed, it seems unlikely that there would ever have been any complaint to the DSB about a

function of expected cost and revenue per licence. The issue considered by the Panel was whether the fact that the 1998 Amendment did not generally change the licensing practices of US CMOs in relation to those establishments that were already exempted under the original homestyle exemption was a reliable indicator of normal exploitation of exclusive rights. The Panel found that it was not, because it was evident that, due to the pre-existing homestyle exemption, those establishments could not be licensed. See Panel Report, *United States – Section 110(5")*, *supra*, footnote 6, para. 6.196. It does not follow from the Panel's finding that the costs associated with licensing have no bearing on the level of licensing. Indeed, the Panel acknowledged "[...] that the extent of exercise or non-exercise of exclusive rights by right holders at a given point in time is of great relevance for assessing what is the normal exploitation with respect to a particular exclusive right in a particular market." See Panel Report, *United States – Section 110(5")*, *supra*, footnote 6, para. 6.188.

50 The European Communities does not specifically question the accuracy of the United States' estimates of the level of licensing which would likely prevail in the United States if Section 110(5)(B) were brought into conformity with the TRIPS Agreement. On the other hand, data provided by the European Communities suggests that the level of licensing in some member States of the European Communities is significantly higher than in the United States. It should be recalled, however, that, before the Panel, the European Communities did not formally claim that the United States was acting inconsistently with the enforcement obligations contained in the TRIPS Agreement. See *supra*, footnote 44.

failure on the part of the United States to take steps to ensure full compliance. This suggests that, at that time, the European Communities accepted the reality that there could never be 100% recovery.

3.33 In the light of the foregoing, the Arbitrators consider that the European Communities could not reasonably expect that, in the United States, all users of copyright works of EC right holders would be licensed and would pay licensing royalties. As a result, the level of royalty income which the European Communities could reasonably expect EC right holders to receive is, in the view of the Arbitrators, limited to licensing revenue from the numbers of users that *would* be licensed.

3.34 The Arbitrators are thus unable to accept the European Communities' view that the level of benefits which the European Communities could reasonably expect to accrue to it under Articles 11*bis*(1)(iii) and 11(1)(ii) equals the royalty income potentially realizable by EC right holders. Indeed, were the Arbitrators to adopt the European Communities' view, the level of EC benefits *nullified or impaired* as a result of Section 110(5)(B) would be *higher* than the level of benefits which would *actually accrue* to the European Communities if Section 110(5)(B) were brought into conformity with the TRIPS Agreement.[51] The Arbitrators consider that such an outcome would be both inconsistent and unwarranted. It would be quite inappropriate for the Arbitrators to award the European Communities benefits which it is not actually losing as a result of the continued application of Section 110(5)(B).[52]

3.35 In conclusion, the Arbitrators will, in this case, determine the level of EC benefits nullified or impaired as a result of Section 110(5)(B) by reference to the royalty income which EC right holders could reasonably be expected to realize if the United States made available the rights set forth in Articles 11*bis*(1)(iii) and 11(1)(ii). For the reasons indicated above, the Arbitrators consider that the royalty income which EC right holders could reasonably be expected to realize does not include the royalty income which EC right holders would forego by not exercising or enforcing their exclusive rights.

---

[51] This is because the royalty income potentially realizable by EC right holders - which the European Communities suggests is what the Arbitrators should assess in this dispute - exceeds the actual royalty income which EC right holders may reasonably be expected to realise once the United States makes available the rights referred to in Articles 11*bis*(1)(iii) and 11(1)(ii).

[52] For the same reason, the Arbitrators cannot agree with the European Communities that it would be absurd for the level of nullification or impairment to be lower in the case of Members with low levels of licensing (due, e.g., to high licensing costs) than it would be in the case of Members with high levels of licensing (due, e.g., to low licensing costs). The level of benefits which would actually accrue to other Members would, likewise, be smaller in the case of Members with low levels of licensing than it would be in the case of Members with high levels of licensing.

B. Royalties Collected Versus Royalties Distributed

3.36 As previously indicated, there is a further and separate conceptual issue which the Arbitrators need to resolve prior to dealing with the details of how to calculate the level of EC benefits which are being nullified or impaired as a result of Section 110(5)(B). That issue goes to the question of whether the royalty income which EC right holders could reasonably be expected to realize is equal to the amount of licensing royalties which would be *collected* by US CMOs from users of works of EC right holders or whether, instead, it is equal to the amount of royalties which would be *distributed* by US CMOs to EC right holders.

3.37 The **European Communities** considers that the Arbitrators should base their determination on the amount of royalties to be paid by the users of copyright works and not on the amount of royalties which US CMOs would distribute to EC right holders. The European Communities notes that the services rendered by US CMOs to EC right holders entail costs for the latter and that these costs reduce the net proceeds of EC right holders. But the European Communities recalls its view that what has to be assessed in the present case is the value of the exclusive rights which are being denied to EC right holders. The costs which US CMOs would incur in administering the rights of EC right holders or the net proceeds accruing to EC right holders are, in the view of the European Communities, irrelevant to the assessment of the economic value of the exclusive rights of EC right holders.

3.38 The European Communities further notes that *all* economic operators incur expenses in collecting receivables because they either need to employ staff for that purpose or else use the services of specialized enterprises. The European Communities argues that, notwithstanding that, the costs related to the collection of receivables from transactions involving goods or services have never been used, in past arbitration proceedings under Article 22.6 of the DSU, to reduce the level of benefits found to be impaired or nullified as a result of an infringement of WTO obligations.

3.39 The **United States** argues that the benefits lost to EC right holders as a result of Section 110(5)(B) are the distributions they otherwise would receive from US CMOs. The United States submits that the benefits lost to EC right holders are not the gross licensing royalties the US CMOs would otherwise collect from licensed users. According to the United States, this is because US CMOs would only distribute *net* licensing royalties to EC right holders. The United States defines net licensing royalties as "licensing royalties collected by the collecting societies minus the costs incurred by the collecting societies". Those costs include the costs resulting from the collection and administration of the rights of copyright holders.

3.40 The United States adds that the European Communities, in focusing only on the payment of fees from US licensees to US CMOs, overlooks the fact that the present case is a trade case. For the United States, what matters are the cross-border payments which EC right holders should be receiving. Thus, in the view of the United States, the level of nullification or impairment suffered by the

European Communities equals the foregone earnings in its current account transactions with the United States, resulting from the inconsistency found between US law and the TRIPS Agreement. The United States recalls in this regard that the current account transaction is the distribution from a US CMO to an EC right holder, and not the payment of a fee by a US licensee to a US CMO.

3.41 The **Arbitrators** note that US CMOs do not distribute to copyright holders the total amount of licensing royalties which they collect from licensed users. This is because the CMOs have to cover the costs which they incur in licensing the rights of copyright holders as well as general operating costs. It follows that the total amount of royalties which US CMOs would distribute to EC right holders if the United States made available to them the rights set forth in Articles 11*bis*(1)(iii) and 11(1)(ii) would be smaller than the total amount of licensing royalties paid to US CMOs by licensed users of works of EC right holders.

3.42 This raises the issue of whether the level of EC benefits which are being nullified or impaired as a result of Section 110(5)(B) should be calculated on the basis of the amount of licensing royalties which would otherwise be *collected* by US CMOs from US licensees or on the basis of the amount of royalties which would be *distributed* by US CMOs to EC right holders.

3.43 In considering this issue, it is useful to take a closer look at the relationship between copyright holders, US CMOs and users of copyright works. As concerns, first, the right holders, they are linked to US CMOs by membership or affiliation agreements.[53] Under such agreements, right holders grant US CMOs the (nonexclusive) right to license users of their copyright works.[54] In return, right holders receive royalty payments from the CMOs in accordance with those societies' distribution policies and methods.[55] The CMOs, for their part, negotiate licensing agreements with the users of the works of right holders they represent. Those negotiations relate, in particular, to the licensing royalties to be paid by licensed users to the CMOs.

3.44 It should be clear from the preceding paragraph that when EC right holders authorize US CMOs to license their rights, they cannot reasonably expect to receive any benefits directly from the licensed users of their works.[56] The benefits

---

53 The Arbitrators note that this is true, at any rate, of the US CMOs which are relevant to this dispute, i.e., ASCAP and BMI.

54 Thus, in cases where CMOs of the type at issue in this dispute are involved, there is no direct link, legal or otherwise, between right holders and licensed users.

55 As already noted, US CMOs deduct the collection, administration and other costs from the licensing royalties collected before making distributions to right holders. Furthermore, it should be pointed out that US CMOs offer so-called blanket licences, which authorise licensed users to use the works of *all* right holders represented by a particular CMO. It is necessary, therefore, for the CMOs to devise distribution formulas in order to asses the royalty payments to be made to individual right holders.

56 EC right holders could receive benefits directly from the users of their copyright works if they were to license those users directly. As previously noted, however, the possibility of direct licensing

which EC right holders, and thus the European Communities, would derive from the exclusive rights set forth in Articles 11*bis*(1)(iii) and 11(1)(ii) would be those resulting from the agreements of EC right holders with US CMOs.

3.45 In order to answer the question of what benefits EC right holders would derive from their agreements with US CMOs, it is necessary, as an initial matter, to be clear about the concept of "benefits". In this regard, the Arbitrators consider that useful guidance may be drawn from the decision of the arbitrators in *EC - Hormones (22.6) (US)*. In that case, the arbitrators determined the level of US benefits nullified or impaired as a result of the European Communities' hormone ban by reference to the total value of US beef or beef products which would have been exported in the absence of the ban.[57]

3.46 With this definition in mind, the Arbitrators now turn to consider what benefits EC right holders would derive from their agreements with US CMOs. As already mentioned, in exchange for granting US CMOs the right to license users, the CMOs would make royalty payments ("distributions") to right holders. It is not in dispute that the payments right holders would receive from US CMOs would be equal to the licensing royalties collected from licensed users of their works, minus the collection and other costs incurred by the US CMOs.

3.47 Like the United States, the Arbitrators are of the view that no particular significance attaches to the fact that the distributions by US CMOs amount to the net licensing revenue of US CMOs. Whatever those distributions may represent for US CMOs, for EC right holders, despite the fact that, in a sense, those distributions are net payments because of the deduction of collection and other costs, they would represent gross receipts and thus benefits resulting from the exclusive rights set forth in Articles 11*bis*(1)(iii) and 11(1)(ii).

3.48 The Arbitrators consider, therefore, that it is the total amount of royalty payments ("distributions") which US CMOs would make to EC right holders (or their representatives) that constitutes the benefits which the European Communities could reasonably expect to accrue to it under Articles 11*bis*(1)(iii) and 11(1)(ii). In more simple terms, it could be said that the benefits which the European Communities could expect to realize are the payments which US CMOs would make to EC right holders after the deduction of collection and administration costs.

3.49 It is true that the CMOs' distributions to EC right holders would be smaller in amount than the licensing royalties collected by US CMOs from users licensed to use the works of EC right holders. However, it does not follow from the fact that US CMOs would be able to *collect* a certain amount of licensing royalties from licensed users that EC right holders would, *ipso facto*, be *entitled*

---

by EC right holders is left out of account for purposes of the present proceedings. See *supra*, footnote 45.

[57] See Decision by the Arbitrators, *EC - Hormones (US) (Article 22.6 - EC) supra*, footnote 39, para. 43.

to receive that amount. As previously pointed out, the payments to be made by US CMOs would depend on the terms of the membership or affiliation agreements between the US CMOs and EC right holders. Under the agreements typically concluded between copyright holders and the US CMOs in question, right holders do *not* receive the full licensing fees collected by US CMOs. The Arbitrators see no reason to assume otherwise in this case.

3.50 The European Communities does not agree that the Arbitrators should determine the amount of royalty payments which US CMOs would make to EC right holders. According to the European Communities, what should be determined is the amount of licensing royalties which would have to be *paid* by users of the works of EC right holders because, in its view, that amount constitutes the value of the exclusive rights which are being denied to EC right holders. The Arbitrators are not convinced by this argument. To recall, the task of the Arbitrators in this case is to assess the level of EC benefits nullified or impaired as a result of Section 110(5)(B), and not to establish the economic value of the exclusive rights which are being denied to EC right holders.[58]

3.51 Even assuming, *arguendo*, the Arbitrators had to establish the economic value of the exclusive rights in question, it is clear that the economic value of those rights would need to be assessed at the level of EC right holders, given that the object of these proceedings is to assess the economic impact of Section 110(5)(B) on the European Communities. For the reasons set out in the preceding paragraphs, the "potential licensing revenue"[59] which could be realized by EC right holders licensing their rights through US CMOs would *not* correspond to the licensing royalties which US licensees would pay to US CMOs.

3.52 The United States considers that the benefits lost to EC right holders as a result of Section 110(5)(B) are the distributions they otherwise would receive from US CMOs. The United States notes that the distributions from US CMOs to EC right holders are reflected on the US current account of international payments. The United States submits, therefore, that the level of EC benefits nullified or impaired should be measured as foregone earnings in the European Communities' current account transactions with the United States.

3.53 The Arbitrators are not persuaded that it is necessary, or even appropriate, in this case to link the issue of the level of EC benefits which are being nullified or impaired to the US current account of international payments. To begin with, the Arbitrators do not see any legal reason why the calculation of the level of payments from US CMOs to EC right holders should necessarily be based on figures stemming from the US current account. The fact that the current account may, in some cases, be usefully relied on to measure the impact of WTO-inconsistent measures does not lead to the conclusion that the current account

---

[58] See also *supra*, footnote 42.

[59] It will be recalled that the European Communities considers that the economic value of the exclusive rights in question is equal to the potential licensing revenue realizable by EC right holders.

should be determining in all cases or that it should be used to the exclusion of other sources of relevant data.[60] Indeed, the United States itself has not based its argumentation before the Arbitrators on current account figures, nor has it provided such figures to the Arbitrators.

3.54 Another reason for approaching current account figures with caution in this case lies in the fact that they may not give sufficiently accurate indications regarding the amount of payments which US CMOs would make to EC right holders. It is the understanding of the Arbitrators that the international transactions which are reflected on the US current account are transactions between residents of the United States and foreign residents. In other words, it is the residency of the parties involved in a particular cross-border transaction rather than their nationality which determines whether and, if so, where that transaction is reflected on the current account. However, what the Arbitrators are concerned with in the present proceedings are payments made by US CMOs to EC nationals, i.e., EC right holders.[61]

3.55 Thus, payments made by US CMOs to EC right holders residing in the United States or to EC right holders residing in, say, Switzerland should, in the view of the Arbitrators, be taken into account in their determination of the level of EC benefits which are being nullified or impaired. Yet those transactions would not be reflected on the US current account as transactions between the United States and the European Communities because the EC nationals concerned would not be EC residents.

3.56 A similar problem would arise in the event of indirect distributions from US CMOs to EC right holders. For instance, EC right holders might rely on US publisher affiliates to represent them in the United States. In such cases, the relevant payments would be those from US CMOs to US publisher affiliates representing EC right holders. These types of payments from US CMOs to US publisher affiliates would not be reflected on the US current account. Yet this does not alter the fact that such payments would be payments to EC right holders.[62] As such, the Arbitrators must take them into account.[63]

---

[60] In the view of the Arbitrators, the mere fact that this case is a "trade case" involving international licensing payments which appear on the US current account does not, in itself, provide a sufficient rationale for why current account figures have to be utilised.

[61] Article 1.3 of the TRIPS Agreement requires Members to accord the treatment provided for in that Agreement to the "nationals of other Members".

[62] In the view of the Arbitrators, such royalty payments would be payments to EC right holders even if EC right holders decided to use or reinvest their revenue in the United States rather than to have it transferred to a member State of the European Communities.

[63] The Arbitrators note that the data they have been provided with concerning distributions by the US CMOs to EC right holders through their US publisher affiliates is somewhat incomplete in that it does not specify the criteria which were applied in compiling it. In the view of the Arbitrators, the data supplied might include distributions to persons that could be considered to be US right holders. The Arbitrators explain at para. 4.46 how they have taken account of this problem in determining the level of such indirect distributions.

3.57 As is evident from the aforementioned examples, were the Arbitrators to employ current account figures, there would be a risk of underestimating the payments which US CMOs would make to EC right holders.[64] In view of that risk, the Arbitrators prefer not to base their determination of the level of benefits lost by the European Communities on data taken from the US current account.[65]

3.58 In the light of the above considerations, the Arbitrators conclude that the level of EC benefits which are being nullified or impaired as a result of Section 110(5)(B) should be assessed on the basis of the amount of royalty payments ("distributions") which would be made by US CMOs to EC right holders or their representatives.

IV. CALCULATION

A. *Outline of the Methodology Followed by the Arbitrator*

1. *"Bottom-up" versus "top-down" Approach*

4.1 The **Arbitrators** recall that, during the proceedings before the Panel, each of the parties suggested a different approach to the calculation of the level of EC benefits nullified or impaired as a result of the operation of Section 110(5)(B). One, referred to as the "bottom-up" approach, was advocated by the European Communities.[65] The other one, called the "top-down" approach, was supported by the United States.[67] The Panel did not take position on which one was the most appropriate to determine the level of nullification or impairment of EC benefits.[68] Before the Arbitrators, the parties elaborated on their respective approaches, which are briefly summarized below.

4.2 Under the "bottom-up" approach, the **European Communities** takes as its starting-point the number of establishments that may qualify for the exemption. Second, the European Communities makes a reduction from that number using the US hypothesis that xx% of all eating and drinking establishments with a surface area below 3,750 square feet actually play music from the radio. Third, it applies to the remaining establishments the appropriate licensing fees selected from the licensing schedules of ASCAP and BMI. The European Communities reaches a level of nullification or impairment of benefits of US$25,486,974.

---

64 Since the Arbitrators have not been provided with information concerning the number of EC right holders residing outside the European Communities or concerning the portion of distributions by US CMOs to US publisher affiliates which the latter would actually transfer to EC right holders, they have no way of knowing whether reliance on current account figures would lead to significantly inaccurate results.

65 The Arbitrators recall that, in any event, the United States has failed to provide US current account figures which would allow the Arbitrators to measure the European Communities' lost earnings.

66 See Panel Report, *United States – Section 110(5"), supra*, footnote 6, paras. 6.253 and 6.256.

67 *Ibid.*, paras. 6.252 and 6.255.

68 *Ibid.*, para. 6.254.

4.3 Under the "top-down" approach, the **United States** takes as its starting-point the three-year average (1996-1998) of the total royalties paid to EC right holders by ASCAP and the total paid by BMI to EC right holders in 1996. Thereafter, it proceeds through successive deductions. It identifies the amount attributable to general licensing. Then it makes a deduction to account for licensing revenue from general licensees that do not meet the statutory definition of an "establishment". Thereafter, it deducts from the licensing revenue the portion that is due to music from sources other than radio and television. Finally, it reduces this amount to account for licensing revenue of eating, drinking and retail establishments which play the radio but do not meet the size and equipment limitations of Section 110(5)(B) and thus do not qualify for that exemption. The United States reaches a level of nullification or impairment of benefits of US$446,000 to US$733,000.

4.4 The **Arbitrators** carefully examined the claims, arguments and evidence submitted by the parties in light of the rules on burden of proof applicable in the context of arbitrations under Article 22.6 of the DSU, as instructed by the parties. The Arbitrators were mindful of the fact that, in arbitration proceedings under Article 22.6, a party contests the level of countermeasures which the other intends to take under paragraphs 2, 3 and 4 of Article 22. It is therefore understandable that the burden be on the party that contests the level of countermeasures to make a *prima facie* demonstration that the methodology and the calculations submitted by the party intending to apply countermeasures are inconsistent with the requirements of Article 22 of the DSU. For instance, in the *European Communities - Hormones* cases, the initial burden was on the European Communities. The present case, however, was referred to the Arbitrators by both parties "by mutual agreement". It is arguable whether or not there is a complainant and a defendant. This said, we note that the agreed procedures submitted by the parties[69] expressly instruct us to follow the allocation of the burden of proof applied in arbitrations under Article 22.6. We also note that the parties agreed that the European Communities would submit a methodology paper ahead of the first written submissions, as in proceedings under Article 22.6. As a result, the Arbitrators decided to allocate the burden of proof accordingly, as in an Article 22.6 case.

4.5 Based upon the record before them, in particular arguments and evidence by the United States demonstrating that the EC methodology was not always appropriate, the Arbitrators consider that the United States established a prima facie case that the methodology and estimates proposed by the European Communities did not result in an appropriate reflection of the level of EC benefits which are being nullified or impaired. In our view, the European Communities failed to rebut this presumption. Therefore, we were not able to accept the methodology

69 See WT/DS160/15.

proposed by the European Communities.[70] We were more convinced by the US alternative. However, we did not accept all the adjustments and deductions made by the United States. In some instances we found them inappropriate and we generally attempted to make a more complete analysis. We further note that, at the request of the Arbitrators, the European Communities and the United States confirmed that the Arbitrators were not bound to choose between the EC or the US methodology, but could develop their own methodology and make their own estimates, on the basis of all arguments and evidence submitted by the parties. Therefore, while using essentially the US methodology, we applied some elements of the EC methodology and estimates in our calculations and made assessments of our own.

4.6 In that context, and having regard to our conclusions in Section III above, we applied the "top-down" approach for the following reasons.

4.7 It is appropriate to start from the number of establishments actually licensed at the time of the entry into force of the 1998 Amendment because this approach offers the advantage of providing us with a starting point grounded on historical, verified facts, even if adjustments may have to be made to assess the level of benefits nullified or impaired on the date of referral of the matter to the Arbitrators.

4.8 This approach also has the advantage of limiting the number of assumptions necessary. In comparison, the European Communities approach would require, in our view, that we base our calculation on what has been described in some Article 22.6 arbitrations as a "counterfactual".[71] We believe that recourse to a counterfactual would only be justified if it was established that the situation predating the 1998 Amendment was itself TRIPS-incompatible.

4.9 The Arbitrators recall that, before the entry into force of the 1998 Amendment, some categories of establishments were already exempted from copyright payments under Section 110(5) of the 1976 Copyright Act. To be exempted, these establishments had to use a single receiving apparatus of a kind commonly used in private homes, hence the term "homestyle exemption" used to

---

[70] See *supra*, Section III.

[71] I.e., the approach followed for instance in Decision by the Arbitrators, *EC - Hormones (US)* (Article *22.6 - EC)* and Decision by the Arbitrators, *EC - Hormones (Canada) (Article 22.6 - EC)*, *supra*, footnote 39, where, in the absence of trade figures relating to a period where the EC regime could be deemed to be WTO-compatible, the arbitrators had to assess what the amount of trade would have been if the European Communities had brought its legislation into conformity at the end of the reasonable period of time it had been granted to do so. In its first submission, the European Communities also claims that the absence of proper protection, even before the 1998 Amendment, of the rights that Section 110(5)(B) denies makes it impossible to look, for comparison purposes, at a historical TRIPS-compatible situation. The European Communities adds that it "had to base its assessment on an 'as-if' basis drawing from other similar situations under US Copyright law and its enforcement."

describe it.[72] Some size requirements also applied to the establishments, based on decisions of courts.[73] With the 1998 Amendment, a subparagraph (B) was added which extended the scope of exemptions under Section 110(5).[74]

4.10 The Arbitrators note that their task is to determine the level of EC benefits nullified or impaired, not to assess the TRIPS-compatibility of any piece of US legislation. Within that framework, they also consider that the most appropriate way to assess the level of EC benefits nullified or impaired is to determine what EC right holders received before the enforcement of the 1998 Amendment – because historical figures are available with respect to that period - and adjust it as appropriate to take into account the evolution of the US market in the sector concerned.

4.11 The Arbitrators are mindful that they should base their calculation on a TRIPS-consistent situation. They recall that the European Communities has claimed that the situation pre-dating the 1998 Amendment (i.e. the exemption of certain establishments under the original homestyle exemption) was not TRIPS-compatible. The European Communities bases its conclusion on the fact that, in its view, the incompatibility of Section 110(5)(B) implies that the original homestyle exemption itself was TRIPS-incompatible.

4.12 The Panel did not make any finding on the original homestyle exemption which, in any event, was no longer in force by the time it issued its report. However, in its analysis of the current Section 110(5)(A) and (B), the Panel did make a number of statements relating to the original homestyle exemption. The Arbitrators recall that the Panel noted the limited percentage of establishments covered by the original homestyle exemption, the restrictions imposed by Section 110(5) and, more specifically, the fact that "playing music by the small establishments covered by the exemption by means of homestyle apparatus has never been a significant source of revenue collection for CMOs."[75] We note in this respect that the European Communities did not, either before the Panel or during these proceedings, sufficiently establish its claim that the economic impact of the original homestyle exemption was considerable.

4.13 The Arbitrators, having regard to the reasons stated by the Panel, concluded that, *even if* the situation pre-dating the 1998 Amendment was TRIPS-inconsistent (a question the Arbitrators do not decide), the impact on the level of EC benefits nullified or impaired of relying on figures excluding those establishments which benefitted from the original homestyle exemption would be limited. Comparatively, trying to take into account in our calculations those establish-

---

[72] Section 110(5) of the 1976 US Copyright Act will hereafter be referred to as the "original homestyle exemption".

[73] For a description of the situation before the 1998 Amendment, see Panel Report, *United States – Section 110(5")*, *supra*, footnote 6, paras. 2.5 to 2.7.

[74] For a description of the situation after the 1998 Amendment, see Panel Report, *United States – Section 110(5")*, *supra*, footnote 6, paras. 2.3, 2.8 to 2.17.

[75] Panel Report, *United States – Section 110(5")*, *supra*, footnote 6, para. 6.271.

ments which were subject to the original exemption would require further estimates, and applying the EC methodology would involve more assumptions and inferences.

4.14 For these reasons, we considered it appropriate not to attempt to include into the total fees paid in relation to EC works the potential revenue from establishments covered by the original homestyle exemption.

4.15 Finally, we note that determining the level of nullification or impairment suffered by a Member requires detailed calculations.[76] In this case, the Arbitrators have encountered particular difficulties due to the lack of precise informa tion available. This problem originated either in the actual absence of specific data for the type of transactions concerned (payment of royalties to EC right holders) or in the lack of co-operation on the part of some of the private entities which may have had the information. The absence of sufficiently specific information played a major role in the choices made by the Arbitrators with respect to the methodology and the calculations. Indeed, since they considered it more appropriate to use figures grounded on facts than deductions or inferences, the Arbitrators generally gave preference to approaches which relied as much as possible on historical figures.

2. *Point in Time at which Benefits Nullified or Impaired should be Assessed*

4.16 The **European Communities** claims that it bases its assessment of nullification or impairment on a static situation based on the most recent figures available. In addition, the European Communities claims that the Arbitrators should assess nullification or impairment at the date the United States should have brought Section 110(5) into conformity with its obligations under the TRIPS Agreement.

4.17 The **United States** bases its calculation on the situation pre-dating the 1998 Amendment. Moreover, it suggests that compensation be based on trade over the 1996-1998 period. However, the United States is of the opinion that the date on which the Panel should assess the level of nullification or impairment of benefits should be the date on which the matter was referred to the Arbitrators.

4.18 In the light of the arguments of the parties, the **Arbitrators** believe that they may have to set a date on which the level of nullification or impairment of EC benefits should be assessed. Indeed, such a level may have varied over time. We note, in this respect, that the circumstances of this arbitration may justify that we adopt a different approach from that followed by arbitrators in arbitrations pursuant to Article 22.6 of the DSU.

4.19 The Arbitrators note that they have been appointed under Article 25 of the DSU. As a result, they do not feel constrained by a number of obligations im-

[76] See the Decision by the Arbitrators, *Brazil – Aircraft (Article 22.6 - Brazil), supra,* footnote 20.

posed on arbitrators in Article 22.6 proceedings. Unlike Article 22.6, which closely relates to compliance (or absence thereof) at the end of the reasonable period of time, Article 25 is silent as to the date on which a matter referred to arbitration should be assessed. However, the Arbitrators are aware that they are not called upon to consider the level of EC benefits which may still be nullified or impaired after the end of the implementation period, but to consider the level of EC benefits which are being nullified or impaired as a result of the current application of Section 110(5)(B).[77] General practice under the DSU has been to consider the facts of a case as at the date of establishment of the panel. In the absence of any specification in our mandate, we believe that it should be assumed that the parties wanted us to assess the level of benefits nullified or impaired on the date the matter was referred to us. In other words, we must determine the level of nullification or impairment of EC benefits over a one-year period ending as closely as possible to 23 July 2001.[78]

4.20 The Arbitrators recall that the European Communities suggested that they follow the approach in the *EC - Hormones* Article 22.6 arbitrations, which would consist of assessing the level of nullification or impairment of benefits in this case on the date when the United States should have brought its legislation into conformity with its WTO obligations. We recall that, in *EC - Hormones*, the arbitrators used a counterfactual and considered that they should assess the level of nullification or impairment of benefits as if the European Communities had brought its legislation into conformity at the end of the reasonable period of time.[79] In the present case, the reasonable period of time was supposed to lapse on 27 July 2001.[80] However, on 24 July 2001, the DSB agreed to an extension until 31 December 2001 or the date on which the current session of the US Congress adjourns, whichever is earlier.[81] In those circumstances, the Arbitrators believe that using the date of the end of the reasonable period of time as cut-off date is not feasible, lest they will add uncertainty to their estimate by making ad-

---

[77] This seems to imply that the level of nullification or impairment that the Arbitrators will assess in this case may be different from that which may exist after the end of the reasonable period of time. This implies further that the amount which will be determined by the Arbitrators may not dispense the parties from an Article 22.6 arbitration.

[78] The reason for the choice of a yearly basis is essentially because compensations or suspensions of concessions or other obligations have been so far calculated on a twelve-month basis.

[79] See the Decision by the Arbitrators, *EC - Hormones (Canada) (Article 22.6 - EC), supra*, footnote 39, para. 37 where the arbitrators stated, that:

> "Upon careful consideration of the claims and arguments set forth by the parties, we consider that our starting-point is as follows: *what would annual prospective Canadian exports of hormone-treated beef and beef products to the EC be if the EC had withdrawn the ban on 13 May 1999*? 13 May 1999 is the date of expiration of the reasonable period of time granted to the EC to implement the panel and Appellate Body reports." (Emphasis in the original).

The arbitrators made the same statement at *para.* 38 of the Decision by the Arbitrators, *EC - Hormones (Canada) (Article 22.6 - EC), supra*, footnote 39,

[80] See WT/DS160/13.

[81] DSB meeting of 24 July 2001, WT/DSB/M/107, p. 13.

ditional assumptions as to the situation at the end of a period which, itself, is not known for sure.

4.21 The Arbitrators also note that the United States claims that we should "make a finding of nullification or impairment based on data from a recent period of time (1996-1998). The parties could then ensure equivalence of the future suspension (or mutually agreed compensation) by using the same period of time in calculating the trade to be adjusted." The United States adds that "by using trade data from the same historical period used in the analysis of harm to compute what concessions should be suspended (or granted as compensation), we can compare commensurate data and minimize the need for speculation."

4.22 The Arbitrators are mindful that their approach may entail adjustments on the basis of deductions or inferences. However, we are of the view that the US approach would be incompatible with what we believe is our mandate, i.e., to assess the level of EC benefits which were being nullified or impaired *at the time the matter was referred to arbitration.*

4.23 With regard to adjustments, the Arbitrators are well aware that they should either use the most recent data available or make appropriate adjustments to reflect the evolution of the market. We note that the United States cautioned us against such adjustments, suggesting that the increase in revenues and distributions posted by ASCAP from 1998 to 2000 – the only figures available for this particular sector - may not reflect accurately the increase in EC right holders' royalties. We agree with the US concern that ASCAP's figures may not reflect the reality of the situation of EC right holders and that other factors may have contributed to ASCAP's increased revenues and distributions. As a result, we will adjust the value of EC right holders' revenue determined on the basis of historical figures by a percentage representative of the annual rate of growth of the US gross domestic product between 1998 and 2001, in order to reflect the evolution in the value of EC rights until the date of referral of the matter to arbitration. We consider that this approach does not contradict our original intent to base our estimate as much as possible on historical figures for two reasons:

(a) adjusting relevant figures regarding the period pre-dating the 1998 Amendment to take into account the evolution of the US market is a necessity since that period has been one of sustained economic growth for the United States. In addition, we have been given no valid reason why we should not make that adjustment; and

(b) using the annual rate of growth of the US gross domestic product between 1998 and 2001 is, in our opinion, a very conservative approach if one compares those figures with those supplied by ASCAP for the same period.

4.24 For these reasons, the Arbitrators deem it appropriate to calculate the level of EC benefits nullified or impaired by the continuing operation of Section 110(5)(B) on a date as close as possible to the date on which the matter was referred to them. In this case, because of the statistical information available, their estimate will be based on the situation on 30 June 2001. For the first six months of the year 2001, we have used the growth rate of 1.7%, which we have calculated from quarterly GDP at current dollar value, seasonally adjusted at annual rates as published by the US bureau of census.[82]

3. *Elements not Considered in the Calculation*

(a) Approach of the Arbitrators

4.25 In its submissions, the **European Communities** suggested that a number of factors which, in its view, could contribute to nullification or impairment of benefits, be disregarded by the Arbitrators because precise data are lacking. This is the case of the detrimental effects of the denial of protection of specific rights in a given work for the exploitation of other rights in this work. Moreover, the European Communities only took into account in its calculations those establishments that use broadcast music (i.e. radio or television music). Despite the fact that, in its opinion, Section 110(5)(B) is also applicable to music transmitted via the Internet, the European Communities did not include this aspect in its calculations.

4.26 In the opinion of the **Arbitrators**, this raises the question of how to reconcile these suggestions with their attempt to reach an estimate which reflects as closely as possible the level of EC benefits nullified or impaired. The Arbitrators recall that in document WT/DS160/15, the parties stated that "they shall accept [the award of the Arbitrators] as the level of nullification or impairment for purposes of any future proceedings under Article 22 of the DSU in this dispute". This seems to imply that our award may not only condition the amount of compensation which the United States may offer to the European Communities under Article 22.2 of the DSU, but also the work of potential arbitrators under Article 22.6, since the latter are required under the DSU to determine whether the level of suspension of concessions or other obligations is *equivalent*[83] to the level of nullification or impairment of benefits.

4.27 As a result, the Arbitrators shall ensure that their determination of the level of nullification or impairment of benefits does not lead to a situation where potential EC suspensions of concessions or other obligations under Article 22.7 would be in fact "punitive", because the level of EC benefits nullified or impaired by the operation of Section 110(5)(B) would have been overestimated.[84]

4.28 More generally, as mentioned in paragraphs 4.15 *supra* and 4.36 *infra*, the Arbitrators in this case did not have sufficiently specific information and either

82 See *infra*, para. 4.72.

83 On the notion of "equivalence", see the Decision by the Arbitrators on *EC - Bananas III (US) (Article 22.6 - EC)*, *supra*, footnote 38, paras. 4.1-4.8.

84 The legal consequences of an overestimation in the case of compensation under Article 22.2 of the DSU are less, since it is not specified that the compensation to be offered should be equivalent to the level of nullification or impairment. Article 22.2 of the DSU simply refer to compensation that is "mutually acceptable".

had to adjust figures or draw inferences. They believe that by trying to incorporate in their calculations elements for which information was insufficient, they run the risk of erring on the side of pure speculation. Therefore, the Arbitrators considered appropriate to accept most of the "simplifications" suggested by the European Communities, such as the exclusion of indirect harm to EC copyright holders or the exclusion of music broadcast through the Internet, provided they were accepted by the United States and to the extent that, in the opinion of the Arbitrators, they did not lead to a higher level of nullification or impairment of benefits. Likewise, when they proceeded to necessary adjustments or deductions, in the absence of figures grounded on facts, the Arbitrators tried to use estimates which were accepted by the parties or otherwise seemed reasonable on the basis of the information available.

(b) Elements not Considered in the Calculation

(i) "Indirect" or "potential" Harm to Other Rights of EC Right Holders

4.29 The **European Communities** recalls that the Panel pointed out that the denial of protection of specific rights in a given work can also have detrimental effects for the exploitation of other rights in this work such as substitution between different uses of the work by a given establishment or a possible erosion of licensing fees for other users. However, the European Communities, given the lack of quantitative data and the uncertainty of causality relations, suggested that the Arbitrators' assessment may not include this "potential" or "indirect" harm to other copyright sources.

4.30 The **United States** did not comment.

4.31 The **Arbitrators** are mindful of the remarks of the Panel that the denial of protection of specific rights in a given work could also have an impact on the exercise of other rights.[85] However, having regard to the arguments of the European Communities and in the light of their own preliminary comments above, the Arbitrators agreed not to incorporate into their calculation the "indirect" or "potential" harm caused to right holders through the substitution of broadcast music by other forms of music, such as recorded music. We consider that we have no reason not to accommodate the request of the European Communities. In particular, we believe that trying to assess the level of benefits nullified or impaired as a result of "indirect" or "potential" harm would most probably entail more assumptions, deductions or inferences, thus increasing the risk of reaching an unreasonable estimate.

4.32 The Arbitrators would like to stress, however, that their position is based on the factual circumstances of this case and the particular purpose of these pro-

[85] See the Panel Report, *United States – Section 110(5), supra*, footnote 6, paras. 6.127, 6.198 and 6.239-6.240.

ceedings, i.e., determining the level of nullification or impairment of EC benefits, not identifying violation. It is without prejudice to whether this type of damage would be considered to nullify or impair benefits accruing directly or indirectly to any Member in another case.

(ii) Activities of SESAC

4.33 The **Arbitrators** recall that, in the United States, three collective management organizations collect fees for copyright holders: ASCAP, BMI, and SESAC. They note that, in their submissions, the parties did not include any data relating to the activities of SESAC. The parties explained in the course of the proceedings that this was essentially because SESAC does not represent any significant number of EC collecting society members and does not distribute significant amounts of royalties to EC right holders.

4.34 We see no reason to put in doubt the information given by both parties about SESAC's representation of EC right holders. Furthermore, considering the difficulties which we would have encountered in assessing the contribution of SESAC, we have decided not to seek to factor SESAC's activities in our calculation. In that case, the reason was nevertheless more related to the limited impact that the exclusion of SESAC would, in the opinion of both parties, have on our calculation.

(iii) Music Broadcast through Internet

4.35 The **Arbitrators** recall that the European Communities, while hinting at the impact of music transmission via Internet in the nullification or impairment of EC benefits, did not include such transmission in its calculation. The Arbitrators are aware of the development of music transmission via Internet. They note, however, that the parties and the Panel essentially addressed the question of transmission via radio or television. For the Arbitrators to ascertain the application of Section 110(5)(B) to broadcasts of music via Internet would require additional findings which, in the light of the position adopted by the European Communities, are not necessary. As a result, the Arbitrators did not consider music broadcast through Internet in their calculation.

B. Calculation

1. General Observations

4.36 Before moving to the calculation of the level of EC benefits which are being nullified or impaired, the **Arbitrators** note that their ability to make an accurate calculation has been limited by the fact that the data provided to them by the two parties were incomplete and included many estimations and assumptions. In their submissions, both parties have recognized this problem, noting that some of the relevant data are in the possession of private parties. As explained above, we sent letters to the two main US CMOs, ASCAP and BMI, requesting actual data on their collections and distributions that would have enabled us to base our calculations on specific information. In response to those letters, we obtained some information from BMI, but due to the conditions attached to its use, we decided not to include it in the record of the case.[86] We also received information from ASCAP and a second submission from BMI. However, having noted that the parties favoured a prompt issue of our award, we decided for the reasons stated *supra* not to take this information into account.[87] Hence, we have had to work on the basis of the incomplete data provided to us by the parties.[88] In order to discharge the mandate given to us by the parties, and in the absence of some important data, we have had to make ourselves a number of estimations and, in some cases, make certain assumptions based on what we perceived to be the most reasonable estimate in the light of the arguments of the parties. In doing so, we have attempted to arrive at a number that is in the right order of magnitude, but we recognize that it may not be entirely accurate.

4.37 We have discussed *supra* the differences between the methodologies suggested by the European Communities and the United States, and the implications that these differences have. We recall that the outcomes of the parties' calculations based on their respective methodologies are quite far apart from each other. The European Communities arrives at the figure of US$ 25,486,974 per year, while the United States suggests that the level of nullification or impairment of benefits to the EC is in the range of US$ 446,000 to US$ 733,000 per year. This discrepancy can, to a large extent, be explained by the conceptual differences between the two approaches.[89]

4.38 As regards the order of magnitude of the annual losses to EC right holders resulting from Section 110(5)(B), we note as an illustration that, according to the information provided by the United States, the total domestic receipts of ASCAP - the biggest of the US CMOs - were over the period 1997-1999 US$ 358,428,000, 377,733,000, and 422,962,000 per year; the growth in the total revenue in 1998 was 5.4% and in 1999 12%. The receipts from the general licensing area, which includes restaurants, bars, retail establishments as well as certain other establishments, in the same years were, respectively, US$ 67,324,000, 68,032,000, and 69,695,000 per year; the growth in these receipts in 1998 was 1.05% and in 1999 2.4%. These figures indicate that, after the entry into force of the 1998 Amendment, there has not been any dip in ASCAP's total domestic receipts or even in the receipts from the general licensing category. Lacking specific data on the receipts originating from the types of establishments

---

[86] See *supra*, para. 1.10.

[87] See *supra*, para. 1.13.

[88] To the extent the parties have submitted data to us on a confidential basis, we have not included that data into the following explanation of our calculation. In those cases, only the results of the various steps in our calculation have been indicated.

[89] See, in particular, our discussion at paras. 3.20 *et seq.* of how the two calculations take into account the level of licensing.

that were affected by the 1998 Amendment (which receipts are included in the broader general licensing category), we nonetheless note that the available data would not support an assumption that there was a significant drop in the licence fees collected from the affected areas. At the same time we note that the rate of increase of the receipts from the general licensing area was modest at a time when the US economy was expanding fast. Furthermore, the receipts from this area grew at a clearly lower rate than the total domestic receipts.

4.39 For the reasons explained *supra*,[90] we have adopted a "top-down" approach as suggested by the United States. Using this approach we have used the historical data on collections prior to the 1998 Amendment that have been available to us. We now proceed to calculate the level of EC benefits which are being nullified or impaired as a result of Section 110(5)(B) on this basis.

2. *Total Royalties Paid to EC Right Holders*

4.40 In their calculation, the Arbitrators have attempted to estimate the amount of royalties that EC right holders received, prior to the entry into force of the 1998 Amendment, for the use of broadcast music from the types of establishments that were newly exempted by that Amendment. For that purpose, we have used the historical data available to us regarding the receipts of the two biggest US CMOs to whom EC right holders have entrusted the licensing of their rights – ASCAP and BMI. As we have noted before, both parties consider that the amount of royalties paid to EC right holders by the third US CMO, SESAC, is insignificant.[91] Therefore, we have not included its receipts into our calculations.

4.41 Relying on this historical data means that our calculation takes into account the licensing income from those establishments that used broadcast music at that time and had acquired a licence from ASCAP or BMI. Our calculation does not include any hypothetical amount of royalties from those establishments that did play broadcast music but had not acquired a licence from the CMOs in question.[92] Relying on the historical data means also that our calculation does not include any hypothetical revenue from such small establishments that were already exempted by the original homestyle exemption at the entry into force of the 1998 Amendment. For the reasons stated above[93], we did not find it necessary to include such establishments in our calculation.

4.42 The **European Communities** provided us with a compilation of quantitative data by ASCAP which includes, for the years 1996-1998, first the amounts of the total domestic distribution to EC CMOs and second distribution to US

90 See *supra*, paras. 4.7 to 4.15.
91 See *supra*, section IV.A, paras. 4.33-4.34.
92 See *supra*, paras. 3.20-3.35.
93 See *supra*, section IV.A.

publisher affiliates for performance of EC works.[94] The European Communities refers to these two categories as, respectively, "direct" and "indirect" distributions to EC right holders. The European Communities notes that the first category does not include the total royalties paid for EC works in the repertoire of ASCAP, because music publishers' share of royalties is overwhelmingly paid directly by ASCAP to EC publishers' US affiliates, rather than through the affiliated EC collecting societies to those EC publishers that are members of those societies. These payments to EC publishers' US affiliates are included in the second category.

4.43 The **United States** has used the three-year averages of these figures provided by ASCAP as the starting-points for its calculations, the "direct" distributions representing the lower range of royalties paid to EC right holders and the sum of "direct" and "indirect" distributions representing the upper range.

4.44 In calculating the amount of revenue that EC right holders received from ASCAP prior to the 1998 Amendment, the **Arbitrators** have taken as their starting-point the sums of "direct" and "indirect" distribution to EC right holders over the period 1996-1998.

4.45 The Arbitrators note that the 1998 Amendment entered into force on 26 January 1999. Therefore, the Amendment did not affect ASCAP's revenues collected before the year 1999. We note that the European Communities and the United States have provided us with relevant data on ASCAP's distributions to EC right holders over the three-year period of 1996-1998, and that the United States has used the average of the distributions in these three years as the starting-points for its calculation. As we are calculating the level of EC benefits nullified or impaired by the Amendment on the basis of historical data, we need to determine an appropriate previous representative period as the starting-point for our own calculation. In this regard, we note that under GATT practice the most recent three-year period not distorted by restrictions has been used in assessing the consistency of a measure.[95] In our case, the most recent representative period would be the three-year period not affected by the 1998 Amendment, namely the years 1996-1998. We believe that using the data made available to us for this three-year period is consistent with the prudent approach which we have decided to follow by using the "top-down" methodology based on historical figures. In determining a single starting-point for our further calculation, we have used the average of the figures concerning these three years. On the one hand, we do note that in this case ASCAP's distributions to EC right holders grew regularly over this period. On the other hand, we have no evidence that this growth is applicable also to the sector at issue in this case and, in any event, three years are generally

[94] Exhibit EC-15 (exhibit US ARB-5), which contains information that was provided to the European Communities in confidence with the request that it not be communicated to private parties.

[95] See the Panel Report on *EEC - Restrictions on Imports of Apples from Chile*, BISD 27S/98, adopted 10 November 1980, para. 4.8. See also the Decision by the Arbitrators, *EC - Bananas III (US) (Article 22.6 – EC), supra*, footnote 38, paras. 5.24 *et seq.*

considered to be insufficient to establish a particular trend in a market. In this sense, using an average for this three-year period would tend to reflect the average revenue at the level of the year 1997 rather than in 1998. We have taken this into account at the final step of our calculation when we have adjusted the outcome of our calculation to reflect the situation at the time of the referral of the issue to the Arbitrators.

4.46 The three-year average of ASCAP's distributions to EC right holders amounts to approximately US$ xxxxxxxx per year. We note that this figure may not be entirely accurate, given that the information made available to us by the parties, on which we based our calculation, may not be complete for the reasons discussed below. Earlier we have noted that direct payments by the US CMOs to EC right holders (i.e., payments that ASCAP and BMI make directly to EC right holders that are their members rather than payments they make to EC CMOs) are relevant for our calculation even if the EC right holders in question were to collect these fees through their US affiliates.[96] However, as regards the confidential data on ASCAP's distributions to EC right holders' US publisher affiliates, we note that we do not have the exact criteria that ASCAP has used in producing its figures. Therefore, there may be a risk that a small part of this figure may represent payments to persons that could not be considered as EC right holders or their representatives. On the other hand, we note that neither the first nor the second category appears to include those payments that ASCAP may make to those individual EC authors that are members of ASCAP and thus receive their royalties directly from it, rather than through EC CMOs. Consequently, the figures provided may be somewhat too high in some respects and too low in others, but we have not attempted to factor in these aspects into our calculations, given that they compensate for each other and that any difference between the two revenues is not likely to be substantial, and that, at any rate, their impact on the overall calculation would be quite limited.

4.47 The **United States** provided us with an estimation of the amount that BMI distributed to EC CMOs in 1996. The United States did not provide any data for the years 1997 and 1998. The **European Communities** does not contest the figure suggested by the United States. The **Arbitrators** have taken this figure as their starting-point in calculating the revenue that EC right holders received from BMI. However, they have made two adjustments to it.

4.48 The **European Communities** argues that if data on BMI's distributions to EC right holders through the EC CMOs were to be used, BMI's distributions to EC right holders' US publisher affiliates should also be taken into account in a similar manner as in the case of ASCAP.

4.49 The **Arbitrators** agree with the European Communities on this point. Lacking any data concerning BMI's distributions to EC right holders' US publisher affiliates, we have made an assumption that the share between BMI's "di-

[96] See *supra*, para. 3.56.

rect" and "indirect" distributions would be the same as the share between ASCAP's corresponding categories of distributions. We have accordingly made the appropriate adjustment to the estimate on BMI's distribution to EC right holders provided by the United States.

4.50 For the reasons explained above[97], in calculating EC right holders' revenue from ASCAP, we have used the average of such revenues for the period 1996-1998. Although we have data from BMI only for the year 1996, we are of the view that in order to be consistent we need also to base BMI figures on similar average from the period 1996-1998. To be able to do so, we have determined BMI's distributions to EC right holders in 1997 and 1998 on the basis of the 1996 estimate, assuming that BMI's distributions grew over that period at the same rate as those of ASCAP. Subsequently, we have calculated the three-year average of these BMI distributions in 1996-1998. For the purposes of our calculation, this figure represents the annual average amount of revenues that EC right holders received from BMI prior to the 1998 Amendment.

4.51 Accordingly, for the purposes of our further calculations, we estimate that BMI's distribution to EC right holders prior to the 1998 Amendment was approximately US$ xxxxxxxx per year.

4.52 Adding up our estimations on ASCAP's and BMI's distributions to EC right holders, we estimate that, prior to the 1998 Amendment, EC right holders received approximately US$ xxxxxxxx per year.

3. Royalties from Eating, Drinking and Retail Establishments

4.53 Having established the annual average of the total amount of royalties EC right holders received prior to the 1998 Amendment, the Arbitrators will now attempt to estimate what share of that revenue came from eating, drinking and retail establishments. We will do this by deducting in two steps the royalties that were received from other types of users.

4.54 First we will estimate what share of the total licensing revenue paid to EC right holders was attributable to the so-called general licensing category. This category includes various types of licensees such as drinking and eating establishments and retail establishments, but it excludes licensing revenue from radio and television broadcasting and concerts. From ASCAP's annual reports for 1996-1998 it can be calculated that an average of 18.45% of the total domestic receipts was attributable to the general licensing category during this period. We have not been provided data that would have allowed us to calculate the corresponding share of BMI's receipts. In the absence of relevant data, we considered it reasonable to apply the same percentage to BMI's receipts. Using this percentage, we calculate that, of the total amount of revenue EC right holders received

[97] See *supra*, para. 4.45.

per year prior to the 1998 Amendment, approximately US$ xxxxxxxx per year were attributable to the general licensing category.

4.55 The general licensing category includes, in addition to eating, drinking and retail establishments, miscellaneous users of background music such as airlines, sports stadiums, motion picture theatres, amusement parks, conventions, telephone music services, colleges and universities, health clubs and background music services. Therefore, we will need to estimate what share of the general licensing revenue is attributable to eating, drinking and retail establishments as defined in Section 110(5)(B). The problem we face is that we have not obtained any specific data on this question. Given that the general licensing category embraces many types of licensed uses, the United States claims that "a more than reasonable estimate is that 50% is attributable to restaurants, bars and retail establishments". We note that the European Communities has not contested this percentage suggested by the United States. Nor has it provided an alternative estimate.

4.56 We consider the US estimate of the percentage to be reasonable in the light of the arguments of the parties. Therefore, we use it in our calculation. Accordingly, we estimate that the amount of revenue received by EC right holders prior to the 1998 Amendment that was attributable to eating, drinking and retail establishments was approximately US$ xxxxxxxx per year.

4. *Royalties Attributable to the Playing of Radio and Television Music*

4.57 The next step is to determine what amount of the revenue collected from eating, drinking and retail establishments was attributable to playing radio and television music as defined in Section 110(5)(B). This requires us to deduct the amount of royalty payments that was attributable to the use of other sources of music that were not exempted under that Section. For this purpose, both parties use in their respective calculations a figure of xx% as representing the share of this revenue that is attributable to the use of radio and television music. This figure is based on data from the National Restaurant Association and the National Licensed Beverage Association.

4.58 In using this figure, the **European Communities** notes that it does not include establishments that play music only from the television, but is not asking the Arbitrators to consider this factor. The **United States** notes that it has used this, in its view, high number to account for the fact that it has been unable to factor television use into the picture.

4.59 The **Arbitrators** note that this figure of xx% is based on actual data and that both parties use it in their respective calculations. The Arbitrators, therefore, decided to use this percentage in their calculation. Accordingly, we calculate that the amount of royalties EC right holders received from eating, drinking and retail establishments prior to the 1998 Amendment that was attributable to radio and television music was approximately US$ 1.55 million per year.

5. *Royalties from Establishments that Meet the Requirements of the Statutory Exemption*

4.60 The Arbitrators have now established the annual average amount of royalties EC right holders received from eating, drinking and retail establishments prior to the 1998 Amendment that was attributable to radio and television music. Next, they need to determine what share of that amount was attributable to establishments that were newly exempted from copyright liability by the 1998 Amendment, i.e., first establishments that were below the size limits of Section 110(5)(B) and thus exempted, and second establishments that were above those size limits but still qualified for the exemption because they met the conditions that concerned the equipment used.[98]

4.61 As regards the first category of establishments, both the **European Communities** and the **United States** use in their calculations the estimate from a 1999 Dun & Bradstreet study according to which 70% of eating establishments, 73% of drinking establishments and 45% of retail establishments fell within the statutory size limits.[99] The United States has calculated that the weighted average of these numbers is 53,9%. The European Communities has not contested the way the United States has counted this weighted average.

4.62 As regards the second category, the **European Communities** estimates that of those establishments that are over the size limits of Section 110(5)(B), only 10% meet the equipment limitations and thus benefit from the exemption. The **United States** notes that, due to lack of data, it has not tried to quantify the number of larger establishments that would meet the equipment limitations. In its rebuttal, it claims that the EC estimate is excessive, but it does not provide an alternative estimate.

4.63 The **Arbitrators** are of the view that they should include the establishments in the second category in their calculation. The problem is that neither party has provided any evidence to support their views. We note that the United States argues that it can be expected that large stores would be especially unlikely to play radio given, *inter alia*, broadcasters' varied programming, and that when businesses of sizes above the statutory limits would use broadcast music it would seem unlikely that a total of six speakers for the entire establishment would be sufficient. However, it would appear to us that the use of specialized music channels does allow businesses to control the atmosphere of a store, and that six speakers might well suffice for an establishment just over the size limit. At any rate, having regard to the arguments of the parties and the information before us, we are of the view that the EC estimate of 10% is already on the low side.

4.64 Using the weighted average of establishments below the statutory size limits provided by the United States, we calculate that an estimated 46.1% of

[98] For details on the size limits of establishments and conditions relating to equipment, see the Panel Report on *United States – Section 110(5")*, *supra*, footnote 6, paras. 2.10-2.14.
[99] See the Panel Report, *United States – Section 110(5")*, *supra*, footnote 6, para. 2.12.

eating, drinking and retail establishments are above the statutory size limits. In our view, the EC estimate according to which 10% of them meet the statutory limits concerning equipment is reasonable. Therefore, we will use this estimate in our calculation. Accordingly, for the purposes of our calculation, we assume that an additional 4.6% of establishments benefit from the exemption under Section 110(5)(B).

4.65 As a result, we estimate that 58.5% of eating, drinking and retail establishments are within the scope of Section 110(5)(B), either by falling within the statutory size limits (53.9%) or, in case their size exceeds those limits, by complying with the statutory equipment limitations (4.6%), and thus benefit from the exemption contained in that Section.

4.66 We note that, at the corresponding point in its calculation, also the United States has deducted from the remaining EC right holders' royalties the percentage that represents the share of establishments that fall within the statutory size limits, namely 53.9% (but not the 4.6% share that represents the share of larger establishments that comply with the statutory equipment limitations). It appears that this methodology of making the 53.9% deduction is not entirely accurate in two respects, although neither of these inaccuracies would appear to have a significant impact on the result of the calculation.

4.67 First, applying this methodology may not be entirely accurate as the exempted smaller establishments were likely to pay lower fees than the larger establishments that were not exempted. However, we have not attempted to factor this aspect into our calculation, given that we have not been provided any data or estimates that would enable us to do so. We also note that when we add 4.6% of the larger establishments into our calculation, we do not factor in the possibility that they may pay higher than average licensing fees. Overall, we believe that these considerations would not have a major impact on our calculation.

4.68 Second, the figure of 53.9% refers to all those establishments that fell within the size limits of Section 110(5)(B). We note that some of the smallest of these establishments were already exempted prior to the 1998 Amendment under the original homestyle exemption and, thus, were not newly exempted by that Amendment. However, as noted above, we have considered it appropriate to exclude from our calculation any hypothetical revenue for the playing of non-dramatic musical works from the establishments covered by the original homestyle exemption, given, *inter alia*, that such revenue would most probably not significantly influence our calculation.[100] Similarly, we are of the view that the fact that the figure of 53.9% includes some establishments that were prior to the 1998 Amendment already exempted under the original homestyle exemption, does not essentially change the outcome of our calculation. To the extent it would have any impact on the outcome, it would compensate for the fact that we did not include revenue from such establishments in our calculations in the first place.

[100] See *supra*, paras. 4.12 and 4.13.

For these reasons, we have not attempted to factor these aspects into our calculation.

4.69 Accordingly, we estimate that, of those royalties that EC right holders received from eating, drinking and retail establishments prior to the 1998 Amendment for the use of radio and television music, 58.5% was attributable to establishments that were newly exempted from copyright liability by that Amendment. This means that of the US$1.55 million per year that EC right holders received from eating, drinking and retail establishments prior to the 1998 Amendment for the use of radio and television music, approximately US$0.91 million was attributable to establishments that were newly exempted by that Amendment.

6. *Further Adjustments*

4.70 As mentioned above, the Arbitrators have taken as the starting-point for our calculations the historical data made available to us on the revenue received by EC right holders prior to the 1998 Amendment. We have attempted to estimate, using the data and estimations provided to us by the parties, the share of those revenues that was attributable to relevant uses of broadcast music by establishments that were newly exempted by that Amendment. However, in our view, these figures have to be adjusted to take into account the evolution of the market between the entry into force of the 1998 Amendment and the date of referral of the matter to the Arbitrators, namely 23 July 2001.[101]

4.71 We recall that our above calculation is based on an average figure calculated on the basis of ASCAP's and BMI's distributions to EC right holders in 1996-1998 (in case of BMI, we had access to data only from 1996, but we assumed an annual growth corresponding to that of ASCAP's distributions). The figure of US$ 0.91 million represents an estimate of the hypothetical level of nullification or impairment in the year 1997, i.e., about one year before the entry into force of the 1998 Amendment. Therefore, in adjusting this figure to reflect the level of EC benefits nullified or impaired at the date of referral of the matter to the Arbitrators, we will need to make an adjustment starting from the end of the year 1997.

4.72 In our view, the most appropriate way to adjust the aforementioned figure is to take into account the growth of the US economy in the same period. For this purpose, we have used the annual rate of growth of the US gross domestic product in current dollars in the relevant period. During this period, the US GDP grew in current-dollar terms at the following rate: +5.6% in 1998; +5.5% in 1999; +6.5% in 2000.[102] For the first six months of the year 2001, we have used the

[101] See *supra*, Section IV.A.2.

[102] See United States Department of Commerce Bureau of Economic Analysis News Release, 28 September 2001, http://www.bea.doc.gov/bea/newsrel/gdp201f.htm.

growth rate of 1.7%, which we have approximated on the basis of quarterly annualized figures of growth rates in current dollars.

4.73 We have adjusted the above figure representing the hypothetical annual average of revenue that EC right holders lost as a result of Section 110(5)(B) at the level of 1997 with the annual growth rate of the US GDP. Accordingly, we calculate that the level of the EC benefits nullified or impaired as a result of Section 110(5)(B) is US$1,1 million per year.

V. AWARD OF THE ARBITRATOR

5.1 For the reasons set out above, the Arbitrators determine that the level of EC benefits which are being nullified or impaired as a result of the operation of Section 110(5)(B) amounts to € 1,219,900 per year.[103]

[103] Exchange Cross Rates, US Dollar to the Euro (11 October 2001), *Financial Times*, 12 October 2001, p. 25.

ANNEX I

TEXT OF THE LETTERS SENT TO ASCAP AND BMI REQUESTING INFORMATION

Dear Ms. Preston/Dear Ms. Bergman,

On 23 July 2001, the European Communities (EC) and the United States mutually agreed pursuant to Article 25.2 of the Understanding on Rules and Procedures for the Settlement Governing the Settlement of Disputes to enter into arbitration to determine the level of nullification or impairment of benefits to the EC as a result of the incompatibility of Section 110(5)(B) of the US Copyright Act with the WTO Agreement on Trade–Related Aspects of Intellectual Property Rights (TRIPS). On 13 August 2001, WTO Members were informed of the composition of the panel of arbitrators.

In order to assist the arbitrators in determining the level of nullification or impairment, I would be grateful if you could reply to the following questions:

1. Could you please provide the following data for each of the years 1997-2000:

(a) the total domestic licensing revenues (excluding licensing revenues from foreign societies);

(b) the total licensing revenues from the general licensing category;

(c) the total licensing revenues from eating and drinking establishments and other establishments as defined in Section 110(5) of the amended US Copyright Act;

(d) the deduction for administrative and collection costs made before the distribution of royalties to right holders;

(e) the total distribution to right holders (excluding the distribution of licensing revenues from foreign societies);

(f) the total distribution to the EC collecting societies;

(g) any other data, if available, that would indicate the amount of distribution to EC right holders directly through your society (rather than through the EC collecting societies), in particular US publisher affiliates for performances of EC works.

2. With reference to question 1(c) above, to the extent you have any information available, could you please indicate the breakdown of the licensing revenue from eating and drinking establishments and other establishments as defined in Section 110(5) of the amended US Copyright Act that fall:

   (i) under the size limits of Section 110(5)(A);

   (ii) between the size limits of Section 110(5)(A) and (B); and

(iii) establishments the size of which is beyond the limits of Section 110(5)(B).

3. Could you please provide any available information on the likely number of establishments that would meet the requirements of Section 110(5)(B) which relay broadcast music.

4. To the extent feasible, please provide your estimation of the share of each category of establishment referred to in Section 110(5) that play broadcast music you are currently licensing.

5. Please provide the rates applicable to the various categories of establishments referred to in Section 110(5).

Needless to say, any information described as confidential in your reply will be treated as such. If you so request, the arbitrators will ensure that only the parties to this case will have access to this information. Moreover, the public version of the arbitrator's report will be edited so as to ensure that it does not contain any confidential data.

I should like to stress that, while there is no obligation for you to reply to the questions above or to submit any of the information requested, your full co-operation would be greatly appreciated.

Since the arbitrators' proceedings are subject to very short deadlines, I would appreciate it very much if you could provide us with any reply by Friday, 14 September 2001.

Yours faithfully,

Ian F. Sheppard
Chairman
Arbitration Panel on
United States – Section 110(5)
of the US Copyright Act

ANNEX II

SPREADSHEET OF CALCULATIONS OMITTED AS CONFIDENTIAL

UNITED STATES – DEFINITIVE SAFEGUARD MEASURES ON IMPORTS OF WHEAT GLUTEN FROM THE EUROPEAN COMMUNITIES

Report of the Appellate Body
WT/DS166/AB/R

United States, *Appellant/Appellee*	Present:
European Communities, *Appellant/Appellee*	Lacarte-Muró, Presiding Member
Australia, *Third Participant*	Abi-Saab, Member
Canada, *Third Participant*	Taniguchi, Member
New Zealand, *Third Participant*	

TABLE OF CONTENTS

I. INTRODUCTION

1. The United States and the European Communities appeal certain issues of law and legal interpretations in the Panel Report, *United States – Definitive Safeguard Measures on Imports of Wheat Gluten from the European Communities* (the "Panel Report").[1] The Panel was established to consider a complaint by the European Communities with respect to a definitive safeguard measure imposed by the United States on certain imports of wheat gluten.

48. On 1 October 1997, the United States International Trade Commission (the "USITC") initiated a safeguard investigation into certain imports of wheat

[1] Panel Report, *United States – Definitive Safeguard Measures on Imports of Wheat Gluten from the European Communities* ("*US – Wheat Gluten*"), WT/DS166/R, adopted 19 January 2001. (the "Panel Report")

gluten.[2] By Proclamation of the President of the United States, dated 30 May 1998, the United States imposed a definitive safeguard measure, in the form of a quantitative restriction on imports of wheat gluten, effective as of 1 June 1998.[3] Products from Canada, a partner with the United States in the North American Free-Trade Agreement ("NAFTA"), and certain other countries were excluded from the application of the safeguard measure.[4] The United States notified the initiation of the investigation, the determination of serious injury, and the decision to apply the safeguard measure to the Committee on Safeguards.[5] The factual aspects of this dispute are set out in greater detail in the Panel Report.[6]

49. The Panel considered claims by the European Communities that, in imposing the safeguard measure on imports of wheat gluten, the United States acted inconsistently with Articles I and XIX of the *General Agreement on Tariffs and Trade 1994* (the "GATT 1994"), and with Articles 2.1, 4, 5, 8, and 12 of the *Agreement on Safeguards*.[7]

50. In its Report, circulated to Members of the World Trade Organization (the "WTO") on 31 July 2000, the Panel concluded that:

> ... the United States has not acted inconsistently with Articles 2.1 and 4 of the *Agreement on Safeguards* or with Article XIX:1(a) of the GATT 1994 in:
>
> > (i) redacting certain confidential information from the published USITC Report; or
> >
> > (ii) determining the existence of imports in "increased quantities" and serious injury.[8]
>
> ...
>
> ... the definitive safeguard measure imposed by the United States on certain imports of wheat gluten based on the United States investigation and determination is inconsistent with Articles 2.1 and 4 of the *Agreement on Safeguards* in that:
>
> > (i) the causation analysis applied by the USITC did not ensure that injury caused by other factors was not attributed to imports; and

---

2 Panel Report, para. 2.2.

3 "Proclamation 7103 of 30 May 1998 – To Facilitate Positive Adjustment to Competition From Imports of Wheat Gluten", United States Federal Register, 3 June 1998 (Volume 63, Number 106), pp. 30359-30360; Panel Report, para. 2.7.

4 *Ibid.*, para. 2.8.

5 Panel Report, paras. 2.3, 2.5 – 2.7.

6 *Ibid.*, paras. 2.1 – 2.10.

7 In its request for the establishment of a panel (WT/DS166/3, 4 June 1999), the European Communities also claimed that the United States had acted inconsistently with Article 4.2 of the *Agreement on Agriculture*. The Panel found that the European Communities had "abandoned" this claim: *Ibid.*, para. 8.221.

8 *Ibid.*, para. 9.1.

> (ii) imports from Canada (a NAFTA partner) were excluded from the application of the measure after imports from all sources were included in the investigation for the purposes of determining serious injury caused by increased imports (following a separate inquiry concerning whether imports from Canada accounted for a "substantial share" of total imports and whether they "contributed importantly" to the "serious injury" caused by total imports).[9]
>
> ...
>
> ... the United States failed to notify immediately the initiation of the investigation under Article 12.1(a) and the finding of serious injury under Article 12.1(b) SA. We further conclude that, in notifying its decision to take the measure after the measure was implemented, the United States did not make timely notification under Article 12.1(c). For the same reason, the United States violated the obligation of Article 12.3 SA to provide adequate opportunity for prior consultations on the measure. Hence, the United States also violated its obligation under Article 8.1 SA to endeavour to maintain a substantially equivalent level of concessions and other obligations to that existing under GATT 1994 between it and the exporting Members which would be affected by such a measure, in accordance with Article 12.3 SA.[10]

51. Having found the United States' safeguard measure to be inconsistent with Articles 2.1 and 4.2 of the *Agreement on Safeguards*, the Panel did not deem it necessary to examine the claims of the European Communities under Article XIX of the GATT 1994, and, in addition, under Article I of the GATT 1994 and Article 5 of the *Agreement on Safeguards*.[11]

52. The Panel recommended that the Dispute Settlement Body ("DSB") request the United States to bring its measure into conformity with the *Agreement on Safeguards*.[12]

53. On 26 September 2000, the United States notified the DSB of its intention to appeal certain issues of law covered in the Panel Report and certain legal interpretations developed by the Panel, pursuant to paragraph 4 of Article 16 of the *Understanding on Rules and Procedures Governing the Settlement of Disputes* (the "DSU"), and filed a Notice of Appeal pursuant to Rule 20 of the *Working Procedures for Appellate Review* (the "*Working Procedures*"). On 6 October 2000, the United States filed its appellant's submission.[13] On 11 October 2000,

---

[9] *Ibid.*, para. 9.2.
[10] Panel Report, para. 9.3.
[11] *Ibid.*, para. 8.220.
[12] *Ibid.*, para. 9.5.
[13] Pursuant to Rule 21 of the *Working Procedures*.

the European Communities filed an other appellant's submission.[14] On 23 October 2000, the European Communities and the United States each filed an appellee's submission.[15] On the same day, Australia, Canada, and New Zealand each filed a third participant's submission.[16]

54. The oral hearing in the appeal was held on 3 November 2000. The participants and third participants presented oral arguments and responded to questions put to them by the Members of the Division hearing the appeal.

II. ARGUMENTS OF THE PARTICIPANTS AND THE THIRD PARTICIPANTS

A. *Claims of Error by the United States – Appellant*

1. *Article 4.2(b) of the Agreement on Safeguards*

55. The United States argues, on appeal, that the Panel erred in finding the United States' causation analysis to be inconsistent with Article 4.2(b) of the *Agreement on Safeguards*. For the United States, the meaning of the word "cause", used in Article XIX:1(a) of the GATT 1994 and Articles 2.1, 4.2(a) and 4.2(b) of the *Agreement on Safeguards*, is "to bring about a result, whether alone or in combination with other factors – not 'to cause on its own.' The plain meaning of 'causal link' in Article 4.2(b), first sentence, is consistent with this understanding of 'to cause.'"[17] The United States believes that the legal standard applied by the USITC satisfies this requirement.

56. The United States also maintains that the Panel did not examine adequately the meaning of the expression "under such conditions" in Article XIX:1(a) of the GATT 1994. Rather than attempt to isolate the causal effects of increased imports, the competent authorities should examine the effects of imports against the background of "the totality of attendant circumstances and existing state of affairs that lead imports to cause serious injury", "including factors that may have rendered a domestic industry more (or less) susceptible to injury."[18] The United States adds that the need to consider the industry as a whole is supported by the fact that "serious injury" refers to an industry's overall condition, rather than to some subset of injury attributable solely to increased imports.

57. Thus, in the United States' view, Article 4.2 does not require the isolation of imports, which the United States contends would, in any event, involve "subjective" speculation.[19] In its view, Article 4.2(b) requires the competent authori-

---

14 Pursuant to Rule 23(1) of the *Working Procedures*.

15 Pursuant to Rules 22 and 23(3) of the *Working Procedures*.

16 Pursuant to Rule 24 of the *Working Procedures*.

17 United States' appellant's submission, para. 54.

18 *Ibid.*, paras. 59 and 60.

19 *Ibid.*, para. 73.

ties to examine other causes of injury to ensure that their effects do not sever the causal link found to exist, after examining the totality of the circumstances, between increased imports and serious injury.[20] The United States asserts that the negotiating history of the *Agreement on Safeguards* bears out this reading of Article 4.2(b).

2. *Article 2.1 of the Agreement on Safeguards*

58. The United States requests the Appellate Body to reverse the Panel's finding that the exclusion of Canadian products from the safeguard measure on wheat gluten is inconsistent with Articles 2.1 and 4.2 of the *Agreement on Safeguards.*

59. In the view of the United States, the Panel's finding that, under Articles 2.1 and 4.2 of the *Agreement on Safeguards*, "there is an implied symmetry with respect to the product that falls within the scope of a safeguard *investigation* and the product that falls within the scope of the *application* of the safeguard measure" [21] (emphasis in original), is inconsistent with the text of the *Agreement on Safeguards*. Article 9.1 of the *Agreement on Safeguards* requires that imports from developing countries be excluded from the application of a safeguard measure, but does not provide for the exclusion of such imports from the investigation, or require any finding that the imports subject to the measure, "in and of themselves," cause serious injury. Furthermore, in *Argentina – Safeguard Measures on Imports of Footwear* ("*Argentina – Footwear Safeguards*"), the Appellate Body found that "Articles 2.1 and 4.1(c) ... do not resolve the matter of the scope of *application* of a safeguard measure." [22] (emphasis in original) The United States stresses that *Argentina – Footwear Safeguards* is distinguishable from this case because the USITC specifically examined the contribution of Canadian imports to the serious injury sustained by the industry and found that these imports played no significant role in that injury. The United States alleges that the Panel ignored legal provisions pertinent to the exclusion from safeguard measures of imports from partner countries in a free-trade area, namely Article XXIV of the GATT 1994 and footnote 1 of the *Agreement on Safeguards*. The United States also contends that the Panel failed to respect the requirement in Article 12.7 of the DSU to set out a "basic rationale" for its treatment of footnote 1.

3. *Articles 8 and 12 of the Agreement on Safeguards*

60. The United States requests the Appellate Body to reverse the Panel's findings regarding notification and consultation. The United States contends that its notifications under Article 12.1, subparagraphs (a), (b) and (c) were submitted

---

[20] *Ibid.*, para. 82.

[21] Panel Report, para. 8.167.

[22] Appellate Body Report, *Argentina – Safeguard Measures on Imports of Footwear* ("*Argentina – Footwear Safeguards*"), WT/DS121/AB/R, adopted 12 January 2000, DSR 2000:I, 515, para. 112.

"immediately" because they provided the required information at a time that allowed Members to review them through the Committee on Safeguards, and allowed interested Members to request consultations. The United States also believes that it complied with Article 12.3 by providing full information on its serious injury finding and the nature of the proposed measure, and by conducting consultations before the final decision.

61. The United States argues that, while the Panel correctly recognized that Articles 8.1, 12.1, 12.2 and 12.3 are interrelated, it failed to recognize that Members may employ a variety of procedures to comply with the obligations imposed under these provisions. For example, Article 12.2 envisions a process whereby Members may submit pertinent information in the Article 12.1(b) notification, in the Article 12.1(c) notification, or in both. There is no requirement that an Article 12.1(c) notification be filed before consultations, as long as prior notifications supplied the necessary information. Similarly, there is no requirement to conduct consultations after the issuance of the decision to apply a safeguard measure, as long as sufficient information was available to conduct consultations at a stage in the process where those consultations would have meaning. Through its notifications, the United States supplied all of the information specified in Article 12.2, including all relevant details of the proposed measure. The United States considers that this information was sufficient to allow for adequate consultations under Article 12.3.

B. Arguments of the European Communities – Appellee

1. Article 4.2(b) of the Agreement on Safeguards

62. The European Communities argues that the Panel correctly concluded that the United States applied a test of causation that is not consistent with Article 4.2(b) of the *Agreement on Safeguards*. The European Communities considers that the Panel did not need to consider explicitly the meaning of the term "to cause" in interpreting Article 4.2(b), since the conclusions it reached on the meaning of Article 4.2(b) are consistent with the ordinary meaning of the terms "to cause", "have caused" and "the causal link", as these terms are used in Article XIX:1(a) of the GATT 1994, and in Articles 2.1, 4.1(a) and 4.1(b) of the *Agreement on Safeguards*. The European Communities adds that the Panel correctly found that the term "under such conditions" in Article XIX:1(a) of the GATT 1994 and Article 2.1 of the *Agreement on Safeguards* refers to the conditions of competition between imported and domestic products rather than, as the United States seems to allege, to the "other relevant factors" that have a bearing on the situation of the industry under Articles 4.2(a) and 4.2(b) of the *Agreement on Safeguards*.

63. The European Communities contends that the Panel correctly recognized that Article 4.2(b) of the *Agreement on Safeguards* requires that increased imports *per se* cause serious injury. As the Appellate Body found in *Argentina – Footwear Safeguards*, Article 4.2(b) sets out a causation analysis that is separate

from, and subsequent to, the injury analysis to be undertaken pursuant to Article 4.2(a).[23] Article 4.2(b) ensures that, when a Member is considering whether to suspend fair trade, it may do so *if, and only if*, the imports are shown to cause serious injury. The practical effect of the United States' interpretation of Article 4.2(b), however, would allow a safeguard measure to be imposed whenever there is serious injury and imports caused *any* injury. The European Communities submits that this cannot be the case, and adds that its own interpretation of Article 4.2(b) is consistent with the object and purpose of the *Agreement on Safeguards*, with the exceptional nature of safeguard measures, and with the negotiating history of the *Agreement on Safeguards*.

64. Lastly, the European Communities submits that, even if the causation standard used by the United States could somehow be considered to be in conformity with Article 4.2(b) of the *Agreement on Safeguards*, the United States in this case nevertheless acted inconsistently with that Article because the USITC undertook no examination whatsoever to ensure that injury caused by other factors was not attributed to imports.

2. *Article 2.1 of the Agreement on Safeguards*

65. As regards the Panel's findings on the exclusion of wheat gluten imports from Canada from the application of the safeguard measure, the European Communities submits that the Panel correctly interpreted Articles 2.1 and 4.2 of the *Agreement on Safeguards* as containing a "symmetry" implied by the terms "a product", "such product" and "the product concerned" in those provisions. Contrary to the argument of the United States, Article 9.1 of the *Agreement on Safeguards* is not inconsistent with the existence of such an "implied symmetry", but is rather the exception to the *Agreement on Safeguards* that proves the rule. The European Communities asserts that the Panel properly recognized that, as in *Argentina – Footwear Safeguards*, the United States could not exclude imports from Canada on the basis of a *global* investigation concerning injury and causation that included imports of wheat gluten *from all sources*. The European Communities highlights that the Panel made a factual finding that the United States had not demonstrated that imports were causing serious injury after the exclusion of imports from Canada and that, as a legal matter, the subsequent causation analysis applied by the USITC regarding imports from Canada did not satisfy the requirements of the *Agreement on Safeguards*.

66. The European Communities adds that Article XXIV of the GATT 1994 is not relevant in this case and that, in any event, the United States has failed to establish that it has satisfied the conditions laid down by the Appellate Body in *Turkey – Restrictions on Imports of Textile and Clothing Products* for the use of

[23] Appellate Body Report, *Argentina – Footwear Safeguards*, *supra*, footnote 22, para. 145.

Article XXIV as a defence.[24] Lastly, the European Communities considers that the Panel set out sufficient reasons for its conclusion that footnote 1 of the *Agreement on Safeguards* did not affect its conclusions in this case.

3. Articles 8 and 12 of the Agreement on Safeguards

67. The European Communities urges the Appellate Body to uphold the findings of the Panel that the United States did not act consistently with Articles 8 and 12 of the *Agreement on Safeguards.* According to the European Communities, the Panel rightly interpreted Article 12 as requiring that all of the procedural steps, findings and decisions set out therein must be made at a date that allows other Members to request consultations, to seek additional information, and to hold meaningful discussions. The United States failed to notify each event listed in Article 12.1 of the *Agreement on Safeguards* in a timely manner. In addition, the notification made by the United States under Article 12.1(b) was not a notification of a "proposed measure" because its title (and therefore its legal basis) was "Article 12.1(b) notification upon making a finding of serious injury or threat thereof " and it contained only non-binding recommendations of the USITC. Articles 8 and 12.3 of the *Agreement on Safeguards* impose a heavy burden regarding consultations and negotiations on a Member proposing to alter unilaterally the balance of negotiated concessions. The European Communities emphasizes that, in this case, the United States acted inconsistently with these provisions because it failed to offer any meaningful opportunity for consultations.

C. Claims of Error by the European Communities – Appellant

1. Article 4.2(a) of the Agreement on Safeguards

68. The European Communities challenges the Panel's interpretation of Articles 4.2(a) and 4.2(b) of the *Agreement on Safeguards* and, in particular, its finding that, in a safeguards investigation, the competent authorities are only required to evaluate factors that are "*clearly* raised … as relevant by the interested parties".[25] (emphasis in original) The European Communities, therefore, requests the Appellate Body to find that the Panel erred in its interpretation of the substantive requirements of Articles 4.2(a) and 4.2(b) of the *Agreement on Safeguards* and to declare, on the basis of the uncontested facts and clear record in the Panel Report, that the United States violated Articles 4.2(a) and 4.2(b) of the *Agreement on Safeguards* because the USITC Report contained no analysis of the protein content of wheat. According to the European Communities, this is the single, most important, factor determining the price of wheat gluten.

---

[24] Appellate Body Report, *Turkey – Restrictions on Imports of Textile and Clothing Products* ("*Turkey – Textiles*"), WT/DS34/AB/R, adopted 19 November 1999, DSR 1999:VI, 2345.

[25] Panel Report, para. 8.69.

69. In the view of the European Communities, the ordinary meaning of Article 4.2(a) is that the competent authorities must gather, search, inquire into, generate and examine systematically *all* the relevant facts that are available – not only those presented to them by interested parties. It would be difficult for the competent authorities to fulfill their obligation under Article 4.2(b) to ensure that imports, taken alone, have caused serious injury, if those authorities were only obliged to evaluate "other factors" raised by interested parties. The European Communities considers that Articles 4.2(c) and 3.1 of the *Agreement on Safeguards* provide additional context to support its conclusion that the competent authorities are under an obligation to investigate *all* relevant factors, and notes that such a conclusion accords with the findings of a recent panel in the context of anti-dumping.[26]

2. *Article 11 of the DSU*

70. The European Communities argues that the Panel erred in its interpretation and application of Article 11 of the DSU. The Appellate Body has established that, pursuant to Article 11 of the DSU, the Panel was obliged to examine *all* the relevant facts and evidence, and to assess whether the USITC provided a reasoned or adequate explanation of how the facts supported the determinations that were made. The Panel, however, applied an inappropriate standard of deference, and failed to provide an adequate and reasonable explanation for its findings. The European Communities asserts that the "Panel failed in this case to make an 'objective' factual and legal assessment of all relevant evidence, because it failed to provide an adequate and reasonable explanation for its findings".[27] The European Communities provides several specific illustrations of the lack of a "sufficient basis" for the findings made.

71. First, the European Communities contends that the Panel erred in endorsing the USITC treatment of "productivity" when the Panel's assessment was based on "data" that could not be verified, and on "statements" made by the competent authorities whose "acts" were under review. In the view of the European Communities, the Panel should have concluded that the United States failed to evaluate overall industry productivity as required by Article 4.2(a) of the *Agreement on Safeguards*.

72. Second, the European Communities argues that the Panel violated Article 11 of the DSU in its review of the USITC determinations on profits and losses. The Panel did not review the financial data nor the allocation methodologies allegedly used by the producers, as these were all part of the confidential informa-

---

[26] Panel report, *Thailand – Anti-Dumping Duties on Angles, Shapes and Sections of Iron or Non-Alloy Steel and H-Beams from Poland* ("*Thailand – H-Beams*"), WT/DS122/R, adopted 5 April 2001, para. 7.236. Thailand has appealed certain issues of law and legal interpretations in that panel report, WT/DS122/4, 23 October 2000.

[27] European Communities' other appellant's submission, para. 25.

tion that the United States declined to submit to the Panel. The Panel's assessment was not "objective" because it was based on "indications" given by the USITC and "clarifications" added by the United States, as well as on the Panel's refusal to "doubt the veracity" of the USITC findings or to "call into question" the scrutiny given by the USITC to data that the Panel never received.[28] The European Communities emphasizes that if the Panel had correctly assessed the facts, it would have reached the conclusion that the USITC had not adequately analysed "profits and losses" in accordance with Article 4.2(a) of the *Agreement on Safeguards*.

73. Third, the European Communities alleges that the Panel erred in not finding that the USITC Report was deficient because, in its causation analysis, the USITC failed to consider the protein content of wheat as a "relevant factor", even though the European Communities' exporters submitted evidence of the relevance of this factor to the USITC, the USITC itself acknowledged the importance of the protein content of wheat, and the Panel had evidence before it of the high correlation between the protein content of wheat and the price of wheat gluten.

74. The European Communities alleges finally that the Panel acted inconsistently with its obligations under Article 11 of the DSU in failing to draw adverse inferences from the refusal of the United States to provide the Panel with information redacted from the USITC Report and other information requested by the European Communities and the Panel. The European Communities requests the Appellate Body to reverse the findings that resulted from such errors, in particular, the Panel's findings that the United States acted consistently with Articles 2.1 and 4 of the *Agreement on Safeguards* in redacting certain confidential information from the USITC Report, and in determining the existence of imports in "increased quantities" and serious injury. For the European Communities, the Panel erred in according significance to the argument of the United States that Article 3.2 of the *Agreement on Safeguards* allows it to withhold information from the Panel. The Panel's failure to obtain the information withheld by the United States on the basis of its allegedly confidential nature, coupled with its failure to draw the necessary adverse inferences from the refusal of the United States, amounted to an error of law.

3. *Judicial Economy*

75. The European Communities asks the Appellate Body to reverse the Panel's exercise of judicial economy in declining to rule on the claim made under Article XIX:1(a) of the GATT 1994. The European Communities argues, on the basis of the Appellate Body Reports in *Argentina – Footwear Safeguards* and *Korea – Definitive Safeguard Measure on Imports of Certain Dairy Products*

[28] European Communities' other appellant's submission, para. 65.

(*"Korea – Dairy Safeguard"*)[29], that a safeguard investigation must include an investigation of "unforeseen developments". In this case, the USITC Report contains no analysis or demonstration of "unforeseen developments". The European Communities concludes that the Panel erred in declining to rule on the Article XIX:1(a) claim, and that the Appellate Body should itself rule on that claim, because, in this case – in contrast to *Argentina – Footwear Safeguards* – the Panel found that the United States' determinations of imports in "increased quantities" and "serious injury" were *not* inconsistent with Articles 2.1 and 4.2 of the *Agreement on Safeguards.*

76. The European Communities also requests the Appellate Body to reverse the Panel's exercise of judicial economy in declining to rule on the claims made under Article I of the GATT 1994 and Article 5.1 of the *Agreement on Safeguards*, and to go on to determine, on the basis of the uncontested facts in the record, that the United States acted inconsistently with these provisions. The Panel's failure to rule on the claim under Article 5.1 of the *Agreement on Safeguards* means that the United States "could simply repeat the serious injury determination and ... proceed to apply the measure in the same way."[30]

D. Arguments of the United States – Appellee

1. Article 4.2(a) of the Agreement on Safeguards

77. The United States urges the Appellate Body to reject the European Communities' appeal on the factors that the competent authorities must assess in their safeguard investigation. According to the United States, the Panel correctly determined that the only information pertinent to a panel's assessment of whether the competent authorities adequately evaluated relevant factors under Article 4.2 of the *Agreement on Safeguards* is information those authorities considered in the course of their investigation. The European Communities, in contrast, argues that the Panel should have relied on information that was not before the USITC. However, the *Agreement on Safeguards* assigns the task of carrying out investigations to competent authorities. Thus, for the United States, a panel examining the "facts of the case" under Article 11 of the DSU must examine and assess what the competent authorities did in the course of *their* investigation, *not* seek to establish additional facts on whether increased imports may or may not have caused serious injury to the domestic industry.

78. According to the United States, the position of the European Communities would undermine the investigative process set out in the *Agreement on Safeguards,* including important procedural protections built into that Agreement. The United States accepts that, in some cases, a panel will need to assess whether

---

[29] Appellate Body Report, *Korea – Definitive Safeguard Measure on Imports of Certain Dairy Products* (*"Korea – Dairy Safeguard"*), WT/DS98/AB/R, adopted 12 January 2000,DSR 2000:I, 3.

[30] European Communities' other appellant's submission, para. 108.

the competent authorities failed to discharge their responsibilities to investigate and to make determinations based on objective evidence. In this case, however, the European Communities seeks to present a panel with information that it, and its wheat gluten producers, failed to present to the USITC. The United States adds that it is not clear that the USITC could itself have obtained the information that the European Communities presented to the Panel.

2. *Article 11 of the DSU*

79. The United States argues that the Panel acted in accordance with Article 11 of the DSU. In the view of the United States, the nature of the examination that a panel must conduct in order to make an objective assessment of the matter before it depends on the nature of the legal obligation at issue. A panel reviewing a matter arising under Article 4 of the *Agreement on Safeguards* must assess whether the competent authorities have, in *their* investigation, evaluated the relevant objective factors, demonstrated a causal link between increased imports and serious injury on the basis of objective evidence, and made a detailed analysis demonstrating the relevance of the factors examined. The only information pertinent to such an assessment is information the competent authorities considered in the course of their investigation and not, as the European Communities argues, information that was not before these authorities.

80. The United States contests the European Communities' claim that the Panel erred in finding that it had a sufficient basis to conduct an objective assessment. For the United States, this argument involves factual findings of the Panel and is thus outside the scope of appellate review. In any event, the United States argues that the Panel properly found that the USITC Report provides adequate, reasoned and reasonable explanations with respect to productivity and profits and losses. The United States contends that the Panel's findings with respect to the USITC consideration of productivity should be upheld because they were based on data and statements contained in the USITC Report regarding worker productivity and industry capital investment. Thus, the Panel correctly found that it is clear from the USITC Report that the USITC examined productivity as required by Article 4.2(a) of the *Agreement on Safeguards*. Similarly, as regards profits and losses, the USITC reviewed the allocation methodologies used by domestic producers and found them to be appropriate, and, before the Panel, the United States clarified and elaborated on the methodologies examined. In the view of the United States, the Panel was not required itself to verify the allocation of profits and losses as part of its objective assessment.

81. The United States further contends that, in its arguments on the protein content of wheat, the European Communities ignores the fact that the USITC fully examined trends in demand, including the possible impact of changes in the protein content. The USITC was only required to evaluate those factors enumer-

ated in Article 4.2(a) of the *Agreement on Safeguards* as well as any other relevant factors "*clearly* raised" by interested parties. The competent authorities are not obliged to "guess" [31] the relevance of factors not raised by the interested parties, particularly when, as here, the interested parties have clearly argued the relevance of some factors but not of others. The United States cautions that the ability of competent authorities to conduct investigations would be undermined if one Member could rely on the failure of its exporters to inform the competent authorities of a relevant factor in order to argue that another Member acted inconsistently with the *Agreement on Safeguards*.

82. The United States considers that the Panel acted within its discretion in declining to draw adverse inferences against the United States. The Appellate Body Report in *Canada – Measures Affecting the Export of Civilian Aircraft* ("*Canada – Aircraft*")[32] does not apply in this case, since the United States did not refuse to provide information. Rather, the USITC was obliged, under Article 3.2 of the *Agreement on Safeguards*, not to disclose confidential business information provided to it by interested parties. The United States also points out that the European Communities has not explained why an inference should have been drawn that the information requested was withheld *because* it was adverse to the United States' position in this case.

3. *Judicial Economy*

83. The United States submits that the Appellate Body should reject the European Communities' claims under Article XIX:1(a) of the GATT 1994, as well as under Article I of the GATT 1994 and Article 5 of the *Agreement on Safeguards*. The United States argues that the Appellate Body cannot examine either of these claims because they both involve factual matters upon which the Panel made no findings, and the relevant facts are disputed. The United States adds that, under Article XIX:1(a) of the GATT 1994, the USITC was not required to conduct a separate investigation and make a specific finding that the surge of wheat gluten imports resulted from "unforeseen developments". The United States also submits that it acted consistently with Article 5.1 and 5.2(a) of the *Agreement on Safeguards* in the application of its safeguard measure.

E. *Arguments of the Third Participants*

1. *Australia*

84. At the oral hearing, Australia recorded its agreement with the Panel's conclusions regarding the causation requirement set out in the *Agreement on Safeguards*, in particular the Panel's statement that "Article 4.2(a) and (b) SA require

---

31 United States' appellee's submission, para. 90.

32 Appellate Body Report, *Canada – Measures Affecting the Export of Civilian Aircraft* ("*Canada – Aircraft*"), WT/DS70/AB/R, adopted 20 August 1999, DSR 1999:III, 1377.

that increased imports *per se* are causing serious injury."[33] Australia considers that the approach proposed by the United States would effectively write the causation requirement out of the *Agreement on Safeguards* and undermine the effectiveness of the rules set out in that Agreement. Australia also urges the Appellate Body to dismiss the European Communities' appeal regarding the Panel's exercise of judicial economy in respect of the claims under Article 5 of the *Agreement on Safeguards* and Article I of the GATT 1994. Australia submits that, as a matter of law, the Appellate Body should not consider this issue unless it is necessary to resolve the dispute. However, in Australia's view, there are insufficient factual findings to allow the Appellate Body to resolve the issue.

2. *Canada*

85. Canada maintains that the Panel erred in concluding that the United States did not act consistently with Articles 2.1 and 4.2 of the *Agreement on Safeguards* by excluding imports of wheat gluten from Canada from the scope of its safeguard measure. Canada notes that, in *Argentina – Footwear Safeguards*, the Appellate Body said that Articles 2.1 and 4.1(c) "do not resolve the matter of the scope of *application* of a safeguard measure."[34] For Canada, it follows that, if the scope of *application* of a safeguard measure cannot be resolved with Article 2.1, then, logically, there can be no general rule of "symmetry" in that provision. The non-application of a safeguard measure to imports from a free-trade area partner is not inconsistent with Article 2.2 of the *Agreement on Safeguards* when – as in this case – a separate investigation determines that such imports are not contributing importantly to the serious injury. Such an approach ensures consistency between the scope of the measure and the products causing the serious injury, and gives the last sentence of footnote 1 to the *Agreement on Safeguards* a meaning consistent with Article XXIV of the GATT 1994. In this regard, Canada adds that the Panel should have examined the relevance of Articles XIX and XXIV of the GATT 1994.

86. As regards the appeal by the European Communities on the Panel's failure to draw adverse inferences from the refusal of the United States to provide certain requested information, Canada recalls that in *Canada – Aircraft*, the Appellate Body recognized that there are circumstances in which a refusal to provide information may be justified. Thus, Canada concludes, panels should exercise extreme prudence in drawing adverse inferences from a refusal to provide documents.

---

[33] Panel Report, para. 8.143.

[34] Appellate Body Report, *Argentina – Footwear Safeguards*, *supra*, footnote 22, para. 112.

3. New Zealand

87. New Zealand submits that the Panel correctly found that the causation analysis applied by the USITC was inconsistent with Article 4.2(b) of the *Agreement on Safeguards*. For New Zealand, Article 4.2(b) requires a direct causal link between increased imports and serious injury. The second sentence of Article 4.2(b) requires that, when there are multiple causes of serious injury, injury due to other factors should not be counted towards, or attributed to, the injury caused by increased imports. For New Zealand, the causation analysis applied by the USITC is inconsistent with this standard because it allows injury caused by other factors to be imputed to increased imports, and licenses the USITC to ignore other factors contributing to serious injury, as long as the contribution of any individual such factor is less important than the contribution of increased imports.

88. As regards the exclusion of imports from Canada from the safeguard measure, New Zealand accepts that a member of a free-trade area may exclude its free-trade area partners from the application of safeguard measures, but insists that where a member of a free-trade area does so, it must, under the terms of the *Agreement on Safeguards*, ensure that the imports to which the safeguard measure is applied are the same imports that cause serious injury. New Zealand agrees with the Panel that, in this case, the United States failed to respect this requirement of "symmetry".

89. New Zealand argues that the Panel wrongly applied the standard of review set out in Article 11 of the DSU by excluding from its consideration evidence that would or should have been known to the competent authorities but was not specifically presented to the USITC by interested parties. New Zealand also submits that the Panel correctly interpreted Article 12 of the *Agreement on Safeguards* and concluded that the United States failed to comply with the notification and consultation requirements set out in that provision. In New Zealand's view, a notification under Article 12.1(c) of that Agreement must contain information concerning the proposed measure and be made at such time as to provide adequate opportunity for prior consultations.

III. ISSUES RAISED IN THIS APPEAL

90. This appeal raises the following issues:

(a) whether the Panel erred in finding, in paragraph 8.69 of the Panel Report, that, under Article 4.2(a) of the *Agreement on Safeguards*, competent authorities are required to evaluate only the "relevant factors" listed in Article 4.2(a) of that Agreement as well as any other "factors" which were "*clearly* raised before [the competent authorities] as relevant by the interested parties in the domestic investigation";

(b) whether the Panel erred in interpreting Article 4.2(b) of the *Agreement on Safeguards* to mean that increased imports "alone", "in and of themselves", or "*per se*", must be capable of causing "serious injury";

(c) whether the Panel erred in finding, in paragraph 8.182 of the Panel Report, that the United States acted inconsistently with Articles 2.1 and 4.2 of the *Agreement on Safeguards*, by excluding imports from Canada from the application of the safeguard measure, after conducting an investigation embracing imports from all sources, including Canada, to determine whether increased imports of wheat gluten were causing or threatening to cause serious injury to the United States industry, and after subsequently conducting a separate examination of the importance of imports from Canada to the situation of the domestic industry;

(d) whether the Panel erred in its interpretation and application of Articles 8 and 12 of the *Agreement on Safeguards*, in particular, by finding that:

   (i) the United States acted inconsistently with its obligations to make "immediate" notification under Article 12.1 of the *Agreement on Safeguards*;

   (ii) the United States acted inconsistently with Article 12.3 of the *Agreement on Safeguards* by failing to provide an adequate opportunity for consultations on the measure prior to its implementation; and

   (iii) the United States acted inconsistently with Article 8.1 of the *Agreement on Safeguards*;

(e) whether the Panel erred in its interpretation and application of Article 11 of the DSU, in particular:

   (i) in its finding on the USITC's treatment of "productivity" in paragraph 8.46 of the Panel Report;

   (ii) in its finding on the USITC's treatment of "profits and losses" in paragraph 8.66 of the Panel Report;

   (iii) by failing to examine the arguments made by the European Communities concerning the overall relationship between the protein content of wheat and the price of wheat gluten; and

   (iv) by declining to draw "adverse" inferences from the refusal of the United States to provide certain allegedly confidential information requested from it by the Panel under Article 13.1 of the DSU; and

(f) whether the Panel erred in its exercise of judicial economy, in paragraph 8.220 of the Panel Report, in not examining the claims of the European Communities under Article XIX:1(a) of the GATT 1994, and also under Article 5 of the *Agreement on Safeguards* and Article I of the GATT 1994.

IV. ARTICLE 4.2(A) OF THE AGREEMENT ON SAFEGUARDS

91. Before the Panel, the European Communities argued that the USITC failed to evaluate "all relevant factors", as required by Article 4.2(a) of the *Agreement on Safeguards*, because the USITC did not examine the relationship between the protein content of wheat and the price of wheat gluten. According to the European Communities, this relationship is the "single, most important, factor determining the price of wheat gluten".[35]

92. The Panel stated that Article 4.2(a) of the *Agreement on Safeguards* "requires a demonstration that the competent authorities evaluated 'all relevant factors' enumerated in Article 4.2(a) as well as other relevant factors."[36] The Panel added:

> We read this requirement in Article 4.2(a) SA as mandating that the investigating authorities evaluate those "factors" enumerated in Article 4.2(a) SA as well as any other relevant "factors" - *in the sense of factors that are clearly raised before them as relevant by the interested parties in the domestic investigation.*[37] (underlining added)

93. The Panel observed that the USITC "considered all the factors expressly enumerated in Article 4.2(a) SA".[38] The Panel also noted that the parties "do not dispute that the USITC [also] considered wages, inventories and price."[39] However, the Panel found that the USITC was not required to examine the relationship between the protein content of wheat and the price of wheat gluten, as regards "the post-1994 segment of the period of investigation", because this issue was not "clearly raised" before the USITC by the interested parties.[40]

94. On appeal, the European Communities argues that the Panel erred in interpreting Article 4.2(a) of the *Agreement on Safeguards* to mean that the competent authorities need only evaluate the "relevant factors" listed in Article 4.2(a), as well as any other "factors" which were "*clearly* raised before them as relevant by the interested parties". According to the European Communities, the competent authorities should investigate "*all* the relevant facts that are available – and not only those presented to them – in order to conduct an assessment of the facts as a whole."[41] (underlining in original)

95. The relevant part of Article 4.2(a) of the *Agreement on Safeguards* reads:

---

[35] European Communities' other appellant's submission, para. 88.
[36] Panel Report, para. 8.69.
[37] *Ibid.*
[38] *Ibid.*, para. 8.41.
[39] *Ibid.*
[40] *Ibid.*, para. 8.125.
[41] European Communities' other appellant's submission, para. 80.

> In the investigation to determine whether increased imports have caused or are threatening to cause serious injury to a domestic industry under the terms of this Agreement, *the competent authorities shall evaluate all relevant factors of an objective and quantifiable nature having a bearing on the situation of that industry*, in particular, the rate and amount of the increase in imports of the product concerned in absolute and relative terms, the share of the domestic market taken by increased imports, changes in the level of sales, production, productivity, capacity utilization, profits and losses, and employment. (emphasis added)

96. We have already had occasion to observe that:

> … Article 4.2(a) of the *Agreement on Safeguards* requires a demonstration that the competent authorities evaluated, at a minimum, each of the factors listed in Article 4.2(a) as well as *all other factors that are relevant to the situation of the industry concerned.*[42] (emphasis added)

97. In this appeal, we are asked to address further the scope of the competent authorities' obligation, under Article 4.2(a), to evaluate "*all* relevant factors". (emphasis added) The word "all" has a broad meaning which, if read alone, would suggest that the scope of the obligation on the competent authorities to evaluate "relevant factors" is without limits or exceptions.[43] However, the word cannot, of course, be read in isolation. As the European Communities acknowledges[44], the text of Article 4.2(a) itself imposes certain explicit qualifications on the obligation to evaluate "all relevant factors" as it states that competent authorities need only evaluate factors which are "objective and quantifiable" and which "[have] a bearing on the situation of that industry".

98. The obligation to evaluate "relevant factors" must also be interpreted in light of the duty of the competent authorities to conduct an "investigation" under the *Agreement on Safeguards*. The competent authorities must base their evaluation of the relevance, if any, of a factor on evidence that is "objective and quantifiable". The competent authorities will, in principle, obtain this evidence during the investigation they must conduct, under Article 3.1, into the situation of the domestic industry. The scope of the obligation to evaluate "all relevant factors" is, therefore, related to the scope of the obligation of competent authorities to conduct an investigation.

---

[42] Appellate Body Report, *Argentina – Footwear Safeguards, supra*, footnote 22, para. 136.

[43] *The New Shorter Oxford English Dictionary*, (Brown, ed.) (Clarendon Press, 1993), Vol. I, p. 52, indicates that, when the word "all" is used as an adjective preceding a noun in the plural form (as in "all … factors"), it means "The entire number of; the individual constituents of, without exception."

[44] European Communities' other appellant's submission, para. 79.

99. We turn, therefore, for context, to Article 3.1 of *Agreement on Safeguards*, which is entitled "*Investigation*". Article 3.1 provides that "A Member may apply a safeguard measure only following an *investigation* by the competent authorities of that Member ...". (emphasis added) The ordinary meaning of the word "investigation" suggests that the competent authorities should carry out a "systematic inquiry" or a "careful study" into the matter before them.[45] The word, therefore, suggests a proper degree of activity on the part of the competent authorities because authorities charged with conducting an inquiry or a study – to use the treaty language, an "investigation" – must actively seek out pertinent information.

100. The nature of the "investigation" required by the *Agreement on Safeguards* is elaborated further in the remainder of Article 3.1, which sets forth certain investigative steps that the competent authorities "*shall include*" in order to seek out pertinent information. (emphasis added) The focus of the investigative steps mentioned in Article 3.1 is on "interested parties", who must be notified of the investigation, and who must be given an opportunity to submit "evidence", as well as their "views", to the competent authorities. The interested parties are also to be given an opportunity to "respond to the presentations of other parties". The *Agreement on Safeguards*, therefore, envisages that the interested parties play a central role in the investigation and that they will be a primary source of information for the competent authorities.

101. However, in our view, that does *not* mean that the competent authorities may limit their evaluation of "all relevant factors", under Article 4.2(a) of the *Agreement on Safeguards*, to the factors which the interested parties have raised as relevant. The competent authorities must, in every case, carry out a full investigation to enable them to conduct a proper evaluation of all of the relevant factors expressly mentioned in Article 4.2(a) of the *Agreement on Safeguards*.[46] Moreover, Article 4.2(a) requires the competent authorities – and *not the interested parties* – to evaluate fully the relevance, if any, of "other factors". If the competent authorities consider that a particular "other factor" may be relevant to the situation of the domestic industry, under Article 4.2(a), their duties of investigation and evaluation preclude them from remaining passive in the face of possible short-comings in the evidence submitted, and views expressed, by the interested parties. In such cases, where the competent authorities do not have sufficient information before them to evaluate the possible relevance of such an "other factor", they must investigate fully that "other factor", so that they can fulfill their obligations of evaluation under Article 4.2(a). In that respect, we note that the competent authorities' "investigation" under Article 3.1 is *not limited* to the investigative steps mentioned in that provision, but must simply "*include*" these steps. Therefore, the competent authorities must undertake additional investiga-

---

45 *The New Shorter Oxford English Dictionary*, *supra*, footnote 43, Vol. I, p. 1410.

46 Appellate Body Report, *Argentina – Footwear Safeguards*, *supra*, footnote 22, para. 136.

tive steps, when the circumstances so require, in order to fulfill their obligation to evaluate all relevant factors.

102. Thus, we disagree with the Panel's finding that the competent authorities need only examine "other factors" which were "*clearly* raised before them as relevant by the interested parties in the domestic investigation." [47] (emphasis added) However, as is clear from the preceding paragraph of this Report, we also reject the European Communities' argument that the competent authorities have an open-ended and unlimited duty to investigate all available facts that might possibly be relevant.[48]

103. In order to complete the Panel's analysis, we now examine the European Communities' claim that the USITC should have examined the overall relationship between the protein content of wheat and the price of wheat gluten as a "relevant factor", under Article 4.2(a) of the *Agreement on Safeguards.* We note that this overall relationship was not "evaluated" by the USITC as a "relevant other factor" under Article 4.2(a) of the *Agreement on Safeguards*. However, the USITC Report is not silent on the importance of the protein content of wheat. The USITC stated that:

> ... *Demand for wheat gluten is closely tied to the protein content of each year's wheat crop*. Should the quantity and quality of *protein* naturally occurring in the wheat supply be *low*, then bakers *consume more wheat gluten* to supplement the lack of protein in the wheat. ... [49] (emphasis added)

The USITC also noted that "when the *protein level in wheat is high, less wheat gluten is demanded* to add to the baking flour."[50] (emphasis added) The USITC observed that a steep rise, in 1994, in the demand for, and price of, wheat gluten "resulted at least in part from a weather-related deficiency in protein content in the wheat crops of the major producing countries, including the United States, during 1993."[51]

104. In our view, the USITC clearly acknowledged that the protein content of wheat has an important influence on the demand for, and the price of, wheat gluten. However, the evidence of record indicates that it is only when the protein content of wheat is *unusually* high or low that this factor merits "evaluation" as a "relevant factor" because it is only in that situation that the protein content of wheat has a noteworthy effect on fluctuations in the demand for, and price of, wheat gluten. The only year of the investigative period in which the protein content of wheat was unusually high or low was in 1993, and this resulted in increased demand and higher prices for wheat gluten solely in 1994. There is no

---

47 Panel Report, para. 8.69.

48 See, *supra*, para. 48, for a summary of the European Communities' argument.

49 USITC Report, p. II-9.

50 *Ibid.*, p. I-23.

51 *Ibid.*, pp. I-22 and I-23.

evidence to suggest that during 1996 and 1997, when the surge in imports occurred[52], the protein content of wheat was unusual to such a degree that this factor had a noteworthy effect on fluctuations in the price of wheat gluten. It follows that there is no reason to conclude that the USITC was required to "evaluate" the protein content of wheat as a particular "relevant factor" under Article 4.2(a) of the *Agreement on Safeguards* in 1996 and 1997.

105. Accordingly, albeit for different reasons, we uphold the Panel's finding that the United States has not acted inconsistently with Articles 4.2(a) and 4.2(b) of the *Agreement on Safeguards* by not examining the overall relationship between the protein content of wheat and the price of wheat gluten with respect to the post-1994 segment of the period of investigation.[53]

V. ARTICLE 4.2(B) OF THE AGREEMENT ON SAFEGUARDS

106. In addressing causation, the Panel described the issue before it as:

> ... whether ... the USITC satisfied the requirements in Article 4.2(b) SA to demonstrate the causal link between the increased imports and the serious injury, and not to attribute to imports injury caused by other factors.[54]

107. The Panel observed that Article 4.2(b) of the *Agreement on Safeguards* "contains an explicit textual link to Article 4.2(a)" of that Agreement. Reading these two provisions together, the Panel opined:

> ... Article 4.2(a) and (b) require a Member: (i) to demonstrate the existence of the causal link between increased imports and *serious* injury; and (ii) not to attribute injury being caused by other factors to the domestic industry at the same time to increased imports. We consider that, read together, these two propositions require that a Member demonstrate that the *increased imports, under the conditions extant in the marketplace, in and of themselves, cause serious injury*. This is not to say that the imports must be the sole causal factor present in a situation of serious injury. There may be multiple factors present in a situation of serious injury to a domestic industry. However, the *increased imports must be sufficient, in and of themselves, to cause injury which achieves the threshold of "serious"* as defined in the Agreement.[55] (underlining added)

108. The Panel reiterated this interpretation in other ways. It stated that:

---

52 USITC Report, p. I-23.
53 Panel Report, para. 8.127.
54 *Ibid.*, para. 8.136.
55 Panel Report, para. 8.138.

> ... where a number of factors, one of which is increased imports, are sufficient *collectively* to cause a "significant overall impairment of the position of the domestic industry", *but increased imports alone are not causing injury that achieves the threshold of "serious"* within the meaning of Article 4.1(a) of the Agreement, the conditions for imposing a safeguard measure are not satisfied.[56] (underlining added)

109. The Panel concluded that "Article 4.2(a) and (b) SA require that increased imports *per se* are causing serious injury."[57]

110. The United States argues, on appeal, that the Panel erred in interpreting Article 4.2(b) to mean that increased imports must be sufficient, in and of themselves, to cause injury that is "serious". It contends that the word "cause" means "to bring about a result, whether alone or in combination with other factors – not 'to cause on its own.' The plain meaning of 'causal link' in Article 4.2(b), first sentence, is consistent with this understanding of 'to cause'."[58] According to the United States, the last sentence of Article 4.2(b) is intended to ensure that other factors do not negate the causal link found to exist, after examining the totality of the circumstances, between increased imports and serious injury.[59]

111. The issue of causation plays a central role in any safeguards investigation. In that respect, Article 4.2(b) of the *Agreement on Safeguards* provides as follows:

> The determination referred to in subparagraph (a) shall not be made unless this investigation demonstrates, on the basis of objective evidence, the existence of *the causal link* between increased imports of the product concerned and serious injury or threat thereof. When *factors other than increased imports are causing injury* to the domestic industry at the same time, *such injury shall not be attributed to increased imports.* (emphasis added)

112. In essence, the Panel has read Article 4.2(b) of the *Agreement on Safeguards* as establishing that increased imports must make a particular contribution to causing the serious injury sustained by the domestic industry. The level of the contribution the Panel requires is that increased imports, looked at "*alone*"[60], "*in and of themselves*"[61], or "*per se*"[62], must be capable of causing injury that is "serious". It seems to us that the Panel arrived at this interpretation through the following steps of reasoning: first, under the first sentence of Article 4.2(b), there must be a "causal link" between increased imports and serious injury; second, the

[56] *Ibid.*, para. 8.139.
[57] *Ibid.*, para. 8.143.
[58] United States appellant's submission, para. 54.
[59] *Ibid.*, para. 82.
[60] Panel Report, para. 8.139.
[61] *Ibid.*, para. 8.138.
[62] *Ibid.*, para. 8.143.

non-"attribution" language of the last sentence of Article 4.2(b) means that the effects caused by increased imports must be *distinguished from* the effects caused by other factors; third, the effects caused by other factors must, therefore, be *excluded* totally from the determination of serious injury so as to ensure that these effects are not "attributed" to the increased imports; fourth, the effects caused by increased imports *alone*, excluding the effects caused by other factors, must, therefore, be capable of causing serious injury.[63]

113. We begin our reasoning with the first sentence of Article 4.2(b). That sentence provides that a determination "shall not be made unless [the] investigation demonstrates ... the existence of *the causal link* between increased imports ... and serious injury or threat thereof." (emphasis added) Thus, the requirement for a determination, under Article 4.2(a), is that "the causal link" exists. The word "causal" means "relating to a cause or causes", while the word "cause", in turn, denotes a relationship between, at least, two elements, whereby the first element has, in some way, "brought about", "produced" or "induced" the existence of the second element.[64] The word "link" indicates simply that increased imports have played a part in, or contributed to, bringing about serious injury so that there is a causal "connection"[65] or "nexus" between these two elements. Taking these words together, the term "the causal link" denotes, in our view, a relationship of cause and effect such that increased imports contribute to "bringing about", "producing" or "inducing" the serious injury. Although that contribution must be sufficiently clear as to establish the existence of "the causal link" required, the language in the first sentence of Article 4.2(b) does *not* suggest that increased imports be *the sole* cause of the serious injury, or that "*other* factors" causing injury must be excluded from the determination of serious injury. To the contrary, the language of Article 4.2(b), as a whole, suggests that "the causal link" between increased imports and serious injury may exist, *even though other factors are also contributing, "at the same time", to the situation of the domestic industry*.

114. It is precisely because there may be several factors, besides increased imports, contributing simultaneously to the situation of the domestic industry that the last sentence of Article 4.2(b) states that competent authorities "shall not ... attribute" to increased imports injury caused by other factors. The opening clause of that sentence indicates, to us, that this sentence provides rules that apply when "increased imports" and certain "other factors" are, together, "causing injury" to the domestic industry "at the same time". The last clause of the sentence stipulates that, in that situation, the injury caused by other factors "shall not be *attributed* to increased imports". (emphasis added) Synonyms for the word "attribute" include "assign" or "ascribe".[66] Under the last sentence of Article 4.2(b), we are

---

63 We base our understanding of the Panel's reasoning on *paras*. 8.138, 8.139, 8.140 and 8.143 of the Panel Report.

64 *The New Shorter Oxford English Dictionary*, *supra*, footnote 43, Vol. I, pp. 355 and 356.

65 *Ibid.*, p. 1598.

66 *The New Shorter Oxford English Dictionary*, *supra*, footnote 43, Vol. I, p. 145.

concerned with the proper "attribution", in this sense, of "injury" caused to the domestic industry by "factors other than increased imports". Clearly, the process of attributing "injury", envisaged by this sentence, can only be made following a separation of the "injury" that must then be properly "attributed". What is important in this process is separating or distinguishing the *effects* caused by the different factors in bringing about the "injury".

115. Article 4.2(b) presupposes, therefore, as a first step in the competent authorities' examination of causation, that the injurious effects caused to the domestic industry by increased imports are *distinguished from* the injurious effects caused by other factors. The competent authorities can then, as a second step in their examination, attribute to increased imports, on the one hand, and, by implication, to other relevant factors, on the other hand, "injury" caused by all of these different factors, including increased imports. Through this two stage process, the competent authorities comply with Article 4.2(b) by ensuring that any injury to the domestic industry that was *actually* caused by factors other than increased imports is not "attributed" to increased imports and is, therefore, not treated as if it were injury caused by increased imports, when it is not. In this way, the competent authorities determine, as a final step, whether "the causal link" exists between increased imports and serious injury, and whether this causal link involves a genuine and substantial relationship of cause and effect between these two elements, as required by the *Agreement on Safeguards*.[67]

116. The need to ensure a proper attribution of "injury" under Article 4.2(b) indicates that competent authorities must take account, in their determination, of the effects of increased imports *as distinguished from* the effects of other factors. However, the need to distinguish between the effects caused by increased imports and the effects caused by other factors does *not* necessarily imply, as the Panel said, that increased imports *on their own* must be capable of causing serious injury, nor that injury caused by other factors must be *excluded* from the determination of serious injury.

117. We consider that Article 4.2(a) of the *Agreement on Safeguards*, which is explicitly referred to in Article 4.2(b), indicates that "other factors" have to be taken into account in the competent authorities' determination of serious injury. Article 4.2(a) sets forth the factors which the competent authorities "*shall evaluate*" in "determin[ing] whether increased imports have caused or are threatening to cause serious injury to a domestic industry...". Under that provision, the competent authorities must evaluate "all relevant factors ... having a *bearing* on the situation of [the] industry". (emphasis added) In evaluating the relevance of a particular factor, the competent authorities must, therefore, assess the "bearing", or the "influence" or "effect"[68] that factor has on the overall situation of the domestic industry, against the background of all the other relevant factors.

---

[67] See, *supra*, para. 67.

[68] *The New Shorter Oxford English Dictionary*, *supra*, footnote 43, Vol. I, pp. 199.

118. The use of the word "all" in the phrase "all relevant factors" in Article 4.2(a) indicates that the effects of *any* factor may be relevant to the competent authorities' determination, irrespective of whether the particular factor relates to imports specifically or to the domestic industry more generally. This conclusion is borne out by the list of factors which Article 4.2(a) stipulates are, "in particular", relevant to the determination. This list includes factors that relate *both* to imports specifically *and* to the overall situation of the domestic industry more generally. The language of the provision does not distinguish between, or attach special importance or preference to, any of the listed factors. In our view, therefore, Article 4.2(a) of the *Agreement on Safeguards* suggests that all these factors are to be *included* in the determination and that the contribution of each relevant factor is to be counted in the determination of serious injury according to its "bearing" or effect on the situation of the domestic industry. Thus, we consider that Article 4.2(a) does not support the Panel's conclusion that some of the "relevant factors" – those related exclusively to increased imports – should be counted towards an affirmative determination of serious injury, while others – those not related to increased imports – should be excluded from that determination.[69]

119. We believe that Articles 4.2(a) and 4.2(b) of the *Agreement on Safeguards* must be given a mutually consistent interpretation, particularly in light of the explicit textual connection between these two provisions. According to the opening clause of Article 4.2(b) – "The determination referred to in subparagraph (a) shall not be made unless..." – *both* provisions lay down rules governing a *single* determination, made under Article 4.2(a). In our view, it would contradict the requirement in Article 4.2(a) to evaluate – and, thereby, include in the determination – the "bearing" or effect *all* the relevant factors have on the domestic industry, if those *same* effects, caused by those *same* factors, were, with the exception of increased imports, to be excluded under Article 4.2(b), as the Panel suggested.

120. We note, in addition, that our understanding of the factors to be taken into account under Articles 4.2(a) and 4.2(b) is borne out by the definition of "serious injury" given in Article 4.1(a). The term "serious injury" is defined as "a significant *overall* impairment in the position of a domestic industry". (emphasis added) The breadth of this term also suggests that all factors relevant to the overall situation of the industry should be included in the competent authorities' determination.

121. We are further fortified in our interpretation of Articles 4.2(a) and 4.2(b) of the *Agreement on Safeguards* by our reading of Article 2.1 of that Agreement. That provision reads:

> A Member may apply a safeguard measure to a product only if that Member has determined, pursuant to the provisions set out below, that *such product is being imported into its territory in such increased quantities*, absolute or relative to domestic production, *and*

---

69 See, *supra*, para. 66, for our summary of the Panel's reasoning.

under such conditions as to cause or threaten to cause serious injury to the domestic industry that produces like or directly competitive products. (emphasis added)

122. Article 2.1 reflects closely the "basic principles"[70] in Article XIX:1(a) of the GATT 1994 and also sets forth "the conditions for imposing a safeguard measure"[71], including those relating to causation. The rules on causation, which are elaborated further in the remainder of the *Agreement on Safeguards*, therefore, find their roots in Article 2.1. According to that provision, a safeguard measure may be applied if a "product is being imported ... *in such increased quantities ... and under such conditions as to cause ...*" serious injury. Thus, under Article 2.1, the causation analysis embraces two elements: the first relating to increased "imports" specifically and the second to the "conditions" under which imports are occurring.

123. Each of these two elements is, in our view, elaborated further in Article 4.2(a). While Article 2.1 requires account to be taken of the "increased quantities" of imports, both in "absolute" terms and "relative to domestic production", Article 4.2(a) states, correspondingly, that "the rate and amount of the increase in imports of the product concerned in absolute and relative terms, [and] the share of the domestic market taken by increased imports" are relevant.

124. As for the second element under Article 2.1, we see it as a complement to the first. While the first element refers to increased imports specifically, the second relates more generally to the "conditions" in the marketplace for the product concerned that may influence the domestic industry. Thus, the phrase "under such conditions" refers generally to the prevailing "conditions", in the marketplace for the product concerned, when the increase in imports occurs. Interpreted in this way, the phrase "under such conditions" is a shorthand reference to the remaining factors listed in Article 4.2(a), which relate to the overall state of the domestic industry and the domestic market, as well as to other factors "having a bearing on the situation of [the] industry". The phrase "under such conditions", therefore, supports the view that, under Articles 4.2(a) and 4.2(b) of the *Agreement on Safeguards*, the competent authorities should determine whether the increase in imports, not alone, but in conjunction with the other relevant factors, cause serious injury.[72]

125. For these reasons, we agree with the first and second steps we identified in the Panel's reasoning; however, we see no support in the text of the *Agreement on Safeguards* for the third and fourth steps of the Panel's reasoning.[73] Therefore, in conclusion, we reverse the Panel's interpretation of Article 4.2(b) of the *Agree-*

70 Preamble to the *Agreement on Safeguards*.

71 Appellate Body Report, *Argentina – Footwear Safeguards, supra*, footnote 22, para. 112.

72 We do not, of course, exclude the possibility that "serious injury" could be caused by the effects of increased imports *alone*.

73 *Supra*, para. 66.

ment on Safeguards that increased imports "alone", "in and of themselves", or "*per se*", must be capable of causing injury that is "serious".[74] And we also reverse the Panel's conclusions on the issue of causation, summarized in paragraph 8.154 of the Panel Report, as these conclusions are based on an erroneous interpretation of Article 4.2(b).

126. As we have reversed the Panel's conclusions regarding causation, we believe that we should now complete the legal analysis on this issue on the basis of the factual findings of the Panel and the undisputed facts in the Panel record. We note that the Panel narrated the findings of the USITC on four potential factors, other than increased imports, for their bearing on the situation of the domestic industry. These were the effects of: "co-product markets", "rising input costs", "importation of wheat gluten by United States domestic producers" and "capacity utilization".[75] Of these four factors, the Panel made most mention of the last, capacity utilization.

127. The uncontested facts of record relating to the capacity utilization of the domestic industry are as follows.[76] During the period of investigation, 1 July 1993 to 30 June 1997, the average available capacity of United States' producers of wheat gluten rose by a little over 68 percent, with 55 percent of that increase being available by 30 June 1995. Total United States' consumption of wheat gluten rose, during the period of investigation, by 17.8 percent. The amount of wheat gluten produced by United States' producers rose by 12 percent during the first three years of the investigative period, before declining to a closing level that was 96 percent of the starting level. In the face of the increase in average capacity and the decrease in production, United States' capacity utilization levels fell from 78.3 percent, in 1993, to 44.5 percent, in 1997. During the investigative period, the volume of imports increased by nearly 38 percent, with the market share of imports rising from 51.4 percent to 60.2 percent.

128. In evaluating increased capacity and capacity utilization levels as "other possible causes of injury", the USITC said:

> ... The domestic wheat gluten market is very competitive. Producers have ample excess capacity to meet higher demand. Also, wheat gluten is a commodity product that sells primarily on the basis of price, and wheat gluten from different sources is highly interchangeable. One new domestic producer, Heartland, entered the market in 1996. In addition, the domestic industry added substantial new capacity early in the period of investigation. This increased capacity was added in anticipation of continued strong growth in domestic demand and consumption. Industry projections of continued growth in demand and consumption were largely cor-

74 Panel Report, paras. 8.138, 8.139 and 8.143.

75 *Ibid.*, paras. 8.147 – 8.150.

76 All the relevant figures are derived from Table C-1, pp. C-3 and C-4, of the USITC Report.

> rect, as apparent consumption increased nearly 18 percent between 1993 and 1997. As indicated above, *but for the increase in imports, the industry would have operated at 61 percent of capacity in 1997, which is much closer to the level at which the industry operated early in the investigative period when it operated reasonably profitably.* We therefore conclude that neither domestic competition nor increased domestic capacity was a more important cause of serious injury than increased imports.[77] (emphasis added)

129. In considering this same issue, the Panel noted certain "assertions" of the United States that the increase in the production capacity of the domestic industry "had a role" in the serious injury suffered by the industry.[78] The Panel then stated:

> ... To us, these assertions constitute an admission by the United States that at least one factor other than increased imports also contributed to the serious injury experienced by the domestic industry. However, we see no indication in the USITC Report that imports were not also held responsible for the injury caused by this factor.[79]

130. We note that the USITC placed particular emphasis on the fact that, "but for the increase in imports", the domestic industry would have operated, in 1997, at nearly 61 percent of available capacity.[80] The USITC emphasizes this fact because, it says, at that rate of capacity utilization, the domestic industry would have been operating "much closer" to rates attained "early in the investigative period", when the industry was reasonably profitable.[81] The USITC, therefore, makes an explicit link between the profitability of the domestic industry and the rate of capacity utilization. We also note that, in arriving at the hypothetical figure of 61 percent capacity utilization, the USITC made certain assumptions which it explained in a footnote to the USITC Report.[82] These assumptions were: first, that total United States' consumption was constant at 1997 levels, representing an 18 percent increase over 1993 levels; second, that the volume of imports was constant throughout the investigative period at 128,337,000 tonnes; and, third, that United States' domestic production satisfied "*all* of the [18 percent] increase in [United States'] consumption".[83] (emphasis added) We observe that, by assuming that domestic producers would supply *all* of the 18 percent increase

---

77 USITC Report, p. I-17.
78 Panel Report, para. 8.151.
79 Panel Report, para. 8.151.
80 USITC Report, p. I-17.
81 *Ibid.* In 1993, the industry operated at 78.3 percent of capacity. In 1994 and 1995 the rates of capacity utilization were 67.4 percent and 56.2 percent, respectively. (USITC Report, Table C-1, p. C-4) The USITC said, at page I-28 of its Report, that the domestic industry was profitable in the period from 1993 – 1995.
82 Footnote 51, p. I-12, USITC Report.
83 *Ibid.*

in consumption, the USITC also assumed a hypothetical market share for imports that *fell* from 51.4 percent to 43.6 percent.

131. At the oral hearing, we asked the participants, the United States and the European Communities, to comment on two additional scenarios, based *exclusively* on the data contained in the USITC Report, that explore further the importance of increases in average capacity and rates of capacity utilization to the situation of the domestic industry. Under the first scenario, the participants both confirmed that the rate of capacity utilization of the domestic industry would have been 74.8 percent *if the average capacity of the domestic industry had remained constant throughout the investigative period and had not increased by 68 percent.*[84] At a rate of 74.8 percent, capacity utilization would have fallen by only 3.5 percent from the 1993 rate of 78.3 percent. In other words, but for the increase in available capacity and *despite the increase in imports*, capacity utilization rates would have remained extremely close to the 1993 rates which allowed the domestic industry to operate profitably.[85]

132. Under the second scenario, both participants confirmed that the rate of capacity utilization of the domestic industry would have been 54.2 percent if the United States' producers, and importers, had held, throughout the entire investigation period, a *constant* market share, by quantity, equal to their respective market shares in 1993. Thus, instead of United States producers supplying *all* of the 18 percent increase in total consumption, as the USITC assumed in reaching its figure of 61 percent, under this scenario, the increase in total consumption was shared between United States' producers and importers according to their respective 1993 market shares.[86] In other words, we assume that the percentage increase in the volume of imports is 17.8 percent, the same as the percentage increase in total United States' consumption, and not 38 percent, the figure by which imports actually increased. In that event, the capacity utilization of the domestic industry would have been, as we said, 54.2 percent. Thus, even if imports had done no more than hold their position on the market, and had increased by less than half of the actual increase, the rate of capacity utilization would have fallen significantly and would have been just about 10 percent higher than the levels actually attained in 1997.

133. Although the United States confirmed, at the oral hearing, our understanding of the rates of capacity utilization in these two additional scenarios, it argued that these figures were irrelevant to the role of increased capacity and capacity utilization as possible other causes. According to the United States, the increases in capacity were largely in place by 30 June 1995, when the surge in imports started to occur. The increase in capacity is, therefore, simply a background cir-

---

[84] In examining this scenario, all other figures are assumed to be as they were in 1997.

[85] The USITC noted, in the passage quoted above, that the domestic industry was reasonably profitable at the levels of capacity utilization attained "early in the investigative period" (*supra*, para. 82).

[86] In examining this scenario, all other figures are assumed to be as they were in 1997.

cumstance and is not a relevant "other factor" causing injury "at the same time" as increased imports, under Article 4.2(b) of the *Agreement on Safeguards*.

134. We note that average available capacity in the domestic industry continued to increase between 30 June 1995 and 30 June 1997, albeit at a slower rate than between 30 June 1993 and 30 June 1995.[87] Thus, increases in capacity *were* occurring at the same time as imports were increasing. However, in any event, the relevance of an "other factor", under Article 4.2(b), depends on whether that "other factor" was, or was not, "causing injury" "at the same time" as increased imports. Therefore, the possible relevance of the increases in capacity added during the period of investigation does not depend on the moment in time when the increases in capacity occurred, but on when the effects of those increases are felt, and whether they are "causing injury" "at the same time" as increased imports. Thus, we do not accept the United States' position that the data in the USITC Report on increases in capacity and on capacity utilization are not relevant under Article 4.2(b) of the *Agreement on Safeguards*.

135. In our view, the two scenarios described above offer a revealing view of the data before the USITC. The first scenario shows that, but for the increase in average capacity, the rate of capacity utilization of the domestic industry would have been only slightly lower in 1997 than it was in 1993; the second scenario shows that, even if the increase in imports had been significantly lower than it actually was, the rate of capacity utilization would, nonetheless, have been significantly lower in 1997 than it was in 1993.

136. The data before the USITC, therefore, suggest that the increases in average available capacity in the domestic industry *may* have been very important to the overall situation of the domestic industry in 1997. We do not suggest that the increase in capacity utilization was *the sole* cause of the serious injury sustained by the domestic industry. Nor do we suggest that the increase in imports had *no* relevance to the situation of the domestic industry. Rather, we submit that the data relied upon by the USITC indicate that the relationship between the increases in average capacity, the increases in imports and the overall situation of the domestic industry was far more complex than suggested by the text of the USITC Report. On this issue, the USITC simply observed that "but for the increase in imports, the [domestic] industry would have operated at 61 percent of capacity in 1997, which is much closer to the level at which the industry operated early in the investigative period when it operated reasonably profitably." [88]

137. We are not satisfied, in light of the data that was before the USITC, that the USITC adequately evaluated the complexities of this issue and, in particular, whether the increases in average capacity, during the investigative period, were

[87] Average available capacity was: 162,856,000 pounds on 30 June 1993; 253,712,000 pounds on 30 June 1995 (an increase of 55.8%); and, 273,895,000 pounds on 30 June 1997 (a total increase of 68.2%). (USITC Report, Table C-1, p. C-4)

[88] USITC Report, p. I-17.

causing injury to the domestic industry at the same time as increased imports. Under Article 4.2(b) of the *Agreement on Safeguards*, it is essential for the competent authorities to examine whether factors other than increased imports are simultaneously causing injury. If the competent authorities do not conduct this examination, they cannot ensure that injury caused by other factors is not "attributed" to increased imports. It follows, in this case, that the USITC has *not* demonstrated adequately, as required by Article 4.2(b), that any injury caused to the domestic industry by increases in average capacity has not been "attributed" to increased imports and, in consequence, the USITC could not establish the existence of "the causal link" Article 4.2(b) requires between increased imports and serious injury.

138. Accordingly, we find that the United States acted inconsistently with its obligations under Article 4.2(b) of the *Agreement on Safeguards*.

VI. ARTICLE 2.1 OF THE AGREEMENT ON SAFEGUARDS

139. Before the Panel, the European Communities claimed that the United States' treatment of imports of wheat gluten from Canada, its partner in the North American Free Trade Agreement ("NAFTA"), was inconsistent with Articles 2.1 and 4.2 of the *Agreement on Safeguards*[89]. On this issue, the Panel concluded that:

> ... in this case, the United States has acted inconsistently with Articles 2.1 and 4.2 SA by excluding imports from Canada from the application of the safeguard measure (following a separate and subsequent inquiry concerning whether imports from Canada accounted for a "substantial share" of total imports and whether they "contributed importantly" to the "serious injury" caused by total imports) after including imports *from all sources* in its investigation of "increased imports" of wheat gluten into its territory and the consequent effects of such imports on its domestic wheat gluten industry.[90] (emphasis in original)

140. On appeal, the United States challenges the Panel's interpretation of Articles 2.1 and 4.2 of the *Agreement on Safeguards,* and argues that the Panel failed to take sufficient account of the fact that, in this case, following its determination that imports from all sources were causing serious injury, the USITC conducted a "separate and subsequent examination"[91], as part of the same investigation, concerning Canadian imports alone. In that examination, the USITC found that, although "imports from Canada account for a substantial share of total imports", those imports were "not contributing importantly to the serious injury caused by

---

89 Panel Report, paras. 8.155 and 8.156.

90 *Ibid.*, para. 8.182.

91 *Ibid.*, para. 8.161.

imports".[92] On the basis of this examination, the USITC recommended that imports from Canada be excluded from any safeguard measure adopted.[93] The United States considers that, for these reasons, it was justified in excluding imports of wheat gluten from Canada from the scope of application of the safeguard measure. The United States adds that the Panel erred in failing to assess the legal relevance of footnote 1 to the *Agreement on Safeguards* and Article XXIV of the GATT 1994 to this issue.

141. In considering the appeal of the United States on this point, we turn first to Article 2.1 of the *Agreement on Safeguards*, which provides that a safeguard measure may only be applied when "such increased quantities" of a "*product* [are] *being imported* into its territory ... under such conditions as to cause or threaten to cause serious injury to the domestic industry". As we have said, this provision, as elaborated in Article 4 of the *Agreement on Safeguards*, sets forth the *conditions* for imposing a safeguard measure.[94] Article 2.2 of the *Agreement on Safeguards*, which provides that a safeguard measure "shall be applied to a *product being imported* irrespective of its source", sets forth the rules on the *application* of a safeguard measure.[95]

142. The same phrase – "product ... being imported" – appears in *both* these paragraphs of Article 2. In view of the identity of the language in the two provisions, and in the absence of any contrary indication in the context, we believe that it is appropriate to ascribe the *same* meaning to this phrase in both Articles 2.1 and 2.2. To include imports from all sources in the determination that increased imports are causing serious injury, and then to exclude imports from one source from the application of the measure, would be to give the phrase "product being imported" a *different* meaning in Articles 2.1 and 2.2 of the *Agreement on Safeguards*. In Article 2.1, the phrase would embrace imports from *all* sources whereas, in Article 2.2, it would exclude imports from certain sources. This would be incongruous and unwarranted. In the usual course, therefore, the imports included in the determinations made under Articles 2.1 and 4.2 should correspond to the imports included in the application of the measure, under Article 2.2.[96]

143. In the present case, the United States asserts that the exclusion of imports from Canada from the scope of the safeguard measure was justified because, following its investigation based on imports from *all* sources, the USITC conducted

[92] USITC Report, p. I-19.
[93] *Ibid.*, p. I-29.
[94] See, *supra*, para. 76; Appellate Body Report, *Argentina – Footwear Safeguards, supra*, footnote 22, para. 112.
[95] *Ibid.*
[96] The United States relies on Article 9.1 of the *Agreement on Safeguards* in support of its argument that the scope of the serious injury investigation need not correspond exactly to the scope of application of a safeguard measure. Article 9.1 is an exception to the general rules set out in the *Agreement on Safeguards* that applies only to developing country Members. We do not consider that it is of relevance to this appeal.

an additional inquiry specifically focused on imports from Canada. The United States claims, in effect, that the scope of its initial investigation, *together with its subsequent and additional inquiry* into imports from Canada, did correspond with the scope of application of its safeguard measure.

144. In our view, however, although the USITC examined the importance of imports from Canada separately, it did not make any explicit determination relating to increased imports, *excluding imports from Canada.* In other words, although the safeguard measure was applied to imports from all sources, *excluding* Canada, the USITC did not establish explicitly that imports from these *same* sources, excluding Canada, satisfied the conditions for the application of a safeguard measure, as set out in Article 2.1 and elaborated in Article 4.2 of the *Agreement on Safeguards.* Thus, we find that the separate examination of imports from Canada carried out by the USITC in this case was not a sufficient basis for the safeguard measure ultimately applied by the United States.

145. Lastly, we note that the United States has argued that the Panel erred in failing to address Article XXIV of the GATT 1994, and in failing to set out a "basic rationale" for finding that footnote 1 to the *Agreement on Safeguards* did not affect its reasoning on this issue. In this case, the Panel determined that this dispute does not raise the issue of whether, as a general principle, a member of a free-trade area can exclude imports from other members of that free-trade area from the application of a safeguard measure.[97] The Panel also found that it could rule on the claim of the European Communities without having recourse to Article XXIV or footnote 1 to the *Agreement on Safeguards.*[98] We see no error in this approach, and make no findings on these arguments.

146. We, therefore, uphold the Panel's finding, in paragraph 8.182 of the Panel Report, that the United States acted inconsistently with its obligations under Articles 2.1 and 4.2 of the *Agreement on Safeguards.*

VII. ARTICLES 8 AND 12 OF THE *AGREEMENT ON SAFEGUARDS*

147. The United States appeals the Panel's findings that the United States acted inconsistently with Articles 12.1(a), 12.1(b), 12.1(c), 12.3 and Article 8.1 of the *Agreement on Safeguards.* The United States contends that the Panel misinterpreted the requirement of "immediate" notification set forth in Article 12.1, erred in its analysis of the relationship between the various obligations set forth in Articles 12.1, 12.2, and 12.3 of the *Agreement on Safeguards*, and wrongly entwined the separate obligations set out in these provisions.

---

[97] Panel Report, 8.183.

[98] *Ibid.*, para. 8.181.

A. *Article 12.1 of the Agreement on Safeguards*

148. Article 12.1 of the *Agreement on Safeguards* provides:

> A Member shall immediately notify the Committee on Safeguards upon:
>
> (a) initiating an investigatory process relating to serious injury or threat thereof and the reasons for it;
>
> (b) making a finding of serious injury or threat thereof caused by increased imports; and
>
> (c) taking a decision to apply or extend a safeguard measure.

Thus, Article 12.1 of the *Agreement on Safeguards* sets out three separate obligations to make notification to the Committee on Safeguards, each of which is triggered "upon" the occurrence of an event specified in one of the three subparagraphs. The chapeau to Article 12.1 stipulates that the notifications must be made "*immediately* ... upon" the occurrence of the triggering events. (emphasis added)

149. Before turning to the United States' appeal of the Panel's findings under each subparagraph of Article 12.1, we begin with the meaning of the word "immediately" in Article 12.1, since it governs timeliness under all three of these subparagraphs. The Panel found that the obligation to notify "immediately" precludes a Member from "unduly delaying the notification of the decisions or findings mentioned in Article 12.1(a) through (c) SA".[99]

150. The United States argues, however, that "immediately" means "without any delay that would interfere with Members' ability to review the measure through the Safeguards Committee or would leave a Member insufficient time to decide whether to request consultations." [100]

151. As regards the meaning of the word "immediately" in the chapeau to Article 12.1, we agree with the Panel that the ordinary meaning of the word "implies a certain urgency".[101] The degree of urgency or immediacy required depends on a case-by-case assessment, account being taken of the administrative difficulties involved in preparing the notification, and also of the character of the information supplied. As previous panels have recognized, relevant factors in this regard may include the complexity of the notification and the need for translation into one of the WTO's official languages.[102] Clearly, however, the amount of time

---

[99] Panel Report, para. 8.194.

[100] United States' appellant's submission, para. 208.

[101] Panel Report, para. 8.193.

[102] Panel report, *Korea – Definitive Safeguard Measure on Imports of Certain Dairy Products*, ("*Korea – Dairy Safeguard*"), WT/DS98/R and Corr. 1, adopted 12 January 2000, DSR "000:I, 49, para. 7.128, as modified by the Appellate Body Report, quoted in para. 8.193 of the Panel Report.

taken to prepare the notification must, in all cases, be kept to a minimum, as the underlying obligation is to notify "immediately".

152. "Immediate" notification is that which allows the Committee on Safeguards, and Members, the *fullest possible period* to reflect upon and react to an ongoing safeguard investigation. Anything less than "immediate" notification curtails this period. We do not, therefore, agree with the United States that the requirement of "*immediate*" notification is satisfied as long as the Committee on Safeguards and Members of the WTO have *sufficient* time to review that notification. In our view, whether a Member has made an "immediate" notification does not depend on evidence as to how the Committee on Safeguards and individual Members of the WTO actually use that notification. Nor can the requirement of "immediate" notification depend on an *ex post facto* assessment of whether individual Members suffered actual prejudice through an insufficiency in the notification period.

153. With this meaning of "immediately" in mind, we turn to the timeliness of the notifications made by the United States under subparagraphs (a) through (c) of Article 12.1.

1. Notification Pursuant to Article 12.1(a)

154. The United States appeals the Panel's finding that the United States did not notify its initiation of a safeguard investigation "immediately", as required by Article 12.1(a) of the *Agreement on Safeguards.*[103]

155. The Panel found that the United States initiated a safeguards investigation regarding imports of wheat gluten on *1 October 1997*, and notified the Committee of Safeguards on *17 October 1997* (that is, 16 days later).[104] The Panel noted the "minimal" information contained in that notification, and held that the United States had not acted consistently with its obligation under Article 12.1(a) to notify its initiation of a safeguard investigation "immediately".[105]

156. On appeal, the United States argues that the notification was submitted "immediately" because it was sufficiently prompt as to allow Members concerned to review the notification and to exercise fully their rights under the *Agreement on Safeguards.* The United States does not argue that there were any particular reasons that a period of 16 days was needed to make this notification.

157. We recall our analysis of the word "immediately".[106] In this case, the United States' notification under Article 12.1(a) consisted of a single page form attaching a notice from the USITC that it had initiated a safeguard investigation concerning wheat gluten. The USITC notice was published in the United States

---

103 Panel Report, para. 8.197.
104 *Ibid.*, para. 8.191; G/SG/N/6/USA/4.
105 *Ibid.*, para. 8.196.
106 *Supra*, paras. 103-106.

Federal Register on 1 October 1997.[107] That same document was not notified to the Committee on Safeguards until 17 October 1997.

158. In these circumstances, we see no basis for concluding that the Panel erred in finding that a notification period of 16 days was not "immediate". We, therefore, uphold the Panel's finding that the United States' notification of its investigation of a safeguard measure did not satisfy the requirement of "immediate" notification under Article 12.1(a) of the *Agreement on Safeguards*.[108]

2. *Notification Pursuant to Article 12.1(b)*

159. The United States appeals the Panel's finding that the United States did not notify its determination of serious injury "immediately", as required by Article 12.1(b) of the *Agreement on Safeguards*.

160. The Panel found that the USITC made a determination of serious injury caused by increased imports on *15 January 1998*, and that the United States notified the Committee on Safeguards of this determination in a communication dated *11 February 1998* (that is, 26 days later).[109] In view of the 26-day time-period taken by the United States to make its notification under Article 12.1(b), the Panel concluded that the United States had not satisfied the requirement to notify its finding of serious injury "immediately".[110]

161. On appeal, the United States makes the same arguments with respect to this finding as it made with respect to the Panel's finding under Article 12.1(a), namely that the notification was submitted "immediately" because it was sufficiently prompt as to allow Members concerned to review the notification and to exercise fully their rights under the *Agreement on Safeguards*. Once again, the United States does not offer any particular justification for the time-period of 26 days.

162. We recall again our analysis of the word "immediately".[111] We also note that the 11 February 1998 notification submitted by the United States consisted, in its entirety, of a single page in which the United States indicated that the USITC Report would follow at a later date.[112] In these circumstances, we see no basis for concluding that the Panel erred in finding that notification in a period of 26 days was not "immediate". We, therefore, uphold the Panel's finding that the notification made by the United States on 11 February 1998 did not satisfy the re-

---

[107] United States Federal Register, 1 October 1997 (Volume 62, Number 190), pp. 51488-51489.

[108] Panel Report, para. 8.197.

[109] G/SG/N/8/USA/2.

[110] Panel Report, para. 8.199.

[111] *Supra*, paras. 103-106.

[112] G/SG/N/8/USA/2. Panel Report., para. 8.191. The USITC Report was sent to the President of the United States on 18 March 1998, and forwarded, along with a revised Article 12.1(b) notification, to the Committee on Safeguards on 24 March 1998. G/SG/N/8/USA/2/Rev.1.

quirement of "immediate" notification under Article 12.1(b) of the *Agreement on Safeguards.*[113]

3. *Notification Pursuant to Article 12.1(c)*

163. The United States also appeals the Panel's finding that the United States did not notify its decision to apply a safeguard measure "immediately", as required by Article 12.1(c) of the *Agreement on Safeguards.*

164. The Panel found that, on *30 May 1998*, the President of the United States decided to apply, effective 1 June 1998, a safeguard measure on imports of wheat gluten and that, on *4 June 1998* (that is, 5 days after the decision was taken), the United States notified the Committee on Safeguards of the decision to apply a safeguard measure.[114] In assessing the timeliness of this notification, the Panel concluded that:

> ... the United States notification of this decision *after the measure had been implemented*, violated the United States obligation under Article 12 SA to make timely notification under Article 12.1 (c) SA of its decision to apply a measure.[115] (emphasis added)

165. The United States appeals this finding on the ground that the Panel erred by interpreting Article 12.1(c) of the *Agreement on Safeguards* as requiring notification of a "decision to apply or extend a safeguard measure" *prior to* implementation of that decision.

166. In examining the ordinary meaning of Article 12.1(c), we observe that the relevant triggering event is the "*taking*" of a decision. To us, Article 12.1(c) is focused upon whether a "decision" has *occurred*, or has been "taken", and not on whether that decision has been *given effect.* On the face of the text, the timeliness of a notification under Article 12.1(c) depends only on whether the notification was immediate.

167. The Panel considered that Article 12.2 of the *Agreement on Safeguards*, which, in its opening clause, specifically refers to notifications made pursuant to Articles 12.1(b) and 12.1(c), provides relevant context in determining the timeliness of notifications under Article 12.1(c). Article 12.2 provides:

> *In making the notifications referred to in paragraphs 1(b) and 1(c),* the Member *proposing* to apply or extend a safeguard measure shall provide the Committee on Safeguards with all pertinent information, which shall include evidence of serious injury or threat thereof caused by increased imports, precise description of the product involved and the *proposed* measure, proposed date of

[113] Panel Report, para. 8.199.

[114] G/SG/N/10/USA/2 and G/SG/N/11/USA/2.

[115] Panel Report, para. 8.207.

> introduction, expected duration and timetable for progressive liberalization. ... (emphasis added)

168. The Panel deduced from this provision that a notification under Article 12.1(c) must be of a "proposed measure" and its "proposed date of introduction", and, on that basis, concluded that a notification under Article 12.1(c) must be made *before* implementation of the "proposed" safeguard measure.[116]

169. Article 12.2 is related to, and complements, Article 12.1 of the *Agreement on Safeguards*. Whereas Article 12.1 sets forth *when* notifications must be made during an investigation, Article 12.2 clarifies *what* detailed information must be contained in the notifications under Articles 12.1(b) and 12.1(c). We do not, however, see the content requirements of Article 12.2 as prescribing *when* the notification under 12.1(c) must take place. Rather, in our view, timeliness under 12.1(c) is determined by whether a decision to apply or extend a safeguard measure is notified "immediately". A *separate* question arises as to whether notifications made by the Member satisfy the content requirements of Article 12.2. Answering this separate question requires examination of whether, in its notifications under *either* Article 12.1(b) *or* Article 12.1(c), the Member proposing to apply a safeguard measure has notified "all pertinent information", including the "mandatory components" [117] specifically enumerated in Article 12.2.

170. Thus, the obligations set forth under Articles 12.1(b), 12.1(c) and 12.2 relate to different aspects of the notification process. Although related, these obligations are discrete. A Member could notify "all pertinent information" in its Articles 12.1(b) and 12.1(c) notifications, and thereby satisfy Article 12.2, but still act inconsistently with Article 12.1 because the relevant notifications were not made "immediately". Similarly, a Member could satisfy the Article 12.1 requirement of "immediate" notification, but act inconsistently with Article 12.2 if the content of its notifications was deficient.

171. In our view, in finding that the United States acted inconsistently with Article 12.1(c) *solely because* the decision to apply a safeguard measure was notified after that decision had been implemented, the Panel confused the separate obligations imposed on Members pursuant to Article 12.1(c) and Article 12.2 and, thereby, added another layer to the timeliness requirements in Article 12.1(c). Instead of insisting on "immediate" notification, as stipulated by Article 12.1(c), the Panel required notification to be made *both* "immediately" *and* before implementation of the safeguard measure. We see no basis in Article 12.1(c) for this conclusion.

172. In consequence, we reverse the Panel's finding that:

> ... the United States notification of this decision after the measure had been implemented, violated the United States obligation under

[116] Panel Report, paras. 8.202, 8.205 and 8.206.

[117] Appellate Body Report, *Korea – Dairy Safeguard, supra*, footnote 29, para. 107.

> Article 12 SA to make timely notification under Article 12.1 (c) SA of its decision to apply a measure.[118]

173. Although we have reversed the Panel's finding on this issue, we believe that we should complete the legal analysis on the basis of the factual findings of the Panel or the undisputed facts in the Panel record.[119] In examining the timeliness of the United States' notification under Article 12.1(c), we recall that the United States made the notification to the Committee on Safeguards in a communication dated 4 June 1998, or 5 days after the President of the United States had "taken the decision" to apply the safeguard measure. Although the Panel did not reach the issue of whether the 4 June notification had been submitted "immediately", it nevertheless stated:

> We note in passing that the delay of 5 days between the decision to apply a safeguard measure and the notification thereof might well satisfy the requirement of immediate notification of Article 12.1 SA.[120]

174. In response to questioning at the oral hearing, the European Communities also accepted that a delay of 5 days "could have been" consistent with the obligation of "immediate" notification under Article 12.1(c).

175. We believe that notification within 5 days was, in this case, consistent with the requirement of "immediacy" contained in Article 12.1(c) of the *Agreement on Safeguards*. In this regard, we consider it relevant that notification was made the day after the decision of the President of the United States was published in the United States Federal Register[121], and during the course of the fourth working day following the taking of the decision.[122]

176. In sum, as regards the findings made by the Panel under Article 12.1 of the *Agreement on Safeguards*, we uphold the Panel's findings, in paragraphs 8.197 and 8.199 of the Panel Report, that the United States did not satisfy the requirements of immediate notification set out in Articles 12.1(a) and 12.1(b);

---

[118] Panel Report, para. 8.207.

[119] For example, in Appellate Body Report, *United States – Standards for Reformulated and Conventional Gasoline* ("*US – Gasoline*"), WT/DS2/AB/R, adopted 20 May 1996, DSR 1996:I, 3, at 17 ff; Appellate Body Report, *Canada – Certain Measures Concerning Periodicals* ("*Canada – Periodicals*"), WT/DS31/AB/R, adopted 30 July 1997, DSR 1997:I, 449, at 468 ff; Appellate Body Report, *European Communities – Measures Affecting the Importation of Certain Poultry Products* ("*EC – Poultry*"), WT/DS69/AB/R, adopted 23 July 1998, DSR 1998:V, 2031, paras. 154 ff; Appellate Body Report, *United States – Import Prohibition of Certain Shrimp and Shrimp Products* ("*US – Shrimp*"), WT/DS58/AB/R, adopted 6 November 1998, DSR 1998:VII, 2755, paras. 123 ff; and, Appellate Body Report, *Australia – Measures Affecting Importation of Salmon* ("*Australia – Salmon*"), WT/DS18/AB/R, adopted 6 November 1998, DSR 1998:VIII, 3327, paras. 117 ff.

[120] Panel Report, para. 8.207.

[121] United States Federal Register, 3 June 1998 (Volume 63, Number 106), pp. 30363-30364.

[122] The decision to apply the measure was taken by the United States President on 30 May, 1998, a Saturday. The measure came into effect on Monday, 1 June, and notification was made on the following Thursday, 4 June 1998.

and we reverse the Panel's finding, in paragraph 8.207 of the Panel Report, that the United States failed to make timely notification under Article 12.1(c) of the *Agreement on Safeguards* of its decision to apply a safeguard measure.

B. Article 12.3 of the Agreement on Safeguards

177. The United States further appeals the Panel's findings that the United States acted inconsistently with Article 12.3 of the *Agreement on Safeguards*. Article 12.3 provides:

> A Member proposing to apply or extend a safeguard measure shall provide adequate opportunity for prior consultations with those Members having a substantial interest as exporters of the product concerned, with a view to, *inter alia*, reviewing the information provided under paragraph 2, exchanging views on the measure and reaching an understanding on ways to achieve the objective set out in paragraph 1 of Article 8.

178. As regards the consistency of the actions taken by the United States with Article 12.3, the Panel stated:

> We found above that the United States did not provide a timely notification under Article 12.1 (c) SA of its proposed final measure since the United States notified its decision to apply a measure three days after the measure had been implemented. *For the same reason,* we find that the United States violated the obligation of Article 12.3 SA to provide adequate opportunity for prior consultations on the measure.[123] (emphasis added)

179. It is clear from the above excerpt that the Panel's conclusion that the United States acted inconsistently with Article 12.3 flowed directly ("for the same reason") from its finding that the United States acted inconsistently with Article 12.1(c). In the previous section, we determined that the Panel erred in concluding that the United States acted inconsistently with Article 12.1(c) of the *Agreement on Safeguards*. Since we have found that the Panel erred in its interpretation of Article 12.1(c), we also believe that the Panel erred in concluding that the United States had "*[f]or the same reason* ... violated the obligation of Article 12.3 SA".

180. The Panel, however, revisited the issue of the adequacy of consultations under Article 12.3 as part of its evaluation of the European Communities' claim under Article 8.1 of the *Agreement on Safeguards*. The Panel found that:

> While the parties have confirmed that consultations did take place on the basis of the United States notifications under Article 12.1(b) concerning the USITC's finding of serious injury and the USITC's

---

[123] Panel Report, para. 8.219.

> recommendations on remedy, no consultations were held on the final proposed measure as approved by the United States President on 30 May 1998. Therefore, the Panel considers that, while consultations may have been held on the basis of the notifications made by the United States under Article 12.1(b) SA, the United States did not provide "an adequate opportunity for prior consultations" on this final proposed measure, within the meaning of Article 12.3 SA.[124]

181. On appeal, the United States argues that it complied with Article 12.3 because, in its notifications under Article 12.1(b) of the *Agreement on Safeguards*, the United States supplied all the information required by Article 12.2 of that Agreement. As a result, the United States contends that, prior to consultations, the European Communities knew the precise product under consideration, the evidence of serious injury caused by increased imports, and all relevant details relating to the proposed measure. The United States concludes, therefore, that it provided the European Communities with an "adequate opportunity for prior consultations", as required by Article 12.3 of the *Agreement on Safeguards*.

182. We note, first, that Article 12.3 requires a Member proposing to apply a safeguard measure to provide an "adequate opportunity for prior consultations" with Members with a substantial interest in exporting the product concerned. Article 12.3 states that an "adequate opportunity" for consultations is to be provided "with a view to": reviewing the information furnished pursuant to Article 12.2; exchanging views on the measure; and reaching an understanding with exporting Members on an equivalent level of concessions. In view of these objectives, we consider that Article 12.3 requires a Member proposing to apply a safeguard measure to provide exporting Members with sufficient information and time to allow for the possibility, through consultations, for a meaningful exchange on the issues identified. To us, it follows from the text of Article 12.3 itself that information on the *proposed* measure must be provided in *advance* of the consultations, so that the consultations can adequately address that measure. Moreover, the reference, in Article 12.3, to "the information provided under" Article 12.2, indicates that Article 12.2 identifies the information that is needed to enable meaningful consultations to occur under Article 12.3. Among the list of "mandatory components" [125] regarding information identified in Article 12.2 are: a precise description of the *proposed* measure, and its *proposed* date of introduction.

183. Thus, in our view, an exporting Member will not have an "adequate opportunity" under Article 12.3 to negotiate overall equivalent concessions through consultations unless, prior to those consultations, it has obtained, *inter alia*, suffi-

---

[124] Panel Report, para. 8.217.

[125] Appellate Body Report, *Korea – Dairy Safeguard, supra*, footnote 29, para. 107.

ciently detailed information on the form of the proposed measure, including the nature of the remedy.

184. With these considerations in mind, we examine whether, in this case, the Panel erred in finding that the United States did not provide the European Communities with an "adequate opportunity for prior consultations" on the proposed safeguard measure, as required by Article 12.3 of the *Agreement on Safeguards.*

185. The Panel found that the United States and the European Communities held consultations on 24 April 1998 and 22 May 1998 [126], and that these consultations were held *on the basis of the information provided by the United States in its notifications under Article 12.1(b)* [127], that is, on the basis of the information contained in the USITC Report. The Panel also found, as a matter of fact, that no consultations were held on the final measure that was approved by the United States President on 30 May 1998.[128]

186. We note that the USITC Report set out a number of "recommendations" to the President of the United States, including:

> ... that, within the overall quantitative restriction, the President allocate separate quantitative restrictions for the European Union, Australia, and "all other" non-excluded countries, taking into account the disproportional growth and impact of imports of wheat gluten from the European Union ...[129]

187. We note that the recommendations made by the USITC did *not* include specific numerical quota shares for the individual exporting Members concerned, and the recommendations imply, without providing details, that the individual quota shares could be less favourable to imports from the European Communities. We consider that these "recommendations" did not allow the European Communities to assess accurately the likely impact of the measure being contemplated, nor to consult adequately on overall equivalent concessions with the United States.

188. Accordingly, we see no error in the Panel's conclusion that the United States' notifications under Article 12.1(b) did not provide a description of the measure under consideration sufficiently precise as to allow the European Communities to conduct meaningful consultations with the United States, as required by Article 12.3 of the *Agreement on Safeguards.*[130]

---

[126] Panel Report, para. 8.218.

[127] *Ibid.*, para. 8.217.

[128] *Ibid.*

[129] USITC Report, p. I-3. See, also, USITC Report, p. I-29.

[130] We note that, in so finding, we do not consider it necessary to determine whether the United States notified a "proposed measure" to the European Communities as required by Article 12.2 of the *Agreement on Safeguards*, as the European Communities did not argue specifically that the United States had acted inconsistently with Article 12.2.

189. We, therefore, uphold the Panel's finding that the United States did not comply with its obligation under Article 12.3 of the *Agreement on Safeguards* to provide an adequate opportunity for prior consultations on the proposed safeguard measure.

C. Article 8.1 of the Agreement on Safeguards

190. The United States also appeals the Panel's finding that it acted inconsistently with its obligations under Article 8.1 of the *Agreement on Safeguards.*[131] Article 8.1 provides:

> A Member proposing to apply a safeguard measure or seeking an extension of a safeguard measure shall endeavour to maintain a substantially equivalent level of concessions and other obligations to that existing under GATT 1994 between it and the exporting Members which would be affected by such a measure, in accordance with the provisions of paragraph 3 of Article 12. To achieve this objective, the Members concerned may agree on any adequate means of trade compensation for the adverse effects of the measure on their trade.

191. Article 8.1 imposes an obligation on Members to "endeavour to maintain" equivalent concessions with affected exporting Members. The efforts made by a Member to this end must be "in accordance with the provisions of" Article 12.3 of the *Agreement on Safeguards.*

192. In view of this explicit link between Articles 8.1 and 12.3 of the *Agreement on Safeguards*, a Member cannot, in our view, "endeavour to maintain" an adequate balance of concessions unless it has, as a first step, provided an adequate opportunity for prior consultations on a proposed measure. We have upheld the Panel's findings that the United States did not provide an adequate opportunity for consultations, as required by Article 12.3 of the *Agreement on Safeguards*. For the same reasons, we also uphold the Panel's finding, in paragraph 8.219 of its Report, that the United States acted inconsistently with its obligations under Article 8.1 of the *Agreement on Safeguards.*

VIII. ARTICLE 11 OF THE DSU

193. At the outset of its findings in this dispute, the Panel articulated a standard of review that was based on Article 11 of the DSU.[132] The Panel said that it would not be appropriate for it to conduct a *de novo* review of the facts of the

---

[131] Panel Report, para. 8.219.

[132] Panel Report, paras. 8.4 and 8.5.

case, nor should it adopt a policy of "total deference" to the findings of the USITC.[133] Instead, the appropriate standard was an "objective assessment".

194. The European Communities agrees, as a general matter, with this articulation of the standard of review. However, it considers that the Panel failed properly to apply this standard of review. The European Communities makes a general assertion that the Panel failed to make an objective assessment "because [the Panel] failed to provide an adequate and reasonable explanation for its findings".[134] In addition, the European Communities asserts that:

> [the] Panel's failure to obtain the relevant information claimed to be confidential by the US and its decline [sic] to draw the necessary adverse inferences from the US's refusal to submit the requested information amount to an error of law that permeates several of the Panel's findings.[135]

For each of these arguments, the European Communities lists a series of paragraphs in the Panel Report which it considers are tainted by these errors.[136] Thereafter, the European Communities sets forth detailed arguments relating to four specific issues under Article 11 of the DSU which we understand are intended to substantiate the general assertions made. The four specific issues are: the treatment of "productivity" under Article 4.2(a) of the *Agreement on Safeguards*; the treatment of "profits and losses" under Article 4.2(a) of the Agreement; the treatment of the protein content of wheat under Article 4.2(a) of the Agreement; and the treatment of confidential information.

195. We note that the European Communities' appeal, insofar as it relates to the findings of serious injury, is limited to its arguments under Article 11 and the Panel's appreciation of the evidence. In addressing these arguments, we will examine the four specific issues highlighted by the European Communities to substantiate its more general assertions. We underline that we are not called upon to examine whether the Panel has properly applied the exacting legal standard in the *Agreement on Safeguards* relating to "serious injury".

196. Before turning to the European Communities specific arguments under Article 11 of the DSU, we recall that, in previous appeals, we have emphasized that the role of the Appellate Body differs from the role of panels. Under Article 17.6 of the DSU, appeals are "limited to *issues of law* covered in the panel report and *legal* interpretations developed by the panel". (emphasis added) By contrast, we have previously stated that, under Article 11 of the DSU, panels are:

> ... charged with the mandate to determine the *facts* of the case and to arrive at *factual findings*. In carrying out this mandate, a panel has the duty to examine and consider all the evidence before it, not

[133] *Ibid.*, para. 8.5.
[134] European Communities' other appellant's submission, para. 25.
[135] *Ibid.*, para. 27.
[136] *Ibid.*, paras. 25 and 27.

just the evidence submitted by one or the other party, and to evaluate the relevance and probative force of each piece thereof.[137] (emphasis added)

197. We have also stated previously that, although the task of panels under Article 11 relates, in part, to its assessment of the *facts*, the question whether a panel has made an "objective assessment" of the facts is a *legal* one, that may be the subject of an appeal.[138] (emphasis added) However, in view of the distinction between the respective roles of the Appellate Body and panels, we have taken care to emphasize that a panel's appreciation of the evidence falls, in principle, "within the *scope of the panel's discretion as the trier of facts*".[139] (emphasis added) In assessing the panel's appreciation of the evidence, we cannot base a finding of inconsistency under Article 11 simply on the conclusion that we might have reached a different factual finding from the one the panel reached. Rather, we must be satisfied that the panel has exceeded the bounds of its discretion, as the trier of facts, in its appreciation of the evidence. As is clear from previous appeals, we will not interfere lightly with the panel's exercise of its discretion.[140]

A. USITC's Treatment of "Productivity"

198. Article 4.2(a) of the *Agreement on Safeguards* refers to "productivity" as one of the enumerated "particular" relevant factors. Before the Panel, the European Communities claimed that the USITC failed properly to evaluate "productivity", as required by Article 4.2(a).[141] The Panel concluded, to the contrary, that "the data and statements pertaining to worker productivity, in conjunction with those on capital investments, in the overall context of the USITC Report, indicate that the USITC *considered* industry productivity as required by Article 4.2(a)." [142] (emphasis added)

---

[137] Appellate Body Report, *Korea – Dairy Safeguard*, *supra*, footnote 29, para. 137.

[138] Appellate Body Report, *EC Measures Concerning Meat and Meat Products (Hormones)* ("*European Communities – Hormones*"), WT/DS26/AB/R, WT/DS48/AB/R, adopted 13 February 1998, DSR 1998:I, 135, at 183, para. 132.

[139] Appellate Body Report, *Korea – Taxes on Alcoholic Beverages* ("*Korea – Alcoholic Beverages*"), WT/DS75/AB/R, WT/DS84/AB/R, adopted 17 February 1999, DSR 1999:I, 3, paras. 161 and 162.

[140] Appellate Body Report, *European Communities – Hormones*, *supra*, footnote 138, at 183 – 188, paras. 131 – 142; Appellate Body Report, *EC – Poultry*, *supra*, footnote 119, paras. 131 –136; Appellate Body Report, *Australia – Salmon*, *supra*, footnote 119, paras. 262 – 267; Appellate Body Report, *Korea – Alcoholic Beverages*, *supra*, footnote 139, paras. 159 – 165; Appellate Body Report, *Japan – Measures Affecting Agricultural Products* ("*Japan – Agricultural Products II*"), WT/DS76/AB/R, adopted 19 March 1999, DSR 1999:I, 277, paras. 140 – 142; Appellate Body Report, *India – Quantitative Restrictions on Agricultural, Textile and Industrial Products* ("*India – Quantitative Restrictions*"), WT/DS90/AB/R, adopted 22 September 1999, DSR 1999:IV, 1763, paras. 149 and 151; and, Appellate Body Report, *Korea – Dairy Safeguard*, *supra*, footnote 29, paras. 137 and 138.

[141] Panel Report, para. 8.43.

[142] *Ibid.*, para. 8.45.

199. As we understand it, the European Communities' appeal, on this point, is that the Panel erred, under Article 11 of the DSU, because the evidence before the Panel was not sufficient to support the conclusion that the "USITC *considered* industry productivity as required by Article 4.2(a)." [143] (emphasis added) In that respect, we note that neither the European Communities nor the United States appeals the Panel's interpretation of the word "productivity" [144] in Article 4.2(a) of the *Agreement on Safeguards*. Therefore, we do not address this question. We also note that the European Communities has not appealed the Panel's finding on the grounds that it erred in interpreting and applying either Articles 3.1 or 4.2(c) of the *Agreement on Safeguards*, which require the competent authorities to provide, respectively, "reasoned conclusions", as well as a "demonstration of the relevance of the factors examined". Nor does the European Communities assert that the Panel's treatment of "productivity" amounted to an error under Article 4.2(a) of the *Agreement on Safeguards*. Instead, the European Communities' appeal on this point is confined to the Panel's appreciation of the evidence under Article 11 of the DSU.

200. The European Communities submits that the Panel could not make an objective assessment of whether the USITC had evaluated "productivity" because the Panel had before it no specific numerical *data* on "productivity".[145] We recall that it is not part of our mandate to examine the facts afresh. Rather, we confine ourselves to determining whether the Panel has made an "objective assessment" of the facts under Article 11 of the DSU.[146]

201. The Panel noted that the USITC had dealt expressly with "worker productivity" and "capital investments".[147] In that respect, the USITC Report stated that worker productivity was at its "lowest level" during the investigative period in 1997 and that "unit labor costs almost doubled during the period examined."[148] It is also clear from the USITC Report that the domestic industry introduced considerable new capacity during the investigative period, which implies significant capital investment.[149] However, as the USITC noted, there "was a significant idling of productive facilities in the industry over the period examined", evidenced by the fall in the rate of capacity utilization.[150] We agree with the Panel that the USITC could have provided a more comprehensive analysis of "productivity".[151] However, although the evidence the Panel relied on is limited in nature, there are, in our view, insufficient grounds for concluding that the Panel erred, under Article 11 of the DSU, in finding that the USITC had "considered industry

[143] *Ibid.*
[144] *Ibid.*, para. 8.44.
[145] European Communities' other appellant's submission, para. 68.
[146] See *supra*, paras. 150 and 151.
[147] Panel Report, para. 8.45.
[148] USITC Report, p. I-14.
[149] *Ibid.*, p. I-12.
[150] *Ibid.*
[151] Panel Report, para. 8.45.

productivity as required by Article 4.2(a)." [152] We, therefore, decline the European Communities' appeal on this point.

B. *USITC's Treatment of "Profits and Losses"*

202. Article 4.2(a) of the *Agreement on Safeguards* refers to "profits and losses" as one of the enumerated "particular" relevant factors. Relying on our statement in *Argentina – Footwear Safeguards*, that Article 4.2 of the *Agreement on Safeguards* requires the competent authorities "adequately [to] explain[ ] how the facts support[ ] the determinations that were made" [153], the European Communities claimed, before the Panel, that the United States acted inconsistently with Article 4.2 because the "USITC [did] not provide an adequate explanation for the determination made" with respect to profits and losses.[154] One aspect of that claim related to the alleged failure of the USITC to explain the methodology that it had applied to allocate profits among wheat gluten, wheat starch, and derived products. These products are all produced from a single raw material input, wheat or wheat flour, using a single production line. The allocation of costs and revenues among these co-products will, therefore, have an influence on the apparent profitability (or losses) made on production of any of the co-products.

203. In addressing the issue of the appropriate methodology, the USITC stated:

> The Commission received usable financial data on wheat gluten operations from three of the four domestic producers of wheat gluten, Midland, Manildra, and Heartland. These three firms accounted for the substantial majority of domestic production of wheat gluten. Each of the companies produces wheat gluten and wheat starch in a joint production process. Each of the companies also produces other by-products or related products, especially alcohol. We carefully considered the arguments made by respondents with respect to the allocations made by domestic producers in providing financial data on their wheat gluten operations. *Based on a careful review of the allocation methodologies used by domestic wheat gluten producers in responding to the Commission's questionnaire, we find those allocations to be appropriate.*" [155] (emphasis added)

204. After referring to this statement, the Panel observed that it had "asked the United States to clarify the nature of the 'careful review' the USITC had performed and to clarify and elaborate upon the 'allocation methodologies' referred

---

[152] *Ibid.*

[153] Appellate Body Report, *Argentina – Footwear Safeguards*, *supra*, footnote 22, para. 121.

[154] Panel Report, para. 8.47.

[155] USITC Report, p. I-13. Footnote 57, attached to this *para.* of the USITC Report, provides "Report at II-20, 19-21 (supporting information on these pages of the report is confidential business information)."

to."[156] The Panel set out, at length, the "clarifications" provided by the United States and noted that the USITC "could have included ... a more detailed explanation as to how and why the USITC considered the allocations to be 'appropriate' ...".[157] However, the Panel concluded that "the *USITC Report provides an adequate, reasoned and reasonable explanation with respect to 'profits and losses'* and that the United States did not act inconsistently with Article 4.2(a) of the *Agreement on Safeguards* in this regard."[158] (emphasis added) In reaching this conclusion, the Panel relied on the statements in the USITC Report quoted above and the "clarifications given by the United States".[159]

205. The European Communities argues, on appeal, that the Panel erred, under Article 11 of the DSU, because it did not have sufficient facts before it to justify its conclusion on this issue. In other words, the evidence did not provide an objective basis for the Panel's conclusion. At the oral hearing, the European Communities drew particular attention to the fact that the *USITC* itself gives only a single sentence explanation to justify its conclusion that the allocation methodologies are "appropriate".[160]

206. We recall that, under Article 3.1 of the *Agreement on Safeguards, the competent authorities* must "publish a *report*" which provides "reasoned conclusions" on "all pertinent issues". (emphasis added) Under Article 4.2(c), that *report* must also contain "a detailed analysis", including "a demonstration of the relevance of the factors examined". We observe that the Panel concluded, on the allocation methodologies, that it was "the *USITC Report*" which "provides an adequate, reasoned and reasonable explanation with respect to 'profits and losses'".[161] (emphasis added) Support for this conclusion must, therefore, be based on evidence drawn from the *USITC Report itself.* The only evidence, in that Report, that the Panel had to support this conclusion was the statement by the USITC that it had "carefully reviewed" and "considered" the allocation methodologies used by the producers.[162] In reaching its conclusion that the *USITC Report* gave an adequate explanation, the Panel placed considerable reliance on the "clarifications" given by the *United States* in response to the Panel's questions on

[156] Panel Report, para. 8.61.
[157] *Ibid.*, paras. 8.61, 8.62 and 8.64.
[158] *Ibid.*, para. 8.66.
[159] *Ibid.*, para. 8.65.
[160] In response to a question at the oral hearing the European Communities referred to the following sentence from the USITC Report: "Based on a careful review of the allocation methodologies used by domestic wheat gluten producers in responding to the Commission's questionnaire, we find those allocations to be appropriate" (USITC Report, p. I-13).
[161] Panel Report, para. 8.66.
[162] See the excerpt from the USITC Report, *supra*, para. 157.

"the nature of the 'careful review' the USITC had performed".[163] These subsequent clarifications obviously do *not* figure in the USITC Report.[164]

207. Although the Panel's conclusion on this issue was that the *USITC Report* contained an adequate explanation of the allocation methodologies, the Panel's reasoning discloses that the Panel clearly did not consider this to be the case. The Panel did not feel able to rely solely or, even, principally, on the explanation actually provided in the USITC Report and, instead, relied heavily on supplementary information provided by the United States in response to the Panel's questions. Indeed, the most important part of the Panel's reasoning on this issue is based on those "clarifications". We consider that the Panel's conclusion is at odds with its treatment and description of the evidence supporting that conclusion. We do not see how the Panel could conclude that the USITC Report *did* provide an adequate explanation of the allocation methodologies, when it is clear that the Panel itself saw such deficiencies in that Report that it placed extensive reliance on "clarifications" that were not contained in the USITC Report.

208. By reaching a conclusion regarding the USITC Report, which relied so heavily on supplementary information provided by the United States during the Panel proceedings – information not contained in the USITC Report – the Panel applied a standard of review which falls short of what is required by Article 11 of the DSU.

209. As a result we conclude that the Panel acted inconsistently with Article 11 in finding, in paragraph 8.66 of the Panel Report, that "the USITC Report provides an adequate, reasoned and reasonable explanation with respect to 'profits and losses' " and, therefore, we reverse this finding.

C. USITC's Treatment of the Protein Content of Wheat

210. Before the Panel, the European Communities argued that the USITC had failed to consider the overall relationship between the protein content of wheat and the price of wheat gluten as a particular "relevant factor" under Article 4.2(a) of the *Agreement on Safeguards*. According to the European Communities, this relationship is "the single, most important, factor determining the price of wheat gluten".[165] The Panel examined the evidence cited by the European Communities in support of its assertion that the issue of the protein content of wheat had been raised before the USITC. The Panel said:

> ... We have examined this evidence cited by the European Community before us. While this evidence demonstrates to us that the issue of the effect of protein premiums on price during 1993-1994

[163] Panel Report, para. 8.61.

[164] In that respect, like the Panel, we note that the USITC could have described the nature of the "careful review" of the allocation methodologies used - as the United States did in its "clarifications" – *without* disclosing confidential *data* provided by the producers (see Panel Report, para. 8.64).

[165] European Communities' other appellant's submission, para. 88.

> was certainly raised by the EU producer respondents as relevant before the USITC, we find that the European Community has not demonstrated to us *as a matter of fact* that the EU producer respondents clearly raised the broader issue of wheat protein premiums as a possible relevant causal factor pertaining to the post-1994 segment of the period of investigation which the European Community raises in these Panel proceedings.[166] (emphasis added)

211. The European Communities alleges that, in making this finding, the Panel failed to make an objective assessment of the facts, as required by Article 11 of the DSU. According to the European Communities, the evidence before the Panel, in the form of EC-Exhibit 10, demonstrated clearly the importance of the relationship between the protein content of wheat and the price of wheat gluten. In light of this evidence, it says, the Panel should have found that the USITC was required to examine this relationship as a relevant other factor, under Article 4.2(a) of the *Agreement on Safeguards*.

212. We recall that we have already examined the European Communities' appeal against the Panel's finding that the competent authorities need not examine "factors" that are neither listed in Article 4.2(a) of the *Agreement on Safeguards* nor clearly raised before the competent authorities as relevant by interested parties.[167] In that section of our findings, we concluded that the competent authorities may be required to evaluate "other factors" which were not "clearly raised" by the interested parties. However, we concluded that the evidence of record suggests that the overall relationship between the protein content of wheat and the price of wheat gluten becomes a relevant other factor, under Article 4.2(a), only when the protein content is *unusually* high or low. We concluded that, as the evidence indicates that the protein content of wheat was *not* unusually high or low during the post-1994 period of investigation, when the surge in imports occurred, the USITC was *not* required to "evaluate" the protein content of wheat as a particular relevant other factor under Article 4.2(a).[168]

213. It seems, to us, that this finding, under Article 4.2(a) of the *Agreement on Safeguards*, also resolves the European Communities' appeal under Article 11 regarding the protein content of wheat. The European Communities argues that the evidence before the Panel should have led the Panel to find that the USITC *was* required to evaluate the overall relationship between the protein content of wheat and the price of wheat gluten as a relevant other factor, under Article 4.2(a), during the post-1994 period of investigation. However, contrary to the European Communities' arguments on this point, we have already found that the evidence of record does *not* indicate that the USITC was required to "evaluate" that rela-

---

[166] Panel Report, para. 8.125.

[167] *Supra*, Section IV, paras. 45 – 59.

[168] The details of our reasoning are set forth, *supra*, para. 58.

tionship as a relevant other factor for that period. We, therefore, decline the European Communities' appeal on this point.

D. Failure to Draw the Appropriate Inferences

214. The Panel requested that the United States supply it with certain factual information.[169] The United States did not submit this information, maintaining that it was business confidential information ("BCI") and that, under Article 3.2 of the *Agreement on Safeguards*, it was entitled to withhold the requested information. The Panel proposed to the parties two different procedures for the protection of BCI. The United States informed the Panel that it could not submit the information under either of these procedures, but would be willing to submit the information to the Panel only. The Panel ruled that it could not accept the information on that basis because, by denying the European Communities access to the information, the Panel would have engaged in *ex parte* communications with the United States.[170] The Panel, however, stated that it was of the view that it could dispose of the case on the basis of the factual record to which it had access.[171]

215. The European Communities argues that the "Panel should have drawn adverse inferences from the US's refusal to provide to the Panel the redacted information from the published USITC report and the other information identified by the EC." [172] The European Communities argues that the Panel should have drawn inferences adverse to the United States with respect to a number of different issues, in particular "productivity" and "profits and losses", where the Panel did not have access to specific numerical data. The European Communities notes that the Panel explicitly acknowledged that having access to the BCI would "have facilitated [its] objective assessment of the facts".

216. We begin by noting our strong agreement with the Panel that a "serious systemic issue" is raised by the question of the procedures which should govern the protection of information requested by a panel under Article 13.1 of the DSU and which is alleged by a Member to be "confidential".[173] We believe that these issues need to be addressed.

217. Next, we recall that we stated, in our original report in *Canada – Aircraft*, that Members of the WTO "are ... under a *duty* and an *obligation* to 'respond promptly and fully' to requests made by panels for information under Article 13.1 of the DSU." [174] (emphasis added) In this case, despite the fact that the Panel proposed to exercise its authority, under Article 12.1 of the DSU, to determine its

[169] Panel Report, para. 8.7.
[170] Panel Report, para. 8.10.
[171] *Ibid.*, para. 8.12.
[172] European Communities' other appellant's submission, para. 38.
[173] Panel Report, para. 8.11.
[174] Appellate Body Report, *Canada – Aircraft*, *supra*, footnote 32, para. 187.

own procedures by adopting two different procedures for the protection of business confidential information, the United States declined to make available to the Panel, and representatives of the European Communities, certain information requested by the Panel under Article 13.1 of the DSU. As the Appellate Body said in *Canada – Aircraft*, the refusal by a Member to provide information requested of it undermines seriously the ability of a panel to make an objective assessment of the facts and the matter, as required by Article 11 of the DSU. Such a refusal also undermines the ability of other Members of the WTO to seek the "prompt" and "satisfactory" resolution of disputes under the procedures "for which they bargained in concluding the DSU." [175] In this specific case, the Panel acknowledged that having access to all of the information requested from the United States "would have facilitated [an] objective assessment of the facts".[176] We, therefore, deplore the conduct of the United States.

218. However, we note that the role of the Appellate Body, on this issue, is limited to determining whether the Panel has erred under Article 11 of the DSU. In that respect, we recall that, in *Canada – Aircraft*, the Appellate Body observed that:

> ... The drawing of inferences is, in other words, an inherent and unavoidable aspect of a panel's basic task of finding and characterizing the facts making up a dispute.[177]
>
> ...
>
> Clearly, in our view, the Panel had the legal authority and the *discretion* to draw inferences from the facts before it – including the fact that Canada had refused to provide information sought by the Panel.[178] (emphasis added)

219. We, therefore, characterized the drawing of inferences as a "discretionary" task falling within a panel's duties under Article 11 of the DSU. In *Canada – Aircraft*, which involved a similar factual situation, the panel did not draw any inferences "adverse" to Canada's position. On appeal, we held that there was no basis to find that the panel had improperly exercised its discretion since "the full *ensemble* of the facts on the record" supported the panel's conclusion.[179]

220. In its appeal, the European Communities places considerable emphasis on the failure of the Panel to draw "adverse" inferences from the refusal of the United States to provide information requested by the Panel. As we emphasized in *Canada – Aircraft*, under Article 11 of the DSU, a panel must draw inferences on the basis of *all of the facts of record* relevant to the particular determination to

---

[175] *Ibid.*, para. 189.

[176] Panel Report, para. 8.12.

[177] Appellate Body Report, *Canada – Aircraft*, *supra*, footnote 32, para. 198.

[178] *Ibid.*, para. 203.

[179] *Ibid.*, paras. 204 and 205.

be made.[180] Where a party refuses to provide information requested by a panel under Article 13.1 of the DSU, that refusal will be one of the relevant facts of record, and indeed an important fact, to be taken into account in determining the appropriate inference to be drawn. However, if a panel were to ignore or disregard other relevant facts, it would fail to make an "objective assessment" under Article 11 of the DSU. In this case, as the Panel observed, there *were* other facts of record that the Panel was required to include in its "objective assessment". Accordingly, we reject the European Communities' arguments to the extent that they suggest that the Panel erred in not drawing "adverse" inferences simply from the refusal of the United States to provide certain information requested from it by the Panel under Article 13.1 of the DSU.

221. In reviewing the inferences the Panel drew from the facts of record, our task on appeal is not to redo afresh the Panel's assessment of those facts, and decide for ourselves what inferences we would draw from them. Rather, we must determine whether the Panel improperly exercised its discretion, under Article 11, by failing to draw certain inferences from the facts before it. In asking us to conduct such a review, an appellant must indicate clearly the manner in which a panel has improperly exercised its discretion. Taking into account the full *ensemble* of the facts, the appellant should, at least: identify the facts on the record from which the Panel should have drawn inferences; indicate the factual or legal inferences that the panel should have drawn from those facts; and, finally, explain why the failure of the panel to exercise its discretion by drawing these inferences amounts to an error of law under Article 11 of the DSU.

222. In this appeal, the European Communities makes, what we regard to be, broad and general statements that the Panel erred by not drawing "adverse" inferences from the facts. Besides the fact that the United States refused to provide certain information requested by the Panel under Article 13.1 of the DSU, the European Communities does not identify, in any specific manner, *which facts* supported a particular inference. Nor does the European Communities identify *what inferences* the Panel should have drawn from those facts, other than that the inferences should have been favourable to the European Communities. Besides the simple refusal of the United States to provide information requested by the Panel, which we have already addressed[181], the European Communities does not offer any other specific reasons why the Panel's failure to exercise its discretion by drawing the inferences identified by the European Communities amounts to an error of law under Article 11 of the DSU. Therefore, we decline this ground of appeal.

---

[180] *Ibid.*

[181] *Supra*, para. 174.

IX. JUDICIAL ECONOMY

223. Before the Panel, the European Communities made a claim under Article XIX:1(a) of the GATT 1994 regarding "unforeseen developments", and also a claim under Article I of the GATT 1994 and Article 5 of the *Agreement on Safeguards* regarding the nature of the remedy. In a single paragraph covering these two claims, the Panel stated:

> ... having determined that the measure at issue is inconsistent with Articles 2.1 and 4.2 SA, and exercising the discretion implicit in the principle of judicial economy, we do not deem it necessary to examine whether the measure at issue is also inconsistent with Article XIX of the GATT 1994 ("unforeseen developments") nor whether the form, level and allocation of the inconsistent measure are in breach of Article 5 SA or Article I of the GATT 1994.[182]

224. The European Communities appeals the Panel's findings on judicial economy. The European Communities asserts that the failure to make a finding regarding the claim on "unforeseen developments" means that there is a flaw in the Panel's findings, under Articles 2.1 and 4.2 of the *Agreement on Safeguards*, concerning increased imports and serious injury. The European Communities also argues that, by failing to address the European Communities' claims under Article I of the GATT 1994 and Article 5 of the *Agreement on Safeguards*, "the Panel has not clarified whether the US could simply repeat the serious injury determination and then still proceed to apply the measure in the same way." [183]

225. We begin by recalling certain of the statements that the Appellate Body has already made regarding the exercise of judicial economy by panels. In *United States – Shirts and Blouses*, we opined:

> Given the explicit aim of dispute settlement that permeates the *DSU*, we do not consider that Article 3.2 of the *DSU* is meant to encourage either panels or the Appellate Body to "make law" by clarifying existing provisions of the *WTO Agreement* outside the context of resolving a particular dispute. *A panel need only address those claims which must be addressed in order to resolve the matter in issue in the dispute.*[184] (emphasis added)

226. However, the "discretion" that a panel enjoys to determine which claims it should address is not without limits.[185] In *Australia – Salmon*, we stated that a "panel has to address those claims on which a finding is necessary in order to

---

[182] Panel Report, para. 8.220.

[183] European Communities' other appellant's submission, para. 108.

[184] Appellate Body Report, *United States – Measure Affecting Imports of Woven Wool Shirts and Blouses from India*, WT/DS33/AB/R and Corr. 1, adopted 23 May 1997, DSR 1997:I, 323, at 340.

[185] Appellate Body Report, *India – Patent Protection for Pharmaceutical and Agricultural Chemical Products*, WT/DS50/AB/R, adopted 16 January 1998, DSR 1998:I, 9, at 35, para. 87.

enable the DSB to make sufficiently precise recommendations and rulings so as to allow for prompt compliance by a Member with those recommendations and rulings ...".[186]

227. In *Argentina – Footwear Safeguards*, we were asked to address a claim on "unforeseen developments" that the panel had not examined. In that appeal, we upheld the panel's finding that Argentina's investigation "was inconsistent with the requirements of Articles 2 and 4 of the *Agreement on Safeguards*." We went on to state:

> As a consequence, there is *no legal basis* for the safeguard measures imposed by Argentina. For this reason, we do not believe that it is necessary to complete the analysis of the Panel relating to the claim made by the European Communities under Article XIX of the GATT 1994 by ruling on whether the Argentine authorities have, in their investigation, demonstrated that the increased imports in this case occurred "as a result of unforeseen developments and of the effect of the obligations incurred by a Member under this Agreement, including tariff concessions ... ".[187]

228. In short, we considered that since the safeguard measure at issue was inconsistent with Articles 2 and 4 of the *Agreement on Safeguards*, there was no need to go further and examine whether, in addition, the measure was also inconsistent with Article XIX:1(a) of the GATT 1994. The inconsistency, as we said, deprived the measure of legal basis.

229. In our view, the same reasoning applies in this case. The Panel found and we have upheld, albeit for different reasons, that the measure is inconsistent with Articles 2.1 and 4.2 of the *Agreement on Safeguards*. Thus, the Panel found, in effect, that the safeguard measure at issue in this case, like the measure at issue in *Argentina – Footwear Safeguard*, has no legal basis. The reasons for which the Panel found an inconsistency with Articles 2.1 and 4.2 of the *Agreement on Safeguards* do not alter that conclusion. The Panel was, therefore, entitled to decline to examine the claim of the European Communities regarding "unforeseen developments". A finding on that issue would not, in our view, have added anything to the ability of the DSB to make sufficiently precise recommendations and rulings in this dispute. We, therefore, see no error in the Panel's exercise of judicial economy as regards the European Communities claim concerning "unforeseen developments".

230. The same reasoning also holds true for the European Communities' claim under Article I of the GATT 1994 and Article 5 of the *Agreement on Safeguards*. As the Panel had found the measure to be inconsistent with Articles 2.1 and 4.2 of the *Agreement on Safeguards*, the Panel was within its discretion in declining to examine these claims. Once again, a finding on this claim would not have added

---

186 Appellate Body Report, *Australia – Salmon*, *supra*, footnote 119, para. 223.

187 Appellate Body Report, *Argentina – Footwear Safeguards*, *supra*, footnote 22, para. 98.

anything to the ability of the DSB to make sufficiently precise recommendations and rulings in this dispute.

231. Finally, the European Communities asserts that, by failing to address these claims, "the Panel has not clarified whether the US could simply repeat the serious injury determination and then still proceed to apply the measure in the same way."[188] It appears, to us, that this argument invites speculation as to how the United States might implement the recommendations and rulings of the DSB. As we said in our Report in *United States – Tax Treatment for "Foreign Sales Corporations"*, "we do not consider that it is appropriate for us to speculate on the ways in which the United States might choose to implement" the recommendations and rulings of the DSB.[189] We, therefore, see no error in the Panel's exercise of judicial economy as regards the European Communities claim concerning Article I of the GATT 1994 and Article 5 of the *Agreement on Safeguards*.

232. For these reasons, we see no error in the Panel's exercise of judicial economy in paragraph 8.220 of the Panel Report.

X. FINDINGS AND CONCLUSIONS

233. For the reasons set out in this Report, the Appellate Body:

(a) upholds the Panel's conclusion, in paragraph 8.127 of the Panel Report, that the United States has not acted inconsistently with its obligations under Articles 4.2(a) and 4.2(b) of the *Agreement on Safeguards*, by declining to evaluate the overall relationship between the protein content of wheat and the price of wheat gluten as a "relevant factor" under Article 4.2(a) of that Agreement; but, in so doing, reverses the Panel's interpretation of Article 4.2(a) of the *Agreement on Safeguards*, in paragraph 8.69 of the Panel Report, that the competent authorities are required to evaluate only the "relevant factors" listed in Article 4.2(a) of that Agreement as well as any other "factors" which were "*clearly* raised before [the competent authorities] as relevant by the interested parties in the domestic investigation";

(b) reverses the Panel's interpretation of Article 4.2(b) of the *Agreement on Safeguards* that increased imports "alone", "in and of themselves", or "*per se*", must be capable of causing "serious injury", as well as the Panel's conclusions on the issue of causation, as summarized in paragraph 8.154 of the Panel Report; finds, nonetheless, that the United States acted inconsistently with its obligations under Article 4.2(b) of the *Agreement on Safeguards*;

---

[188] European Communities' other appellant's submission, para. 108.

[189] Appellate Body Report, *United States – Tax Treatment for "Foreign Sales Corporations* ("*US – FSC*"), WT/DS108/AB/R, adopted 20 March 2000, DSR 2000:III, 1619, para. 175.

(c) upholds the Panel's finding, in paragraph 8.182 of the Panel Report, that the United States acted inconsistently with its obligations under Articles 2.1 and 4.2 of the *Agreement on Safeguards*, by excluding imports from Canada from the application of the safeguard measure, after conducting an investigation embracing imports from all sources, including Canada, to determine whether increased imports of wheat gluten were causing or threatening to cause serious injury to the United States industry, and after subsequently conducting a separate examination of the importance of imports from Canada to the situation of the domestic industry;

(d) upholds the Panel's findings, in paragraphs 8.197 and 8.199 of the Panel Report, that the United States acted inconsistently with its obligations under Articles 12.1(a) and 12.1(b) of the *Agreement on Safeguards*;

(e) reverses the Panel's finding, in paragraph 8.207 of the Panel Report, that the United States acted inconsistently with its obligations under Article 12.1(c) of the *Agreement on Safeguards*; finds that the United States acted consistently with its obligations under Article 12.1(c) of that Agreement to notify "immediately" its decision to apply a safeguard measure;

(f) upholds the Panel's finding, in paragraph 8.219 of the Panel Report, that the United States acted inconsistently with its obligations under Article 12.3 of the *Agreement on Safeguards*, and, in consequence, upholds the Panel's finding, in paragraph 8.219 of the Panel Report, that the United States acted inconsistently with its obligations under Article 8.1 of the *Agreement on Safeguards*;

(g) finds that the Panel did not act inconsistently with Article 11 of the DSU:

   (i) in concluding, in paragraph 8.45 of the Panel Report, that the USITC had "considered industry productivity as required by Article 4.2(a)" of the *Agreement on Safeguards*;

   (ii) in finding, in paragraph 8.127 of the Panel Report, that the USITC was not required to evaluate the overall relationship between the protein content of wheat and the price of wheat gluten as a "relevant factor", under Article 4.2(a) of the *Agreement on Safeguards*, during the post-1994 period of investigation; and,

   (iii) in declining to draw "adverse" inferences from the refusal of the United States to provide certain allegedly confidential information requested from it by the Panel under Article 13.1 of the DSU;

(h) finds that the Panel acted inconsistently with Article 11 of the DSU in finding, in paragraph 8.66 of the Panel Report, that "the USITC

Report provides an adequate, reasoned and reasonable explanation with respect to 'profits and losses'" and, therefore, reverses this finding; and

(i) finds no error in the Panel's exercise of judicial economy, in paragraph 8.220 of the Panel Report, in not examining the claims of the European Communities under Article XIX:1(a) of the GATT 1994, and also under Article 5 of the *Agreement on Safeguards* and Article I of the GATT 1994.

234. The Appellate Body *recommends* that the DSB request that the United States bring its safeguard measure found in this Report, and in the Panel Report as modified by this Report, to be inconsistent with the *Agreement on Safeguards*, into conformity with its obligations under that Agreement.

9 780521 829793